Italian Yearbook of Human Rights 2011

P.I.E. Peter Lang

Bruxelles · Bern · Berlin · Frankfurt am Main · New York · Oxford · Wien

Interdepartmental Centre on Human Rights
and the Rights of Peoples, University of Padua

Director
Antonio Papisca

Research and editing committee
Andrea Cofelice, Paola Degani,
Pietro de Perini, Paolo De Stefani,
Marco Mascia, Antonio Papisca, Claudia Pividori

Editors
Centro interdipartimentale di ricerca
e servizi sui diritti della persona e dei popoli,
Università degli Studi di Padova
via Martiri della Libertà, 2
35137 Padua

tel. 040.8271817; fax 049.8271816

annuario@centrodirittiumani.unipd.it
www.italianhumanrightsyearbook.eu
http://unipd-centrodirittiumani.it/en/

Italian Yearbook of Human Rights 2011

Human Rights Studies
No.1

Università degli Studi di Padova | Interdepartmental Centre on Human Rights and the Rights of the Peoples

UNESCO Chair "Human Rights, Democracy and Peace"

Regione del Veneto

Archivio Pace Diritti Umani – peace human rights

Cover picture: © *The ideal city (interpolation)*, 2011, Venezia, Marsilio Editori.

First Italian edition: *Annuario italiano dei diritti umani 2011*, 2011, Venezia, Marsilio Editori. Translation Italian-English by Janet Sethre.

1 avenue Maurice, B-1050 Brussels, Belgium
info@peterlang.com; www.peterlang.com

ISSN 2034-9610
ISBN 978-90-5201-858-4 (Paperback)
ISBN 978-3-0352-6181-3 (eBook)
D/2012/5678/38

CIP available from the British Library, GB.

Bibliographic information published by "Die Deutsche Nationalbibliothek"
"Die Deutsche Nationalbibliothek" lists this publication in the "Deutsche Nationalbibliografie"; detailed bibliographic data is available on Internet at <http://dnb.d-nb.de>.

Table of Contents

Acronyms

AGCOM	The Communications Regulatory Authority (Autorità per le garanzie nelle comunicazioni)
AISE	External Intelligence and Security Agency (Agenzia Informazioni e Sicurezza Esterna)
ANCI	Association of Italian Municipalities
CARA	Reception Centre for Asylum Seekers (Centro di accoglienza per richiedenti asilo)
CAT	Convention against Torture and Other Cruel, Inhuman or Degrading Treatment or Punishment
CDA	Reception Centre (Centro di accoglienza)
CEDAW	Convention on the Elimination of All Forms of Discrimination against Women
CFREU	Charter of Fundamental Rights of the European Union
CFSP	Common Foreign and Security Policy of the European Union
CICLOPE	Inter-Ministerial Committee for the Coordination of the Fight against Paedophilia (Comitato interministeriale di coordinamento per la lotta alla pedofilia)
CIDU	Inter-Ministerial Committee for Human Rights (Comitato interministeriale per i diritti umani)
CIE	Identification and Expulsion Centre (Centro di Identificazione ed Espulsione)
C.l.	Constitutional law (Legge costituzionale)
CM	Committee of Ministers of the Council of Europe
CNEL	National Council on Economy and Labour (Consiglio nazionale dell'economia e del lavoro)
CoE	Council of Europe
COHOM	Human Rights Working Group of the Council of the European Union
CPED	International Convention for the Protection of All Persons from Enforced Disappearance
CPT	European Committee for the Prevention of Torture and Inhuman or Degrading Treatment or Punishment
CPTA	Centres for Temporary Stay and Assistance (Centri di permanenza temporanea e assistenza)
CRC	Convention on the Rights of the Child

CRPD	Convention on the Rights of Persons with Disabilities
CSDP	Common Security and Defence Policy of the European Union
DG	Directorate-General
D.p.c.m.	Decree of the President of the Council of Ministers (Decreto del Presidente del Consiglio dei Ministri)
D.p.r.	Decree of the President of the Republic (Decreto del Presidente della Repubblica)
ECHR	European Convention on Human Rights
ECJ	Court of Justice of the European Union
ECOSOC	United Nations Economic and Social Council
ECRI	European Commission against Racism and Intolerance
ECSR	European Committee on Social Rights
ECtHR	European Court of Human Rights
EEAS	European External Action Service
EIDHR	European Instrument for Democracy and Human Rights
EP	European Parliament
ESC-R	European Social Charter (Revised)
ESDP	European Security and Defence Policy
EU	European Union
EUROJUST	Judicial Cooperation Unit of the European Union
EUROPOL	European Police Office
FRA	Fundamental Rights Agency of the European Union
FRONTEX	European Agency for the Management of Operational Cooperation at the External Borders of the Member States of the European Union
FRP	Fundamental Rights Platform
FNS	Italian National Press Association (Federazione Nazionale Stampa Italiana)
GA	General Assembly of the United Nations
HR/VP	European Union High Representative for Foreign Affairs and Security Policy and European Commission Vice-President
ICCPR	International Covenant on Civil and Political Rights
ICERD	International Convention on the Elimination of All Forms of Racial Discrimination
ICESCR	International Covenant on Economic, Social and Cultural Rights
ICRMW	International Convention on the Protection of the Rights of All Migrant Workers and Members of Their Families
ILO	International Labour Organisation

INDIMI	National Institute for the Rights of the Child (Istituto nazionale per i diritti dei minori)
L.	Law
Lgs.d.	Legislative decree (Decreto legislativo)
L.d.	Law-decree (Decreto legge)
MIUR	Ministry of Education, University and Research (Ministero dell'istruzione, dell'università e della ricerca)
NAM	Needs Assessment Mission (ODIHR)
NGO	Non-governmental organisation
ODIHR	Office for Democratic Institutions and Human Rights (OSCE)
OHCHR	United Nations Office of the High Commissioner for Human Rights
OP-CAT	Optional Protocol to the Convention against Torture
OSCE	Organisation for Security and Cooperation in Europe
P.l.	Provincial law
PACE	Parliamentary Assembly of the Council of Europe
R.l.	Regional law
SIOI	Italian Society for International Organization (Società italiana per l'organizzazione internazionale)
TAR	Regional administrative tribunal (Tribunale amministrativo regionale)
TEU	Treaty of the European Union
TFEU	Treaty on the Functioning of the European Union
UNAR	National Office against Racial Discrimination (Ufficio per la promozione della parità di trattamento e la rimozione delle discriminazioni fondate sulla razza e sull'origine etnica)
UNDEF	United Nations Democracy Fund
UNESCO	United Nations Educational, Scientific and Cultural Organisation
UNFPA	United Nations Population Fund
UNHCR	United Nations High Commissioner for Refugees
UNICEF	United Nations Children's Fund
UNRWA	United Nations Relief and Works Agency for Palestine Refugees in the Near East
UPI	Union of Italian Provinces
UPR	Universal Periodic Review

Preface

Building the first edition of a national *Yearbook* on human rights has been a highly demanding task, both in substance and method.

It has involved reporting on a reality which touches the very foundations of the legal system and civil co-existence: the Universal Declaration of Human Rights tells us, indeed, that "recognition of the inherent dignity and of the equal and inalienable rights of all members of the human family is the foundation of freedom, justice and peace in the world".

Our task here has also been to lay out a blueprint for future editions. We have not built over a void, though.

Nowadays, thanks above all to international organisations, both governmental and non-governmental, we can call upon a "glocal" information and monitoring network to give us data both on human rights violations around the globe and guarantee mechanisms available at various levels. In this context of industrious civic and political engagement, however, Italy has not had available a yearly publication capable of reporting on its institutional position on human rights issues in a systematic, comprehensive way, with special attention toward the Country's many international obligations, and toward the complex system of interweaving relations tying it to supra-national monitoring bodies.

With this *Yearbook* we aim to fill this gap. It is the fruit of research conducted within the *Centro interdipartimentale sui diritti della persona e dei popoli dell'Università di Padova* (Interdepartmental Centre on Human Rights and the Rights of Peoples of the University of Padua). The research and editing team includes Andrea Cofelice, Paola Degani, Pietro de Perini, Paolo De Stefani, Marco Mascia, Director of the Centre, and myself, as coordinator. We have worked in awareness that the complexity of the universe under our observation would necessitate clear choices in content and method. The research and editing group, together with the entire Human Rights Centre, assumes full responsibility for those choices. We have not recurred to a language of denunciation, but rather, of information at the service of institutional truth and respect for the canons of scientific reporting.

This work was made possible thanks to tangible support from the Region of Veneto, which also deserves distinction as the first Region in Italy – and, perhaps, in the world – to endorse a regional law containing a provision formally recognising peace as a fundamental right of the human person and of peoples: the so-called "peace human rights norm". The law's text, which refers both to the Italian Constitution and international law principles, was passed in 1988 and renewed in 1999.

The Padua Human Rights Centre can boast leadership in its own right. Founded in 1982, it is the first structure of its kind created in Italy within the university system: one of the first in Europe and, indeed, the world. In 1997 the Centre promoted the creation of the European Master in Human Rights and Democratisation, an academic structure which today works in partnership with 41 prestigious European universities. The Centre also produces the review "Pace diritti umani-Peace human rights", published by Marsilio, and it manages both the Region of Veneto Archive bearing the same denomination and the Jean Monnet European Centre of Excellence on Intercultural Dialogue, Human Rights and Multi-level Governance. The Human Rights Centre itself continues in its commitment to carry out programmes in collaboration with the Council of Europe, UNESCO, the United Nations High Commissioner for Human Rights, and the European Commission.

Solidly sustained by its fruitful academic experience, the Centre shares responsibility with the UNESCO Chair on Human Rights, Democracy and Peace at the University of Padua in offering this *Yearbook* to public institutions operating at various levels, as well as to civil society groups in Italy, beginning with schools and volunteer associations, and of course to international organisations.

The *2011 Yearbook* has been realised on the 150th anniversary of Italian Unity. We hope that Italy will forge ahead on the road to a law-based civilisation marked by respect for the supreme value of human dignity, and by the rights inhering in it. We must remember that Italy is the homeland of Cesare Beccaria, Norberto Bobbio, Giuseppe Capograssi and the most worthy Antonio Rosmini, who wrote: "the person is the human right subsistent". We must also remember that Italy hosted the signing of international treaties which are both destinations and starting-points for constructing a peaceful and just international order as proclaimed by art. 28 of the Universal Declaration: *opus iustitiae pax*. They include the 1950 European Convention for the Protection of Human Rights and Fundamental Freedoms, called "Convention of Rome"; the 1961 European Social Charter, called the "Turin Charter", on the 100th anniversary of Italian Unification; the 1998 Statute of the International Criminal Court, or "Rome Statute". Nor must we forget that in 1993 Italy played a fundamental role in proposing, before the United Nations Security Council, the creation of an International Criminal Tribunal for the Former Yugoslavia.

These are stones in a mosaic of exemplary identity, if only we can see them: key elements in the total picture of a full-dimension humanistic identity, as the image of the ideal city appearing on the cover of the *Yearbook* intends to signify and evoke.

Padua, 13 June 2011

Antonio Papisca

Professor Emeritus of the University of Padua

Chairholder, UNESCO Chair in Human Rights, Democracy and Peace at the same University

Introduction

1. "The Republic recognises and guarantees the inviolable rights of the person, both as an individual and in the social groups where human personality is expressed. The Republic expects that the fundamental duties of political, economic and social solidarity be fulfilled".

Art. 2 of the Constitution of the Italian Republic is in full accordance with the Universal Declaration of Human Rights, in particular with art. 1, which proclaims: "all human beings are born free and equal in dignity and rights. They are endowed with reason and conscience, and must act towards one another in a spirit of brotherhood".

The principles of a "new", human-centric international law were enshrined in the United Nations Charter and in the Universal Declaration of Human Rights, and have developed through numerous international instruments, starting – on a universal level – with the two International Covenants of 1966 regarding, respectively, civil and political rights, and economic, social and cultural rights; and – on a regional – European level – with the 1950 Convention on the Protection of Human Rights and Fundamental Freedoms.

The Italian constitutional system is in perfect harmony with the main principles set forth in those legal sources. The principle of equality and the related principle of interdependence and indivisibility of all the human rights, according to which economic, social and cultural rights are just as fundamental as civil and political rights, finds substantial acknowledgement in art. 3 Const.: "all citizens have equal social dignity and are equal before the law, without distinction of sex, race, language, religion, political opinion, or personal and social condition. It is the task of the Republic to remove obstacles of an economic and social nature which, in limiting in fact freedom and equality among citizens, prevent the full development of the human being and the real participation of all workers in the political, economic and social organisation of the Country".

The Preamble to the Universal Declaration reads: "recognition of the inherent dignity and of the equal and inalienable rights of all members of the human family is the foundation of freedom, justice and peace in the world". Art. 11 of the Italian Constitution acknowledges the founding nature of this message and translates it into a solemn commitment for positive peace: "Italy rejects war as an instrument of aggression against the freedom of other peoples and as a means for the settlement of international disputes. Italy agrees, on conditions of equality with other States, to the limitations of sovereignty that may be necessary to a world order ensuring peace and justice among nations. Italy promotes and encourages international organisations furthering such ends".

The fact that Italy has ratified most international human rights instruments, whether universal or European, attests to its commitment to carrying forward the rule of law and democratic principles in the name of universal ethics.

The obligations deriving from those legal instruments are numerous and complex. Within a dynamics tending toward the perennial improvement of norms and institutions, in fact, one must continually adapt this or that part of the internal legal system; one must continually update and enrich case-law, and further public policies which are consistent with the logic of "positive measures".

2. The aim of this *Yearbook* is to provide data updated till the end of 2010, in order to make known how the Italian State fulfils the obligations assumed with the formal ratification of conventions and protocols, and how it responds to comments, remarks, recommendations and sentencing by the pertinent international bodies.

The *Yearbook*'s report should therefore allow the reader to assess the real willingness of Italy to enter into constructive dialogue with those international authorities.

The rather sparse number of human rights yearbooks published in other Countries generally falls into one of two categories. First, there are publications of a more decidedly academic nature in which the institutional, political and normative developments in human rights issues are illustrated and assessed from a variety of viewpoints, using differing methodological and disciplinary perspectives. This is the case of the *European Yearbook on Human Rights*, edited by a pool of academic institutions such as the European Training and Research Centre for Human Rights and Democracy at the University of Graz, the Austrian Institute for Human Rights, the European Inter-University Centre for Human Rights and Democratisation, with headquarters in Venice, the Ludwig Boltzman Institute of Human Rights in Vienna. It contains a series of essays written in a multi-disciplinary perspective, dedicated to the European Union, the Council of Europe, OSCE and civil society organisations. There are also more descriptive yearbooks which systematically present data relative to the state of the art of human rights in a given Country or region without, however, neglecting synthetic assessments concerning specific aspects of the reality dealt with. This is the case, for example, of *Les droits de l'homme en France. Regards portés par les instances internationales*, a periodical publication edited by the French Human Rights Commission.

The *Italian Yearbook of Human Rights*, similar, in many respects, to the French one, is intended as a sort of "log" recording the implementation of international human rights law in Italy.

In the framework of Italy's human rights infrastructure, there is tardiness in some sectors, while others reflect an original, innovative character.

Today Italy is still devoid of "National Human Rights Institutions" in line with the so-called "Paris Principles", included in the resolution 48/134 adopted by the United Nations General Assembly on 20 December 1993[1]: such institutions would take form as a National Human Rights Commission and a National Ombudsman. Numerous human rights bodies of the United Nations have addressed Italy strongly recommending that it create such institutions; among others, the Committee on the Rights of the Child (2003), the Committee on Economic, Social and Cultural Rights (2004), the Human Rights Committee (civil and political rights) (2005), the Committee against Torture (2007), the Committee on Racial Discrimination (2008). The recommendation addressed to Italy by the Human Rights Council during the Universal Periodic Review (UPR), held in 2010, was particularly noteworthy. The Council of Europe, in particular its Commissioner for Human Rights, has repeatedly made similar recommendations.

Since 2002, this issue has been a priority for Italian non-governmental organisations, in particular those acting through the *Comitato per la promozione e protezione dei diritti umani*, a network of 83 non-governmental organisations and associations created with the purpose of promoting and supporting the legislative process aiming to endow Italy with an independent "national human rights institution" in line with the "Paris Principles". This civil society committee works with exemplary competence and passion. Recently it published the "First Monitoring Report of NGOs and associations of the Comitato per la promozione e protezione dei diritti umani: Italy a year after recommendations from the UN Human Rights Council" (*Primo Rapporto di monitoraggio delle organizzazioni non-governative e associazioni del Comitato per la protezione e promozione dei diritti umani. L'Italia a un anno dalle raccomandazioni del Consiglio ONU per i diritti umani*).

Italy's delay in creating an independent national human rights institution cannot find justification in the fact that, in any event, it already

1 On 12 July 2011, the Parliament approved law No. 112, establishing the National Commissioner for the Rights of Children and Adolescents. On 19 July 2011, the Senate had approved the law No. 2720, instituting the National Commission for the Promotion and Protection of Human Rights, but this instrument is still a draft, pending at the House of Representatives.

has specific bodies dealing with human rights, both in the Parliament and the Executive spheres. But none of these bodies has the structural and functional traits of a human rights institution in conformity with the fore-mentioned "Paris Principles".

Since 1978, the Inter-Ministerial Committee for Human Rights (CIDU) is functioning at the Ministry of Foreign Affairs. Its main task is to prepare the periodical reports which the Italian State is obliged to submit to the pertinent international monitoring bodies. The CIDU underwent restructuring in 2007, the same year when a Committee of Ministers for Strategic Orientation in Human Rights Protection was created. Since 2008, the Chairman of this body has been the Minister for Equal Opportunities, but up to now, the Committee has never met.

It should also be reminded that in 1984, by decree of the President of the Council of Ministers issued on 31 January, a Human Rights Commission was created at the Presidency of the Council of Ministers; it functioned until 2002. Formed by a small number of members appointed *intuitu personae*, it had an *ad personam* consultative role in advising the President of the Council of Ministers. Its tasks were to "acquire most extensive information regarding facts which may endanger the fundamental, universally recognised human rights, anywhere in the world", and to "assist the President of the Council of Ministers in such informative activity in order to foster proper initiatives by the Italian Government". The Commission's attention was therefore directed entirely toward other Countries, running the risk of interfering in competencies of the Ministry of Foreign Affairs. Its endeavours for developing an institutional system specifically dedicated to promoting and protecting human rights in Italy were inconsequential. Its last membership included Virginio Rognoni (Chairman, former Minister of Interior), Giovanni Conso (former President of the Constitutional Court), Carlo Russo (former member of the European Court of Human Rights), Mario Alessi (former President of CIDU) and Antonio Papisca (Director of the Human Rights Centre of the University of Padua). Its last act in 2001 was to address a "note" to the President of the Council of Ministers urging the creation of national human rights institutions as insistently requested by the United Nations and the Council of Europe. The attempts made in this direction by Mr Rognoni obtained no results. Therefore, the Commission decided in 2002 to self-dissolve.

The list of Parliamentary bodies includes the following: the Senate's Extraordinary Commission for the Protection and Promotion of Human Rights; the Permanent Committee on Human Rights, created in 2008 by the Foreign Affairs Commission of the House of Representatives; the Parliamentary Commission for Childhood and Adolescence. On 7 July 2009 a consultancy began functioning, named Parliament-Government

Observatory Monitoring the Promotion and Protection of Fundamental Rights.

As documented in the pages of this *Yearbook*, in 2010, Parliament witnessed the presentation of 6 bills on Italy's adaptation to international human rights norms, plus 32 motions, 4 interpellations, 6 questions receiving oral response, 81 questions receiving written response, 18 questions before Commissions, 6 resolutions before Commissions, 9 agenda items before the Assembly and 3 agenda items before Commissions, on issues concerning the internationally recognised human rights.

Even though the year 2010 saw, among other negative events, a substantial abolition of the office of municipal Ombudsman, Italy's formal commitment toward creating national human rights institutions has not ceased. It was expressly reiterated in the letter of candidacy for membership in the United Nations Human Rights Council during the period 2007-2010 (see para. 29, referring to Universal Periodic Review). However, it should be pointed out that this commitment recently tends to be expressed in a much more generic manner compared to the 2007 letter of candidacy which had led Italy to the Human Rights Council for the period 2007-2010. Fortunately, this change in tone did not prevent the United Nations General Assembly from appointing Italy to the Human Rights Council for the second time, in May 2011.

3. In the various international contexts in which it participates, Italy does not abstain from making its position known. In 2010, its participation in the 65th session of the United Nations General Assembly was marked by the presentation of a draft resolution on strengthening the United Nations Crime Prevention and Criminal Justice Programme, and by the sponsoring of 29 out of 52 resolutions regarding human rights issues adopted by the Assembly. As for the Human Rights Council, Italy participated as full member in two regular sessions and in the special session concerning Haiti. Nor, all told, has Italy failed in its financial commitments supporting various United Nations bodies and specialised agencies active on the human rights front. Italy allocated approximately 11.5 million dollars for UNHCR, 16 million for UNESCO (plus 9.5 million more in voluntary contributions), and 19.7 million for the International Labour Organisation (ILO). Both as regards the ILO and the UN, Italy's contribution amounts to roughly 5% of their budgets. However, for the first time, contrary to its long-standing practice, Italy did not allot any funds for the United Nations Office of the High Commissioner for Human Rights.

Participation in UPR proceedings will later be addressed in a more detailed way.

Italy is currently subject to monitoring, in particular, by seven out of nine United Nations Committees created under international Conventions, the so-called "Treaty Bodies": Human Rights Committee; Committee on Economic, Social and Cultural Rights; Committee on the Elimination of Racial Discrimination; Committee on the Elimination of Discrimination against Women; Committee against Torture; Committee on the Rights of the Child; Committee on the Rights of Persons with Disabilities.

The Committee on Enforced Disappearances and the Committee on Migrant Workers still remain cut off from the monitoring machinery, since Italy has not ratified their respective Conventions. Moreover, while awaiting ratification of the Protocol to the Convention against Torture, Italy is not subject to monitoring by the Sub-Committee on Prevention of Torture.

Punctuality in submitting reports, which are edited by the Inter-Ministerial Committee for Human Rights, is still a sore point for Italy. Indeed, if attention is set to the latest reports submitted to the different Committees, it results that the delay accumulated by Italy with respect to the deadline ranges from a minimum of three months (joint report III-IV on children's rights) to a maximum of five years (joint report XIV-XV on eliminating racial discrimination); in other cases, the delay generally lasts for around two years.

As before mentioned, in 2010 Italy was subjected to the UPR proceeding. At the end of the review, the Human Rights Council addressed the Italian Government with 92 recommendations on measures to adopt in order to improve the national system for promoting and protecting human rights. Italy *fully accepted* 78 recommendations (44 of which considered as already implemented or in the phase of implementation); it *partially accepted* 2 recommendations, and *rejected* 12. Approximately 13% of the recommendations were not accepted: a lower number compared to other European States, including the United Kingdom (30%), the Netherlands (25%), Germany and Norway (20%).

Considering the number of international legal instruments and related monitoring bodies, the reporting system is undoubtedly demanding for States. However, periodic accounting is proving highly effective, also due to the fact that in cases of non-compliance by the States involved, the critical assessments and recommendations recur time after time, inexorably, in a context marked by publicity and by attentive participation on the part of national and international non-governmental organisations. Needless to point out that the reiteration of critical points helps to delineate weak points in the national human rights systems. Limiting the discussion to the fore-mentioned United Nations Committees, the most frequent recommendations addressed to Italy concern, e.g., the need to create a national independent human rights institution; inclusion of the crime of "torture" in the criminal code; the launching of rapid, impartial, effective inquiries when police are accused of excessive use of force; the prevention of any form of racial discrimination, and punishment for those who incite ethnic or racial hate; the reinforcement of human rights protection for specific categories of persons: migrants, asylum-seekers, Roma and Sinti, persons in a state of detention.

4. Aside from assessment linked to periodic reporting, that also include bodies operating in the sphere of the Council of Europe such as the European Committee of Social Rights, the Committee of the Convention on the Exercise of Children's Rights, the Committee for the Prevention of Torture, Italy is subject to the judicial machinery driven by the European Court of Human Rights.

Italian citizens have gradually become more and more familiar with this last instrument, so that Italy now figures among the most assiduous suppliers of cases to the European Court. At the end of 2010, there were 10,208 claims pending against Italy, or 7.3% of the Court's overall judicial burden. In case number, Italy was preceded by Russia (over 40,000 cases pending), Turkey (over 15,000), Romania (nearly 12,000) and Ukraine (10,434).

Several cases involving Italy – given the widespread notoriety of the events and the importance of the controversy they inspire – attract the attention of the public and the media, and help keeping attention alive toward the fundamental role of the European Court of Human Rights. However, most of the case-load is made up of scattershot appeals regarding issues already dealt with by the Court, in which the Italian institutions intervened late or in an insufficient manner. Indeed, Italy continues to be the object of numerous claims touching, for example, on the excessive duration of judicial proceedings, trials by default in particular; and on protection of property rights in cases of expropriation. A particularly worrying tendency which occasionally emerged during 2010 is the failure to satisfy requests for provisional measures issued by the Strasbourg Court, in particular, suspension of the repatriation order against appellants. The European Council's Committee of Ministers has urged Italy to show greater respect for such orders; non-compliance with them might imply violation of the European Convention on Human Rights itself.

The importance assigned to European Court case-law has grown considerably within the Italian judicial system: the year 2010 has already provided signs of this tendency not only in Constitutional Court verdicts, but also in Cassation case-law and in the jurisprudence of single judges involved.

The impact of the European Human Rights Court case-law may soon grow in importance, parallel to the process of encompassing human rights in the law and in the judicial machinery of the European Union. In fact, with the full equalisation of the EU Charter of Fundamental Rights with the binding value of the Lisbon Treaty provisions, and with the prospect of the EU's adhesion to the European Convention on Human Rights, the way is open to a melding of the two systems – the supra-national with the inter-governmental – as regards controlling States' behaviours in the specific human rights field. This enlargement of the European human rights space has direct consequences for the administration of justice in Italy; it implies the increasingly direct, immediate impact of international human rights standards, not only as "norms interposed" when judging the constitutional legitimacy of a law, but also as provisions destined to prevail systematically over incompatible internal norms.

Then, the monitoring of Italy by supra-national jurisdictional and non-jurisdictional authorities reveals both light and dark areas. Some of the critical situations have already been mentioned: the condition of Roma, Sinti and irregular immigrants; the trauma of pushing back migrants at sea; the situation of prisons; intolerance and xenophobia. Such issues were focused on during special visits made to Italy in 2009 by Thomas Hammarberg, the Council of Europe Human Rights Commissioner, and in 2010, by the United Nations High Commissioner for Human Rights, Navanethem Pillay. Other critical issues include pluralism in the media, television in particular; and the correlative freedom of information and political participation. The consultancies and monitoring bodies of the Council of Europe, and of the OSCE as well, have dedicated close attention to this problem in referring to specific laws of recent years.

5. Despite its formal commitment toward the prompt ratification of international human rights conventions and protocols, and the progress made toward recognising the peculiar strength of international legal sources in relation to internal law, the Italian legal system still reveals serious shortcomings in making normative and institutional infrastructures capable of full compliance with international standards, starting once again with the lack of an overall blueprint for creating national human rights institutions. Italy is also amiss in promoting – through laws or other normative acts, and suitable policies – a real adaptation of the system and its institutional apparatus to the provisions of important international conventions, even when it has ratified them and issued their execution. One instance of a duly ratified international convention to which Italy has, nonetheless, not yet completely adapted, concerns the Statute of the International Criminal Court. Perhaps, the most glaring case – given, too, the fact that for over twenty years it has remained unsolved – is that of the Convention against Torture (CAT).

As is well known, the Convention against Torture and Other Cruel, Inhuman or Degrading Punishments or Treatments, adopted in 1984, came into force in Italy in 1989. In art. 4 it requires each Member State to "ensure that all acts of torture are offences under its criminal law" and to punish them adequately. In its first report on the implementation of the Convention submitted to the Committee against Torture (1991), the Italian government declared that it was not obliged to make any change in its criminal system, since the crime as defined by the Convention substantially corresponded to such crimes as battery, injury, private violence, threats and kidnapping, not to mention a series of incriminations aimed at protecting citizens against abuse by the authorities (art. 606-609, penal code); and the common aggravating circumstance of abuse of power applies as well (art. 61, No. 9, penal code). Besides automatically recognising the applicability of the international customary law (*ius cogens*) against torture, the Italian Constitution establishes principles regarding personal freedom, fundamental rights and freedoms, the provision of punishment, etc., which are clearly incompatible with torture. However, the fact remains that the specific crime of torture in line with the definition provided by art. 1 of the 1984 Convention is not defined in the Italian legislation (art. 185-*bis* of the wartime military criminal code, introduced in 2002, foresees an autonomous crime of torture, but the various laws authorising ratification and containing the order of execution of the international instruments against torture do not appear suitable to introducing a directly applicable incriminating norm).

In the course of various legislatures, there has been no shortage of draft laws aiming to include – among crimes against the person, or against moral freedom – a criminal norm in line with the 1984 Convention. In fact, in 2006, the House of Representatives had approved a bill introducing an art. 613-*bis* into the criminal code, aiming to punish by imprisonment from three to twelve years "anyone who, with violence or grave threats, inflicts serious physical or mental harm or cruel, inhuman or degrading treatment on another person, with the purpose of obtaining from that person or a third person information or confession concerning an act which that person or a third person has committed or is suspected of having committed; or with the purpose of punishing a person for an act which he himself or a third person has committed or is suspected of having committed; or for reasons of racial, political, religious or sexual discrimination".

This text, actually expanded the concept of "torture" as it appears in the 1984 Convention, since it viewed the crime as an ordinary offence. Instead, the Convention presents the offence as a specific crime for which only a public official can be punished: the act of torture must have been committed, ordered, instigated or tolerated or not repressed, by that official. In the conception that was shared in the Italian House of Representatives, instead, the culprit's being a public official was an aggravating circumstance. The crime of torture was therefore identified by the particular malice associated with it, implying the intent to capture information, force confession, or illegitimately discriminate against or punish the victim. Again in line with the 1984 Convention, the proposed law excluded any form of immunity, including diplomatic immunity; and – in the perspective of universal jurisdiction – established punishment even for offences taking place outside Italy.

Early closure of the legislature has prevented the Senate from giving final approval to the proposed law. In the current period of office of the legislature, No. XVI, the bill which Parliament failed to pass in 2006, as well as other similar bills, was again proposed in 2009 and at the beginning of 2010 by various members of Parliament in both the House of Representatives and Senate, in the wake of dramatic news events arousing public attention to the dangers of mistreatment and even actual torture threatening persons stopped or detained by the police (among the most emblematic, the case of Stefano Cucchi); and in light of Italy's possible involvement in the illegal practice of "extraordinary rendition" (the cases of Abu Omar and Abou Elkassim Britel, mentioned in the European Parliament's resolution of 14 February 2007 concerning the presumed involvement of European Countries in CIA illegal transfer and detention of prisoners, had still not been clarified by the of 2010). Unfortunately, however, as months have passed, such initiatives seem to have disappeared into thin air.

Few now nourish any doubt about the need, both political and juridical, to introduce a specific crime of torture in the criminal code.

Most Countries do define such a crime, grouped among offences subject to the machinery of the European arrest warrant. EC regulation 1236/2005, duly transposed by Italy, punishes the production of and commerce in instruments usable for torture or and for capital punishment. From 2004 until 2008 the Italian State contributed approximately 120,000 euros per year to the United Nations Fund for the Victims of Torture.

The European Human Rights Court has remained adamantly contrary to any form of torture, affirming the responsibility of States Party to the European Convention on Human Rights and Fundamental Freedoms even when the probability of torture of an individual in their custody was attributable to the behaviour of Third States. Italy has aligned itself with this firm stance. In declarations made prior to its appointment as member of the United Nations Human Rights Council, and during the UPR proceedings, the Italian Government has often mentioned its intention to ratify as soon as possible the Optional Protocol to CAT.

Furthermore, it seems clear, though the connection is not strictly necessary, that the prevention of torture can be more easily achieved if national norms clearly define this crime. However, as above mentioned, at the end of 2010 the State had not yet ratified the Protocol, though in 2007 it had promised to do so.

Important reasons of principle and of practice, then, argue in favour of defining explicit punishment for the crime of torture in the Italian criminal code. Urgent requests in this sense have been addressed by the Council of Europe's Committee for the Prevention of Torture (CPT).

Therefore it is surprising to see that in the *Addendum* to the final document of the Universal Periodic Review (which took place the meeting of 9 June 2010), the recommendations made by the Netherlands, the Czech Republic, and New Zealand to define the crime of torture in legislation were rejected by the Italian Government, ostensibly for the reason that "even though it is not typified as one specific offence under the Italian criminal code, both the constitutional and legal framework already punish acts of physical and moral violence against persons subject to restrictions of their personal liberty. Both provide sanction for all criminal conducts covered by the definition of torture, as set forth in art. 1 [of the 1984 Convention]". These are the same arguments already used in 1991 (first report on the implementation of the CAT submitted to the Committee); apparently the Government sees no need for further action.

6. Different remarks can be made in regard of the struggle against human trafficking and grave forms of exploitation affecting workers, and of protection measures favouring the victims of such odious crimes. Undoubtedly, Italy has distinguished itself in these areas since the 1990s, showing strong commitment on the operative level. Even on the international level, it has proven the value of its approach in protecting the fundamental rights of human trafficking victims, looking well beyond the victims' role as witnesses in judicial proceedings.

It is necessary both to guarantee the rights of victims, and meet needs linked to activities of crime prevention and, above all, repression, in a "multi-agency" key (institutionalised cooperation among police, judiciary and social actors). Reconciling these two demands has proven not only operatively possible, but fully in line with indications contained in the most significant instruments adopted in this sphere by the United Nations, the Council of Europe, OSCE and the European Union. Since March 1998, in a wider scope of intervention affecting immigration law, Italy presented a legislative instrument which has proven useful on many fronts: art. 16 of law 6 March 1998, No. 40, which later became art. 18 of the Consolidated act on immigration (legislative decree No. 286, 25 July 1998). This law has allowed to approach the goals established by various international directives, in particular reinforcing the repression of human trafficking, while considering the protection instrument not only as machinery compatible with the fight against criminal organisations, but also as an incentive favouring repressive action. Art. 18 sets forth the possibility, for the *Questore* (Head of the Police in each Province), to issue a special residence permit to foreigners who are victim to violence or severe exploitation, when they are in danger because of their attempt to free themselves of conditioning by a criminal association, or because of declarations they have made during criminal proceedings. On request or by prior approval by the *Procuratore della Repubblica* (Prosecutor), the permit allows such victims to participate in programmes of assistance and social integration. Conditions of violence or exploitation may be ascertained during police operations, inquiries or proceedings referring to crimes connected to prostitution or other grave offences; or during intervention by social services. This residence permit lasts six months and can be renewed for one year (or longer), for the same reasons, or for reasons of employment; or it may be converted into a residence permit for students.

As years have passed, the application of this legislation has made possible not only to assist and reintegrate thousands of persons who were victim to situations of severe subjection and exploitation, but also to foster the development of important investigative activities leading to numerous arrests and condemnations.

Law 228/2003 (Measures against human trafficking) emended the criminal code as regards art. 600 (Reduction to or holding in slavery or servitude), 601 (Human trafficking) and 602 (Buying and selling of slaves). This emending law, along with law 146/2006 ratifying the Convention of Palermo of 2000 (on transnational organised crime) and its additional Protocols, are the most significant norms concerning this complex area.

As regards the year 2010, with law 2 July 2010, No. 108 (authorising ratification and ordering the execution of the Council of Europe Convention on Action against Trafficking in Human Beings, signed in Warsaw on 16 May 2005, plus norms adapting internal legislation), other changes have been made in the fore-mentioned penal code articles; and a series of aggravating circumstances have been added. However, the ratifying law does not actually appear to give "full and total implementation" to the Warsaw Convention. In particular, while art. 13 of the Convention establishes a period of recovery and reflection of at least thirty days during which the presumed human trafficking victim cannot be expelled from the Country, no such provision appears in the Consolidated act on immigration; nor is this situation hypothesised by the

European Union's "repatriation directive", which establishes different times and terms.

Moreover, art. 26 of the Convention allows the Parties to "provide for the possibility of not imposing penalties on victims for their involvement in unlawful activities, to the extent that they have been compelled to do so". Like other elements, this provision has not been fully transposed into the adapting norms; it is not encompassed by the hypothesis of "physical coercion" nor "state of need".

It should be stressed that – as this *Yearbook* makes abundantly clear – the treatment of immigrants, asylum-seekers, refugees and foreigners illegally present on Italian territory still remains a sore point in the Italian human rights scenario. In fact, no international or European authority monitoring human rights in Italy fails to note shortcomings and problems afflicting this sphere. The condition of irregular migrants is a constant source of worry as regards protection of their rights. To the demand for such protection, Italy is still slow to provide structured response, rather than mere emergency measures: response in full respect of international standards. The numerous possible facets of the foreigner's condition (regular or irregular, migrant or refugee, adult or minor, etc.) are discussed in several sections of this *Yearbook*, confirming the absolute centrality of this issue in the sphere of human rights.

7. In a situation showing the persistent inadequacy of Italy's relationship with international human rights law and its machinery, the existence of structures and processes dealing with human rights at subnational level proves the Country's commitment in fostering the establishment of an appropriate national infrastructure. The preceding pages do provide some reference to such virtuous reality. This includes, for example, the reinforcement of legislation aiming to repress human trafficking and exploitation, as well as recent norms opposing violence against women, specifically in the form of "stalking". It should be focused, in particular, on two virtuous developments which are currently burgeoning in Italy: the growth of an active, conscientious role on the part of local and regional government institutions as regards policies and positive measure in the very field of human rights, and consolidation of human rights teaching and education in the school system.

One fact pertaining to commitment by local governments is, in many ways, unique in the world: unique as to content, unique in its strong territorial bonds. Since 1991, a number of Municipalities, Provinces and Regions have endowed themselves with statutes and bills containing a provision which explicitly refers both to the Italian Constitution and to international law of human rights. The standard text of the so-called "peace human rights norm" included in those instruments reads: "The Municipality (the Province, the Region) recognises peace as a fundamental right of the person and of peoples, according to the principles of the Italian Constitution and the international law enshrining the promotion and the protection of human rights".

This norm exists today in the statutes of 2,086 Italian Municipalities with over 5,000 inhabitants, 97 Provinces and 13 Regions. The statutes of 842 Municipalities, 56 Provinces and 8 Regions mention at least one international and/or European human rights instrument (United Nations Charter, Universal Declaration of Human Rights, the two International Covenants of 1966, the European Union Charter of Fundamental Rights, the Convention on Children Rights, etc.). 14 out of 20 Regions have adopted specific laws concerning human rights promotion, international cooperation and international solidarity.

On a sub-national level, then, local authorities have crafted exceptional formal acknowledgment of international norms. In so doing, they have confirmed the idea that the Universal Declaration of Human Rights is the fundamental norm for any legal system, at any level. In addition, local and regional authorities often play a substantial role in monitoring and reporting. More and more often, local authorities tend to become a precious source of information and best practices. They also tend to become partners in international cooperation, helping the State institutions in their commitment to international human rights obligations. This is a good example of a dynamics of healthy subsidiarity, leading human rights promotion from below to become an organically structured, multi-level system in Italy.

The positive aspects of this process make the national leadership gaps all the more visible and unacceptable, lacking adequate institutions and measures capable of shedding light, in the international context, on the civil society heritage which so enriches Italy.

On the positive side, it should be pointed out that in the United Nations context, Italy recently contributed to the substantive effectiveness of international law in the specific field of human rights education and training. Needless to stress that education is the primary safeguard for human rights, first of all, because it works to prevent their violation. The Universal Declaration highlights this concept by proclaiming itself "as a common standard of achievement for all peoples and nations, to the end that every individual and every organ of society, keeping this Declaration constantly in mind, shall strive by teaching and education to promote respect for these rights and freedoms". From 2008 to 2011 Italy actively participated in an initiative by the United Nations Human Rights Council aiming to set out a "United Nations Declaration on Human Rights Education and Training". Together with France, Costa Rica, the Philippines, Morocco, Senegal, Slovenia and Switzerland, it took part in a special orientation and support "platform". The final

Declaration draft was adopted by the Human Rights Council with resolution 16/1 of 23 March 2011, and forwarded for approval to the United Nations General Assembly. This new legal (soft law) instrument is motivated by the wish to send a strong message to the international community in order to increment every effort in the field of human rights education and training through the shared commitment of all interested subjects. The strategic relevance is clearly reflected by Declaration art. 1: "Everyone has the right to know, seek and receive information about all human rights and fundamental freedoms and should have access to human rights education and training". Human rights education and training, then, are themselves recognised as a specific fundamental right within the overall framework of the human right to education pursuant to art. 26 of the Universal Declaration and to art. 13 of the International Covenant on Economic, Social and Cultural Rights.

It should be noted that in the Council of Europe sphere as well, the topic of human rights education is assuming more and more importance, as reflected in the Committee of Ministers' Recommendation of 11 May 2010, including the "European Charter on Education for Democratic Citizenship and Human Rights Education". In virtue of this instrument, that foresees a monitoring follow-up system, the Member States of the Council of Europe are asked to collaborate with one another also in setting out specific national programmes.

Italy's participation in the current international norm-making process significantly coincides with a renewed commitment in the very field of education, especially thanks to the introduction in the school system – beginning in the year 2008-2009 – of a specific teaching entitled "Citizenship and Constitution", pursuant to law 169/2008 and to recent rules enacted with school reform.

On 27 October 2010 a circular letter by the Ministry of Education, University and Research launched a call in schools at all levels for planning and experimenting innovative organisational and teaching itineraries focusing precisely on this new teaching. In response, the Ministry received 3,202 projects, of which 104 were selected, with the involvement of 4,366 schools, 367 of which were awarded prizes. As a matter of empirical evidence, the Italian schools show a high level of interest toward this undertaking. The heading "human dignity" and "fundamental rights" have now become central to training programmes for teachers.

The current grass roots educational mobilisation is preceded and now accompanied by a burgeoning of human rights curricula in universities, which began in 1982, when the Interdepartmental Centre on Human Rights and the Rights of Peoples of the University of Padua started functioning. As in 2010, the Italian university system is endowed with 125 teaching courses relating to human rights, distinguished in 60 Faculties of political science, 30 Faculties of law, and with 5 human rights centres, 13 doctoral programmes and 7 Master degree programmes.

There are good premises in Italy for eventually succeeding in developing a human rights-based civic education with a strong international-universalist dimension as defined in the pioneering Recommendation by UNESCO of 19 November 1974 "concerning education for international understanding, cooperation and peace, and education relating to human rights and fundamental freedoms", recently improved by the fore mentioned new instruments of the United Nations and the Council of Europe. Hopefully it could also be envisaged the development of a fruitful educational and training pact between schools at various levels, – beginning with primary schools – and university institutions, in shared awareness that a human rights educational strategy will unite them all in pursuing the best interest of pupils and of the whole society.

8. The *Italian Yearbook of Human Rights* is divided into four main Parts, sub-divided into chapters dedicated to the adaptation of internal law to international human rights norms, to the national human rights infrastructure, to Italy's relationship with the international human rights machinery, to Italian human rights case-law and to international human rights case-law directly involving Italy. Their consecutive reading should yield a comprehensive picture of the human rights situation in Italy, both in a normative, "infrastructural" light and as regards the real enactment of policies and initiatives fostering human rights promotion and protection. The degree of detail and in-depth discussion pursued in each Part of the *Yearbook* may hopefully allow to make transversal, targeted readings, which can be developed by consulting the Index.

The diachronic arc considered is the year 2010. However, since this is the first issue of a publication aiming to become periodical, the research and editing team in agreement with the Interdepartmental Centre on Human Rights and the Rights of Peoples of the University of Padua (Human Rights Centre), decided to report succinctly data pertaining to previous years in order to contextualise activities of 2010 within the larger, evolutionary framework in which they were performed. This methodological choice is particularly clear in Part III, dedicated to "dialogue" between Italy and regional or international organisations; here, in the absence of specific activities performed in 2010, the *Yearbook* recalls other recent reports, visits, recommendations and initiatives.

Another methodological choice lies in the fact that the information provided in the first three Parts are taken from documents of public dominion, mostly traceable to the official websites of the various organisations considered. It is partly for this reason that all the documents mentioned in the *Yearbook* can be consulted on an *ad hoc* online database at the website of the Regional Archive "Pace Diritti Umani-Peace Human Rights", managed by the Human Rights Centre of the University of Padua. The database was created thanks to the assistance of Luca Gazzola and the four volunteers from the National Civil Service at the Human Rights Centre: Stefano Iachella, Federica Napolitano, Claudia Turetta and Letizia Virgis.

Part I of the *Yearbook* illustrates the degree to which international and European norms have been included in the internal law system. The review progresses systematically, starting from the universal level (norms and machinery of the United Nations, UNESCO, ILO, international humanitarian law instruments) and finally reaching the regional level, constituted by norms and machinery of the Council of Europe, European Union, OSCE. The same progressive criterion is used in presenting the internal legislation which acknowledges principles and obligations contained in international legal instruments, starting from the Italian Constitution and ending with a survey of the sub-national (municipal, provincial and regional) legislation.

Part II is dedicated to Italy's human rights infrastructure, and is divided into three chapters. The first presents the structure, functions and activities of Parliamentary and Government bodies, independent authorities (guarantors), civil society organisations and academic institutions. The second chapter refers to the sub-national level, and surveys the unique, variegated local and regional human rights infrastructure, and the related national coordinating structures. The third chapter concentrates on the activities of the Region of Veneto in the field of human rights, peace and international solidarity. The particular emphasis on this exemplary sub-national reality is inspired by the pioneering commitment of the Region of Veneto, beginning with regional law 18/1988, in promoting a universal culture of human rights.

Part III surveys Italy's position in relation to the international and European monitoring machinery: Committees, Commissions, Special Rapporteurs and Representatives, etc. Ample space is given to the assessments and recommendations addressed to the Italian Government by those bodies, as the result of specific missions and activities of periodic reporting. Further focus is on Italy's role within those organisations, and on contribution given by its representatives in promoting human rights both at regional and global level. This Part is divided into five chapters. The first focuses on the United Nations system: General Assembly, Human Rights Council, particularly on the Universal Periodic Review process, Treaty Bodies. The second chapter is dedicated to the Council of Europe: it offers an overview of activities and initiatives focusing on the European Convention of Human Rights, European Convention against Torture, the European Committee on Social Rights, which in 2010 issued a "decision" over a class action brought against Italy, the Human Rights Commissioner and the European Commission against Racism and Intolerance (ECRI). The third chapter, specifically dedicated to the European Union, presents the innovations introduced with the coming into force of the Lisbon Treaty on 1st December 2009, concerning the responsibilities and functions of EU institutions and organs in human rights matters, both within the EU and in the relationship with third Countries. This chapter completes material presented in Part I as regards the Council of Europe and the European Union norms and case-law during 2010. The fourth chapter refers to the Organisation for Security and Cooperation in Europe (OSCE), and its bodies committed to promoting the human dimension of security: particularly those concerned with freedom in the media and the protection of national minorities. The fifth and final chapter of Part III examines international humanitarian and criminal law, highlighting the degree of Italy's adaptation to it, and listing international peace missions that took place in 2010 involving participation by Italian security forces.

Finally, Part IV provides a selection from national and international case-law regarding Italy during 2010. In both its chapters, cases are subdivided according to the topics addressed by the various sentences. The two chapters deal respectively with internal case-law – of the Constitutional Court, the Court of Cassation, and individual lower courts –, and case-law of the European Court of Human Rights as regards claims brought against Italy. A targeted reading of case-law can also be made by looking up single cases appearing in the Index at the end of this volume, which extensively lists the key details of the decisions cited.

With this layout, the *Yearbook* calls upon the attention primarily of those who are serving in public institutions at all levels, so that they may gain ideas from the overview presented in order to fill normative and operational gaps, of course accordingly with the sound principle "*de lege semper perficienda*": the law must be perennially perfected. It also calls upon the attention of those working within the academia, schools, and all other civil society environments, which take to heart the growth of a true axio-practical culture of human rights and fundamental freedoms.

Part I

Implementation of International Human Rights Law in Italy

International Human Rights Law

There are 132 international legal instruments in force dedicated to protecting and promoting human rights, on a global scale and at the regional level, according to the listing annually edited by UNESCO (*Major Human Rights Instruments*). Tens of other instruments adopted under the aegis of other international organisations can be added, which help orient States' policies, often with a high degree of effectiveness. The first Part of this *Yearbook* is dedicated to recapitulating the most relevant international human rights instruments which Italy has fully accepted, incorporating them by ratification and order of execution into its domestic legal system. In this Part are listed as well international instruments which Italy has signed but not ratified, and those which have not yet become the object of any acceptance initiative. The overview of Italy's international obligations in this area takes into account conventions of universal scope, often adopted in the sphere of the United Nations or its specialised Agencies, conventions adopted by regional organisations to which Italy belongs, and European Union treaties and legislation. The resulting information is preliminary to the presentation of the national normative system – the Italian Constitution, and State and regional legislation – carried out in the next chapter.

In the charts below, the international instruments which establish obligations for Italy in human rights matters are grouped according to the international organisation adopting those instruments, and to thematic area. For each treaty, the official title, the date of adoption and the date of its coming into force are detailed as well as the date of Italy's signature and deposit of the ratification instrument, if applicable. The deposit of made after an act of the Italian Parliament authorised ratification of the treaty and issued the order of execution.

I. Legal Instruments of the United Nations

The following charts indicate the principle instruments touching on human rights matters (variously designated as conventions, protocols, covenants or treaties) adopted by the United Nations and its specialised Agencies, in particular the UN Educational, Scientific and Cultural Organisation (UNESCO) and the International Labour Organisation (ILO).

The issues dealt with by such international agreements include the prohibition and prevention of discrimination, torture and other cruel, inhuman or degrading punishment or treatment, genocide, war crimes and crimes against humanity, slavery, forced labour and human trafficking. The agreements also deal with the fight against terrorism, freedom of information and expression, rights of specific groups of persons (foreigners, refugees, displaced or stateless persons, workers, women, children, persons with disabilities, victims of armed conflict).

A. Conventions Ratified by Italy

Treaty Title	Adoption and opening for signature	Entry into force (as of 31/12/2010)	Signature	Deposit of instrument of ratification
a) General Instruments				
International Covenant on Economic, Social and Cultural Rights	16/12/1966	03/01/1976	18/01/1966	15/09/1978
International Covenant on Civil and Political Rights	16/12/1966	23/01/1976	18/01/1966	15/09/1978
Optional Protocol to the International Covenant on Civil and Political Rights	16/12/1966	23/03/1976	30/04/1976	15/09/1978
Second Optional Protocol to the International Covenant on Civil and Political Rights, aiming at the abolition of the death penalty	15/12/1989	11/01/1991	13/02/1990	14/02/1995
b) Instruments concerning particular subjects				
Prevention of discrimination				
International Convention on the Elimination of All Forms of Racial Discrimination	07/03/1966	04/01/1969	13/03/1968	05/01/1976
ILO Convention (No. 100) concerning Equal Remuneration for Men and Women Workers for Work of Equal Value	29/06/1951	23/05/1953		08/06/1956
ILO Convention (No. 111) concerning Discrimination in Respect of Employment and Occupation	25/06/1958	15/06/1960		12/08/1963
Genocide, war crimes, crimes against humanity				
Convention on the Prevention and Punishment of the Crime of Genocide	09/12/1948	12/01/1951		04/06/1952
Rome Statute of the International Criminal Court	17/07/1998	01/07/2002	18/07/1998	26/07/1999
Terrorism				
Convention for the Suppression of Terrorist Bombings	15/12/1997	23/05/2001	04/03/1998	16/04/2003

Convention for the Suppression of the Financing of Terrorism	09/12/1999	10/04/2002	13/12/2000	27/03/2003
Torture and other cruel, inhuman or degrading treatment or punishment				
Convention against Torture and Other Cruel, Inhuman or Degrading Treatment or Punishment	10/12/1984	26/06/1987	04/02/1985	12/01/1989
Slavery, traffic in persons, forced labour				
Protocol amending the Slavery Convention signed at Geneva on 25 September 1926	07/12/1953	07/12/1953		04/02/1954
Supplementary Convention on the Abolition of Slavery, the Slave Trade, and Institutions and Practices Similar to Slavery	07/09/1956	30/04/1957	07/09/1956	12/02/1958
Convention for the Suppression of the Traffic in Persons and of the Exploitation of the Prostitution of Others	21/03/1950	25/07/1951		18/01/1980
ILO Convention (No. 29) concerning Forced or Compulsory Labour	21/06/1930	01/05/1932		18/06/1934
ILO Convention (No. 105) concerning the Abolition of Forced Labour	25/06/1957	17/01/1959		15/03/1968
Freedom of information and expression				
UNESCO Convention on the Protection and Promotion of the Diversity of Cultural Expressions	20/10/2005	18/03/2007		19/02/2007
Education				
UNESCO Convention against Discrimination in Education	14/12/1960	22/05/1962		06/10/1966
UNESCO Protocol Instituting a Conciliation and Good offices Commission to be Responsible for Seeking the settlement of any Disputes which may Arise between States Parties to the Convention against Discrimination in Education	10/12/1962	24/10/1968		06/10/1966
c) Instruments concerning the protection of particular groups				
Foreigners, refugees, stateless				
Convention relating to the Status of Refugees	28/07/1951	22/04/1954	23/07/1952	15/11/1954
Protocol relating to the Status of Refugees	31/01/1967	04/10/1967		26/01/1972
Convention relating to the Status of Stateless Persons	28/09/1954	06/06/1960	20/10/1954	03/12/1962

Workers				
ILO Convention (No. 11) concerning the Rights of Association and Combination of Agricultural Workers	12/11/1921	11/05/1923		08/09/1924
ILO Convention (No. 87) concerning Freedom of Association and Protection of the Right to Organise	09/07/1948	04/07/1950		13/05/1958
ILO Convention (No. 98) concerning the Application of the Principles of the Right to Organise and to Bargain Collectively	01/07/1949	18/07/1951		13/05/1958
ILO Convention (No. 122) concerning Employment Policy	09/07/1964	15/07/1966		05/05/1971
ILO Convention (No. 135) concerning Protection and Facilities to be Afforded to Workers' Representatives in the Undertaking	23/06/1971	30/06/1973		23/06/1981
ILO Convention (No. 141) concerning Organisations of Rural Workers and Their Role in Economic and Social Development	23/06/1975	24/11/1977		23/06/1981
ILO Convention (No. 151) concerning Protection of the Right to Organise and Procedures for Determining Conditions of Employment in the Public Service	27/06/1978	25/02/1981		28/02/1985
Women				
Convention on the Political Rights of Women	31/03/1953	07/07/1954		06/03/1968
Convention on the Elimination of All Forms of Discrimination against Women	18/12/1979	03/09/1981	17/07/1980	10/06/1985
Optional Protocol to the Convention on the Elimination of Discrimination against Women	06/10/1999	22/12/2000	10/12/1999	22/09/2000
Children				
Convention on the Rights of the Child	20/11/1989	02/09/1990	26/01/1990	05/09/1991
Optional Protocol to the Convention on the Rights of the Child on the involvement of children in armed conflict	25/05/2000	12/02/2002	06/09/2000	09/05/2002
Optional Protocol to the Convention on the Rights of the Child on the sale of children, child prostitution and child pornography	25/05/2000	18/01/2002	06/09/2000	09/05/2002

ILO Convention (No. 138) concerning Minimum Age for Admission to Employment	26/06/1973	19/06/1976		28/07/1981
ILO Convention (No. 182) concerning the Prohibition and Immediate Action for the Elimination of the Worst Forms of Child Labour	17/06/1999	19/11/2000		07/06/2000
Persons with disabilities				
Convention on the Rights of Persons with Disabilities	13/12/2006	03/05/2008	30/03/2007	15/05/2009
Optional Protocol to the Convention on the Rights of Persons with Disabilities	13/12/2006	03/05/2008	30/03/2007	15/05/2009
Fighters, prisoners and civilians				
Geneva Convention (I) for the Amelioration of the Condition of the Wounded and Sick in Armed Forces in the Field	12/08/1949	21/10/1950	08/12/1949	17/12/1951
Geneva Convention (II) for the Amelioration of the Condition of Wounded, Sick and Shipwrecked Members of Armed Forces at Sea	12/08/1949	21/10/1950	08/12/1949	17/12/1951
Geneva Convention (III) relative to the Treatment of Prisoners of War	12/08/1949	21/10/1950	08/12/1949	17/12/1951
Geneva Convention (IV) relative to the Protection of Civilian Persons in Time of War	1208/1949	21/10/1950	08/12/1949	17/12/1951
Protocol Additional to the Geneva Conventions of 12 August 1949, and relating to the Protection of Victims of International Armed Conflicts (Protocol I)	08/06/1977	07/12/1978	12/12/1977	27/02/1986
Protocol Additional to the Geneva Conventions of 12 August 1949, and relating to the Protection of Victims of Non-International Armed Conflicts (Protocol II)	08/06/1977	07/12/1978	12/12/1977	2702/1986
Protocol additional to the Geneva Conventions of 12 August 1949, and relating to the Adoption of an Additional Distinctive Emblem (Protocol III)	08/12/2005	14/01/2007	08/12/2005	29/01/2009

B. Conventions Signed by Italy but Not (yet) Ratified

Treaty Title	Adoption and opening for signature	Entry into force (as of 31/12/2010)	Signature	
a) General Instruments				
Optional Protocol to the International Covenant on Economic, Social and Cultural Rights	10/12/2008	Not yet in force	28/09/2009	
b) Instruments concerning particular subjects				
Terrorism				
International Convention for the Suppression of Acts of Nuclear Terrorism	13/04/2005	07/07/2007	14/09/2005	
Torture and other cruel, inhuman or degrading treatment or punishment				
Optional Protocol to the Convention against Torture and Other Cruel, Inhuman or Degrading Treatment or Punishment	18/12/2002	22/06/2006	20/08/2003	
International Convention for the Protection of All Persons from Enforced Disappearance	20/12/2006	23/12/2010	03/07/2007	
c) Instruments concerning the protection of particular groups				
Women				
Convention on Consent to Marriage, Minimum Age for Marriage and Registration of Marriages	10/12/1962	09/121964	20/12/1963	

C. Conventions Not Signed by Italy

Treaty Title	Adoption and opening for signature	Entry into force (as of 31/12/2010)		
b) Instruments concerning particular subjects				
Prevention of discrimination				
International Convention on the Suppression and Punishment of the Crime of Apartheid	30/11/1973	18/07/1976		
ILO Convention (No. 156) concerning Equal Opportunities and Equal Treatment for Men and Women Workers: Workers with Family Responsibilities	23/06/1981	11/08/1983		
International Convention against Apartheid in Sports	10/12/1985	03/04/1988		

OIL Convention (No. 169) concerning Indigenous and Tribal Peoples in Independent Countries	27/06/1989	05/09/1991		
Genocide, war crimes, crimes against humanity				
Convention on the non-applicability of statutory limitations to war crimes and crimes against humanity	26/11/1968	11/11/1970		
Education				
UNESCO Convention on Technical and Vocational Education	10/11/1989	29/08/1991		
c) Instruments concerning the protection of particular groups				
Foreigners, refugees, stateless				
Convention on the Reduction of Statelessness	30/08/1961	13/12/1975		
Workers				
International Convention on the Protection of the Rights of All Migrant Workers and Members of Their Families	18/12/1990	01/07/2003		
Women				
Convention on the Nationality of Married Women	20/02/1957	11/08/1958		

II. Legal Instruments on Disarmament and Non-proliferation

A. Conventions Ratified by Italy

Treaty Title	Adoption and opening for signature	Entry into force	Signature	Deposit of instrument of ratification
Protocol for the Prohibition of the Use of Asphyxiating, Poisonous or Other Gases, and of Bacteriological Methods of Warfare	17/06/1925	08/02/1928	17/06/1925	03/04/1928
Treaty Banning Nuclear Weapon Tests in the Atmosphere, in Outer Space and Under Water	05/08/1963	10/10/1963	08/08/1963	10/12/1964
Nuclear Non-proliferation Treaty	01/07/1968	05/03/1970	28/01/1969	02/05/1975
Convention on the Prohibition of the Development, Production and Stockpiling of Bacteriological (Biological) and Toxin Weapons and on their Destruction	10/04/1972	26/03/1975	10/04/1972	30/05/1975

Convention on Prohibitions or Restrictions on the Use of Certain Conventional Weapons Which May be Deemed to be Excessively Injurious or to Have Indiscriminate Effects	10/10/1980	02/12/1983	10/04/1981	20/01/1995
Protocol on Non-Detectable Fragments (Protocol I)	10/10/1980	2/12/1983	10/04/1981	20/01/1995
Protocol on Prohibitions or Restrictions on the Use of Mines, Booby-Traps and Other Devices (Protocol II), as amended by the Review Conference	10/10/1980	02/12/1983	10/04/1981	20/01/1995
Protocol on Prohibitions or Restrictions on the Use of Incendiary Weapons (Protocol III)	10/10/1980	02/12/1983	10/04/1981	20/01/1995
Protocol on Blinding Laser Weapons (Protocol IV)	13/10/1995	30/07/1998		13/01/1999
Protocol on Explosive Remnants of War (Protocol V)	28/11/2003	12/11/2006		11/02/2010
Amendment art. 1 of the Convention on Prohibitions or Restrictions on the Use of Certain Conventional Weapons Which May be Deemed to be Excessively Injurious or to Have Indiscriminate Effects	21/12/2001	18/5/2004		01/09/2004
Convention on the prohibition of the development, production, stockpiling and use of chemical weapons and on their destruction	13/01/1993	29/04/1997	13/01/1993	08/12/1995
Comprehensive Nuclear Test-Ban Treaty	10/09/1996	Not yet in force	24/09/1996	01/02/1999
Convention on the Prohibition of the Use, Stockpiling, Production and Transfer of Anti-personnel Mines and on their Destruction	18/09/1997	01/03/1999	03/12/1997	23/04/1999

B. Conventions Signed by Italy

Treaty Title	**Adoption and opening for signature**	**Entry into force**	**Signature**	
Convention on Cluster Munitions	30/08/2008	01/08/2010	03/12/2008	

III. Legal Instruments of the Council of Europe

A. Conventions Ratified by Italy

Treaty Title	Adoption and opening for signature	Entry into force	Signature	Deposit of instrument of ratification
a) General instruments				
Convention for the Protection of Human Rights and Fundamental Freedoms	04/11/1950	03/09/1953	04/11/1950	26/10/1955
Protocol to the Convention for the Protection of Human Rights and Fundamental Freedoms	20/03/1952	18/05/1954	20/03/1952	26/10/1955
Protocol No. 4 to the Convention for the Protection of Human Rights and Fundamental Freedoms, securing certain rights and freedoms other than those already included in the Convention and in the first Protocol thereto	16/09/1963	02/05/1968	16/09/1963	27/05/1982
Protocol No. 6 to the Convention for the Protection of Human Rights and Fundamental Freedoms concerning the Abolition of the Death Penalty	28/04/1983	01/03/1958	21/10/1983	29/12/1988
Protocol No. 7 to the Convention for the Protection of Human Rights and Fundamental Freedoms	22/11/1984	01/11/1988	22/11/1984	07/11/1991
Protocol No. 13 to the Convention for the Protection of Human Rights and Fundamental Freedoms, concerning the abolition of the death penalty in all circumstances	03/05/2002	01/07/2003	03/05/2002	03/03/2009
Protocol No. 14 to the Convention for the Protection of Human Rights and Fundamental Freedoms, amending the control system of the Convention	13/05/2004	01/06/2010	13/05/2004	07/03/2006
European Agreement relating to Persons participating in Proceedings of the European Commission and Court of Human Rights	06/05/1969	17/04/1971	08/01/1974	06/01/1981
European Agreement relating to persons participating in proceedings of the European Court of Human Rights	05/03/1996	01/01/1999	05/03/1996	06/03/1998
European Social Charter	18/10/1961	26/02/1965	18/10/1961	22/10/1965

Additional Protocol to the European Social Charter	05/05/1988	04/09/1992	05/05/1988	26/05/1994
Protocol amending the European Social Charter	21/10/1991	Not yet in force	21/10/1991	27/01/1995
Additional Protocol to the European Social Charter Providing for a System of Collective Complaints	09/11/1995	01/07/1998	09/11/1995	03/11/1997
European Social Charter (revised)	03/05/1996	01/07/1999	03/05/1996	05/07/1999
Convention for the Protection of Individuals with regard to Automatic Processing of Personal Data	28/01/1981	01/10/1985	02/02/1983	29/03/1997
Convention on Cybercrime	23/11/2001	01/07/2004	23/11/2001	05/06/2008
Council of Europe Convention on Action against Trafficking in Human Beings	16/05/2005	01/02/2008	08/06/2005	29/11/2010
b) Instruments concerning particular subjects				
Terrorism				
European Convention on the Suppression of Terrorism	27/01/1977	04/08/1978	27/01/77	28/02/86
Torture				
European Convention for the Prevention of Torture and Inhuman or Degrading Treatment or Punishment	26/11/1987	01/02/1989	26/11/1987	29/12/1988
Protocol No. 1 to the European Convention for the Prevention of Torture and Inhuman or Degrading Treatment or Punishment	04/11/1993	01/03/2002	30/10/1996	08/03/1999
Protocol No. 2 to the European Convention for the Prevention of Torture and Inhuman or Degrading Treatment or Punishment	04/11/1993	01/03/2002	30/10/1996	08/03/1999
c) Instruments concerning the protection of particular groups				
Foreigners, refugees, stateless				
European Agreement on Transfer of Responsibility for Refugees	16/10/1980	01/12/1980	07/07/1981	08/11/1985
Convention on the Participation of Foreigners in Public Life at Local Level	05/02/1992	01/05/1997	05/02/1992	26/05/1994
Migrant workers				
European Convention on the Legal Status of Migrant Workers	24/11/1977	01/05/1983	11/01/1983	27/02/1995

Minorities				
Framework Convention for the Protection of National Minorities	01/02/1995	01/02/1998	01/02/1995	03/11/1997
Children				
European Convention on the Exercise of Children's Rights	25/01/1996	01/07/2000	25/01/1996	04/07/2003

B. Conventions Signed by Italy

Treaty Title	Adoption and opening for signature	Entry into force	Signature	
a) General Instruments				
Protocol No. 12 to the Convention for the Protection of Human Rights and Fundamental Freedoms	04/11/2000	01/04/2005	04/11/2000	
b) Instruments concerning particular subjects				
Bioethics				
Convention for the protection of Human Rights and dignity of the human being with regard to the application of biology and medicine: Convention on Human Rights and Biomedicine	04/04/1997	01/12/1999	04/04/1997	
Additional Protocol to the Convention for the Protection of Human Rights and Dignity of the Human Being with regard to the Application of Biology and Medicine, on the Prohibition of Cloning Human Beings	12/01/1998	01/03/2001	12/01/1998	
Additional Protocol to the Convention on Human Rights and Biomedicine concerning Transplantation of Organs and Tissues of Human Origin	24/01/2002	01/05/2006	28/02/2002	
Additional Protocol to the Convention on Human Rights and Biomedicine, concerning Biomedical Research	25/01/2005	01/09/2007	25/01/2005	
Terrorism				
Protocol amending the European Convention on the Suppression of Terrorism	15/05/2003	not yet in force	15/05/2003	
Council of Europe Convention on the Prevention of Terrorism	16/05/05	01/06/2007	08/06/2005	

c) Instruments concerning the protection of particular groups				
Minorities				
European Charter for Regional or Minority Languages	05/11/1992	01/03/1998	27/06/2000	
Children				
Council of Europe Convention on the Protection of Children against Sexual Exploitation and Sexual Abuse	25/10/2007	01/07/2000	07/11/2007	

C. Conventions Not Signed by Italy

Treaty Title	Adoption and opening for signature	Entry into force		
b) Instruments concerning particular subjects				
Prevention of discrimination				
Additional Protocol to the Convention on cybercrime, concerning the criminalisation of acts of a racist and xenophobic nature committed through computer systems	28/01/2003	01/03/2006		
Genocide, war crimes, crimes against humanity				
European Convention on the Non-Applicability of Statutory Limitation to Crimes against Humanity and War Crimes	25/01/1974	27/06/2003		
b) Instruments concerning the protection of particular groups				
Victims of crime				
European Convention on the Compensation of Victims of Violent Crimes	24/11/1983	01/02/1988		
Foreigners, refugees, stateless				
Council of Europe Convention on the avoidance of statelessness in relation to State succession	19/05/2006	01/05/2009		

IV. European Union Law

The legal framework offered by European Union law is a binding point of reference for the Italian legislator, whether national or regional (see art. 117(1)). Its importance has expanded progressively into areas ever more contiguous to the central nucleus: protection of the rights of the person. This section presents a short overview of EU law, focusing particularly on the Treaty on the European Union (TEU), the Treaty on the Functioning of the European Union (TFEU) and the European Union Charter of Fundamental Rights (CFREU). As for EU-derived law, only measures adopted during 2010 will be dealt with. Again with reference to 2010 only, some case law of the European Court of Justice (ECJ) are mentioned, which either concern the protection of fundamental rights, or directly involve Italy.

A. Treaties

Through the Treaties and its secondary legislation, the European Union has progressively endowed itself with increasingly extended and specific norms for the promotion and protection of human rights. A decisive step towards the inclusion of international human rights norms and principles within the EU was taken in 2000, with the adoption of the Charter of Fundamental Rights of the European Union, adapted in some formal aspects in 2007 so it could be referred to as a binding instrument in the Treaty of Lisbon, which marks the most recent reform of the EU. Also the EU Court of Justice's work in interpreting EU treaties and secondary legislation is of fundamental importance; the Court was the first entity to arouse awareness on the need to integrate human rights into the European juridical framework (see Part III, European Union, IV).

Before the CFREU, the European Union had adopted a certain number of instruments containing important reference to human rights, including the Declaration of the Ministers of Foreign Affairs on Human Rights of 21 July 1986, the Community Charter on the Fundamental Social Rights of Workers, on 9 December 1989; The Luxemburg Council of Europe Declaration on Human Rights on 29 June 1991; the Declaration of Vienna on the 50th anniversary of the Universal Declaration of Human Rights, on 10 December 1998.

The 1992 Treaty of Maastricht, which established the European Union, introduced provisions affirming the principles of freedom, democracy, respect for human rights and the fundamental freedoms, and the rule of law as basic to the Union. Its text already contained reference to the binding value, for the Union and Community Law, of the principles established in the Council of Europe's European Convention for the Protection of Human Rights and Fundamental Freedoms (ECHR), and in the constitutional traditions common to the Member States.

The following Treaty of Amsterdam (1997) reinforced the impact of such norms by introducing a procedure for determining the existence of a serious and persistent breach made by a State of the fundamental human rights principles. The procedure could end in suspending the accused State from exercising some rights deriving from the EU membership.

After the failure to ratify the Treaty establishing a Constitution for Europe (which foresaw further expansion of the importance given to human rights protection among the Union's goals and principles), the Treaty of Lisbon, which came into force on 1 December 2009, rearranged the European Union's legal basis around two fundamental instruments: the Treaty on the EU and the Treaty on the Functioning of the European Union. They both contain important references to human rights. In addition, the CFREU was assigned the same legal force as the EU founding treaties.

The Preamble and art. 2 of the TEU proclaim the rights of the person and human dignity as the founding values of the European construction, while TEU art. 3 places peace and human rights among the essential aims of the Union, in both its internal activity and its international relations. TEU art. 21 states that respect for the dignity of the human being and the principle of the universality and indivisibility of human rights, respect for the principles of equality and solidarity, for the United Nations Charter, for the principles of democracy and the rule of law, form the foundation of the EU's international action.

TEU art. 6 explicitly recognises the human rights declared in the CFREU, which has equal legal value as the TEU and the TFEU. Art. 6 foresees as well the EU's accession to the ECHR (by unanimous vote of the Council, after approval by the European Parliament and with successive ratification by States: see TFEU art. 218, paragraphs 6 and 8), and acknowledges that the human rights mentioned in the ECHR, like those resulting from the constitutional traditions common to Member States, are general principles upholding the Union system. TUE art. 7 disciplines the procedure by which the Council – with a four-fifths majority and after deliberation by the European Parliament – can declare the existence of a State's serious and persistent breach of the EU values referred to in TEU art. 2 and, with a qualified majority vote, can decide to suspend some of the rights deriving from membership in the Union.

In delineating the democratic foundations of the EU, TEU art. 9-12 implicitly allude to the importance of civil and political rights within the European Union. TEU art. 11, in particular, introduces for European citizens the possibility to invite that the Commission to present a proposal on matters which seem to call for normative intervention by the EU. To present such a petition, citizens must first gather support from at least one million persons of various nationalities.

TFEU art. 18-25 concern European citizenship, which is added to national citizenship (and therefore does not merely "complement" it, as expressed in the preceding Maastricht-Amsterdam text). The articles define a series of rights (recognised by the CFREU as well) to which all citizens of Member States are entitled, without discrimination: the right to move and reside freely within the Member States' territory, the right to vote and stand as candidates in European and municipal elections in their State of residence, the right to diplomatic and consular assistance by any State Party, the right to present petitions to the European Parliament and apply to the European Ombudsman. The fight against any form of discrimination (not only discrimination relating directly to matters of EU competency) is assumed as a possible area of EU measures, after unanimous approval by the Council

The fundamental rights are central to many areas of Union action. This occurs in a particularly tangible manner in the sphere of TFEU Title V, dedicated to the space of freedom, security and justice (TFEU art. 67-89) and placed under the jurisdictional supervision of the ECJ. The issues encompassed in this sector concern:

- the abolition of controls on persons when crossing the internal borders (TFEU art. 77), asylum and subsidiary or temporary protection (TFEU art. 78), and immigration from third Countries (TFEU art. 79);
- judicial cooperation in civil matters: mutual recognition of judgments, cross-border service of judicial and extrajudicial documents, cooperation in the taking of evidence, development of alternative methods of dispute settlement, etc. As regards measures having family law implications, a unanimous Council vote is required;
- judicial cooperation in criminal matters: recognition of judgments, cooperation among prosecutor's offices, definition of "European" offences and relative sanctions (on such offences it is envisaged the establishment of a European Prosecutor's Office; this is an area for enhanced cooperation between States; coordinating action also proceeds through EUROJUST; any States may suspend the ordinary legislative procedure, and verify consensus within the Council);
- police cooperation: this includes data collection, treatment and analysis; training, etc. In this sector, as well, States may develop forms of enhanced cooperation; cooperation also proceeds by way of EUROPOL, which has been qualified as an EU Agency since 1 January 2010.

Title VII as well (TFEU art. 101 ff.) contains important provisions touching on human rights matters. The text refers to the domestic market, and introduces common norms on competition, taxation and harmonisation among legislations. It expressly excludes from the scope of the approximation of laws measures fiscal provisions and the rights of employed persons; instead, legislations must harmonise in the field of intellectual property rights.

Title X, on social policy, opens with recognition of the fundamental social rights as defined by the 1961 European Social Charter and the 1989 Communitarian Carter of Fundamental Social Rights of Workers. Areas of intervention by the EU include improvement of the working environment and conditions, information and consultation of workers, equality between men and women and combating social exclusion. Linked to the EU's competence in the social field is the functioning of the European Social Fund (Title XI, TFEU art. 162 ff.).

Human rights issues are also prominent in such EU spheres of competence as the employment (TFEU art. 145-150), the education, vocational training, youth and sports (both introduced by the Lisbon Treaty: TFEU art. 165-166), consumer protection (TFEU art. 169), energy policies (TFEU art. 194), and civil protection (TFEU art. 196).

The TEU and the TFEU both recognise the towering significance of the human rights dimension in the Union's external action (see TEU art. 21), which encompasses the common foreign and security policy of the Union (TEU art. 23-46). The principles and goals of democracy, rule of law, universality and indivisibility of human rights, as well as the eradication of poverty, the preservation of peace (in line with the United Nations aims), environmental protection, development cooperation, etc., must be respected both in external action and in relation to the external aspects of any other Union policy. As regards cooperation with third Countries, and humanitarian aid, the Union acts to complement and reinforce the action of States Parties, pursuing, in particular, the goal of reducing and eradicating poverty (TFEU art. 208).

As noticed above, the coming into force of the Lisbon Treaty has also implied attribution to the EU Charter of Fundamental Rights (CFREU) of the same legal value as the Treaties. The 50 articles of its substantive part include provisions pertaining to fundamental rights. Some provisions already existed in the TEU and TFEU, while others replicate provisions of the ECHR. The fundamental rights are classified under six headings: dignity, freedom, equality, solidarity, citizenship, justice. Art. 51 of the CFREU states that the Charter's norms apply to institutions, bodies and offices and agencies of the EU, and to its Member States only as far as they are implementing EU law. The provisions do not modify limits of EU law nor establish any new powers to the Union. When the Charter recognises rights already guaranteed by the ECHR, these are considered protected to the degree established by the ECHR itself. The principles of the CFREU may be a source of inspiration not only for EU bodies and institutions, but also for State legislators and Governments, when they implement EU law. The CFREU norms may be invoked at the judicial level only in order to interpret acts pertaining to the sphere of EU law, or in order to verify their legality.

B. EU Law Developments and Case-law in 2010

During the year 2010, the EU adopted regulations and directives relevant for the human rights question, both as regards situations outside Union territory and in relation to internal issues.

Regulations have been adopted in order to update the list of individuals and bodies subject to sanctions in execution of United Nations Security Council resolutions against the terrorist networks of Al-Qaeda and the Taleban, and to update the punitive measures against other terrorist organisations. In addition, EU regulations were used during 2010 in order to renew measures against persons wanted by the International Criminal Tribunal for the ex-

Yugoslavia and those individuals who protects those at large as well as to implement restrictive measures established by the United Nations against such Countries as Somalia, Liberia, Zimbabwe, Ivory Coast, the Democratic Republic of Congo, Lebanon, North Korea, Myanmar, Guinea, Eritrea and Belarus. With a decision adopted in the sphere of the Common Foreign and Security Policy, the Council also established restrictive measures against Iran and the region of Trans-Dnistria (Republic of Moldova). As regards the war on terrorism, the EU concluded an agreement with the United States on the processing and transfer of Financial Messaging Data from the European Union to the United States for purposes of the Terrorist Finance Tracking Program ("Official Journal of the EU", 27 July 2010).

As concerns internal EU affairs, on 20 December 2010, Council regulation 1259/2010 was adopted, establishing an enhanced cooperation in the area of laws applying to divorce and separations; another important measure is directive 2010/64/EU, issued on 20 October 2010 by the European Parliament and the Council, on the right to interpretation and translation during criminal proceedings.

Critical measures in the field of immigration include: Council decision 2010/252/EU, 26 April 2010, supplementing the Schengen borders code as regards surveillance of the sea external borders in the context of FRONTEX, the European Agency for the Management of Operational Cooperation at the External Borders of the Member States of the EU; and the Commission's Communication on the Action Plan on unaccompanied minors for the period 2010-2014 (COM(2010)213 final). During 2010 a proposal for a regulation reforming FRONTEX was presented by the Commission (COM(2010) 61 final).

As regards privacy issues, the Commission adopted a communication on *A Global Approach to the Protection of Personal Data in the European Union* (COM(2010) 609 final). Another important privacy measure is the Commission's Communication regarding the use of body scanners in EU airports (COM(2010) 311).

The Commission also addressed the issues of persons with disabilities, with the Communication on the *European Strategy on Disability 2010-2020: A Renewed Commitment to a Barrier-Free Europe* (COM(2010)636 final), of the Roma people, with a Communication on social and economic integration of the Roma in Europe (COM (2010)133 final), and of equality between men and women, adopting the *Women's Charter*, a Declaration by the European Commission on the occasion of the 2010 International Women's Day and in commemoration of the Beijing Conference on Women (COM(2010)78 final).

In December 2009 the EU acceded to the International Convention on the Rights of Persons with Disabilities. Later on, a code of conduct was signed by the Council, Member States and the Commission (published in the "Official Journal" on 15 December 2010) setting out internal norms for the implementation of the Convention by the European Union, and regulating forms of EU representation in the bodies established by the treaty.

On 7 July 2010 the EU Commission launched negotiations in view of its accession to the ECHR.

The European Court of Justice applied the Charter of Fundamental Rights in various judgments during 2010, so enriching its human rights case-law.

Several judgments are worthy of note. Case C-555/07 of 19 January 2010 (*Kücükdeveci*) concerns age discrimination against a woman worker (German legislation offers lower guarantees for dismissed workers if they are young). The judgment of 9 November 2010 (cases C-92/09 and C-93/09) protects the right to privacy of those benefiting of financial contribution from the European Agricultural Fund and the European Agricultural Fund for Rural Development; some beneficiaries complained that their names and the sums they had received had been published and made available to anyone. In addition, several judgments have been issued concerning the conformity to EU law – including principles of the CFREU – of norms imposing restrictions affecting persons linked to terrorist organisations or regimes violating International Law.

In 2010 several suits reached a conclusion filed by the Commission against Italy for its failure to comply with European norms, or to transpose Union directives pertinent to human rights into its internal legislation. At the end of 2010, approximately 140 suits were pending against Italy for infraction; in 2009 the number had reached 153.

In the case C-297/08, of 4 March 2010, the European Court of Justice recognised that Italy has failed to fulfil its obligations deriving from directive 2006/12 of the European Parliament and the Council, on waste, since it has not adequately managed waste disposal in Naples and Campania. The Court points out that from the available data, it clearly appears that in the Campania Region, the Italian State has not succeeded in fulfilling its obligation, deriving from art. 4, No. 2 of directive 2006/12, to prevent the abandonment, dumping and uncontrolled disposal of waste; and that the worrying situation of waste accumulating in the streets has exposed the health of the population to certain risk, in violation of art. 4, No. 1 of the same directive.

In case C-491/08, the Court ascertained the Italian State's failure to comply with directive 92/43/CEE ("habitat directive") relative to the site Is Arenas, in the province of Oristano; although being declared a site of EU interest, the area has been included in a plan of tourist facility development which has compromised its conservation.

In case C-379-/10 (claim submitted on 29 July 2010), the Commission sued the Italian State alleging the incompatibility with EU law of Italian legislation (law 13 April 1988, No. 117) which excludes any responsibility by the State towards a citizen in case of miscarriage of justice in applying EU law, except in cases of criminal intent or gross negligence on the part of the judge.

Italian Law

I. The Constitution of the Italian Republic

The Italian Constitution came into force on 1 January 1948; it declares the democratic nature of the Italian Republic, "founded on work" and on the rule of law. The recognition of the inviolable rights and of substantial (and not merely formal) equality of all citizens and human beings, regardless of their condition, stands out clearly among the fundamental principles of the Constitutional Charter (see art. 2 and 3 Const.). These provisions are complemented by the recognition of the right to work (art. 4 Const.), the rights of linguistic minorities (art. 6 Const.), the freedoms guaranteed to the Catholic Church and all to other religious confessions (art. 7 and 8 Const.); the Constitution also features the commitment to the development of culture and of scientific and technical research and to the protection of the natural landscape and the historical and artistic heritage of the Country (art. 9 Const.). The Charter includes as well the right of foreigners to seek asylum in Italy, and their right not to be extradited for political offences (art. 10 Const., paragraphs 3 and 4). Moreover, the norm in art. 11 Const. provides constitutional grounds to the right to peace and to international solidarity.

Besides these basic principles, the entire First Part of the Constitution (art. 13-54) is dedicated to the fundamental rights of the person.

The rights have their correlated duties: e.g. art. 4, para. 2 Const. (the duty to contribute to societal progress); 18, para. 2 Const. (interdiction of secret and politico-military associations); 21, para. 6 Const. (ban on publications or manifestations contrary to public decency); 28 Const. (civil liability of State officers); 30, para. 1 (parents' duties toward their children); 33, para. 5 (State examinations prescribed for admission to and graduation from schools and for qualification to exercise a profession); art. 34, para. 2 (at least eight years of compulsory education); 41, para. 2 (ban on carrying out economic activities conflicting with social utility or contrary to human security, freedom and dignity); 42, para. 3, 43 and 44 Const. (obligation to comply with expropriation provisions or restrictions affecting private property, economic activities or land property); art. 48, para. 2 Const. (exercising the right to vote is a civic duty); as well as art. 52, 53 and 54 Const., on respectively defence of Homeland, tax duties and loyalty to the Republic (also see art. 28 and 30 Const.).

The inviolable rights recognised in Part One of the Constitution are classified according to four areas. The first regards civil relations (art. 13-28 Const.). It comprises personal freedom and freedom from any personal inspection, detention or search, from physical or moral violence, and from illegal extra-judicial detention; privacy of home and correspondence; freedom of movement and residence; the right to peaceful assembly and association; the right to freely profess religious beliefs and to religious association; the right to freely express one's opinions; the right to preserve one's legal capacity, citizenship and name; the right not to be imposed of obligations of personal or financial nature not prescribed by law; the right to bring case before a court, the right to defence during legal proceedings and the right to reparation in case of judicial error; the right to be judged by a tribunal previously established by law, the right not to be punished for an act that did not constitute a criminal offence at the time it was committed and not to be inflicted a punishment not prescribed by a law; the right not to be extradited for political offences; the right not to be punished for an act committed by a different person, and not to be subject to inhuman treatments or capital punishment.

The second group rights regard ethico-social relations (art. 29-34 Const.). This group encompasses the rights of the family and equality between spouses, the right (constituting a duty as well) to maintain, instruct and educate children, banning any discrimination against children born out of wedlock; the right of families, mothers, children and young people to social protection; the right to health, held by individuals as well as by the community; the right not to undergo obligatory health care treatments (except in cases defined by the law), or in any case contrary to the dignity of the person; the freedom in scientific research and teaching; the right to education and the freedom to set up educational structures at no cost to the State; the right of universities and similar institutions to be autonomous; the right to be admitted to schools and to be awarded scholarship, through open selections.

The third area concerns economic relations (art. 35-47 Const.). It deals not only with the fundamental right to work pursuant to art. 4 Const., but also the workers' right to job protection and professional training; the right to emigrate; the right to fair wages and equal remuneration, to a weekly rest period and paid annual holidays, to maximum daily working hours established by law; the woman's right not to undergo discrimination in employment and to working conditions protective of women and children; the right not to work below the age limit set by the law; the right of working minors not to undergo discrimination; the right – ensured by entities and institutions established or supported by the State – of social assistance for those unable to work; the right to welfare benefits in case of accident, illness, disability, old age, or involuntary unemployment; the right to education and professional or vocational training for persons with disabilities; right to establish and participate in trade unions; the right to strike; the right to carry out private enterprises; the right to private property, including inheritance rights; the right to carry out economic activity in cooperative form and in artisan enterprises; the right of workers to collaborate in the management of enterprises; the right to access to credit, the ownership of housing and directly cultivated land, and the right to invest in the stock market.

The last area concerns political relations (art. 48-52 Const.). Citizens are entitled to the right to vote; the vote is personal, equal, free and secret (special measures are mentioned for citizens residing outside Italy). All citizens have the right to freely associate in political parties, the right to submit petitions to the Parliament, the right of equal access to public offices and elective positions (which justifies the adoption of measures promoting equal opportunities between men and women); those elected have the right to retain their previously held job. Political relations also envisage the duty to defend the homeland, contribute to public expenditure, and be loyal to the Country, which are mentioned above.

Other rights of a Constitutional nature derive from provisions contained in the Second Part of the Constitution, dedicated to the institution system of the Republic.

In recent years, the Constitution has undergone reforms regarding such issues as the governance of Regions, Provinces and Municipalities (Title V, Part II – Constitutional law 22 November 1999, No. 1 and Constitutional law 18 October 2001, No. 3); the "Parliamentary immunity system" (c.l. 29 October 1993); equal opportunities in public office (c.l. 30 May 2003, No. 1); and "fair trial" (c.l. 23 November 1999, No. 2).

II. National Legislation

During the year 2010, the Parliament and the Government passed a number of legislative acts (laws, decree-law, legislative decrees) regarding issues addressing – directly or indirectly – the internationally recognised human rights. Any selection of such acts cannot help but be incomplete and tentative. The list in the following pages therefore represents a preliminary approach to the issue. It focuses on the internal and international impact made by various normative acts in matters directly pertinent to the themes and policies most obviously associated with the protection of international civil, political, economic, social, and cultural human rights.

State and sub-State institutions

Lgs.d. 28 May 2010, No. 85 (Attribution of patrimony proper to Municipalities, Provinces, Metropolitan areas and Regions, pursuant to art. 19 of law 5 May 2009, No. 42).

Lgs.d. 26 November 2010, No. 26 (Provisions for determining standard costs and standard needs for Municipalities, Metropolitan areas and Provinces).

EU stabilisation and association agreements

L. 13 August 2010, No. 151 (Stabilisation and Association Agreement between the European Communities and their Member States, of the one part, and the Republic of Serbia, of the other part, with Attachments, Protocols and a final Act with attached declarations, made in Luxembourg on 29 April 2008).

L. 8 June 2010, No. 97 (Stabilisation and Association Agreement between the European Communities and their Member States, of the one part, and the Republic of Bosnia-Herzegovina, of the other part, with Attachments, Protocols and a final Act with attached declarations, made in Luxembourg on 16 June 2008).

Minorities

Lgs.d. 19 November 2010, No. 262 (Norms implementing the special statute of the Autonomous Region Trentino-Alto Adige, modifying and complementing the legislative decree of 16 December 1993, on protection of the Ladina, Mochena and Cimbra communities in the Province of Trent).

Lgs.d. 14 May 2010, No. 86 (Norms implementing the special statute of the Autonomous Region Trento-Alto Adige, on recognition of equal value to certifications attesting knowledge of Italian and German languages).

The judiciary in general

L. 22 February 2010, No. 24 (Conversion into law of decree-law 29 December 2009, No. 193, bearing urgent intervention in matters pertaining to the functioning of the judiciary system).

Lgs.d. 4 March 2010, No. 28 (Implementation of art. 60, law 18 June 2009, No. 69, on mediation aimed at settling civil and commercial disputes).

L. 23 June 2010, No. 98 (Conversion into law, with amendments, of decree-law 28 April 2010, No. 63, on urgent provisions regarding foreign States' immunity from Italian jurisdiction and the appointment of bodies representing Italians residing abroad).

Lgs.d. 2 July 2010, No. 104 (Implementation of art. 44, law 18 June 2009, No. 69, bearing: Delegation to the Government for restructuring the administrative judicial procedure).

Offences, criminal proceedings, penitentiary matters

L. 3 December 2009, No. 188 (Ratification and order of execution of the additional Protocol to the Convention on Extradition of 9 December 1987 between the Italian Republic and the Argentine Republic, signed in Rome on 31 March 2003)[1].

L. 5 March 2010, No. 46 (Ratification and order of execution of the Treaty on Transferring Convicted Persons between the Government of the Italian Republic and the Government of the Dominican Republic, signed at Santo Domingo on 14 August 2002).

L. 6 April 2010, No. 52 (Conversion into law, with amendments, of decree-law 12 February 2010, No. 10, bearing: Urgent provisions on criminal jurisdiction on persons accused of committing serious crimes that create social alarm).

L. 7 April 2010, No. 51 (Provisions on legitimate impediments to court appearance)[2].

L. 4 June 2010, No. 96 (Provisions on the fulfilling of obligations deriving from Italy's EU membership – "Community law" 2009 – art. 52: Delegation to the Government for enacting EU framework decisions – 1. The Government is delegated to adopt, within twelve months after the coming into force of this law, legislative decrees bearing the norms necessary to enact the following draft decisions: a) framework decision 2001/220/JHA by the Council, of 15 March 2001, on the position of the victim during penal proceedings […]

Lgs.d. 7 September 2010, No. 161 (Provisions for aligning internal legislation with framework decision 2008/909/JHA, on the application of the principle of mutual recognition to judgments in criminal matters imposing custodial sentences or measures involving deprivation of liberty for the purpose of their enforcement in the EU).

Lgs.d. 26 October 2010, No. 192 (Provisions implementing the special statute of the Valle d'Aosta/Vallée D'Aoste Region: transfer of competence in matters of penitentiary medicine and health care).

Lgs.d. 19 November 2010, No. 252 (Provisions implementing the special statute of the Autonomous Trentino-Alto Adige Region: health care services for detainees and other persons residing in penitentiary institutions).

Lgs.d. 23 December 2010, No. 274 (Provisions implementing the special statute of the Friuli-Venezia Giulia Region: penitentiary health care services).

---

1 The Protocol refers to the possibility, in certain circumstances, of recognising default criminal judgments.

2 With judgment 13 January 2011, No. 23, the Constitutional Court declared the Constitutional illegitimacy of art. 1, para. 3 and 4 of the law, aimed at protecting the highest State officials from judiciary proceedings, thus substantially reducing the law's scope.

Public order and security

L. 31 March 2010, No. 50 (Conversion into law, with amendments, of decree-law 4 February 2010, No. 4, on the establishment of a National Agency for managing sequestrated and confiscated assets of criminal organisations).

L. 22 May 2010, No. 73 (Conversion into law, with amendments, of decree-law 25 March 2010, No. 40, bearing urgent fiscal and financial measures concerning the fight against international and national fiscal fraud, including fraud in the form of caroselli and cartiere ("carousel trader" or "missing trader"), the strengthening and rationalisation of tax collection, partly as implementation of EU law, and the allocation of recovered money to incentive schemes to increase market demand in given sectors).

L. 29 July 2010, No. 120 (Provisions on road safety).

L. 13 August 2010, No. 136 (Extraordinary anti-Mafia plan and delegation to the Government to enact anti-Mafia legislation).

L. 13 October 2010, No. 175 (Provisions to prevent persons subjected to criminal preventive measures from participating to electoral campaigns).

L. 26 November 2010, No. 199 (Provisions concerning home detention in replacement of prison detention for those sentenced to a year of imprisonment or less).

L. 17 December 2010, No. 217 (Conversion into law, with amendments, of decree-law 12 November 2010, No. 187, on urgent measures for security).

Education, cultural rights

Legs.d. 15 March 2010, No. 44 (National transposition of directive 2007/65/EC on the coordination of certain provisions laid down by law, regulation or administrative action in Member States concerning the pursuit of television broadcasting activities).

L. 29 June 2010, No. 100 (Conversion into law, with amendments, of decree-law 30 April 2010, No. 64, urgent provisions on entertainment and cultural activities).

L. 8 October 2010, No. 170 (New norms on specific learning difficulties in school).

L. 23 December 2009, No. 202 (Ratification and order of execution of the Agreement between the Government of the Italian Republic and the United Nations on the status of the UN System Staff College in Italy, signed in Turin on 16 September 2003, with amendments made in Turin on 28 September 2006).

L. 30 December 2010, No. 240 (Norms concerning the governance of universities, academic personnel and its recruitment, and delegation to the Government support the quality and efficiency of the university system).

Human trafficking, protection of disaster victims

L. 2 July 2010, No. 108 (Ratification and order of execution of the Council of Europe Convention against the Trafficking of Human Beings, signed in Warsaw on 16 May 2005, and norms for its domestic implementation).

L. 7 July 2010, No. 106 (Provisions in favour of survivors and victims' family members of the railway disaster at Viareggio).

Development cooperation

L. 5 March 2010, No. 30 (Conversion into law, with amendments, of decree-law 1 January 2010, No. 1, urgent measures to extend development cooperation activities in support of peace and stabilisation processes, as well as international operation of Italian armed forces and the police; urgent measures for the implementation of the European External Action Service, and on military administrative issues).

L. 3 August 2010, No. 126 (Conversion into law, with amendments, of decree-law 6 July 2010, No. 102, urgent measures to extend development cooperation activities in support of peace and stabilisation processes, as well as international operation of Italian armed forces and the police).

The military system and peace-keeping missions

L. 12 November 2009, No. 162 (Establishment of a "Memorial Day honouring soldiers and civilians who lost their lives in international peace-keeping missions").

L. 5 March 2010, No. 30 – see above, Development Cooperation.

Lgs.d. 15 March 2010, No. 66 (Military code)[3].

L. 14 May 2010, No. 84 (Ratification and order of execution of the Declaration of Intent Between the Kingdom of Spain, the French Republic, the Ital-

[3] In the Military Code, human rights are explicitly mentioned in the provisions on conscientious objection (art. 2097: "Those who out of obedience to their conscience, in exercising the right to freedom of opinion, conscience and religion recognised by the Universal Declaration of Human Rights and by the International Covenant on Civil and Political Rights, and opposing the use of arms, do not accept enrolment in the Armed Forces or in the State Police, may fulfil their draft obligations, even in times of war or serious international crisis, by performing civil service in substitution of military service; while different in nature from military service, and autonomous with respect to it, the civil service does not differ from it as it responds to the same Constitutional duty to defend the homeland, and is disciplined in light of the goals envisioned by the fundamental principles of the Constitution"). Human rights also emerge in the provision allowing for the enrolment to Italian military academies and institutes of foreigners provided that their Country: "a) is not currently affected by any embargo decided by the UN or the European Union; b) the United Nations and/or the European Union has not ascertained any violation of the international human rights convention [sic: this seems to refer to the International Covenant on Civil and Political Rights, of 1966; editor's note]; c) the Country – while receiving Italian assistance in cooperation toward development – does not allot resources to the military budget that are excessive *vis-à-vis* the national defence needs".

ian Republic, the Kingdom of The Netherlands and the Portuguese Republic, concerning creation of a European Gendarme Force, signed at Noordwijk on 17 September 2004, and the Treaty between the Kingdom of Spain, the French Republic, the Italian Republic, the Kingdom of The Netherlands and the Portuguese Republic, establishing the European Gendarmerie Force EUROGENDFOR (EGF), signed at Velsen on 18 October 2007).

L. 3 August 2010, No. 126 – see above, Development cooperation

Industrial property rights

Legs.d. 13 August 2010, No. 131 (Modifications of legislative decree 10 February 2005, No. 30, on the industrial property code, pursuant to art. 19, law 23 July 2009, No. 99).

Work

Lgs.d. 25 January 2010, No. 5 (National transposition of directive 2006/54/EC on the implementation of the principle of equal opportunities and equal treatment of men and women in matters of employment and occupation).

L. 30 December 2010, No. 238 (Fiscal incentives towards workers' return to Italy).

Environment, health, animal welfare

Lgs.d. 25 January 2010, No. 16 (National transposition of directives 2006/17/EC and 2006/86/EC, implementing directive 2004/23/EC as regards traceability requirements, notification of serious adverse reactions and events and certain technical requirements for the coding, processing, preservation, storage and distribution of human tissues and cells).

L. 1 February 2010, No. 19 (Accession by the Italian Republic to the Convention on Civil Liability for Bunker Oil Pollution Damage, with Attachment, signed in London on 23 March 2001, and implementation norms).

Lgs.d. 15 February 2010, No. 31 (Disciplining localisation, construction and functioning on Italian territory, of nuclear plants producing electric energy, plants producing nuclear fuel, storing systems for irradiated fuel and radioactive waste, plus reparation measures and public information campaigns, pursuant to art. 25, law 23 July 2009, No. 99).

L. 15 March 2010, No. 38 (Provisions guaranteeing access to palliative treatment and pain therapy).

Lgs.d. 15 March 2010, No. 47 (Penal provisions for violating provisions in regulation EC 1523/2007, banning the placing on the market and the import to, or export from, the Community of cat and dog fur, and products containing such fur).

Lgs.d. 13 August 2010, No. 155 (Enactment of directive 2008/50/EC on ambient air quality and cleaner air for Europe).

L. 19 July 2010, No. 111 (Conversion into law, with amendments, of decree-law 20 May 2010, No. 72, urgent measures for extending deadlines in matters concerning the environment and transport on wheels, and in the determination of CO_2 emission quotas).

L. 4 November 2010, No. 201 (Ratification and order of execution of the European Convention for the protection of pet animals, signed in Strasbourg on 13 November 1987, and implementation norms).

Persons with disabilities

L. 24 June 2010, No. 107 (Measures for recognising the rights of deaf-and-blind persons).

L. 12 July 2010, No. 109 (Provisions on the admission of persons affected by favism into the Armed Forces and the police).

III. Municipal, Provincial and Regional Statutes

In March 1991, after the adoption of law 8 June 1990, No. 142 (Local authorities system), during the Assembly of the National Coordination of Local Authorities for Peace and Human Rights in Perugia, the Human Rights Centre of the University of Padua launched a proposal for including in the new statutes of Italian Municipalities and Provinces a norm on peace and human rights explicitly referring to the Constitution and to International Human Rights Law.

The original wording of this norm – known as the "peace human rights norm" – appears in art. 1 of Veneto regional law 30 March 1988, No. 18 (updated today by regional law 55/1999) on "Regional measures for the promotion of a culture of peace". It reads:

> 1. The Region of Veneto, consistent with the Constitutional principles sanctioning the repudiation of war as a means of resolving international controversies, and the promotion of human rights, the democratic freedoms and international cooperation, recognises peace as a fundamental human and peoples' right.
>
> 2. To this end it promotes the culture of peace through cultural, research, education, cooperation and information initiatives aimed at making Veneto a land of peace.
>
> 3. In order to achieve these goals, the Region takes direct initiatives and fosters intervention by local authorities, associations, cultural institutions, volunteer groups and international cooperation groups present in the Region.

A study carried out by the Human Rights Centre of the University of Padua and financed by the Region of Veneto – M. Mazzucchelli, *Pace e diritti umani nei Comuni, nelle Province e nelle Regioni. L'infrastruttura normativa e istituzionale* (Peace and human rights in Italian Municipalities, Provinces and Regions. Normative and institutional infrastructure), Padua: Cleup, 2011 – offers a detailed picture of the diffusion, in Italy, of this specific normative reference. The study examines the statutes of the 2,372 Italian Municipalities with over 5,000 inhabitants, of the 104 ordinary Provinces, of the two Provinces with special autonomy, and of the 20 Regions with ordinary or special statutes. The data presented are updated to the end of September 2009, when the monitoring ended

The study shows that the "peace human rights norm", in its original wording or in analogous forms, has been included in the statutes of 2,086 of the 2,372 Municipalities examined, of 97 Provinces and 13 Regions.

Another set of data emerging from this study concerns the international norms and principles on human rights and territorial self-government, explicitly mentioned in the statutes examined

On the municipal level, there are 846 statutes referring to one or more international legal instruments, in particular the Charter of the United Nations (120), the Universal Declaration of Human Rights (154), the International Covenant on Civil and Political Rights (23), the International Covenant on Economic, Social and Cultural Rights (20), the International Convention on the Rights of the Child (200), the EU Charter of Fundamental Rights (30), and the European Charter on Local Self-Government (516). For instance, excerpts extracted from three municipal statutes read as follows:

Municipality of Vicenza (Vicenza, Statute adopted in 1991, modified in 2002)

art. 2 (Peace and cooperation)

1. The Municipality, in conformity to the Constitutional principles and to international norms which recognise the innate rights of human persons, state the repudiation of war as a means of resolving international controversy, and promote cooperation among peoples, recognises peace as a fundamental right of the person and of peoples.

2. To this end the Municipality promotes a culture of peace and human rights through initiatives in cultural and research, education and information initiatives, with the support from associations promoting solidarity with the poorest persons and populations [...]

4. The Municipality, in referring to the Universal Declaration of Human Rights approved by the UN, recognises the value of human life and promotes any initiative offering tangible solidarity toward any person, regardless of their physical, psychic, economic or social condition, their political or religious convictions, their race or their age.

art. 4 (Services for citizens)

[...] 2-bis. The Municipality, in conformity to the International Convention of the United Nations, draws inspiration for its action from the promotion of rights and of opportunities for children and adolescents, in an institutional framework recognising the Mayor as the "Ideal Ombudsman of children".

Municipality of Felino (Parma, Statute adopted in 2001)

art. 4 (Functions of the Municipality)

[...] 1. The Municipality represents the entire population residing on its territory, whose needs it meets in a unitary manner, with respect for ethnic and cultural traits; it promotes its harmonious development and its civil, social and economic progress, guaranteeing citizens' participation in political decision-making and administrative activity, with no discrimination.

[...] 5. The Municipality, in exercising its functions, is inspired by the principles of the Universal Declaration of Human Rights approved by the United Nations General Assembly on 10 December 1948, and pursues the political and social goals sanctioned by the Constitution of the Republic.

Municipality of Palagonia (Catania, Statute adopted in 2003)

art. 1 bis (Democratic traditions)

1. The Municipality draws its inspiration from the respect for the civil and democratic traditions of its community; it recognises the traditions' ideals of peace and its values based on justice, solidarity and human cooperation; it contributes to the construction of European unification by promoting cooperation among local authorities in a national or European perspective.

2. It favours meeting and mutual understanding among peoples, ethnic groups and individuals in respect for the human person and for different cultural, historical and religious traditions.

art. 14 bis (Ethical code)

The Municipal Council adopts the guiding values and the principles declared in the Constitution of the Italian Republic, the Universal Declaration of Human Rights, the European Union Charter of Fundamental Rights and the Rio Declaration on environment and development.

At the provincial level, such international legal instruments are referred to in the statutes of 57 Provinces with ordinary autonomy, in particular the Charter of the United Nations (9), the Universal Declaration of Human Rights (5), the International Covenant on Civil and Political Rights (1), the International Convention on the Rights of the Child (4), the EU Charter on Fundamental Rights (6) and the European Charter on Local Self-Government (44). For instance, excerpts extracted from three municipal statutes read as follows:

Province of Lodi (Statute adopted in 1998, modified in 2005)

art. 2 (Fundamental principles)

1. The Province of Lodi exercises its functions in conformity with the political and social goals declared in the Constitution of the Republic, in respect for the principles established in the Universal Declarations of human rights and on the rights of the child, and in the European Charter on Local Self-Government.

Province of Macerata (Statute adopted in 2001)

art. 1 (Goals)

The Province of Macerata, as an autonomous local authority intermediating between Municipalities and the Region, represents its community, protects community interests, and promotes and coordinates community development according to the principles of subsidiarity and solidarity, guided by the values of the Constitution, of the Convention for the Protection of Human Rights and Fundamental Freedoms, of the European Charter on Local Self-Governments; by State laws and laws of the Marche Region; and by the historical, cultural and civil identity of its population.

Province of Potenza (Statute adopted in 2007)

art. 3 (Provincial goals)

[…] 3. In particular, the Province, in harmony with the fundamental principles stated by the Constitution and by the laws of the State, and in conformity with the principles of the European Charter on Local Self-Government and the Nice Charter of rights, in respect for cultural tradition and for the affirmation and appreciation of the historic, civil and moral identity of the Lucan people, promotes and spreads the values underlying the European Union, through cooperation and collaboration between provincial bodies and communitarian institutions.

Finally, eight regional statutes currently in force refer to at least one international legal instrument: Abruzzo, Apulia, Calabria, Lazio, Lombardy, Marche, Piedmont, and Umbria.

The instruments mentioned are the Charter of the United Nations (1), the Universal Declaration of Human Rights (5), the International Convention for the Rights of the Child (1), the EU Charter on Fundamental Rights (5), the European Convention for the Protection of Human Rights and Fundamental Freedoms (1) and the European Charter on Local Self-Government (1). Extracts from three regional statutes stand as examples:

Region of Lazio (Statute adopted in 2004)

art. 6 (Fundamental rights and values)

1. The Region adopts the principles guiding the Universal Declaration of Human Rights.

2. It recognises the primacy of the person and of life and protects the rights of children and adolescents stated by the international conventions, as well as the rights of the elderly to a dignified, independent existence within the family and social sphere.

3. It safeguards and appreciates the right to freedom, and guarantees the equality of every member of Lazio's community in exercising the civil, social, economic and political rights stated by the Constitution and by the European Union Charter of Fundamental Rights [...]

Region of Piedmont (Statute adopted in 2005)

Preamble

Piedmont, an Autonomous Region in the unity and indivisibility of the Italian Republic, within the framework of the European Union principles, guided by the principles of the Universal Declaration of Human Rights, declaring its loyalty to the Constitutional Charter founded on values proper to the Liberation and to the democracy reconquered by our Country; [...].

Region of Apulia (Statute adopted in 2004)

art. 1

[...] The Region of Apulia favours self-government by its inhabitants and pursues their welfare and security guided by the principles of the Universal Declaration of Human Rights, the European Convention on Human Rights, the European Union Charter on Fundamental Rights and the Italian Constitution [...].

IV. Regional Laws

The Italian Regions and Autonomous Provinces have not only included the "peace human rights norm" and references to international legal instruments in their statutes; over time, they also have adopted a series of laws concerning the human rights-related issues considered in this *Yearbook*. The following list gives a representative selection of rights-based laws in force, divided according to topics; for each Region, laws are listed chronologically. The list shows laws adopted since the creation of the regional authority.

Peace, human rights, development cooperation, fair trade

R.l. Abruzzo 14 December 1989, No. 105 (Realisation of Development Co-operation Activities in developing Countries), modified with r.l. Abruzzo 20 April 1965, No. 63.

R.l. Abruzzo 18 December 1990, No. 98 (Activities of the Region of Abruzzo for the development of a culture of peace).

R.l. Abruzzo 17 October 2005, No. 29 (Promotion and diffusion of a culture of peace and human rights education)

R.l. Abruzzo 28 March 2006, No. 7 (Provision for the diffusion of fair trade in Abruzzo).

R.l. Apulia 25 August 2003, No. 20 (Partnership in cooperation).

R.l. Basilicata 8 May 1996, No. 26 (Regional measures for peace and cooperation among peoples), modified and integrated with r.l. 4 November 1996, No. 54.

R.l. Basilicata 24 April 2009, No. 10 (Participation by Basilicata in the Foundation "Città della Pace per i Bambini" – Basilicata, ONLUS), modified with r.l. Basilicata 25 October 2010, No. 30.

R.l. Campania 7 April 2000, No. 12 (Promotion and diffusion of a culture of peace and human rights education).

R.l. Emilia-Romagna 24 June 2002, No. 12 (Regional measures for cooperation with developing Countries and Countries in transition, international solidarity, and the promotion of a culture of peace).

R.l. Friuli-Venezia Giulia 30 October 2000, No. 19 (Measures for promoting on the local and regional level, of development cooperation and international partnership activities).

R.l. Lazio 7 April 2000, No. 19 (Regional initiatives for development cooperation, for international collaboration and solidarity).

R.l. Lazio 24 December 2008, No. 25 (Promotion and implementation of initiatives fostering disarmament processes and a culture of peace).

R.l. Liguria 20 August 1998, No. 28 (Measures for development cooperation, international solidarity and peace).

R.l. Liguria 13 August 2007, No. 32 (Regulation and measures for the development of fair trade in Liguria).

R.l. Lombardy 5 June 1989, No. 20 (Lombardy for peace and development cooperation).

R.l. Marche 18 June 2002, No. 9 (Regional activities for the promotion of human rights, the culture of peace, development cooperation and international solidarity).

R.l. Marche 29 April 2008, No. 8 (Measures supporting and promoting fair trade).

R.l. Molise 29 August 2005, No. 29 (Regional measures concerning cooperation with developing Countries and Countries in transition, international solidarity and the promotion of a culture of peace).

R.l. Piedmont 17 August 1995, No. 67 (Regional measures for the promotion of a culture and an education of peace for international cooperation and solidarity).

R.l. Sardinia 11 April 1996, No. 19 (Provisions on cooperation with developing Countries and international cooperation).

R.l. Tuscany 30 July 1997, No. 55 (Measures for the promotion of a culture of peace).

R.l. Tuscany 23 March 1999, No. 17 (Measures promoting activities of international cooperation and partnership, at regional and local levels).

R.l. Tuscany 23 February 2005, No. 37. (Provisions fostering the diffusion of fair trade in Tuscany).

R.l. Tuscany 9 February 2010, No. 6 (Institution of a "Day for a Global Fair Development").

P.l. Bolzano 9 March 1991, No. 5 (Development Cooperation).

P.l. Trent 10 June 1991, No. 11 (Promotion and diffusion of the culture of peace).

P.l. Trent 15 March 2005, No. 4 (Actions and measures for international solidarity in the Autonomous Province of Trent).

R.l. Umbria 27 October 1999, No. 26 (Regional measures for the promotion of international development cooperation and solidarity among peoples).

R.l. Umbria 27 October 1999, No. 28 (Foundation "Umbria for Peace")

R.l. Valle d'Aosta 17 April 2007, No. 6 (New provisions for development cooperation and international solidarity regional measures).

R.l. Veneto 30 March 1988, No. 18 (Regional measures for the promotion of a culture of peace), abrogated with r.l. Veneto 16 December 1999, No. 55.

R.l. Veneto 28 December 1998, No. 33 (European Master in Human Rights and Democratisation).

R.l. Veneto 16 December 1999, No. 55 (Regional measures for the promotion of human rights, a culture of peace, development cooperation and solidarity), modified with r.l. Veneto 22 January 2010, No. 6.

R.l. Veneto 22 January 2010, No. 6 (Measures in support of fair trade organisations, and modifications of r.l. 55/1999).

Equal opportunities

R.l. Abruzzo 18 May 2000, No. 88 (Permanent Commission for the realisation of equal opportunities and legal and substantial equality between men and women, and the promotion of affirmative actions).

R.l. Apulia 9 June 1980, No. 70 (Establishment of a regional women's consultancy).

R.l. Apulia 30 April 1990, No. 16 (Regional Commission for equal employment opportunities between men and women).

R.l. Apulia 21 March 2007, No. 7 (Provisions concerning gender policies and services reconciling daily life with work demands in Apulia).

R.l. Basilicata 26 November 1991, No. 27 (Provisions concerning the creation of a Regional Commission for equality and equal opportunities between men and women).

R.l. Calabria 26 January 1987, No. 4 (Establishment of a Commission for equal rights and equal opportunities between men and women).

R.l. Campania 4 May 1987, No. 26 (Establishment of a regional Commission for the realisation of equal rights and opportunities between men and women).

R.l. Emilia-Romagna 27 January 1986, No. 3 (Establishment of a Commission for the realisation of equality between men and women).

R.l. Emilia-Romagna 28 July 2004, No. 15 (Participation by the Region Emilia-Romagna in creating the association Women of the Mediterranean, Southeast and east Europe network).

R.l. Friuli-Venezia Giulia 21 May 1990, No. 23 (Establishment of a Regional Commission for equal opportunities between men and women), modified with r.l. Friuli-Venezia Giulia 24 May 2004, No. 17.

R.l. Lazio 25 November 1976, No. 58 (Establishment of a Regional women's consultancy on equal opportunities).

R.l. Liguria 1 August 2008, No. 26 (Integration of equal opportunities policies between men and women in the Region of Liguria).

R.l. Liguria 10 November 2009, No. 52 (Provisions against discrimination based on sexual orientation or gender identity).

R.l. Lombardy 2 May 1992, No. 16 (Establishment and functions of a regional commission for the realisation of equality between men and women).

R.l. Marche 18 April 1986, No. 9 (Regional Commission for equal opportunities between men and women).

R.l. Molise 13 April 2000, No. 23 (New regulation for the regional Commission for equality and equal opportunities).

R.l. Piedmont 12 November 1986, No. 46 (Regional Commission for the realisation of equal opportunities).

R.l. Piedmont 29 October 1992, No. 43 (Information, promotion and diffusion of affirmative actions for the realisation of equal opportunities between men and women).

R.l. Piedmont 18 March 2009, No. 8 (Integration of equal opportunities and gender equality policies in the Piedmont Region and provisions on the setting up of gender budgeting?).

R.l. Sardinia 13 June 1989, No. 39 (Establishment of a regional Commission for the realisation of equality between men and women).

R.l. Sardinia 3 November 2000, No. 20 (Establishment of a consultancy of the women elected in Sardinia).

R.l. Sicily 7 May 1977, No. 27 (Establishment of a Regional women's Consultancy).

R.l. Tuscany 15 December 2009, No. 76 (Regional Commission for equal opportunities).

R.l. Tuscany 2 April 2009, No. 16 (Gender citizenship).

P.l. Bolzano 10 August 1989, No. 4 (Measures for the realisation of equal opportunities between men and women).

P.l. Trent 10 December 1993, No. 41 (Measures for the realisation of equal opportunities between men and women).

P.l. Trent 23 July 2004, No. 7 (Provisions in matters of education, culture and equal opportunities).

P.l. Trent 9 March 2010, No. 6 (Measures against gender violence and for the protection of women who are victim to it).

R.l. Umbria 15 April 2009, No. 6 (Establishment of a Centre for equal opportunities and for the implementation of gender policies in the Region of Umbria).

R.l. Valle d'Aosta 23 December 2009, No. 53 (Provisions concerning the regional Consultancy for equal opportunities and the equality Councillor).

R.l. Veneto 29 April 1987, No. 13 (Establishment of a consultancy of the women elected in Veneto).

R.l. Veneto 30 December 1987, No. 62 (Establishment of a regional commission for the realisation of equality between men and women).

Migrations, Roma and Sinti

R.l. Abruzzo 13 February 1990, No. 10 (Measures in favour of Abruzzi citizens living outside Italy and non-EU Member States citizens living in Abruzzo), modified with r.l. Abruzzo 28 April 1995, No. 79.

R.l. Abruzzo 13 December 2004, No. 46 (Measures in support of foreign immigrants).

R.l. Apulia 11 May 1990, No. 29 (Measures in favour of non-EU Member States immigrants in Apulia).

R.l. Apulia 4 December 2009, No. 32 (Measures on the acceptance, civil coexistence and integration of immigrants in Apulia).

R.l. Basilicata 19 June 1981, No. 13 (Establishment of a regional emigration Consultancy).

R.l. Basilicata 13 April 1996, No. 21 (Measures in support of non-EU workers in Basilicata and establishment of the Regional Immigration Commission).

R.l. Calabria 9 April 1990, No. 17 (Regional measures concerning emigration and immigration), integrated with r.l. Calabria 1 March 1994, No. 9.

R.l. Campania 1 March 1984, No. 10 (Regional measures on emigration and immigration).

R.l. Campania 3 November 1994, No. 33 (Measures supporting the rights of foreign immigrants in Campania coming from non-EU Member States).

R.l. Emilia-Romagna 21 February 1990, No. 14 (Regional initiatives in favour of emigration and immigration – New norms on the establishment of a Regional consultancy on emigration an immigration), modified with r.l. Emilia-Romagna 24 March 2004, No. 5.

R.l. Friuli-Venezia Giulia 14 March 1988, No. 11 (Provisions protecting the Roma culture within the territory of the Autonomous Region of Friuli-Venezia Giulia), modified with R.l. Friuli-Venezia Giulia 24 June 1991, No. 25.

R.l. Friuli-Venezia Giulia 10 September 1990, No. 46 (Creation of a regional body on migrants' issues).

R.l. Lazio 24 November 1986, No. 48 (Regional measures on emigration and immigration).

R.l. Liguria 10 June 1993, No. 27 (New provisions on emigration and establishment of a regional consultancy on emigration).

R.l. Liguria 20 February 2007, No. 7 (Provisions on the reception and social integration of foreign immigrant citizens, men and women).

R.l. Lombardy 5 May 1975, No. 67 (Regional measures concerning migratory movements).

R.l. Lombardy 4 July 1988, No. 38 (Measures protecting non-EU Member States immigrants in Lombardy, and their families).

R.l. Marche 26 May 2009, No. 13 (Provisions supporting rights and integration for immigrated foreign citizens).

R.l. Piedmont 9 January 1987, No. 1 (Regional measures concerning migratory movements).

R.l. Piedmont 8 November 1989, No. 64 (Regional measures in favour of non-EU Member States immigrants resident in Piedmont).

R.l. Piedmont 10 June 1993, No. 26 (Measures in favour of the gypsy population).

R.l. Sardinia 24 December 1990, No. 46 (Measures favouring the promotion of living conditions of non-EU workers in Sardinia).

R.l. Sicily 6 June 1984, No. 38 (Provisions in favour of emigrant workers and their families).

R.l. Tuscany 22 March 1990, No. 22 (Measures protecting the rights of non-EU Member States immigrants in Tuscany), modified with r.l. Tuscany 21 December 1995, No. 109.

R.l. Tuscany 22 April 1991, No. 14 (Funds for rescue operations directed toward refugees, displaced persons, prisoners and populations involved in exceptional events due to armed conflict, disaster and conditions of malnourishment or health and hygiene problems).

R.l. Tuscany 12 January 2000, No. 2 (Measures concerning Roma and Sinti people).

R.l. Tuscany 8 June 2009, No. 29 (Norms for the reception, participative integration and protection of foreign citizens in the Region of Tuscany).

R.l. Trentino-Alto Adige 30 May 1993, No. 11 (Measures in favour of populations from non-EU Member States affected by war or calamity, or in harrowing economic and social conditions).

P.l. Trent 2 May 1990, No. 13 (Measures concerning non-EU Member states immigrants).

P.l. Trent 29 October 2009, No. 12 (Measures favouring the integration of Sinti and Roma groups residing in the Province of Trent).

R.l. Umbria 27 June 1973, No. 28 (Regional Consultancy on emigration and immigration. Regional solidarity fund in favour of emigrant or immigrant workers and their families), modified with r.l. Umbria 10 December 1974.

R.l. Umbria 22 June 1979, No. 31 (New provisions in favour of emigrant workers and their families).

R.l. Umbria 10 April 1990, No. 18 (Measures in favour of non-EU immigrants), modified with r.l. Umbria, 5 December 1974, No. 40.

R.l. Umbria 6 August 2004, No. 18 (Health care measures in favour of non-EU Countries in severe difficulty as regards health care).

R.l. Veneto 19 June 1984, No. 28 (Regional measures concerning emigration and immigration), modified with r.l. Veneto 30 January 1990, No. 9.

R.l. Veneto 22 December 1989, No. 54 (Measures protecting the Roma and Sinti cultures).

R.l. Veneto 30 January 1990, No. 9 (Measures in the immigration sector).

R.l. Veneto 23 November 2006, No. 25 (Creation of a technical commission to study the territorial and social impact of migratory movements in the Region of Veneto).

Ombudsman and Children's Commissioners

R.l. Abruzzo 2 June 1988, No. 46 (Convention with UNICEF for the establishment of the "Commissioner for Children").

R.l. Abruzzo 20 October 1995, No. 126 (Establishment of the Ombudsman).

R.l. Apulia 9 July 1981, No. 38 (Establishment of the Ombudsman).

R.l. Apulia 10 July 2006, No. 19 (Regulation of the integrated social service network for the dignity and welfare of men and women in Apulia).

R.l. Basilicata 19 February 2007, No. 5 (New regulation on the regional Ombudsman).

R.l. Basilicata 29 June 2009, No. 18 (Establishment of the regional Commissioner for children and adolescents).

R.l. Calabria 16 January 1985, No. 4 (Establishment of the regional Ombudsman of the Region of Calabria).

R.l. Calabria 12 November 2004, No. 28 (Commissioner for children and adolescents).

R.l. Campania 11 August 1978, No. 23 (Establishment of the Ombudsman of the Region of Campania).

R.l. Campania 24 July 2006, No. 17 (Establishment of the Commissioner for children and adolescents).

R.l. Emilia-Romagna 17 February 2005, No. 9 (Establishment of the Commissioner for children and adolescents), modified with r.l. Emilia-Romagna 6 February 2007, No. 1.

R.l. Emilia-Romagna 16 December 2003, No. 25 (Provisions concerning the regional Ombudsman).

R.l. Friuli-Venezia Giulia 24 June 1993, No. 49 (Provisions in support of families and in protection of minors).

R.l. Lazio 28 February 1980, No. 17 (Establishment of the Ombudsman).

R.l. Lazio 28 October 2002, No. 38 (Establishment of the regional Commissioner for children and adolescents).

R.l. Liguria 5 August 1986, No. 17 (Establishment of the Ombudsman), modified with r.l. Liguria 6 October 2009, No. 38.

R.l. Liguria 16 March 2007, No. 9 (Regulation of the office of regional Commissioner for the rights of children and adolescents) modified with r.l. Liguria, 6 October 2009, No. 38.

R.l. Lombardy 18 January 1980, No. 7 (Establishment of the Ombudsman of the Region of Lombardy).

R.l. Lombardy 30 March 2009, No. 6 (Establishment of the role and office of the Commissioner for children and adolescents).

R.l. Marche 28 July 2008, No. 23 (Authority guaranteeing respect for the rights of adults and children – Regional Ombudsman).

R.l. Molise 14 April 2000, No. 26 (Establishment of the Ombudsman).

R.l. Molise 2 October 2006, No. 32 (Establishment of the Commissioner for children).

R.l. Piedmont 9 December 1981, No. 50 (Establishment of the Ombudsman).

R.l. Piedmont 9 December 2009, No. 31 (Establishment of the regional Commissioner for children and adolescents).

R.l. Sardinia 17 January 1989, No. 4 (Establishment of the Ombudsman in Sardinia).

R.l. Tuscany 27 April 2009, No. 19 (Regulation regarding the regional Ombudsman).

R.l. Tuscany 1 March 2010, No. 26 (Establishment of the Commissioner for children and adolescents).

P.l. Bolzano 26 June 2009, No. 3 (Commissioner for children and adolescents).

P.l. Bolzano 4 February 2010, No. 3 (The Ombudsman in the Autonomous Province of Bolzano).

P.l. Trent 20 December 1982, No. 28 (Establishment of the Ombudsman).

P.l. Trent 11 February 2009, No. 1 (Modification of the p.l. regarding the Ombudsman – Tasks of the Ombudsman concerning children and adolescents).

R.l. Umbria 27 November 2007, No. 30 (New regulation for the Regional Ombudsman).

R.l. Umbria 21 July 2009, No. 18 (New regulation for the regional Commissioner for children and adolescents).

R.l. Valle d'Aosta 28 August 2001, No. 17 (Regulation on functioning of the Ombudsman's office).

R.l. Veneto 6 June 1988, No. 28 (Establishment of the Ombudsman).

R.l. Veneto 9 August 1988, No. 42 (Establishment of the Commissioner for children and adolescents).

Part II

The Human Rights Infrastructure in Italy

National Human Rights-related Bodies

International human rights law requires States to set up structures adequately specialised in promoting and protecting fundamental rights. In this regard, a distinction shall be made between, on one hand, strictly governmental bodies and, on the other, independent structures directly emanating from civil society. The latter in particular, through channels different from those classically used by governmental powers, aim at participating in policy-making, promoting and developing a human rights culture as well as preventing violations.

In this perspective, the "Paris Principles", adopted by the UN General Assembly with resolution 48/134 of 20 December 1993, provide a thorough list of requirements for "National Human Rights Institutions", explicitly understood as independent institutions of civil society. A subsequent agreement underwritten by the United Nations, the Council of Europe, the OSCE and the European Union, decided that such institution be established in the form of *National Human Rights Commission* and *National Ombudsman.* They must be set up by legislative act (preferably of a constitutional nature) and their members should, in principle, result from decisions adopted not by the executive power, but by parliamentary organs. National human rights institutions' members have consultative, informative and monitoring functions.

As today, Italy has not yet established neither a National Human Rights Commission nor a National Ombudsman. However, since 2005 several bills have been proposed in this sense. For updated information, which will appear in greater detail in the 2012 edition of the *Yearbook*, see footnote No. 1 in the Introduction. In this chapter the composition, mandate and activities of the following institutions will be illustrated:

– *Parliamentary bodies*: the Extraordinary Commission for the Promotion and Protection of Human Rights of the Italian Senate; the Permanent Committee on Human Rights instituted within the Foreign Affairs Commission (III) of the Italian House of Representatives; the Parliamentary Commission for Childhood and Adolescence; the Parliament-Government Observatory Monitoring the Promotion and Protection of Fundamental Rights.

– *Governmental bodies*: the Committee of Ministers for Orientation and Strategic Guidance on Human Rights; the Inter-ministerial Committee for Human Rights (CIDU), set up within the Ministry of Foreign Affairs; the departments and bureaus of the Ministry of Justice and the Ministry of Labour and Welfare, specifically involved in human rights matters; the Department for Equal Opportunities under the auspices of the Presidency of the

Council of Ministers; the National Council on Economy and Labour (CNEL); the National Observatory on Childhood and Adolescence; the National Committee on Bioethics; the National Observatory Monitoring the Condition of Persons with Disabilities; the Committee on Foreign Children; the Commission for Intercountry Adoptions; the National Commission for UNESCO.

– *Independent authorities*: the Communications Regulatory Authority; the Italian Data Protection Authority; the Commission Guaranteeing the Implementation of the Law on Strikes Affecting Essential Public Services.

Finally, Italy's national human rights infrastructure is completed by academic institutions promoting not only research, but also education and training in human rights issues, and by several non-governmental organisations, some of which function through networking.

I. Parliamentary Bodies

A. *Senate: Extraordinary Commission for the Protection and Promotion of Human Rights*

The Senate's Extraordinary Commission for the Protection and Promotion of Human Rights was set up during the 14th legislature (motion 20, 1 August 2001) and is the fruit of long experience by the Committee against Capital Punishment (1996-2001). Since the Commission is not of a permanent nature, it must be instituted formally at the beginning of each legislature and the Senate did so both during the 15th legislature (motion 20, 12 July 2006) and the 16th legislature (motion 13, 26 June 2008). In the latter motion, the Senate decided to proceed with the establishment of a permanent human rights commission.

On 5 December 2001, in the framework of the inquiry on mechanisms and systems of protection of human rights at the national and international level, the first Extraordinary Commission held a hearing with Prof. Antonio Papisca, Director of the Human Rights Centre of the University of Padua.

The incumbent Commission is made up of 25 members, present in proportion to the numerical presence of the various parliamentary groups to which they belong. Among these members, the Commission elects the bureau, made up of the Chair, two Vice Chairs and two Secretaries. In 2010 the Commission was composed as follows: *Chair*: Pietro Marcenaro; *Vice Chairs*: Lorenzo Bodega, Ulisse Di Giacomo; *Secretaries*: Franco Mugnai, Marco Perduca; *Members:* Silvana Amati, Emanuela Baio, Franco Cardiello, Emilio Colombo, Barbara Contini, Roberto Della Seta, Egidio Digilio, Roberto Di Giovan Paolo, Salvo Fleres, Andrea Fluttero, Cosimo Gallo, Mariapia Garavaglia, Cosimo Latronico, Rita Levi-Montalcini, Massimo

Livi Bacci, Rosa Angela Mauro, Colomba Mongiello, Francesco Pardi, Fedele Sanciu, Giancarlo Serafini.

The Commission has the task of studying, observing and taking initiatives on issues concerning the protection and promotion of internationally recognised human rights. To this end, it can establish relations with institutions of other Countries and with international bodies; carry out missions in or outside Italy, in particular with foreign parliaments, even – if necessary – in order to establish agreements fostering human rights or to facilitate other forms of collaboration; it can carry out informational procedures and formulate proposals and Assembly reports; and provide its advisory opinions on proposed legislation as well as on matters deferred to other commissions.

Along the years, the Commission has been campaigning for the abolition of capital punishment throughout the world; the introduction of the crime of torture into domestic law; the protection of children's rights; the promotion and implementation of the right to asylum; the fight against human trafficking; the fight against racism, xenophobia and discrimination against minorities; and the prohibition against forms of mutilation. It has created networks among Italian institutions, non-governmental organisations and associations working to protect human rights.

In particular, in 2010 the Commission continued the inquiry, launched the previous year, on mechanisms and systems of protection of human rights existing in Italy as well as abroad. To achieve its research goal it hosted 35 hearings attended by representatives of associations and organisations, local administrators as well as eminent experts. Particularly worthy of note were the hearings with Navanethem Pillay, the United Nations High Commissioner for Human Rights (10 March 2010); with Shirin Ebadi, winner of the Nobel Peace Prize (20 July 2010), as well as two hearings with the Undersecretary of State for Foreign Affairs, Vincenzo Scotti, on the Universal Periodical Review of Italy (14 April and 19 May 2010).

Important themes discussed during the hearings were: in-depth examination of the human rights situation emerging in conditions of degradation and difficult co-existence in rural and urban areas of Italy; conditions of Roma and Sinti communities in Italy and other European Countries; conditions in centres for migrants, such as Identification and Expulsion Centres (CIE), Reception Centres for Asylum Seekers (CARA) and Receptions Centres (CDA); fight against female genital mutilation; status of migrant workers; conditions of Italian detainees; human rights situation in Iran, North Korea, Occupied Palestinian Territories and Somalia.

B. House of Representatives: Permanent Committee on Human Rights

The international protection of human rights is one of the focal point of the activities carried out by the Commission for Foreign and European Union Affairs (3rd Commission) of the House of Representatives. Using hearings as its main instrument, the Commission ensures continual updating for Parliament on the status of human rights in various parts of the world and, with this goal in mind, in July 2008 it created the Permanent Committee on Human Rights.

The Committee is made up as follows: *Chair*: Furio Colombo; *Vice Chair*: Gianluca Pini; *Secretary*: Manuela Repetti; *Members*: Margherita Boniver, Nunzia De Girolamo (until 2009), Paolo Guzzanti (until 2009), Riccardo Migliori, Fiamma Nirenstein, Enrico Pianetta, Alessandro Ruben, Mario Barbi, Marco Fedi, Matteo Mecacci, Fabio Porta, Gianni Vernetti, Roberto Cota (until 16 June 2010), Fabio Evangelisti, Ferdinando Adornato and Riccardo Antonio Merlo.

The Commission for Foreign and European Union Affairs asked the Permanent Committee to carried out an inquiry on violations of human rights throughout the world, with a particular attention to violations affecting minorities. The inquiry, began on 1 October 2008, is still in progress. In 2010, eleven meetings were held, giving voice to both institutional representatives – Italian and international – and to delegates from international associations and organisations for the promotion and protection of human rights.

The inquiry offered the opportunity to foster the parliamentary discussions on the Universal Periodic Review (UPR) of Italy, which took place on 9 February 2010. The meeting of the Permanent Committee on that date gave voice to representatives from the Italian section of Amnesty International, who in that occasion informed the Government it had submitted to the Human Rights Council a document containing data on the status of human rights in Italy, together with a series of recommendations addressed to the Italian Government. In the following hearing of 16 February 2010, the Chair of the Inter-Ministerial Committee for Human Rights, Valentino Simonetti, reported on the results of the first phase of the UPR. The United Nations High Commissioner for Human Rights, Navanethem Pillay, participated in the hearing of 1 March 2010, taking care to mention the outcomes of the UPR of Italy. Finally, during the hearing of 20 May 2010, before the adoption of the final UPR Report of Italy, a hearing was held with the Undersecretary of State for Foreign Affairs, Vincenzo Scotti, who reported on the Government's position regarding responses to be given to the 92 recommendations addressed to Italy during the UPR.

In the framework of the inquiry, the following hearings are worth of mention:

- 18 March 2010: hearing with Caspian Makan, human rights activist in Iran, on the status of human rights in that Country;
- 8 April 2010: hearing with representatives of Canadian indigenous peoples belonging to the organisation *Friends and Relatives of Disappeared* on violations of human rights which took place in residential schools for Native Americans, functioning until 1996;
- 13 April 2010: hearing with Filippo Grandi, Commissioner-General of the United Nations Relief and Works Agency for Palestine Refugees in the Near East (UNRWA);
- 18 May 2010: hearing with Emmanuel Raison, coordinator of the International Human Rights Bureau of Action Colombia, an international network of non-governmental organisations concerned with human rights issues in Colombia; participants discussed the need to protect human rights defenders in that Country;
- 26 May 2010: hearing with human rights activists from the Democratic People's Republic of Korea, and with a delegate from the non-governmental organisation *Anti-Human Crime Investigation Committee*, whose activities aim at stimulating intervention by the International Criminal Court for crimes against humanity perpetrated in DPRK;
- 6 July 2010: hearing with representatives of Amnesty International on the presentation of the annual report on the status of human rights in the world;
- 28 October 2010: hearing with Marco Pannella, Chair of the Non-Violent Transnational Trans-Party Radical Party's Senate, concerning the death penalty inflicted on the former Deputy President of Iraq, Tareq Aziz, and events of the war in Iraq;
- 21 December 2010: hearing with Father Moissié Zerai, Eritrean priest and President of the agency Habeshia, involved in the rescue of around 250 Eritrean citizens who, travelling from Libya in the attempt to reach Israel, fell into the hands of bandits and human traffickers, and were detained in prison camps located into the Egyptian territory, in the region of Sinai.

The Permanent Committee on Human Rights also carries out preparatory work in relation to the activities of the Foreign Affairs Commission following, in particular, the development of human rights-related bill on which the *plenum* of the Commission will be called to deliberate. In connection with this function, during the hearing of 27 January 2010, the Permanent Committee on Human Rights began the formal examination of the report concerning activities carried out by the Inter-Ministerial Committee for Human Rights during the year 2008 (doc. CCXI, No. 2).

During the hearing of 20 January 2010, the Chair of the Committee reported on the results of the meeting of the Parliament-Government Observatory monitoring the Promotion and Protection of Human Rights, which took place in Rome on 24 November 2009. The outcomes of the subsequent Observatory meeting (the 4th) were presented to the Committee during the hearing of 28 July 2010.

C. Bicameral bodies: Parliamentary Commission for Childhood and Adolescence

The Parliamentary Commission for Childhood and Adolescence was set up by law 23 December 1997, No. 451, although its denomination and competencies were modified by law 3 August 2009, No. 112.

The Commission is composed of 20 Senators and 20 Representatives appointed, respectively, by the Chair of the Italian Senate and the Chair of the Italian House of Representatives, proportionately to the total number of members in the various parliamentary groups. The Commission then elects its Chair, two Vice Chairs and two Secretaries. In 2010 the Commission was composed as follows: *Chair*: Alessandra Mussolini; *Vice Chairs*: Annamaria Serafini, Gabriella Carlucci; *Secretaries*: Laura Allegrini, Marco Calgaro; *members from the House*: Mariella Bocciardo, Sandro Brandolini, Luisa Capitanio Santolini, Daniela Cardinale, Giulia Cosenza, Anita Di Giuseppe, Arturo Iannaccone, Beatrice Lorenzin, Barbara Mannucci, Donella Mattesini, Gabriella Mondello, Carla Castellani (replaced by Alessandro Pagano after 30 Sept. 2010), Massimo Polledri, Mariarosaria Rossi, Daniela Sbrollini, Amalia Schirru, Sandra Zampa; *Members from the* Senate: Giuliana Carlino, Mauro Ceruti, Stefano De Lillo, Giuseppe Esposito, Alessandra Gallone, Antonio Gentile, Rita Ghedini, Mirella Giai, Claudio Gustavino, Piergiorgio Massidda, Donatella Poretti, Fabio Rizzi, Maria Rizzotti, Luciana Sbarbati.

Essentially, the Commission is entrusted with a supervisory and policy-making role related to the actual enforcement of international agreements and laws on children's rights. In particular, in exercising its consultative powers, the Commission gathers data, fosters the exchange of information and promotes effective synergies with bodies and institutions both in and outside of Italy involved in protecting children and adolescents; with associations, non-governmental organisations and all other subjects operating in the field; and with groups dealing with adoptions and foster care. It may also present to the two Houses of Parliament observations and proposals concerning the effects of current legislation, its limitations, and any need to adapt it in order to ensure compliance with European Union law and with the rights enshrined in the United Nations Convention on the Rights of the Child.

In 2010, The Commission carried out three inquiries respectively on: unaccompanied foreign minors, already started in 2008 with a hearing involving representatives of Save the Children Italia; children protection in the field of communication, already started in 2008; issues in the implementation of policies designed for the promotion of childhood and adolescence, carrying out 11 hearings in October 2010.

The latter inquiry stemmed from the Commission's interest in gathering data prior to the examination, as established by art. 2 of law 23 December 1997, No. 451, of the 3rd national biennial plan of action to protect rights and development of underage individuals, prepared by the National Observatory on Childhood and Adolescence. In concluding the examination, carried out during the hearings of 26 and 28 October 2010, the Commission expressed its approval, along with various observations.

D. Parliament-Government Observatory Monitoring the Promotion and Protection of Fundamental Rights

The Observatory (*Osservatorio Parlamento-Governo per il monitoraggio dello stato di promozione e tutela dei diritti fondamentali*) is a consultative body created on 7 July 2009. It meets when necessary in order to report on Italy's international activity in the field of human rights. Members of the Observatory include representatives from the Senate's Extraordinary Commission for the Protection and Promotion of Human Rights, from the House of Representatives Permanent Committee on Human Rights, from the Ministry of Foreign Affairs and from the Inter-Ministerial Committee for Human Rights.

Between 2009 and 2010, the Observatory held four meetings. During the last one, held on 13 July 2010, participants discussed the outcome of the Universal Periodical Review of Italy, plus specific topics linked to the 65th session of the UN General Assembly, such as the abolition of female genital mutilation and capital punishment, the protection of religious freedom, the project for an international Conference on inter-ethnic cities, the plight of Eritrean refugees in Libya and the situation of political prisoners in Cuba.

E. Chronology of Parliamentary initiatives concerning human rights

This section presents a chronology of the 2010 most relevant Parliamentary initiatives in the field of human rights, subdivided as bills, motions, interpellations, questions receiving oral response, questions receiving written response, questions before Commissions, resolutions before Commissions, Assembly agendas. The source of reference for this compilation is the website *openparlamento* (http://parlamento.openpolis.it). For each initiative it is indicated the proposer or first signer, the code (in particular, the letter "C" indicates that the act was presented at the House of Representatives while the letter "S" indicates it was presented at the Senate), the heading, the date of presentation and its most recent updating.

Bills

Date	Initiative	Latest update
05/01/2010	Rita Bernardini (PD) – C.3094 Introduction of art. 593-bis, penal code, on the crime of torture, plus other norms concerning torture	09/02/2010 assigned (examination not yet begun)
01/03/2010	Angelino Alfano (PdL) and others – S.2043 Ratification and execution of the Council of Europe Convention on Action against Trafficking in Human Beings, signed in Warsaw on 16 May 2005, plus national implementing legislation	14/04/2010 approved
15/04/2010	Angelino Alfano (PdL) and others – C.3402 Ratification and execution of the Council of Europe Convention on Action against Trafficking in Human Beings, signed in Warsaw on 16 May 2005, plus national implementing legislation	03/06/2010 passed as law
10/06/2010	Domenico Di Virgilio (PdL) – C.3538 Establishment of the Parliamentary Commission for the Promotion and Protection of Human Rights	29/07/2010 assigned (examination not yet begun)
22/06/2010	Domenico Gramazio (PdL) – S.2251 Rules concerning prohibition against producing, importing and selling merchandise produced by forced labour	20/07/2010 assigned (examination not yet begun)
13/10/2010	Roberto Della Seta (PD) – S.2372 Rules concerning prohibition against producing, importing and selling merchandise produced by forced labour or slave labour	13/10/2010 still to be assigned

Motions

Date	Initiative	Latest update
11/01/2010	Augusto Di Stanislao (IdV) – C.1/00301 Situation of Italian prisons	12/01/2010 accepted
22/01/2010	Carlo Ciccioli (PdL) – C.1/00321 Respect for human rights in Iran	09/03/2011 new signers
09/02/2010	Leoluca Orlando (IdV) – C.1/00327 Violence in Democratic Republic of Congo	16/02/2010 accepted
10/02/2010	Gianpiero D'Alia (UDC-SVP) – S.1/00233 Prison situation	17/02/2010 accepted
11/02/2010	Jean Leonard Touadi (PD) and others – C.1/00328 State of emergency and war in Democratic Republic of Congo	16/02/2010 accepted

16/02/2010	Margherita Boniver (PdL) – C.1/00329 Military and humanitarian crisis in Democratic Republic of Congo	16/02/2010 accepted
23/02/2010	Maurizio Gasparri (PdL) – S.1/00242 Peace process in the Middle East and role of UN	13/05/2010 Delayed for future hearing
01/03/2010	Giuseppe Francesco Maria Marinello (PdL) – C.1/00334 Government commitment in favour of religious freedom and against persecution of Christians in the world	11/01/2011 concluded
02/03/2010	Francesco Pardi (IdV) – S.1/00250 Government immigration policy	02/03/2010 not accepted
04/03/2010	Margherita Boniver (PdL) – C.1/00338 Situation of political dissidents and those imprisoned for crimes of opinion in Cuba	10/06/2010 accepted
11/03/2010	Matteo Mecacci (PD) – C.1/00344 Situation of political dissidents and those imprisoned for crimes of opinion in Cuba	10/06/2010 rejected
13/04/2010	Elisabetta Zamparutti (PD) – C.1/00357 Government commitment to request that the Iranian Government free movie director Panahi	20/05/2010 new signers
03/06/2010	Fabio Evangelisti (IdV) – C.1/00376 Government commitment to overcome, through the EU coordination, the ideological conflict with Cuba	10/06/2010 accepted
07/06/2010	Aurelio Salvatore Misiti (Mixed) and others – C.1/00379 Human rights and freeing of Cuban prisoners	10/06/2010 accepted
07/06/2010	Francesco Tempestini (PD) – C.1/00381 Limitations on fundamental rights in Cuba	10/06/2010 approved
07/06/2010	Michele Giuseppe Vietti (UDC) – C.1/00383 Respect for civil and human rights in Cuba	10/06/2010 accepted
04/08/2010	Maria Antonietta Farina Coscioni (PD) – C.1/00426 Global prohibition against female genital mutilation	04/08/2010 presented
04/08/2010	Emanuela Baio Dossi (Mixed) – S.1/00305 Italy's position on the millennium development goals	new signers
15/09/2010	Roberto Della Seta (PD) – S.1/00308 Prevent execution of Sakineh Mohammadi Ashtani	16/09/2010 repeat request
15/09/2010	Stefano Pedica (IdV) – S.1/00309 Promotion and protection of fundamental rights in Iran	15/09/2010 presented
13/10/2010	Gianni Vernetti (Mixed) – C.1/00452 Free Nobel Peace Prize winner Liu Xiaobo	09/11/2010 concluded
13/10/2010	Anna Finocchiaro (PD) and others – S.1/00316 Free Nobel Peace Prize winner Liu Xiaobo from prison	new signers
20/10/2010	Maurizio Gasparri (PdL) – S.1/00322 Free Nobel Peace Prize winner Liu Xiaobo from prison	20/10/2010 presented
26/10/2010	Stefano Pedica (IdV) – S.1/00330 Free Nobel Peace Prize winner Liu Xiaobo from prison	26/10/2010 presented
27/10/2010	Pietro Marcenaro (PD) – S.1/00332 Foster political dialogue among military junta of Myanmar, opposition forces and ethnic groups	27/10/2010 presented

08/11/2010	Matteo Mecacci (PD) – C.1/00485 Treaty Italy-Libya: need for changes to protect human rights	09/11/2010 not accepted
08/11/2010	Roberto Antonione (PdL) – C.1/00484 Treaty Italy-Libya: human rights protection and clandestine immigration	09/11/2010 not accepted
08/11/2010	Aurelio Salvatore Misiti (Mixed) and others – C.1/00482 Libya: human rights protection and protection of Italian companies involved in the reconstruction of Libyan infrastructures	09/11/2010 accepted
09/11/2010	Gianni Vernetti (Mixed) and others – C.1/00487 Free Nobel Peace Prize winner Liu Xiaobo	09/11/2010 accepted
18/11/2010	Italo Bocchino (FLI) and others – C.1/00495 Protection of human rights and religious freedom in the world, in particular sub-Saharan Africa and Middle East	11/01/2011 concluded
19/11/2010	Souad Sbai (PdL) and others – C.1/00498 Promote measures for protecting Christian minorities in the world	19/11/2010 presented
23/11/2010	Stefano De Lillo (PdL) – S.1/00350 Foster respect for human rights and religious freedom in Pakistan	03/03/2011 repeat request

Interpellations

Date	Initiative	Latest update
25/02/2010	Luigi Compagna (PdL) – S.2/00166 Freedom of expression for journalist Vittorio Feltri	25/02/2010 presented
13/04/2010	Elisabetta Zamparutti (PD) – C.2/00673 Violation of women's rights in Yemen	15/04/2010 concluded
20/04/2010	Francesco Tempestini (PD) – C.2/00680 Facts regarding arrest and later liberation of 3 Emergency humanitarian workers in Afghanistan	22/04/2010 concluded
19/10/2010	Luigi Compagna (PdL) – S.2/00270 Domestic implementation of the resolution on the promotion and protection of human rights	19/10/2010 presented

Questions receiving oral response

Date	Initiative	Latest update
09/03/2010	Maurizio Gasparri (PdL) – S.3/01209 Respect for human rights by Iran	15/03/2010 Modified for delegated Minister
13/07/2010	Filippo Berselli (PdL) – S.3/01418 Lapidation of an Iranian woman condemned for adultery	13/07/2010 presented
08/09/2010	Angelo Compagnon (UDC) – C.3/01212 Riots in Identification and Expulsion Centres (Centro di Identificazione ed Espulsione, CIE))	08/09/2010 presented
15/09/2010	Stefano Ceccanti (PD) – S.3/01499 Protect the universal values of pluralism and democracy beyond the freely professed religious faith	03/03/2011 concluded

13/10/2010	Pierluigi Mantini (UDC) and others – C.3/01278 Free Nobel Peace Prize winner Liu Xiaobo	13/10/2010 presented
16/11/2010	Mariapia Garavaglia (PD) – S.3/01757 Re-establish legality in labour relations and guarantee respect for human rights	16/11/2010 presented

Questions receiving written response

Date	Initiative	Latest update
04/01/2010	Rita Bernardini (PD) – C.4/05592 Special report on push-back operation of migrants prepared by the European Committee for the prevention of torture and inhuman or degrading treatment or punishment	03/05/2010 concluded
11/01/2010	Rita Bernardini (PD) – C.4/05640 Situation in the Altamura prison	12/04/2010 repeat interrogation
11/01/2010	Rita Bernardini (PD) – C.4/05666 Situation in the Cagliari prison	12/04/2010 repeat interrogation
12/01/2010	Francesco Ferrante (PD) – S.4/02496 Protect human rights in prisons and in Identification and Expulsion Centres (Centri di identificazione ed Espul-sione)	12/01/2010 presented
18/01/2010	Maurizio Turco (PD) – C.4/05742 Code of conduct on politico-military aspects of security	12/04/2010 repeat interrogation
20/01/2010	Leoluca Orlando (IdV) – C.4/05793 Situation for Kurds in Turkey	05/07/2010 concluded
11/02/2010	Francesco Maria Amoruso (PdL) – S.4/02686 Call Iran to respect human rights and democracy of internal opposition forces	11/02/2010 presented
17/02/2010	Donatella Poretti (PD) – S.4/02718 Illegal practices based on racial profiling by police of Milan	17/02/2010 presented
25/02/2010	Giuseppe Francesco Maria Marinello (PdL) – C.4/06286 Case of medical malpractice at Cervello hospital, Palermo	25/02/2010 presented
01/03/2010	Riccardo Migliori (PdL) – C.4/06296 Initiatives on political-diplomatic level in favour of human rights in Cuba	01/03/2010 presented
02/03/2010	Francesco Ferrante (PD) – S.4/02781 Suicide in Vibo Valentia prison	02/03/2010 presented
18/03/2010	Elisabetta Zamparutti (PD) – C.4/06568 Prohibit commerce of instruments used by law enforce-ment personnel which might improperly be used for torture	113/07/2010 concluded
23/03/2010	Francesco Ferrante (PD) – S.4/02907 Manufacturers of instruments of torture present in Italy	23/03/2010 presented
23/03/2010	Francesco Ferrante (PD) – S.4/02920 Inquiry on the death of Giuseppe Uva	26/03/2010 modified for delegated Minister
30/03/2010	Rita Bernardini (PD) – C.4/06608 Overcrowding in the Saluzzo prison (Cuneo)	12/04/2010 repeat interrogation

31/03/2010	Augusto Di Stanislao (IdV) – C.4/06690 European External Action Service (EEAS)	31/03/2010 presented
07/04/2010	Francesco Ferrante (PD) – S.4/02974 Suicide in Sulmona prison	07/04/2010 presented
14/04/2010	Teresa Armato (PD) – S.4/03011 Guarantee right to asylum	14/04/2010 presented
27/04/2010	Elisabetta Zamparutti (PD) – C.4/06937 Grant political asylum to Turkish citizen Avni Er	01/07/2010 repeat interrogation
11/05/2010	Domenico Scilipoti (Iniz. Resp.) and others – C.4/07117 Right to health and respect for human dignity in psychiatric hospitals	07/03/2011 concluded
20/05/2010	Pietro Tidei (PD) – C.4/07276 Overcrowding, degradation and inadequacy of Italian prisons	20/05/2010 presented
03/06/2010	Isabella Bertolini (PdL) – C.4/07455 Woman condemned and then absolved for practicing infibulation	03/06/2010 presented
09/06/2010	Rita Bernardini (PD) – C.4/07524 Protect rights of the 2 Algerians who attempted suicide in the Identification and Expulsion Centre at Ponte Galeria	29/06/2010 repeat interrogation
07/07/2010	Renato Farina (PdL) – C.4/07938 Guarantee respect for human rights and the right to asylum for Eritrean refugees	19/11/2010 concluded
08/07/2010	Roberto Della Seta (PD) – S.4/03421 Guarantee human rights for the 300 Eritreans seeking political asylum	29/07/2010 concluded
03/08/2010	Roberta Pinotti (PD) – S.4/03585 Italian system for protecting victims of human trafficking and combating criminality	03/08/2010 presented
08/09/2010	Rita Bernardini (PD) – C.4/08398 Guarantee civil and human rights for non-European citizens held in Identification and Expulsion Centres	08/09/2010 presented
08/09/2010	Rita Bernardini (PD) – C.4/08508 Situation in the local prison of Piazza Armerina, Province of Enna	08/09/2010 presented
08/09/2010	Rita Bernardini (PD) – C.4/08468 Suicide of a prisoner in the prison of Rebibbia, Rome	08/09/2010 presented
08/09/2010	Rita Bernardini (PD) – C.4/08399 Suicide in Brindisi prison	08/09/2010 presented
14/09/2010	Rita Bernardini (PD) – C.4/08531 International Covenant on the Protection of the Rights of All Migrant Workers and Members of Their Families	31/01/2011 concluded
15/09/2010	Roberto Della Seta (PD) – S.4/03652 Respect for the civil and human rights of Russian oligarch Khodorkovsky	21/09/2010 modified for delegated Minister
15/09/2010	Augusto Di Stanislao (IdV) – C.4/08596 Italian commitment to fostering human rights dialogue	26/10/2010 concluded

15/09/2010	Marco Zacchera (PdL) – C.4/08572 Human rights protection in Myanmar	19/11/2010 concluded
15/09/2010	Augusto Di Stanislao (IdV) – C.4/08583 Harsh condition of women and girls in Afghanistan	31/01/2011 concluded
15/09/2010	Augusto Di Stanislao (IdV) – C.4/08594 Failure to present a bill for ratifying the Protocol to UN Convention against Torture.	22/02/2011 concluded
28/10/2010	Giulio Camber (PdL) – S.4/03977 Solution of problems relating to the rights of Istrian exiles	28/10/2010 presented
28/10/2010	Jean Leonard Touadi (PD) and others – C.4/09230 Violation of human rights in occupied cities of Morocco	05/05/2011 concluded
02/11/2010	Roberto Della Seta (PD) – S.4/03982 Condemnation of the Eritrean dictatorship	02/11/2010 presented
03/11/2010	Marco Perduca (PD) – S.4/04006 Progress made in accepting 300,000 requests for regularisation in province of Brescia	03/11/2010 presented
10/11/2010	Rita Bernardini (PD) – C.4/09360 Severe degradation of Forlì prison	10/11/2010 presented
10/11/2010	Rita Bernardini (PD) – C4./09358 Resolve problems in Bologna detention centre for minors	10/11/2010 presented
10/11/2010	Augusto Di Stanislao (IdV) – C.4/09372 Intervention in favour of Somalia to stop the phenomenon of "child soldiers"	22/02/2011 concluded
10/11/2010	Augusto Di Stanislao (IdV) – C.4/09354 Involvement of minors in armed conflict	10/11/2010 presented
10/11/2010	Augusto Di Stanislao (IdV) – C.4/09368 Italian position and contribution to policy-making by UN Human Rights Council	31/01/2011 concluded
11/11/2010	Rita Bernardini (PD) – C.4/09394 Information on situation in prison at Carinola, Caserta	11/11/2010 presented
16/11/2010	Rita Bernardini (PD) – C.4/09441 Health care for drug-addicted and mentally ill prisoners	16/11/2010 presented
17/11/2010	Matteo Mecacci (PD) – C.4/09481 Urge the Uganda Government to combat crimes of homophobia	17/11/2010 presented
18/11/2010	Giuliano Barbolini (PD) – S.04126 Demand that Morocco respect the human rights of the Saharawi people	18/11/2010 presented
18/11/2010	Rita Bernardini (PD) – C.4/09544 Urgent intervention to improve conditions of the Identification and Expulsion Centre at Ponte Galera, Roma	18/11/2010 presented
19/11/2010	Rita Bernardini (PD) – C.4/09577 Resolve the degraded living conditions of Somali political refugees in the former embassy of Somalia	19/11/2010 presented
19/11/2010	Pierluigi Castagnetti (PD) – C.4/09589 Promote full freedom of the press in the Russian Federation	15/02/2011 concluded

22/11/2010	Rita Bernardini (PD) – C.4/09625 Guarantee adequate health care for Mr Mainardi in the Messina prison	22/11/2010 presented
22/11/2010	Rita Bernardini (PD) – C.4/09629 Resolve problems of security and human resources in Ancona prison	22/11/2010 presented
29/11/2010	Rita Bernardini (PD) – C.4/09781 Information on Favignana prison, Trapani, and on possible punitive attitudes toward prisoners	29/11/2010 presented
29/11/2010	Rita Bernardini (PD) – C.4/09774 Case of a prisoner detained at Bad' e Carros, Nuoro	29/11/2010 presented
29/11/2010	Rita Bernardini (PD) – C.4/09771 Critical situation of Lamezia Terme prison	29/11/2010 presented
06/12/2010	Salvatore Fleres (PdL) – S.4/04196 Case of Mr Mainardi, elderly and ill, detained in Messina Gazzi prison	06/12/2010 presented
06/12/2010	Giuseppe Valditara (Mixed) and others – S.4/04190 Emergency situation in the local prison of Mantua	06/12/2010 presented
06/12/2010	Giuseppe Valditara (Mixed) and others – S.4/04188 Grant refugee status to Joshua Jean Paul, Nigerian homosexual	06/12/2010 presented
07/12/2010	Tomaso Zanoletti (PdL) – S.4/04246 Combat criminal organisations that practice human trafficking	07/12/2010 presented
13/12/2010	Rita Bernardini (PD) – C.4/09950 Lack of water in Ranza prison, San Gimignano, province of Siena	13/12/2010 presented
13/12/2010	Rita Bernardini (PD) – C.4/09947 Serious shortcomings and degradation in penitentiaries of Basilicata	13/12/2010 presented
13/12/2010	Rita Bernardini (PD) – C.4/09943 Grave situation, Mammagialla prison, Viterbo	13/12/2010 presented
13/12/2010	Rita Bernardini (PD) – C.4/09905 Overcrowding in prison Santa Maria Maggiore, Venice	13/12/2010 presented
14/12/2010	Augusto Di Stanislao (IdV) – C.4/09978 Rights and regularisation of migrant workers	14/12/2010 presented
14/12/2010	Calogero Mannino (Mixed) and others – C.4/09977 Commit Egyptian Government to respecting human rights of Eritrean refugees in Egypt	14/12/2010 presented
14/12/2010	Augusto Di Stanislao (IdV) – C.4/09985 Guarantee protection and respect for human rights of Camp Ashraf residents	28/04/2011 concluded
14/12/2010	Marco Zacchera (PdL) – C.4/09994 Verify whether in Libya the rights of refugees and migrants are respected	10/03/2011 concluded
14/12/2010	Marco Zacchera (PdL) – C.4/09995 Initiatives aimed at improving the situation in Eritrea	10/03/2011 concluded

14/12/2010	Marco Zacchera (PdL) – C.4/09997 Information on the situation of Eritrean, Somali, Sudanese and Ethiopian refugees living in Egypt	10/03/2011 concluded
14/12/2010	Marco Perduca (PD) – S.4/04269 Arrest of Biram Dah Abeid and other human rights defenders in Mauritania	15/12/2011 repeat interrogation
15/12/2010	Matteo Mecacci (PD) – C.4/10034 Release of Biram Dah Abeid and the other human rights defenders arrested in Mauritania	10/03/2011 concluded
21/12/2010	Rita Bernardini (PD) – C.4/10145 Health care in prison for Salvatore Coci	21/12/2010 presented
21/12/2010	Rita Bernardini (PD) – C.4/10128 Suicide attempt by Fabrizio Bruzzone in prison of Genoa Pontedecimo	21/12/2010 presented
21/12/2010	Rita Bernardini (PD) – C.4/10127 Death in prison of Saidiou Gadiaga Elhdj	21/12/2010 presented
21/12/2010	Rita Bernardini (PD) – C.4/10125 Conditions in Foggia prison	21/12/2010 presented
21/12/2010	Rita Bernardini (PD) – C.4/10121 Overcrowding of prisoners and other problems, Messina prison	21/12/2010 presented
21/12/2010	Marco Perduca (PD) – S.4/04298 Release of Biram Dah Abeid and the other human rights defenders arrested on 13 December in Mauritania	21/12/2010 presented
21/12/2010	Francesco Ferrante (PD) – S.4/04299 Renew expiring residence permit of non-European workers for additional 24 months and improve care for detainees	21/12/2010 presented
22/12/2010	Magda Negri (PD) – S.4/04315 Homicides, violence and torture committed against young women in Mexico	22/12/2010 presented

Questions before Commissions

Date	Initiative	Latest update
19/01/2010	Leoluca Orlando (IdV) – C.5/02352 Situation in Africa	20/01/2010 concluded
19/01/2010	Sandro Zampa (PD) – C.5/02522 Role of the Minister of Foreign Affairs in relation to cooperation with Haiti	20/04/2010 concluded
24/02/2010	Alessia Maria Mosca (PD) – C.5/02546 Overcrowding in Monza prison	24/02/2010 modified for assigned commis-sion
01/03/2010	Matteo Mecacci (PD) – C.5/02565 Update on proposed initiatives by the Italian Government fostering freedom of the press in the Russian Federation	20/04/2010 concluded
30/03/2010	Dario Ginefra (PD) – C.5/02692 Protection of Turkish journalist Avny Er	26/05/2010 concluded

13/04/2010	Fiamma Nirenstein (PdL) – C.5/02731 Iran sitting at the UN Human Rights Council	20/04/2010 concluded
15/04/2010	Delia Murer (PD) – C.5/02761 Guarantee health care for clandestine foreigners throughout all the national territory	16/02/2011 new signers
27/04/2010	Fabio Evangelisti (IdV) – C.5/02807 Measures favouring release of Saharawi activists	28/04/2010 concluded
19/05/2010	Dario Ginefra (PD) – C.5/02919 Clarify situation in Albania	23/06/2010 concluded
07/07/2010	Matteo Mecacci (PD) – C.5/03194 Release of dissidents in Cuba	14/07/2010 concluded
19/07/2010	Renato Farina (PdL) – C.5/03253 Inquiry on respect for human rights in Venezuela	29/07/2010 concluded
28/07/2010	Renato Farina (PdL) – C.5/03298 Release Juan Juan Almeida	28/07/2010 modified for assigned commission
29/07/2010	Mario Tullo (PD) – C.5/03325 Intervention in favour of victims of human trafficking and fight against criminality	29/07/2010 modified for assigned commission
27/10/2010	Carmen Motta (PD) – C.5/03675 Right to self-determination of the Saharawi people	27/10/2010 modified for assigned commission
17/11/2010	Susanna Cenni (PD) – C.5/03843 Difficult situation for staff and prisoners in Ranza prison, province of Siena	17/11/2010 modified for assigned commission
25/11/2010	Aldo Di Biagio (FLI) and others – C.5/03890 Respect for human rights in Tunisia	25/11/2010 modified for assigned commission
13/12/2010	Francesco Tempestini (PD) – C.5/03946 Take action to free Eritrean refugees who have fallen into the hands of a gang of human traffickers	14/12/2010 concluded
21/12/2010	Emanuele Fiano (PD) – C.5/03988 Suicide of a prisoner in Sollicciano prison	21/12/2010 modified for assigned commission

Resolutions before Commissions

Date	Initiative	Latest update
06/05/2010	Fabio Evangelisti (IdV) – C.7/00325 Process of political transition towards a multi-party democracy in Cuba	06/05/2010 presented
24/05/2010	Francesco Tempestini (PD) – C.7/00338 Freedom of access and movement in territories of the Western Sahara	21/07/2010 accepted

08/06/2010	Rossana Lidia Boldi (Lega) – S.7/00049 Duty to define human trafficking as a crime	08/06/2010 approved
17/11/2010	Augusto Di Stanislao (IdV) – C.7/00440 End recruiting of child soldiers in Afghanistan	17/11/2010 presented
29/11/2010	Roberto Menia (FLI) and others – C.7/00447 Violation of human rights in Tunisia	29/11/2010 presented
13/12/2010	Stefano Stefani (Lega) – C.7/00452 EU Eastern Partnership	14/12/2010 accepted

Assembly agendas

Date	Initiative	Latest update
24/02/2010	Pietro Marcenaro (PD) – S.9/02002/005 Sustain all political and cooperative actions aiming to promote improvement of the woman's condition in Afghanistan	24/02/2010 accepted
05/05/2010	Alessandro Pagano (PdL) – C.9/03350-A/069 Multi-functional naval platforms for rescue operations	05/05/2010 accepted
03/06/2010	Rita Bernardini (PD) – C.9/03402/001 Implement the special assistance programme for victims of human trafficking	03/06/2010 accepted
28/07/2010	Furio Colombo (PD) – C.9/03638/154 Italian volunteers in international human rights organisations	28/07/2010 accepted
28/07/2010	Sandro Gozi (PD) – C.9/03638/160 Disbursement of Italian funds to international organisations	28/07/2010 accepted
27/10/2010	Marco Perduca (PD) – S.9/02179/001 Request at the European level to interrogate Minsk vigorously over the issue of respect for human rights	27/10/2010 presented
27/10/2010	Marco Perduca (PD) – S.9/02264/001 Respect for human rights in Belarus and support for the University of humanistic studies active in Vilnius	27/10/2010 accepted
19/11/2010	Marco Beltrandi (PD) – C.9/03778-A/146 Condition development cooperation aid to the respect of sexual and reproductive rights	19/11/2010 accepted
07/12/2010	Pietro Marcenaro(PD) – S.9/02464/058 Set up of an independent Authority on human rights	07/12/2010

Commission agendas

Date	Initiative	Latest update
27/07/2010	Stefano Pedica (IdV) – S.0/2291/01/0304 Assessment of agreements with Countries violating human rights	28/07/2010 concluded
29/09/2010	Marco Perduca (PD) – S.0/2264/01/03 Condition suspension of sanctions against Belarus authorities	29/09/2010 concluded
01/12/2010	Donatella Poretti (PD) – S.0/2464/58/05 Development cooperation only to Countries respecting sexual and reproductive rights	01/12/2010 accepted

II. Governmental Bodies

A. Committee of Ministers for Orientation and Strategic Guidance on Human Rights

The Committee was established on 13 April 2007 by a decree of the President of the Council of Ministers (d.p.c.m.) and is composed as follows: President of the Council of Ministers, Minister of Rights and Equal Opportunities, Minister of Foreign Affairs, Minister of Defence, Minister of Justice, Minister of Interior, Minister of Education, University and Research, Minister of Labour and Social Welfare, Minister of Social Solidarity, Minister of European Policies, Minister of Family Policy, Undersecretary of State to the Presidency of the Council of Ministers – Secretary to the Council of Ministers.

Since 2008, in virtue of d.p.c.m. 13 June 2008, the Committee has been chaired by the Minister for Equal Opportunities. The Committee adopts guidelines and orientation relating to human rights issues, and serves as steering and coordinating body of the Inter-Ministerial Committee for Human Rights (CIDU) and other bodies carrying out institutional activities in the field of human rights.

B. Ministry of Foreign Affairs: Inter-Ministerial Committee for Human Rights (CIDU)

The Ministry of Foreign Affairs hosts several Directorates-General (DG) and bureaus specifically involved in human rights, disarmament and cooperation. The Undersecretary delegated to deal with topics related to the United Nations system and to human rights and fundamental freedoms is Enzo Scotti.

DG for Political Affairs and Security: Office I – United Nations system and reform, peacekeeping operations and preventive diplomacy; Office II – Human rights advocacy and international humanitarian law, Council of Europe; Office V – Disarmament and arms control, nuclear, biological and chemical non-proliferation, Office of the National Authority for the Ban of Chemical Weapons; Office VI – Organisation for Security and Cooperation in Europe.

DG for the European Union: Office III – European space of freedom, justice and security; free movement of people and migratory flows towards the European Union.

DG for Development Cooperation: Office I – Development cooperation policies within the European Union; Office II – Multilateral development cooperation; Office VI – Emergency and humanitarian aid; Office VIII: Planning and monitoring of the cooperation budget; gender issues, rights of children and persons with disabilities.

The Inter-Ministerial Committee for Human Rights (CIDU), established by decree of the Minister of Foreign Affairs on 15 February 1978, act No. 519, is particularly important; its composition was updated by d.c.p.m. on 11 May 2007. It is chaired by an agent of the diplomatic service appointed by the Minister of Foreign Affairs: in June 2010 the chairmanship passed from Valentino Simonetti to Diego Brasioli.

The CIDU's members include representatives of the Presidency of the Council of Ministers, of various Ministries and of numerous institutions (such as the National Council on Economy and Labour (CNEL); the Association of Italian Municipalities (ANCI); the Conference of Presidents of the Regions and Autonomous Provinces; the Union of Italian Provinces (UPI); the National Commission for UNESCO; the Italian Committee for UNICEF; the Italian Society for International Organisation (SIOI); as well as three eminent personalities in the field of human rights.

The CIDU has the following tasks: to promote measures necessary for ensuring full compliance with international obligations already assumed, or that must be assumed by Italy upon ratification of the conventions it has signed; to monitor nation-wide compliance with international agreements; to draft all reports Italy is requested to submit to the United Nations and other multilateral bodies; to prepare the yearly report on the status of human rights promotion and protection in Italy the Ministry of Foreign Affairs must present to the Parliament in accordance to art. 1, Law 19 March 1999, No. 80; to maintain and develop pertinent relations with organisations of civil society which are actively involved in promoting and protecting human rights.

On 26 July 2010, the Minister of Foreign Affairs reported to the Italian House of Representatives on activities carried out by the Interministerial Committee for Human Rights as well as on the human rights situation in Italy in the year 2009 (doc. CXXI, No. 3). The report briefed the Parliament on cooperation activities with human rights mechanisms of the United Nations, the Council of Europe and the European Union, both in relation to the reporting obligation and to field-missions. In this regard, in 2009 CIDU performed the following activities:

United Nations

- presentation of the 3rd Periodic Report to the Convention on the Rights of the Child;
- drafting of the 6th Periodic Report to the Convention for the Elimination of All Forms of Discrimination against Women and of the national report for the UPR mechanism of the Human Rights Council;
- updating of the 14th-15th Periodic Report to the Convention against Racial Discrimination;
- drafting of the 5th Periodic Report to the International Covenant on Economic, Social and Cultural Rights and to the International Covenant on Civil and Political Rights;

- follow-up to the visit in Italy (from 3-14 November 2008) of the Working Group on Arbitrary Detention.

Council of Europe

- updating of the 3rd Report on Italy adopted by the European Commission against Racism and Intolerance;
- follow-up to the 5th periodical visit to Italy of the European Committee for the Prevention of Torture (14-26 September 2008);
- *ad hoc* visit to Italy of the European Committee for the Prevention of Torture (27-31 July 2009);
- *ad hoc* visit to Italy of the Council of Europe Commissioner for Human Rights, Thomas Hammarberg (13-15 January 2009).

European Union

– Response to the 2009 Report on Italy of the EU Fundamental Rights Agency (FRA).

In addition, the report sums up Italy's responses, formulated via CIDU, to specific requests for information and questionnaires sent to Italy by various bodies of the United Nations, the Council of Europe and the Organisation for Security and Cooperation in Europe (OSCE). In this connection, Italy replied to the following questionnaires or inquiries:

- urgent appeal from the UN Special Rapporteur on the promotion and protection of the right to freedom of opinion and expression and the Special Rapporteur on the situation of human rights defenders, concerning protective measures taken to guarantee the safety of the writer/human rights defender Roberto Saviano (January 2009);
- questionnaire from the UN Special Rapporteur on the sale of children, child prostitution and child pornography, requesting information on the legislative framework to fight such phenomena (March 2009);
- joint questionnaire from various UN Special-procedure mandate holders (Special Rapporteur on torture and other cruel, inhuman and degrading treatment of punishment, Special Rapporteur on the promotion and protection of human rights while countering terrorism, Working Group on Arbitrary Detention, Working Group on Enforced Disappearance), concerning policies and measures aimed at fighting terrorism adopted by Italy from 2001 on (April 2009);
- letter from the Chair of the Council of Europe European Committee for the Prevention of Torture, seeking information on the conditions of persons detained at Lampedusa's centre for immigrants (April 2009);
- request for information from the OSCE Office for Democratic Institutions and Human Rights (ODIHR), on the failure to grant the Roma community the status of historico-linguistic minority (May 2009);

- letter from the Chair of the Council of Europe European Committee for the Prevention of Torture seeking information on the push-back operations of migrants at sea (July 2009);
- request for information by the United Nations Office of the High Commissioner for Human Rights in relation to the national framework for protection and promotion of human rights of persons with disabilities (October 2009).

C. Ministry of Justice

Within the Ministry of Justice there are various departments and bureaus specifically involved with human rights. The most relevant are:

– *Office for studies, research, legislation and international relations* (Office of the Head of Department – Department of penitentiary administration): focused on coordinating activities with international organisations devoted to the protection and promotion of human rights of adult prisoners; it takes care of the application procedure of complaints lodged by inmates to the European Court of Human Rights;

– *Office II*: (DG for litigation and human rights – Department of legal affairs): it is actively involved in examining cases pending before the European Court of Human Rights and in procedures relating to compliance with international obligations, and to the incorporation into domestic law of provisions of international instruments;

– *Office III: Protection and support for the rights of minors. Promotion of measures in favour of subjects who risk the greatest degree of social exclusion* (DG for enforcement of judgments – Department of juvenile justice): dedicated to promoting and protecting the rights of unaccompanied foreign minors and of persons at risk of social exclusion;

– *Area I: Promotion of measures favouring minors at risk of social exclusion* (Office III Protection and support for the rights of minors. Promotion of measures in favour of subjects who risk the greatest degree of social exclusion – DG for the enforcement of judgments – Department of juvenile justice): in collaboration with the Ministry of Welfare and the Conference between State and Regions (*Conferenza Stato-Regioni*), it prepares a report to Parliament on adoptions pursuant to law 149/2001; it helps preparing the National Plan in collaboration with the Inter-Ministerial Committee for the Coordination of the Fight against Paedophilia (CICLOPE); it also collaborates with CIDU, with the Committee on Foreign Children, and with the Central coordinating body for the protection of unaccompanied minors coming from European Countries;

– *Area II: Protection of children's rights* (Office III Protection and support for the rights of minors. Promotion of measures in favour of subjects who risk the greatest degree of social exclusion – DG for the enforcement of judgments – Department of juvenile justice): it is dedicated to promoting and protecting the rights of minors, in collaboration with decentralised and territorially-based services, as well as protecting the rights of children pursuant to the United Nations Convention on the Rights of the Child.

D. Ministry of Labour and Welfare

The Ministry of Labour and Welfare's structure includes several departments and bureaus specifically involved with human rights. Of particular note:

– *DG for the protection of working conditions* (Technical bureau of the national Committee for equality between men and women; Division II – International affairs; Division III – Safety and health at work; Division VI – Law on prevention of work accidents and working conditions; Division VII – Labour disputes in agricultural and service sectors, protection of union rights, strikes in essential public service sectors);

– *DG for social inclusion, social rights and the corporate social responsibility* (Division II – Policies for social inclusion and social cohesion; Division III – Policies for children and adolescents; Division IV – Policies for persons with disabilities. Corporate social responsibility);

– *DG for immigration* (Division II – Immigration policies; Division III – Integration policies and international affairs; Division IV – Policies for foreign minors);

– *DG for volunteer work, associations and social groups* (Division I – Social organisations and general affairs; Division II – Associations; Division III – Voluntary work).

E. Department for Equal Opportunities: UNAR and Observatory for the Fight against Paedophilia and Child Pornography

The Department for Equal Opportunities, instituted under the auspices of the Presidency of the Council of Ministers, is dedicated to planning and coordinating legal, administrative and research initiatives in all areas pertaining to equal opportunities policies. It is directed by the Minister-without-portfolio for Equal Opportunities (in 2010 this was Maria Rosaria Carfagna).

The Department was instituted by d.p.c.m. No. 405 of 28 October 1997, later amended by d.p.c.m. of 30 September 2004. It is composed of four offices:

– *Office of international affairs and social measures:* it oversees initiatives aimed at adapting national legislation to international requirements; manages relations with the European Union, the United Nations, the Council of Europe and OSCE; fosters initiatives and activities against the exploitation and sexual abuse of minors, offering them assistance and protection, and working to combat paedophilia and child pornography; enacts measures linked to human trafficking and female genital mutilation;

– *Office of general affairs and protection measures*: it oversees activities implementing policies aiming to combat sexual and gender violence and acts of persecution such as stalking; it furthers activities combating discrimination against persons with disabilities;

– *Office for equality and equal opportunities, strategic intervention and communication*: it works in programming, planning and managing initiatives furthering equality and equal programmes; promotes and manages initiatives fostering female entrepreneurship; coordinates and monitors initiatives linked to the programming and use of European structural funds and resources for underused areas. Worth to mention, the Department presented several proposals for coordinated action with other institutions, including foreign Countries, aimed at combating phenomena of particular concerns such as violence in general, stalking, and human trafficking.

– *National Office against Racial Discrimination* (UNAR).

UNAR was instituted by legislative decree No. 215 on 9 July 2003, in compliance with the European Community directive 2000/43/CE. Its mission is to guarantee observance of the principle of equal treatment for individuals, to monitor the efficacy of current instruments against discrimination, and to help abolish forms of discrimination based on race or ethnic origin, while analysing their diversified impact on gender, and their connection with other forms of racism, of a cultural and religious nature.

UNAR's mandate includes: assisting victims of discriminatory behaviour lodging complaints, on both the administrative and judicial level; carrying out inquiries in order to verify the existence of discriminatory phenomena; adopting policies for affirmative action contrasting racial discrimination, in collaboration with non-profit associations; spreading instruments of protection by way of awareness-raising actions and communications; formulating recommendations and opinions on issues linked to racial and ethnic discrimination; preparing two yearly reports, respectively addressing Parliament and the President of the Council of Ministers; promoting studies, research, training courses and exchange of experiences in collaboration with non-governmental organisations and other associations working in the field, with the aim to setting up guidelines or codes of conduct in the fight against racial and ethnic discrimination.

During the year 2010, according to data provided by UNAR in the *Report to the President of the Council of Ministers on activities carried out in 2010*, the Office received 540 pertinent complaints regarding cases of racial discrimination, 405 of them (75%) were brought to conclusion thanks to a conciliation procedure; for 13.1%, an investigation is still in progress, while for 7.4% legal proceedings monitored by the Office are underway. Several cases, meanwhile, have been referred to the Observatory for protection against discriminatory acts and to the Postal Police (both linked to the Ministry of Interior) or else to the national Equality Councillor. 20% of these complaints regard the mass media; other areas touch on public life (17.8%), the supply of services by public agencies (16%), labour (11.3%), housing (8.9%), leisure time (8%), the supply of services by public companies (5.4%), schools and education (3.3%), the access to financial services (3.3%), law enforcement (2.4%), public transport (2.4%) and health care.

During 2010 UNAR also set up a widespread network of *territorial centres* against racism, in synergy with local and regional authorities and the civil society, with the aim to develop centres and observatories pursuant to art. 44 of legislative decree No. 286, 25 July 1998 (Consolidated act on immigration). To this end, and in acceptance of specifically formulated recommendations addressed to Italy during the Universal Periodic Review, on 16 November 2010 an inter-ministerial technical group was set up, open to representatives of local authorities. The group, coordinated by UNAR, was given a clear mandate to record, analyse and organise data referring to activities carried out by the various central and local administrations aiming to prevent and combat xenophobia and racism. Eventually, it is hoped, a national plan of action should result.

As regards the involvement of *non-governmental organisations* and social groups, starting from May 2010, eight regional hearings were held (in Lazio, Campania, Sicily, Calabria, Lombardy, Piedmont, Tuscany, Emilia-Romagna) involving 93 associations and agencies enrolled in the Register set up pursuant to legislative decree 215/2003. This has provided an updated picture of the real situation in various territories as well as defined best practises and common problems. A memorandum of understanding with unions and management against racial discrimination in the workplace has been adopted.

In 2010 the following activities for the awareness-raising, promotion and information have been carried out: the *Action week against racism*, encompassing over 30 initiatives throughout Italy and promoted in collaboration with local authorities and non-governmental organisations; the *National week against violence*, promoted in October in all Italian schools; *Diversity as value*, hosted in connection with 2007-2013-*PROGRESS*, a European plan for employment and social solidarity; the Council of Europe campaign *DOSTA!* for the fight to prejudice and stereotypes against Roma and Sinti; *Foreign women against all discriminations*, a campaign against complex forms of discrimination.

Among other activities carried out by UNAR in 2010, it is also worth noting:

- the elaboration of *thematic focuses* targeting young people, associations and foreign women; the realisation of *ad hoc* measures such as a social network of young voluntary workers (www.retenear.it) and various awareness campaigns;
- in the framework of the European Social Fund, the definition of a comprehensive strategy for *protecting Roma and Sinti communities* through an innovative and experimental model of governance in Convergence Objective Regions (Apulia, Calabria, Campania and Sicily), favouring a larger participation of those communities;
- development of activities aiming to combat "*institutional*" *discrimination* and discrimination linked to the sphere of everyday public life, stemming from administrative actions based on unequal treatment and carried out by central or local public administrations, starting with those sparked off by political movements and by the public use of racist expressions in political speech, not to mention forms of discrimination fostered by the media (Internet in particular).

Finally, in October 2009 UNAR published a call for proposals, funded with 900,000 euros, inviting civil society organisations to present ideas for the promotion of *positive actions* aimed at avoiding or countering situations of disadvantage linked to race or ethnic origin. The call, in particular, set out three strategic sectors: the development of microenterprises and enterprises managed by immigrant women; the promotion of the fight against racial discrimination among the younger generations; the prevention and fight against racial discrimination through the development of foreign communities associations and networking. In July 2010, 25 of out the 300 projects submitted to UNAR were selected. Most of the planned initiatives started in the first half of September of the same year.

In addition to the four offices mentioned above, the following joint bodies also link up to the Department for Equal Opportunities: the Inter-Ministerial Commission for the Support of Victims of Trafficking, Violence and Serious Exploitation (assisted, since January 2010, by the Technical Roundtable on Human Trafficking, composed of representatives from the most relevant institutions and organisations concerned with the trafficking of human beings, as well as several experts; this technical group is in charge of elaborating a national plan of action against human trafficking and/or guidelines coordinating pertinent measures taken up on the national level); the Commission for the Prevention and Abolition of the Practice of Female Genital Mutilation; the Commission Assessing the Legitimacy of Specific Actions in Favour of Persons with Disabilities (it keeps a register of associations and institutions entitled to take legal action on behalf of persons with disabilities who are victims of discrimination); the Commission for Equal Opportunities between Men and Women; the Committee for Female Entrepreneurship; the Commission for Health Studies; the Inter-Ministerial Committee for the Coordination of the Fight against Paedophilia (CICLOPE); the Observatory against Paedophilia and Child Pornography.

The Observatory against Paedophilia and Child Pornography was created pursuant to the law 3 August 1998, No. 269 (Provisions against the exploitation of prostitution, pornography and sex tourism harming minors, seen as new forms of slavery) amended by law 6 February 2006, No. 38. Its task is to gather and monitor data and information relating to activities carried out by public administrations for the prevention and repression of abuse and sexual exploitation of minors. Among its other tasks, the Observatory must prepare a *National plan for the prevention and repression of sexual exploitation of minors*; it submits the plan to CICLOPE for approval.

In May 2010 the Ministry for Equal Opportunities presented to the Parliament the report, prepared by the Observatory, on the coordinating activities established by art. 17, paragraph 1 of law 3 August 1998, No. 269. The Observatory is chiefly committed to managing a database with information provided by pertinent administrations, enabling it to monitor the abuse and sexual exploitation of minors, child pornography and actions undertaken to prevent and repress such phenomena.

At the international level, in 2010 the Observatory participated in numerous initiatives, such as:

- the European programmes *Safer Internet 2009-2013*, a plan of intervention regarding the new media and protection of minors: this project encompassed a *Safer Internet Day 2010* meant to further web security (9 February 2010);
- the *Annual meeting on children's rights*, held on 10 March 2010 in Geneva during the 13th session of the United Nations Human Rights Council;
- the European Commission plan *Prevention and Fight Against Crime 2007-2013*, including the project *Developing methods for identifying and supporting children who have been sexually exploited in order to produce paedo-pornographic images*, in collaboration with Save the Children, CISMAI – the Italian Coordination of services against child abuses – as well as the Postal Police.

F. National Council on Economy and Labour (CNEL)

CNEL is a body provided for in art. 99 of the Constitution. Since 2005, the Chair has been Antonio Marzano; he was re-confirmed by the Council of Ministers in July 2010, for the 9th council period (2010-2015).

Its function is essentially consultative. It expresses opinions on request of the Parliament, the Government and the Regions; on its own initiative it prepares comments and recommendations on proposed legislation, reports, studies and in-depth analysis.

The CNEL structure includes an Assembly, a Chair's office and committee, several specialised Commissions (among which a Commission for social policy and a Commission for European and international policies), as well as several committees and bodies: e.g. the Committee on immigration; the Committee on union representation in public employment; the Observatory on social economy; the Socio-economic Observatory on crime; the Coordinated Committee of consultants on the south; the National body of coordination for policies of foreign citizens' social integration at the local level.

During 2010 CNEL prepared 37 documents, including:

- 12 documents containing observations and proposals, notably *Women's employment in Italy*; *Official Development Assistance: conditions of efficacy and proposals for improving it*; *The social enterprise*;
- 11 reports, including the *Preliminary Report on the levels and quality of assistance given by public administrations to citizens and enterprises*; the *Report on labour relations in Italy and Europe 2008-2009*; the 7th report on *Indexes of integration of immigrants in Italy*;
- 5 studies, inquiries and researches, notably *Are we ready to give young people a home? Inquiry on the housing situation of under thirty-five-year old in Italy*; *Planning economic development in Italian Regions*; *Types of knowledge*;
- 4 volumes on meetings and conference proceedings;
- 2 texts on preliminary agreements for inter-institutional collaboration;
- a *communiqué* on the topic *Involvement of organised civil society in the framework of European Strategy 2020. Declaration of the Presidents and Secretaries-General of the Economic and Social Councils (CES) of Member States and of the European Economic and Social Committee. Brussels, 16 September 2010*;
- an informative dossier;
- the *Chair's general directive for the implementation of the Council programme and guidelines for administrative action in 2010.*

G. National Observatory on Childhood and Adolescence

The Observatory performs a role of coordination among central administrations, local and regional agencies, associations, professional groups and non-governmental organisations dedicated to children's issues.

It was instituted by law 23 December 1997, No. 451, and is currently regulated by decree of the President of the Republic (d.p.r.), No. 103, 14 May 2007, which assigns it joint chairship by the Ministry of Labour and Welfare and the Undersecretary of State to the Presidency of the Council of Ministers mandated of family policies. It is made up of representatives from national and local public administrations, institutions, professional orders, no profit organisation as well as experts in the field of children's rights.

D.p.r. 103/2007 assigns the Observatory the task of preparing three important documents regarding the condition of children and adolescents in Italy:

– The *National Plan of action and intervention for the protection of rights and development of subjects in developmental age.* Prepared every two years, it presents the fundamental guidelines and concrete commitments the Government intends to undertake in order to protect children and adolescents in Italy. Before being formally adopted by a d.p.r., the Plan of Action must be approved by the Parliamentary Commission for childhood and adolescence. Since its institution, the Observatory has prepared two Plans of Action, respectively for the period 2000-2001 and 2002-2004; in addition, from October 2007 to October 2009 it drew up a 3rd Plan of Action (2009-2011), which the Parliamentary Commission for childhood and adolescence licensed in October 2010. The new plan focuses on the right to participate and to enjoy a child-oriented environment; on the pact for intergenerational equity; on the struggle against poverty; on minors in an intercultural society; on Roma, Sinti and Travellers minors; on the machinery for the protection of children's rights and the integrated system of social services.

– The *Report on the condition of children and adolescents in Italy*, which aims to provide an updated picture of the aspects and phenomena characterising the condition of children and adolescents in Italy, and of the system of social services and measures for promoting and protecting the rights of children and adolescents. The latest report published by the Observatory refers to the two-year period 2008-2009. It presents an analysis of several domains such as social participation; intergenerational relations; condition of Roma, Sinti and Travellers children; intercultural society; the fight against poverty and social exclusion; the machinery for the protection of children's rights and the integrated system of social services.

– The *Periodic Report to the United Nations Convention on the Rights of the Child*, pursuant to art. 44 of the Convention. The latest Report, merging the 3rd and 4th Reports, was sent by Italy in January 2009, and is still awaiting discussion by the Committee (see Part III, the United Nations System, V, F).

In carrying out its various functions, the National Observatory makes use of the National Centre of Documentation and Analysis for Childhood and Adolescence, which has the task of documenting, analysing, researching, monitoring and training. The chair of the Centre in 2010 was Francesco Paolo Occhiogrosso; the Coordinator of scientific activities, Valerio Belotti.

More specifically, the National Centre of Documentation carries out the following tasks:

- collecting and disseminating regional, national, European and international laws, as well as statistical data and scientific studies;
- creating an annually updated map, based on information provided by regional authorities, of public, private and non-governmental social services, including assistance and health care, and of financial resources dedicated to children on the national, regional and local level;
- analysing the situation of childhood and adolescence in Italy, including the conditions of foreign minors;
- preparing an outline, based on National Observatory directives, of the biennial report on the condition of children in Italy, and of the Government report to the United Nations Committee on the Rights of the Child on the domestic implementation of the Convention on the Rights of the Child;
- formulating proposals, even upon request of local authorities, for the creation of pilot projects aiming to improve children living conditions as well as the assistance to mothers during the perinatal period.

H. National Committee on Bioethics

The National Committee on Bioethics carries out roles of consultancy *vis-à-vis* the Government, Parliament and other institutions, formulating opinions and motions on legislative and administrative instruments dealing with bioethical issues. It also has the role of information and awareness raising in relation to ethical and legal problems that may arise in connection with progress in scientific research and technological applications on life.

The Committee was established by the d.p.c.m. of 28 March 1990. It is composed of the following bodies: President (Francesco Paolo Casavola, President Emeritus of the Constitutional Court); Vice Presidents (Riccardo Di Segni, Chief Rabbi of Rome; Lorenzo d'Avack, Professor of Philosophy of Law; Luca Marini, Professor of International Law; Laura Palazzoni, Professor of Philosophy of Law); Office of the President (made up of the President and the Vice Presidents); Assembly.

The Committee is organised in 9 working groups, respectively dealing with: ethics committees; conscientious objection; synthetic biology; neurosciences and enhancement; neglected areas of medicine; pharmacological experimentation in developing Countries; bioethics and plastic surgery; the right to know one's origins in the case of medically assisted procreation; human health, nutrition and animal welfare.

The Committee also has the task of formulating proposals for legislative acts. The Committee's documentation offers in-depth focus and reflection on issues of an ethical and legal nature which emerge along with the evolution of knowledge in the life sciences field. According to their nature and purpose, Committee documents may be classified as follows: opinions (approved by the Assembly after in-depth study carried out by working groups); motions (documents of an urgent nature, approved by a two-thirds majority of Assembly participants); responses (Committee documents offering recommendations on issues raised by institutions or individuals).

During 2010, no motion or response was approved; instead, the following topics of discussion were hosted: Neurosciences and human experimentation: bioethical problems (17 December 2010); Identification of the human body: bioethical aspect of biometrics (26 November 2010); Improper use of placebo (29 October 2010); Bioethics and education in schools (16 July 2010); Life conditions of women in the third and fourth age: bioethical aspects of social health care (16 July 2010); Suicides in prison: bioethical trend (25 June 2010); Criteria for the ascertainment of death (224 June 2010); Secrecy in drug regulatory system procedures (28 May 2010); Kidney donation from a living donor to a stranger (23 April 2010); Ethics, sports and doping (25 March 2010); Minor's sexual differentiation disorders: bioethical aspects (25 February 2010).

In addition, on 15 July 2010 a preliminary agreement was signed between the Presidency of the Council of Ministers – National Committee on Bioethics and the Ministry of Education, University and Research, advocating common initiatives for including bioethics in the school curriculum.

Finally, on 29 April 2010, the Committee promoted the 7th National school conference on bioethics, on the topic *Possibilities and limits of genetic investigations* (Pontedera, PI). Similar national conferences have been organised yearly, beginning in 2001, by the Italian Institute of Bioethics, in collaboration with university structures and bioethics centres. Targeting high school students, and actively promoted by the Committee, the conferences aim to transmit theoretical knowledge on the history, principles and problems of bioethics, and lead students to acquire the "bioethical competencies" necessary to confront, as responsible citizens, the ethical challenges posed by scientific progress.

I. National Observatory Monitoring the Condition of Persons with Disabilities

The Observatory is a consultative body giving techno-scientific support in defining and implementing disability-related policies.

It was instituted by law 3 March 2009, No. 18, at the Ministry of Labour, Health and Welfare. It is chaired by the Ministry of Labour and includes a maximum number of 40 members, who are appointed by ministerial decree and represent central administrations involved in defining and implementing disability-related policies; regional and local authorities; social security institutions; the National Statistics Institute; trade unions; and most representative associations and organisations of persons with disabilities, joined by a maximum number of five experts of proven experience in the field of disabilities. The strategic and scientific guidance of the Observatory's activities is provided by a Technical and Scientific Committee.

The Observatory's tasks include the following: to promote the implementation of the United Nations Convention on the Rights of Persons with Disabilities and to prepare, together with CIDU, the national report for the monitoring procedure established by that Convention; to prepare a biennial plan of action on disability implementing national and international laws; to promote and develop statistic-based studies and research that may contribute to defining priorities and needs.

The Observatory is regulated by the inter-ministerial decree of 6 July 2010, No. 167, which entered into force on 23 October 2010. The Observatory will remain active for three years beginning on that date. The current members of the Observatory were appointed by the successive ministerial decree of 30 November 2010.

In 2010 the composition of the Observatory was the following: Orietta Maizza (Department of Public Administration and Innovation of the Presidency of the Council of Ministers); Alessandra de Marco (Department for Equal Opportunities of the Presidency of the Council of Ministers); Angelo Mari (Department of Family Policies of the Presidency of the Council of Ministers); Daniela Bas (Ministry of Foreign Affairs); Massimo Marconi (Ministry of Economy and Finance); Corrado Loschiavo (Ministry of Infrastructure and Transport); Raffaele Tangorra (Ministry of Labour and Social Policy); Fiammetta Landoni (Ministry of Health); Massimo Zennaro (Ministry of Education, University and Research); Fabio Cembrani (Conference of Regions and Autonomous Provinces); Raffaele Goretti (Conference of Regions and Autonomous Provinces); Francesco Lo Trovato (UPI); Paolo Anibaldi (ANCI); Anna Radi (INPS); Ivano Mannucci (INPDAP); Saverio Gazzelloni (ISTAT); Antonina Daita (CGIL); Silvia Stefanovichj (CISL);

Sergio Ricci (UIL); Giovanni Scacciavillani (UGL); Fabio Pontrandolfi (Confindustria); Tommaso Daniele (UIC and FAND); Ida Collu (ENS and FAND); Franco Bettoni (ANMIL and FAND); Alessandro Bucci (UNMS and FAND); Giovanni Pagano (ANMIC and FAND); Pietro Vittorio Barbieri (FAIP and FISH); Giampiero Griffo (EDF, DPI and FISH); Antonio Cotura (FIADDA and FISH); Ivo Manavella (ANFFAS and FISH); Donata Vivanti (Autismo Italia, EDF and FISH); Giuseppe Trieste (FIABA); Sergio Silvestre (COORDOWN); Nicola Spinelli (UNIAMO F.I.R.M. Onlus); Fulvio De Nigris (Gli Amici di Luca); Paola Menetti (Legacoopsociali and Forum Terzo Settore); Ugo Campagnaro (Federsolidarietà Regione Veneto, Forum Terzo Settore); Carlo Francescutti (expert); Matilde Leonardi (expert); Mario Melazzini (expert). The techno-scientific Committee included Matilde Leonardi (Committee coordinator), Raffaele Tangorra, Fiammetta Landoni, Raffaele Goretti, Paolo Anibaldi, Giovanni Pagano, Pietro Vittorio Barbieri, Carlo Francescutti, Mario Melazzini.

The initial meeting of the Observatory took place on 16 December 2010.

J. Committee for Foreign Children

The Committee for Foreign Children is the inter-ministerial body instituted by the legislative decree 25 July 1998, No. 286, with the aim to monitor modes of residence for foreign minors temporarily present on Italian territory, and to coordinate the activities of administrations involved.

Initially instituted under the auspices of the Presidency of the Council of Ministers, it currently operates at the Ministry of Labour and Welfare. It includes nine representatives, one for each of the following ministries: Ministry of Social Solidarity, Ministry of Foreign Affairs, Ministry of Interior, Ministry of Justice; two representatives from the Association of Italian Municipalities (ANCI), one representative from the Union of Italian Provinces (UPI), two delegates from the most representative associations concerned with issues of the family and unaccompanied minors.

The lgs.d. 25 July 1998, No. 286 (amended by lgs.d. of 13 April 1999, No. 113) and the regulations of the Committee for Foreign Minors (adopted by d.p.c.m. on 9 December 1999, No. 535) define the competencies of this body in relation to two categories of foreign minors: *unaccompanied minors present in the territory* and *minors temporarily admitted.*

As regards *unaccompanied minors present in the territory*, the Committee monitors accommodation arrangements for foreign minors; ascertains the status of the unaccompanied minor; takes initiatives and carries out research in order to identify the family members of minors, even in their Country of origin or in third Countries, seeking collaboration from the competent public administrations and appropriate national and international organisations (in particular, the International Organisation for Migration). It takes a census of unaccompanied minors who are present in Italy. The Committee may then adopt two kinds of measures: the first one is "no repatriation", which amounts to mobilising the integration process of the person into Italian national territory; the second one is an "assisted repatriation" in order to protect the children's right to family unity. As regards the first measure, the local territorial authorities are called upon to manage and monitor intervention. The most frequent choice made for unaccompanied minors is to place them in protected communities in Italy.

As regards *temporarily admitted minors*, the Committee decides, according to predetermined criteria, upon request of organisations, associations or Italian families concerning the temporarily admission of children in the framework of humanitarian programmes; the Committee then makes decisions for the minors' repatriation. It keeps a register of minors already admitted in the framework of humanitarian programmes and predefines criteria for assessing requests for the admission of other minors.

In 2010, 4,438 unaccompanied foreign minors were referred to the Committee's attention, including 4,016 males (90.5%) and 422 females (9.5%). The main Countries of origin were Afghanistan (around 21%), Morocco (15%), Egypt (11%), Albania (9%), and Bangladesh (6%).

In the same year, 19,280 minors were admitted in the framework of 1,056 humanitarian hospitality programmes proposed by 237 associations active on the national territory. The majority of these minors were from Belarus (13,894); the other main Countries of origin were Ukraine (3,514), Bosnia-Herzegovina (718), the Russian Federation (639) and Algeria (Sahrawi, 290). The Italian Regions admitting the greatest number of minors were Lombardy (4,167), Veneto (1,873), Emilia-Romagna (1,863), Piedmont (1,687), Campania (1,428), Lazio (1,289), Tuscany (1,271), Sicily (1,123) and Apulia (1,065).

K. Commission for Intercountry Adoptions

Art. 6 of the Hague Convention on the Protection of Minors and Co-operation in Respect of Intercountry Adoption, adopted on 29 May 1993 and entered into force on 1 May 1995, requires State parties to establish a central authority guaranteeing that adoptions of foreign children occur in respect for the principles established by the Convention itself. In order to comply with this requirement, Italy, via ratifying law 31 December 1998, No. 476, instituted the Commission for Intercountry Adoptions, operative through the Presidency of the Council of Ministers. The Commission is Italy's central authority implementing the Hague Convention.

The Commission has the following tasks: to propose the conclusion of bilateral agreements in matters of international adoption; whether directly or in coordination with other public authorities, to take all measures capable of facilitating adoption procedures and of preventing improper material profit when an adoption takes place; to authorise bodies considered capable of furthering international adoption procedures, of keeping a register of adoptions and overseeing their enactment; to see that the adoption responds to the child's best interest; to authorise the child's entry and permanent residence with the goal of adoption; to promote training initiatives for those operating or who intend to operate in the field of adoption; to preserve the documents and information relative to the procedure, including those regarding the child's origin and medical history and the identity of his natural parents; to arrange for a biennial report to Parliament on the progress of international adoptions, on progress in applying the Hague Convention and on the conclusion of any bilateral agreements with Countries which have not signed the Convention. The report is presented by the President of the Council of Ministers or by the delegated Minister.

The Commission is composed of a Chair, appointed by the President of the Council of Ministers (in 2010 this was Carlo Giovanardi, Undersecretary of State), and by the following members: three representatives of the Presidency of the Council of Ministers; a representative of the Ministry of Foreign Affairs; a representative from the Ministry of Education; a representative from the Ministry of Labour and Welfare; a representative from the Ministry of Interior; two representatives from the Ministry of Justice; a representative from the Ministry of Health; a representative from the Ministry of Economy; four representatives from the Conference between State and Regions (*Conferenza Stato-Regioni*); three representatives from family associations; experts in the field.

According to data provided by the Commission, 2010 saw the highest number of adoptions concluded by Italian couples: the Commission issued authorisation for the entry in Italy of 4,130 children, coming from 58 Countries, compared to 3,964 of the previous year, with an increase of 4.2%. 3,241 couples successfully carried out an adoption procedure in 2010, compared to 3,082 in 2009. The average waiting period for completing an international adoption (calculated from the moment when the application is passed to the authorised agency to the moment when the Commission authorises entry) is 26 months.

Among the children adopted in 2010, 56.7% were males and 43.3% females. Their average age was 6 years, slightly more than in 2009 (5.9 years). Data regarding age groups shows that more than a third (36.1%) were of an age between 1 and 4 years; 43.8% between 5 and 9 years; and 13.5% 10 years or older, while 6.5% were less than one year old. In this last age group, the number of females far exceeds the number of males.

Children from European Countries made up 43.7% of the total, followed by children from the Americas (27.3%), Asia (18.2%), and finally, Africa (10.7%). The Country of origin for most of the adopted children was the Russian Federation, with its 707 children receiving permission for entry (amounting to 17.12% of the total); followed by Colombia, with 592 children (14.33%), Ukraine, with 426 (10.31%), Brazil, with 318 (7.70%), Ethiopia, with 274 (6.63%), Vietnam, with 251 (6.08%), and Poland, with 193 (4.67%). In all, 2,761 children reached Italy from 7 different Countries. They amount to around 67% of children authorised entry during the year for the purpose of adoption.

During 2010, 746 couples (amounting to 23% of the total) adopted pairs or groups of two or more siblings, amounting to an overall number of 1,635 children. Finally, it can be noted that as many as 639 children, amounting to 15.5% of the total number of children adopted, are classified as children with special needs: afflicted by serious, often incurable pathologies, such as neurological and mental diseases, or in need of special therapies which may lead to recovery.

In the area of international relations, in 2010 the Commission carried out several missions abroad: in Colombia and Bolivia, during the month of May, in the Hague in June, and in Vietnam and Canada in December.

In addition, during that year the Commission financed 31 "subsidiarity" projects, including one in the geographic area of Europe, 12 in the geographic area of Asia, 7 in the geographic area of Africa and 11 in the geographic area of Latin America, proposed by authorised agencies. The missions aimed to prevent and combat the phenomenon of children's abandonment in their Country of origin, by implementing measures allowing them to remain in their family of origin and, more generally, in the community to which they belong. To this end, stronger participation must be offered by local associations, families and youths.

Finally, in 2010 the Commission prepared four research documents (*A journey in schools*; *The quality of waiting during international adoption*; *Pathways of international adoption: the families' viewpoint*; *Together at school*), and promoted a European meeting, taking place in Florence in June, on the theme *Resilience and autobiographic approach in international adoptions – Scholastic integration, adolescence, adoption of siblings*.

L. National Commission for UNESCO

The Commission was established by inter-ministerial decree on 11 February 1959, at the Ministry of Foreign Affairs, two years after Italy entered the Organisation, and pursuant to art. 7 of the UNESCO Charter.

Its composition has been regulated and updated by a series of successive decrees, the most recent one dating back to 24 May 2007. Members of the Commission include representatives from Parliament, the Presidency of the

Council of Ministers, various Ministries, public and private agencies, local authorities and civil society.

The Commission's mission is to promote the implementation of UNESCO programmes in Italy; to spread the ideals of the Organisation, especially among the younger generations; to disseminate information on its principles, goals and activities, thus stimulating action by institutions, the civil society and the world of culture, education and science. The Commission also offers consultancy relative to relations between the Government and UNESCO.

In 2010, the Chair appointed by the Ministry of Foreign Affairs was Giovanni Puglisi, while Lucio Alberto Savoia was Secretary General.

During 2010, the Commission for UNESCO promoted a series of activities – seminars, meetings, school conferences, contests, exhibitions, laboratories, performances – in various Italian cities, celebrating such events as the International Year of Biodiversity, the International Year for the Rapprochement of Cultures, and the Decade of Education for Sustainable Development 2005-2014. It also celebrated several international United Nations Days.

In 2010 the National Commission also activated specific school projects, notably a programme teaching respect for cultural diversity; a programme teaching respect for intellectual property and copyrights, in collaboration with the Italian Society of Authors and Publishers (SIAE); a learning project on the immaterial cultural heritage, in collaboration with the Ministry of Education, University and Research; a project on the cultural and landscape heritage, in collaboration with the Italian Fund for the Environment (FAI).

Finally, on 11 February the National Commission for UNESCO participated in the first technical meeting of the Committee for the Application of the UNESCO Convention for the Safeguarding of the Intangible Cultural Heritage. Members of this latter Committee included the following Ministries: Cultural Heritage and Activities, Foreign Affairs, Environment, Territory and Sea, Education, University and Research.

III. Independent Authorities

The independent authorities include: the Communications Regulatory Authority (AGCOM); the Italian Data Protection Authority; Commission Guaranteeing the Implementation of the Law on Strikes Affecting Essential Public Services; Authority Protecting Free Competition and the Market (Antitrust Authority); the Italian Companies and Stock Exchange Commission (CONSOB); Institute for the Vigilance on Private Insurance and Insurances of Collective Interest (ISVAP); the Regulatory Authority for Electricity and Gas; Authority for the Vigilance on Contracts for Public Works, Services and Supplies. In the following paragraphs the three Authorities most directly involved in the promotion and protection of human rights will be examined.

A. Communications Regulatory Authority (AGCOM)

AGCOM was set up by the law 31 July 1997, No. 249. It is composed of the following bodies: *Chair* (in 2010 this was Corrado Calabrò); *Infrastructure and Networks Commission*, made up of four Commissioners (in 2010 these were Michele Lauria, Sebastiano Sortino, Gianluigi Magri and Antonio Martusciello: the latter since July); *Services and Products Commission*, made up of four Commissioners (in 2010 these were Stefano Mannoni, Nicola D'Angelo, Roberto Napoli and Enzo Savarese); *Council*, made up of the Chair and all the Commissioners.

AGCOM has a double mandate: to ensure correct competition among market actors and to guarantee the fundamental freedoms of citizens in the area of communications, particularly as regards the protection of minors. In this area, AGCOM not only sanctions violation of provisions envisaged in legislative decree 31 July 2005, No. 177 (Consolidated act on radio and television) and in the self-regulatory code on TV and minors approved on 29 November 2002, but it has also adopted various other measures through the years, including:

- *Deliberation 165/06/CSP* of 22 November 2006, calling on public and private radio and television broadcasters and providers of radio and television programmes to respect the principle of human dignity in the area of entertainment, including respect for religious feelings, with particular attention towards criteria of correctness in participants' language and behaviour, towards displays of physical and verbal violence, and towards sexual allusions or displays tending to offend human dignity;
- *Deliberation 23/07/CSP* of 22 February 2007 on respect for the fundamental human rights and the prohibition of programmes presenting pornographic scenes;
- *Deliberation 13/08/CSP* of 31 January on correct ways of presenting legal proceedings in television broadcasts: those responsible are urged to avoid disproportionate, excessive and/or blatantly biased media coverage.

According to information from the annual activities report of 2010 covering the period 1 May 2009-30 April 2010, the Authority dedicated particular attention to monitoring broadcasts and imposing sanctions, with the aim to protect minors and media users. To this end, during the period considered, it initiated 73 inquiries involving local and national broadcasters, aiming to ascertain any violation that might warrant the imposition of penalties; 34 proceedings ended in ordinances of injunction, including: 16 for violation of art. 4, clause 1, letter b), legislative decree of 31 July 2005, No. 177 (adequate coverage on national territory); 3 for violation of art. 4, clause 1, letter b) of legislative decree 177 and the self-regulatory code on TV and minors together with art. 34, clause 3 of l.d. 177 (prohibition against broadcasting films prohibited to persons under 14 years of age, from 7 a.m. to 10:30 p.m.); 9 for violation of art. 1, clause 26, of l.d. 23 December 1996, No. 650 (prohibition against international and audio text services presenting forms or content of an erotic, pornographic or obscene nature, between 7 a.m. and midnight).

As for the regulatory dimension, during a meeting on 28 October 2009, the Authority approved the general guidelines on further obligations binding the general public radio and television services which were functional to the renewal of the national service contract for the three-year period 2010-2012. Then, on 12 November, after consulting the Ministry for Economic Development, the Authority approved deliberation 614/09/CONS, whose art. 7 requires RAI (Radiotelevisione Italiana), in its programming, to adopt measures capable of protecting minors, not only during the scheduled period declaredly adapted to their needs (from 4 p.m. to 8 p.m.), but in the entire period dedicated to family viewing, from 7 a.m. to 10 p.m. Except during late-night broadcasting, RAI must not only scrupulously respect current primary and secondary norms, including discipline foreseen by the self-regulatory code on TV and minors; it must also avoid transmitting programmes containing scenes of gratuitous violence which may disturb the younger public of viewers. In the same deliberation, with the goal of protecting minors, the Authority also attempted to widen obligations binding public broadcasters: it introduced the requirement that the RAI Code of Ethics encompass the self-regulatory code on televising criminal proceedings, the code on media and minors, the code on broadcasting sports commentary (see art. 34 of the Consolidated act on radio and television), and a code of good conduct containing specific norms on "reality" shows.

Finally, by deliberation 194/09/CONS, the Authority approved a project for editing a *White Book on relations between the media and minors.* Through an inter-disciplinary approach, this study aims to explore the synergic relationship between the multi-media offering, in all its integrated aspects, and the social behaviour of minors, adolescents in particular.

B. Italian Data Protection Authority

The Data Protection Authority (*Autorità garante per la protezione dei dati personali*) was instituted by legislative decree No. 675, 31 December 1996, later substituted by legislative decree 30 June 2003, No. 196 (Personal Data Protection Code), with the aim to ensure protection of the fundamental rights and freedoms and respect for the dignity of persons, in the treatment of personal data. This joint body is made up of four members elected by Parliament, who remain in office for a seven-year non-renewable mandate. The current joint body entered office on 18 April 2005 and includes Francesco Pizzetti (Chair), Giuseppe Chiaravalloti (Vice Chair), Mauro Paissan and Giuseppe Fortunato.

> The Authority's tasks include: verifying that the processing of personal data complies with laws and norms and, if necessary, informing persons named as holders of data or responsible for holding data, of modifications to be adopted in order to respect compliance; examining indications and complaints, and procedures for redress by affected persons; partially or entirely prohibiting data treatment, or arranging to block personal data whose treatment might seriously harm the person involved, given its nature or the modes and/or effects of its treatment; adopting provisions foreseen by personal data norms: in particular as regards general authorisation for the treatment of sensitive data; promoting the signing of ethical codes and codes of conduct in various areas (consumer credit, journalistic activity, etc.); if advisable, informing the Government of the need to adopt new norms in given sectors; formulating opinions on request by the President of the Council of Ministers or by any Minister, regarding regulation and administrative acts affecting the protection of personal data; preparing a yearly report addressed to Parliament and the Government, on activities performed, and on current progress in the application of privacy norms; informing citizens and increasing public awareness relative to the treatment of personal data and to data security measures.

During 2010 the Authority adopted several measures protecting the fundamental rights of persons in processing personal data. Particular attention was given to the following areas:

- *Sensitive and judicial data.* Contraception and minors: prohibition against parents' access to prescriptions (17 November 2010); Online arrest warrant: permission, but giving only essential data (29 September 2010);
- *Journalism and other manifestations of thought.* Articles published on the Web: prohibition against diffusing sensitive data (1 July 2010); Prohibition against seeking out adopted children on TV (6 May 2010); Diffusion of income data by daily newspapers (18 February 2010); Sexual violence and the right to give news (28 January and 11 February 2010);
- *Internet and the new media.* In-company e-mail and employee privacy (21 January 2010); Data-collecting via Internet for promotional purposes: those affected must always give their consent (15 July 2010);

- *Minors.* On TV, greater protection for minors who are victims of violence (16 September 2010); School: prohibition against communicating personal data of minor-age students (13 May 2010);
- *Sport.* Soccer fan identity card: greater guarantees for the team supporters (10 November 2010).

In 2010, the Authority also adopted *Guidelines on the processing of personal data while reproducing judgements and other decisions of judicial authorities for purposes of legal information* (2 December), and the *General provisions on video-surveillance* (8 April). Finally, the Authority participated in the 32nd International Conference of Data Protection and Privacy Commissioners, held in Jerusalem from 27 to 29 October 2010.

C. Commission Guaranteeing the Implementation of the Law on Strikes Affecting Essential Public Services

The Commission was instituted by the law of 12 June 1990, No. 146, modified from law 11 April 2000, No. 83. It comprises nine members designated by the Chairs of the House of Representatives and the Senate among experts in matters of Constitutional law, labour law and industrial relations, and appointed by decree of the President of the Republic. In 2010 the office of Commissioner was composed of Giovanni Pitruzzella (Chair), Roberto Alesse, Pietro Boria, Gaetano Caputi, Alessandro Forlani, Elena Montecchi, Iolanda Piccinini, Nunzio Pinelli and Salvatore Vecchione.

The Commission has the following tasks:

– assessing the capacity of indispensable services as defined in accords among the social parties and in self-regulatory codes, to guarantee conciliation between exercising the right to strike, and enjoyment of the constitutionally guaranteed human rights; if services are judged as insufficient, the Commission shall specifically motivate an overall proposal for services considered indispensable, and submit it to the parties involved;

– expressing judgment on interpretative or applicative issues regarding the content of self-regulatory agreements or codes, upon joint request by the parties or on its own initiative (upon joint request by the parties involved, the Commission may provide arbitration concerning the controversy);

– requesting that those calling the strike delay the date of abstention from work if the Commission intends to attempt conciliation, or if it judges that the abstention violates legal and/or contractual obligations required for exercising a strike in essential public services;

– immediately pointing out to potential strikers, any violations of norms that may emerge regarding the giving of notice beforehand, maximum duration, attempts at preventive cooling-off and conciliation procedures, exemption periods, minimum intervals between one call to strike and the next, and any other limitation regarding the phase preceding collective abstention;

– indicating any overlapping that might emerge between interruptions or reductions in alternative public services affecting the same group of users because of collective abstentions proclaimed by different trade unions, and urging those whose call to strike has been communicated after other calls, to put off abstention until a later date;

– notifying the authority competent to order strikers back to work, of situations where a strike or collective abstention from work might give rise to an imminent, probable danger harming constitutionally protected human rights;

– taking note of behaviour by administrations or enterprises that provide essential public services in clear violation of the law or of procedures foreseen by collective agreements or contracts; or of illegitimate behaviour that in any way may cause or worsen conflicts;

– assessing behaviour by the parties involved and, if any non-compliance or violation of legal or contractual obligations emerges regarding indispensable services, inflicting penalties pursuant to art. 4 of law 146/1990, as modified from art. 3 of law 83/2000, obliging the employer to apply disciplinary sanctions.

According to information from the report on Commission activities, published in June 2010, during the period from 1 January 2009 to 30 April 2010, the Commission received 2,626 strike proclamations, especially in sectors most prone to conflict, such as transportation (with 1,026 calls to strike). Relative to such strikes, the Commission adopted 790 deliberations immediately indicating the illegitimacy of the strike proclamations and of participating in strike action (amounting to around 30% of all strikes). The rate of compliance with such indications was high: 74.24% in 2009, 61.71% in the first quarter of 2010. The calls to strike mostly coincided with controversy on the company or local level, while the number of abstentions from work on the national level was lower.

900 strikes were revoked (nearly a third of the total); 507 revocations occurred following preventive measures taken by the Commission (amounting to 56% of all revocations). In the transportation sector, in particular, out of 1,026 calls to strike, there were 407 revocations. In this sector the Commission repeatedly intervened to prevent the strike, bringing about more than 200 revocations.

As regards violations communicated to the parties during preventive intervention, generally speaking, the norms most frequently violated were those touching on the interval between strikes and on the cooling-off process, both introduced by law 83/2000, still beset by several problems of interpretation and application. In the period considered, moreover, the Commission adopted 23 acquittals and 30 sanctioning deliberations (half of which during the first four months of 2010), applying sanctions amounting to a total of around 146,000 euros. The wide gap between the number of strikes called and the sanctions applied reflects the Commission's tendency to favour preventive powers of intervention rather than sanctioning powers. The latter, in fact, affected only irregular strikes of which the Commission was informed only immediately before the date when the strike took place, or afterwards.

Finally, the Commission held 52 hearings with representatives of the social sectors in 2009 (35 with union representatives, 14 with employers' representatives, and 3 with both); 21 hearings were held in the first four months of 2010 (13 with labour unions, 3 with enterprises and 5 in conjunction).

IV. Non-governmental Organisations

In Italy there are numerous non-governmental organisations active in protecting human rights. Some of them, organised in networks on the national and international level, have gained the consultative status before international organisations and actively participate in the organisations activities. By 30 September 2010 there were 93 non-governmental organisations in Italy having consultative status with the United Nations Economic and Social Council (ECOSOC), including 9 with general status, 66 with special status and 18 with "roster" status. 196 non-governmental organisations with headquarters or representative offices in Italy enjoy consultant status with the Council of Europe.

In addition, some of the most important international non-governmental organisations have a local branch in Italy. They include Amnesty International, the International Federation on Human Rights, Save the Children, Médecins sans Frontières, Action Aid. The Italian associations *Nessuno tocchi Caino* and *Non c'è pace senza giustizia* attract great international attention. Particularly worthy of note, as well, is the *Comitato per la promozione e protezione dei diritti umani*, a network of 83 non-governmental organisations working to promote human rights, created in January 2002 by initiative of the Fondazione Basso (Basso Foundation), with the support of a group of human rights experts. In 2010, Barbara Terenzi acted as coordinator, while Carola Carazzone was the main spokesperson.

The following organisations belong to the network: Associazione italiana genitori (A.GE), Associazione genitori di omosessuali (AGEDO); Agenzia della pace; AGESCI; Associazione nazionale famiglie adottive a affidatarie (ANFAA); Associazione nazionale oltre le frontiere, (ANOLF); ANTIGONE; Archivio dell'immigrazione; Archivio disarmo; ARCI; Arcigay; Articolo 21; Associazione per gli studi giuridici sull'immigrazione (ASGI); Associazione Eleonora Pimentel; Assopace; Atd quarto mondo;

Associazione universitaria per la cooperazione internazionale (AUCI); AUSER; Banca Etica; Befree; Casa dei diritti sociali; CGIL; Chiamalafrica; Centro italiano aiuti all'infanzia (CIAI); Centro interconfessionale per la pace (CIPAX); Coordinamento di iniziative popolari di solidarietà internazionale (CIPSI); Consiglio italiano per i rifugiati (CIR); CISL; Coordinamento italiano dei servizi contro il maltrattamento e l'abuso all'infanzia (CISMAI); Comitato internazionale per lo sviluppo dei popoli (CISP); CittadinanzAttiva; Consiglio nazionale sulla disabilità (CND); Comitato per i diritti umani; Comitato Singh Mohinder; Donne in nero; Ebrei per la pace; EMA; Federazione delle chiese evangeliche in Italia (FCEI); Fondazione Basso, Fondazione Centro Astalli; Fondazione internazionale Don Luigi Di Liegro; Fondazione Labos; Fondazione volontariato giovani e solidarietà (FVGS); Giovani per un mondo unito; Gruppo Martin Buber;Istituto cooperazione economica internazionale (ICEI); Consorzio italiano di solidarietà (ICS); Istituto internazionale di scienze mediche, antropologiche e sociali (IISMAS); IMS; INTERSOS; INTER-VITA; IRMA; Istituto Medicina del Soccorso; La gabbianella; LAW; Lega internazionale per i diritti e la liberazione dei popoli; Legambiente nazionale; Libera; MeD.eA; Medici contro la tortura (MEDU); MOVIMONDO; OLTRE BABELE; PAX CHRISTI segreteria nazionale; Ponte della memoria; Progetto continenti; Rete educare ai diritti umani; Save the Children; Terre des hommes; UBI MINOR; Unione delle donne in Italia (UDI); UIL; UNICEF Italia; Unione forense per la tutela dei diritti dell'uomo; Università del terzo settore (UniTs); VIDES internazionale; VIS; Women's International League for Peace and Freedom (WILPF) Italia.

The Committee's main goal is to stimulate and support the Italian legislative process in order to create an independent National Institution for Human Rights, in full compliance with the standards promoted by the United Nations General Assembly (resolution 48/134 of 20 December 1993) and the "Paris Principles". In addition, the Committee is committed to the promotion of human rights culture, with particular attention towards specific aspects of the Italian and European situation.

Alongside activities linked to the creation of the national institution for human rights, since 2005 the Committee has systematically monitored the human rights situation in Italy. This supervisory activity, focusing on civil and political, economic, social and cultural rights in an integrated perspective, has as its source of reference the legal framework of the two related international covenants. A specific monitoring Group, composed of 60 non-governmental organisations and associations and coordinated by VIS, has been created with support from the Fondazione Basso. The first results of this monitoring process were presented on 20 June 2007 (the day when Italy formally became a member of the United Nations Human Rights Council), through publication of a report entitled *Report on the monitoring of recommendations to the Italian Government by the UN Committee on Economic, Social and Cultural Rights (26 November 2004) and the UN Committee on Human Rights (2 December 2005) relative to Italy's progress in complying with the international Covenants on Economic, Social and Cultural Rights and on Civil and Political Rights, and with other instruments of international law.*

During 2010 the Committee contributed to the UPR of Italy (Geneva, February 2010, see the specific section of Part III), submitting to the Office of the High Commissioner for Human Rights, in August 2009, an informative report on the status of human rights in Italy; the report was widely discussed during the Review. In March a delegation from the Committee, composed of Carola Carazzone, Barbara Terenzi, Arianna Saulini (Save the Children; coordinator of the working group on the Convention for the Rights of the Child), and Maria Grazia Caputo (permanent representative in Geneva of the international institute Maria Ausiliatrice and of VIDES) took part in the 7th session of the working group on the UPR discussing the Italian report.

Later, the Committee launched a national monitoring campaign open to all non-governmental associations and organisations in Italy, targeting the 92 recommendations addressed to Italy during the Universal Periodic Review. This campaign was divided into two phases: the first saw preparation of a supplementary report presented in Geneva during the regular session of the Human Rights Council in June 2010, when the recommendations addressing Italy were adopted. The second phase included the preparation of a non-governmental follow-up report on recommendations, to be presented during the year 2011.

V. Human Rights Teaching and Research in Italian Universities

In recent years, the Italian academia has shown a growing attention towards research and training in the subject of human rights. Human rights are now part of many teaching programmes and university curricula, ranging from undergraduate and post-graduate courses to research programmes in a number of scientific sectors. A preliminary attempt at mapping university institutions and research centres specifically dedicated to human rights is here presented. A list human rights-oriented courses offered in bachelor, master, postgraduate and doctoral degree, active or started up in 2010, is also presented. Proceeding in a partial, pragmatic manner, it has been possible to mention only those courses and structures formally named as involving "human rights" or equivalent denominations. The outcome is a non-exhausting, although quite complete, presentation of the currents state of affairs in the field of human rights education in the Italian academia.

Data relating to graduate degrees, single courses and doctorate programmes can be found on the website of the Ministry of Education, university and research (section "teaching programmes" at http://offf.miur.it).

University institutions and research centres

University	Name	Founding Year
University of Padua	Interdepartmental Centre on Human Rights and the Rights of Peoples	1982
University of Salento	Inter-university Centre on Bioethics and Human Rights	1992
41 European universities in partnership	European Inter-University Centre for Human Rights and Democratisation (EIUC)	2002
University of Naples	Centre for Studies on Human Rights in the era of globalisation and conflicts	2003
University of Ca' Foscari, Venice	Interdepartmental Human Rights Research Centre (CIRDU)	2003

Undergraduate programmes

University	Name	Scientific Area
University of Padua	Political Science, International Relations, Human Rights	L-36: Political science and International Relations

Master degrees

University	Name	Scientific Area
University of Bergamo	Human Rights and the Ethics of International Cooperation	LM-81: Cooperation development sciences
University of Bologna	International Cooperation, Protection of Human Rights and Ethno-cultural Heritage in the Mediterranean and Eurasia	LM-81: Cooperation development sciences
University of Padua	Institutions and Policies of Human Rights and Peace	LM-81: International relations

Teachings

University	Department	Teachings
Aldo Moro University of Bari	Law	Human rights
		Human rights – theory of fundamental rights
		International protection of human rights
		International protection of human rights – human rights protection in the European Convention on Human Rights
	Foreign Languages and Literatures	International protection of human rights
University of	Educational Sciences	Teaching human rights

Bergamo		Teaching on marginalisation and human rights
	Humanities	Teaching on human rights and international cooperation
University of Bologna	Cultural Heritage Conservation	Rights and training in international cooperation
		Human rights and history of international law
		International human rights law and European law on cooperation
		Public law and protection of fundamental rights
	Law	Fundamental rights
	Political Science	International protection of human rights (seminar)
	Statistical Science	Human rights, constitutions, institutions
		Human rights and new individual rights
University of Cagliari	Law	Constitutional law, governance and human rights protection
	Political Science	History of political thought on human rights
University of Calabria	Economics	Sociology of migrations and human rights
		Human rights theory
		Protection of rights
	Political Science	Institutions and rights in the European Union
		History of human rights and citizenship
University of Catania	Political Science	Philosophy of social rights
University of Ferrara	Law	International protection of human rights
University of Florence	Economics	International law, human rights and armed conflict
	Law	Legal systems and protection of rights
		Welfare state and human rights
	Educational Sciences	Human rights
	Political Science	Citizenship-related rights and self-Government units
		Civil society and religious rights
		International protection of human rights
University of Genoa	Law	Civil and social rights
	Political Science	European protection of human rights
University of L'Aquila	Economics	Theory of interpretation and human rights
University of Macerata	Law	Social and citizenship-related rights
	Letters and Philosophy	Philosophy of rights and cultures
	Political Science	Human rights and rights of difference
		Philosophy of human rights
University of Messina	Political Science	International organisation and human rights

University of Milan	Law	Rights in action: case analysis on fundamental rights
	Political Science	Equality, differences and rights
		Theories on fundamental rights
		International protection of human rights
University of Milan-Bicocca	Law	European Constitutional law (fundamental rights)
		International protection of human rights
	Sociology	Cooperation and human rights protection
		Rights and European citizenship
Sacro Cuore University	Law	Human rights
	Political Science	International protection of human rights
University of Modena and Reggio Emilia	Law	Theory and practice of human rights
University of Molise	Economics	Citizenship and citizenship-related rights
	Human and Social Sciences	Human rights and globalisation
Second University of Naples	Law	International protection of human rights
	Political Studies and Jean Monnet Advanced European and Mediterranean Studies	Constitutions and fundamental rights in Arab-Islamic systems
		Protection of rights in multi-cultural States
Federico II University of Naples	Economics	International protection of human rights
University of Padua	Law	Human rights
	Political Science	Economic and social rights
		Fundamental rights and European citizenship
		Human rights
		Human rights and the status of women
		Human rights and international justice
		Sport and human rights in the European Union law
		Governance of human rights in Italian and comparative Constitutional law
		Philosophy of human rights
		Philosophy of human rights (advanced)
		Globalisation of human rights and promotion of women
		Human rights, monitoring, electoral observation, peace-keeping
		Public policy and human rights
		Sociology of criminal law, prevention of deviance, prison conditions and rights of detainees
		General sociology and sociology of human rights

		History of human rights politics
		Economic development and human rights
		International human rights protection
		International human rights protection (advanced)
University of Palermo	Educational Science	Human rights theory and practice
		International protection of human rights
	Political Science	Human rights and multi-culturalism
		Human rights and international criminal law
		Philosophy of human rights
		Organisation, justice and protection of human rights
		European political thought and human rights
University of Pavia	Law	Protection of fundamental rights
	Political Science	Gender studies: history of feminist movements-achievements of rights
University of Perugia	Law	Protection of fundamental rights
	Educational Sciences	Modern state, rights of citizens and peoples
	Political Science	Human rights and international crime
		International law and human rights
Amedeo Avogadro University of Eastern Piemonte-Vercelli	Political Science	Democracy, rights, religions
		European fundamental rights
University of Pisa	Mathematical, Physical and Natural Sciences	Monitoring, assessment and protection of human rights
La Sapienza University of Rome	Communications	Communications of rights and active citizenship
	Political Science	Human rights
		Human rights and international jurisdictions
		Human rights and cooperation strategies
Roma Tre University	Political Science	Rights and constitutional freedoms
		International organisation and protection of human rights
		Protection and promotion of minors' rights in international and European relations (seminar)
		Protection of fundamental rights in comparative law
Guido Carli LUISS-Free International University of Social Studies	Political Science	International protection of human rights

University of Salerno	Law	Human rights
	Letters and Philosophy	Citizenship and rights
University of Siena	Political Science	International protection of human rights
University of Teramo	Law	Human rights
University of Turin	Law	Philosophy of human rights
		Fundamental rights guarantees
		The European Court of Human Rights
		Social order, juridical hermeneutics and protection of fundamental rights
	Political Science	Citizenship, social rights, justice
		Human rights and globalisation
		International organisation and protection of human rights
		International economic organisations and human rights
		Vulnerable groups and human rights protection
		History of human rights
University of Trieste	Law	International legal instruments for the protection human rights
	Political Science	Human rights
	Advanced School of Modern Languages for Interpreters and Translators	Comparative human rights
University of Udine	Law	Human rights theory
Carlo Bo University of Urbino	Law	Human rights
		International protection of human rights
Ca' Foscari University of Venice	Letters and Philosophy	Human rights and policies of citizenship SP.
		Human rights and policies of citizenship SP. I
		Human rights and policies of citizenship SP. II
	Foreign Languages and Literatures	International law and human rights

Source: Ministry of Education, University and Research

Doctoral programmes (academic years 2009-2010 and 2010-2011)

University	Name	Area of Scientific Discipline
University of Cassino, Department of Public law	Human Rights Protection in national constitutional courts and other European courts case-law	IUS/08, IUS/09, IUS/10, IUS/13, IUS/14, IUS/21, IUS/12, IUS/20, IUS/16
University of Florence, Department of Theory and History of Law	Theory and history of law – Theory and history of human rights	IUS/18, IUS/19, IUS/20
Federico II University of Naples, Department of international studies and the European Political and Institutional System	International legal order and protection of individual rights	IUS/13, IUS/14, IUS/11, IUS/12
Federico II University of Naples, Department of Roman Law, History and Theory of Law	Philosophy of law: art and technique of jurisprudence – Hermeneutics of human rights	IUS/19, IUS/20
University of Palermo, Department of Studies on Politics, Law and Society	Human rights: evolution, protection and limits	IUS/01, IUS/09, IUS/12, IUS/20, SPS/02, IUS/13, IUS/19, IUS/10, SPS/09, SECS-P/01, IUS/O8
Amedeo Avogadro University of Eastern Piedmont, Department of Law and Economics	Local autonomies, public services and citizenship's rights	IUS/05, IUS/08, IUS/09 IUS/10, IUS/21
Scuola Superiore Sant'Anna in Pisa	Politics, human rights and sustainability	SPS/01, SPS/06, IUS/13, IUS/03, IUS/14, SPS/04, SECS-P/02, SECS-P/06, SECS-P/08
La Sapienza University of Rome, Department of State Theory	International Order and Human Rights	IUS/13, IUS/14, IUS/08, IUS/07, IUS/01
Libera Maria Santissima Assunta University – LUMSA, Department of Law	Fundamental rights and freedoms in contemporary legal systems	IUS/01, IUS/11, IUS/13, IUS/17, IUS/20, IUS/18, IUS/07
	International adoptions: issues on the protection of fundamental human rights	IUS/01, IUS/11, IUS/13
University of Salerno, Department of Law on Civil and Economic Relations in Contemporary Legal Systems	Comparative human rights	IUS/01, IUS/02, IUS/07, IUS/13, IUS/14, IUS/16, IUS/17
University of Teramo, Department of Public Legal Studies	Protection of fundamental rights – Italian and European public law	IUS/08, IUS/09, IUS/10, IUS/21
Carlo Bo University of Urbino, Department of Legal Science	Human rights and fundamental social rights	IUS/01, IJUS/02, IUS/07, IUS/10, IUS/11, IUS/13, IUS/15, IUS/16, IUS/17, IUS/18, IUS/19, IUS/12, SECS-P/03

Master degree programmes – postgraduate

University	Name	Level
European Inter-University Centre for Human Rights and Democratisation (EIUC, 41 European partner universities)	European Master's Degree in Human Rights and Democratisation E.MA	I
University of Bologna	Human rights and humanitarian intervention	I
Sant'Anna School of Advanced Studies of Pisa	Human rights and conflict management	I
University of Siena	European joint master of human rights and genocide studies	I
La Sapienza University, Rome	International protection of human rights	II
Libera Maria Santissima Assunta University – LUMSA, Department of Law	Bioethics and human rights	II
Roma Tre University	Peace studies: international cooperation, human rights and policies of the European Union	II

Concluding, it shall be mentioned that the Italian university system hosts three UNESCO Chairs specifically dealing with human rights: the Chair "Human rights, democracy and peace", instituted in 1999 at the University of Padua; the Chair "Human rights and the ethics of international cooperation", instituted in 2003 at the University of Bergamo; and the Chair "Bioethics and human rights", instituted in 2009 at the Pontifical University Regina Apostolorum, European University of Rome (see Part III, the United Nations System, VI, B).

Among the non-academic research and training centres of particular relevance it is worth recalling: National Institute for children's rights (INDIMI); International Institute of Humanitarian Law in San Remo; Committee on Human Rights of the Italian Society for International Organisation (SIOI); Lelio Basso International Foundation for the Rights and Liberation of Peoples (Fondazione Basso); and the Italian Bar Association for the Protection of human rights (Unione forense per la tutela dei diritti dell'uomo).

Human Rights Structures at a Sub-national Level

On the municipal, provincial and regional levels, by virtue of the inclusion of the "peace human rights norm" in thousands of municipal, provincial and regional statutes, and of the adoption of special regional laws linked to this topic (see Part I, Italian law, III and IV), several consultancies, municipal cultural offices, departments and bureaus dedicated to human rights, peace, equal opportunities, development cooperation, fair trade and international solidarity have been established in Italy; not to mention the Ombudsman's offices and independent commissioners for children's rights. In addition, the Regions of Veneto, Emilia-Romagna and Campania have set up regional Archives for the collection, elaboration and diffusion of documentation, studies and informational resources on the topic of peace and human rights.

I. Peace Human Rights Offices in Municipalities, Provinces and Regions

Some of the results presented in the volume *Pace e diritti umani nei Comuni, nelle Province e nelle Regioni. L'infrastruttura normativa e istituzionale* (see Part I, Italian law, III) regard the Italian Municipalities with a population over 5,000, and the Provinces adhering to the National Coordination of Local Authorities for Peace and Human Rights, as well as the Regions and Provinces with special autonomy. This report aims to verify the existence, in each authority, of governmental bodies (cultural offices, mandates assigned to the Presidency of the local authority) and administrative structures (areas, sectors, services, bureaus) expressly called upon to plan and implement policies linked to peace and human rights.

Municipalities

The research shows a tendency of a certain number of Municipalities adhering to the National Coordination, to set up permanent specialized structures. Among others, they include the Municipalities of Perugia (Perugia), Albinea (Reggio Emilia), Riccione (Ravenna), Pavullo nel Frignano (Modena), Vicenza (Vicenza), Padua (Padua), Grottammare (Ascoli Piceno), Portoferraio (Livorno) and Trevi (Perugia).

Besides painting a clear picture of such municipal infrastructures promoting peace and human rights, the report points out that many Municipalities are committed to carry out activities for the promotion of such issues through inter-municipal or inter-provincial coordination, in collaboration with public bodies, associations and other actors involved in the field of human rights.

Provinces

As regards the peace human rights infrastructure on the provincial level, the report reveals that 53 out of 104 Provinces with ordinary autonomy have joined the National Coordination of Local Authorities for Peace and Human Rights.

All the Provinces participating in the National Coordination and belonging to the Regions of Veneto, Friuli-Venezia Giulia, Liguria, Tuscany, Umbria, Marche, Campania and Calabria present both administrative structures and governmental bodies dedicated to human rights and peace issues. In the remaining Provinces the situation varies: in some cases there is an administrative structure, but not a specific Councillor's office; in others, the opposite is true.

In all, 41 Provinces have set up a governmental body dedicated to peace and human rights, while 39 have set up an administrative structure promoting human rights issues.

Regions and Autonomous Provinces

The report finds that 16 regional authorities provide a peace human rights infrastructure; such Regions have arranged to set up both a governmental body and an administrative structure dedicated to these issues, in harmony with the provisions on peace and human rights included in their statutes; or, in the absence of similar statutory arrangements, in compliance with regional laws on human rights issues. The Regions which lack any infrastructure specifically fostering peace and human rights are Friuli-Venezia Giulia, Molise and Sicily. The Region of Calabria has arranged to create a specific human rights Councillor's office, but no administrative structure. Both the Autonomous Provinces of Bolzano and Trent have set up specific peace/human rights infrastructures.

II. The Ombudsman in Municipalities, Provinces and Regions

The data presented in this section appear in a research report entitled *La tutela non giurisdizionale dei diritti umani con particolare riferimento alla difesa civica (Non-jurisdictional protection of human rights with particular reference to the mandate of the Ombudsman)*, 2009, edited by prof. Paolo De Stefani, Human Rights Centre of the University of Padua, on assignment of the Department for Equal Opportunities of the Presidency of the Council of Ministers. The report presents an analytical mapping of the Ombudsman's role in Italy, referring not only to the laws instituting the Ombudsman in the statutes of Municipalities with over 5,000 inhabitants, Provinces and Regions and in regional laws (or provincial laws, in the case of the Autonomous Provinces of Bolzano and Trent); but also to the existence of an Ombudsman holding office and/or to a bureau supporting the Ombudsman's activity under the administrations studied by the report. The data presented are updated to 31 October 2008, when the monitoring ended.

It is to be noticed that the financial law for 2010 (law 23 December 2009, No. 191) – as amended by law decree 25 January 2010, No. 2, converted into law 42/2010 – has ordered the Municipalities, according to clause 186 of art. 2, to eliminate the figure of the municipal Ombudsman in order to limit public spending. The law states that his function may be assigned to the provincial Ombudsman, who, accordingly, becomes "territorial Ombudsman".

Municipalities

On the municipal level, the report reveals the existence of 2,156 Municipalities whose statute provides for the establishment of an Ombudsman, out of 2,372 Municipalities with a population over 5,000 inhabitants. Therefore, 90% of the Municipalities identified by the research methods used have favoured the possibility of setting up such an institution (at least on a normative basis): a possibility offered, first, by art. 8 of law 8 June 1990, No. 142, and newly disciplined by art. 11 of legislative decree 267/2000 (Consolidated act of laws on the structuring of local authorities), which abrogates the preceding law.

As regards the number of incumbent municipal Ombudspersons at the time of the survey, it appears that such normative dispositions have been applied in 852 Municipalities, amounting to 39.5% of the total number of Municipal authorities foreseeing such an institution in their statute.

In addition, the report sets the data against the backdrop of total resident population, in order to calculate the percentage of people potentially served by the Ombudsman. The result shows that Municipal authorities which normatively provide for an Ombudsman in their statute, cover 95.6% of the population residing in Municipalities with more than 5,000 inhabitants; and that in bodies where an Ombudsman actually holds office, the portion of population potentially served is 57.11%.

As regards the gender dimension of incumbent Ombudspersons, the monitoring indicates that 563 are males (66.07%) and 289 females (33.93%), showing a ratio approximating 2 to 1.

Provinces

With regards to the mapping of the Provinces, which are subject to the same above-mentioned legislative dispositions regarding Municipalities (legislative decree 267/2000), it results that 98 authorities out of 104 have instituted the figure of the Ombudsman in their statute. The six Provinces which, at the time of the survey, had not yet done so belong to five different Regions: Tuscany (1 Province), Sicily (1), Sardinia (1), Veneto (1) and Friuli-Venezia Giulia (2).

According to the research report, an Ombudsman is incumbent in 42 Italian Provinces, amounting to 42.85%. In addition, the analysis of the Ombudsman law's implementation according to geographic region shows that some regional territories, though enjoying total *normative* coverage by Ombudsman services, actually lack *real* coverage.

Results show that 96.81% of the total population are *normatively* protected by dispositions regarding the Ombudsman, but only 53.6% of this number are *effectively* protected by any active service.

As regards gender, the ratio between male provincial Ombudspersons and female ones is approximately 3 to 1 (32 males and 10 females).

During 2010, many Provinces, in applying the above-mentioned law 191/2009, have instituted the figure of the territorial Ombudsman with a mandate to guarantee impartiality and best practises in public administrations, both in provincial matters and in issues of municipal competence. The Municipalities involved have therefore assigned territorial Ombudsman the tasks formerly assumed by the recently suppressed municipal Ombudspersons.

Regions and Autonomous Provinces

The development of the Ombudsman role in the Regions and in the Autonomous Provinces of Trent and Bolzano, differs with respect to most Italian Municipalities and Provinces in that these authorities have no explicit, general normative provision instituting the office of Ombudsman. However, beginning in 1974, the Ombudsman has started developing on this level of governance through regional laws (or provincial ones, in the case of Trent and Bolzano), deriving the legitimation from art. 97 and 3 of the Italian Constitution. Only in more recent times has the Ombudsman begun to take root firmly, and on a statutory level, in the Autonomous Regions and Provinces. The report yielding this data therefore refers both to regional laws, and to any specific dispositions contained in regional statutes.

17 Italian Regions have a law instituting the Ombudsman, as do both the Autonomous Provinces. The Region of Sicily and the Region of Trentino-Alto Adige do not; while in the Region of Friuli-Venezia Giulia the Ombudsman law was abrogated with the 2008 law re-allotting public spending (r.l. 14 August 2008, No. 9).

The research shows that ten Regions have provided specific statutory norms regarding the Ombudsman figure; in all ten cases the statutes are new, adopted from 2003 on in compliance with the most recent Constitutional modifications. The statutes of the Autonomous Provinces, on the contrary, do not foresee this institution.

In 2010 there are 12 incumbent regional Ombudspersons – in Abruzzo, Basilicata, Emilia-Romagna, Lazio, Liguria, Lombardy, Marche, Molise, Piedmont, Tuscany, Valle d'Aosta and Veneto – while there is one for each Autonomous Province. The regional Ombudspersons of Liguria and Tuscany, like the Ombudsman of the Autonomous Province of Bolzano, are women.

III. Ombudsman National Coordination

The Regions and Autonomous Provinces Ombudsman National Coordination is a consultative body working to harmonize and enhance the institutional role of the Ombudsman in Italy, and to guarantee every citizen, regardless of where he or she resides, protection in dealing with the public administration at any level, whether State, regional or local.

Besides creating effective liaisons with Parliament and the Italian Government, the Coordination promotes the full application of treaties and of European and international human rights law, in particular the European Union Charter of Fundamental Rights; and it develops relations with the European Ombudsman and with the Ombudspersons of EU Member States. In addition, it fosters coordination in all Regions with the Ombudspersons at every territorial level, in order to widen the scope of their role and to enhance standards for the protection of individual rights and common interests; and it organises pertinent research and study programmes. The Coordination is made up of the incumbent Ombudspersons in the Regions and in the Autonomous Provinces, joined by several Ombudspersons from local authorities, who are chosen by the Assembly of incumbent local Ombudspersons. The Coordination operates through the bureau of an Ombudsman elected collegially from time to time; it has headquarters in Rome, at the Network of the Presidents of the Assembly, of Regional Councils, and Autonomous Provinces (*Conferenza dei Presidenti dell'Assemblea, dei Consigli regionali e delle Province autonome*) where it normally meets.

During the period considered in this publication, the National Coordinator was firstly the Ombudsman of the Marche Region, Samuele Animali; successively, the Coordinator was the Ombudsman of Veneto, Vittorio Bottoli, appointed on 20 September 2010; followed by the appointment of Antonio Caputo, Ombudsman of Piedmont.

Among its most notable acts of 2010, on 31 May, the National Coordination adopted a resolution regarding law 26 March 2010, No. 42 (Conversion into law of amended legislative decree 25 January 2010, No. 2, requiring urgent measures affecting local authorities and Regions). As mentioned above, this law requires Municipalities to suppress the office of the Ombudsman. In its resolution, the Coordination points out that the Ombudsman must not be an optional, but instead, a form of protection available to anyone; and that the financial reform further penalises citizens, who can no longer resort to an institution near to them. The Coordination expresses hope that all citizens will be guaranteed the right to make a complaint to an Ombudsman; and that suppression of the municipal Ombudspersons will be reconsidered when discussing the new code for local authorities. As long as current legislation is valid, the Coordination urges Regions, Provinces and Municipalities to commit themselves to appointing an Ombudsman in the Provinces where it is still lacking.

Finally, on 21 June, the National Coordination signed a memorandum of understanding with the Human Rights Centre of the University of Padua, to launch the activities of the Italian Institute of the Ombudsman (*Istituto italiano dell'Ombudsman*). This initiative aims to promote research and training on the Ombudsman role and human rights, in collaboration with national, European and international institutions, and to increase the visibility and efficacy of the Ombudsman in Italy, the only Country in the EU unable to count on a national non-judicial system for the protection of human rights (since it lacks both a National Ombudsman and a National Human Rights Commission).

IV. Network of Children's Commissioners

The Network of Children's Commissioners (Conferenza dei Tutori e dei Garanti dell'infanzia e dell'adolescenza) was established in Naples on 30 April 2010, following a meeting attended by the then Regional Commissioners for children and adolescents of Lazio (Francesco Alvaro), Molise (Nunzia Lattanzio), Marche (Samuele Animali), Veneto (Lucio Strumendo) and Friuli-Venezia Giulia (Edouard Ballaman).

> The main goal of this body is to promote throughout the national territory best practices as observed by various regional protection bodies during their experience on the ground. The Network also aims to raise awareness among local groups concerning children's rights, by instituting and appointing re-

gional Commissioners; to foster and promote preliminary agreements among actors dealing with children and adolescents; and to advocate the presence of at least one representative from the Network at the National Observatory and at the National Centre of Documentation and Analysis on Children and Adolescents.

The Commissioner of Lazio was unanimously appointed as the first Network's Coordinator. Coordinators should remain in office for one year, by rotation, and should convene the other regional Commissioners at least once every four months.

V. National Coordination of Local Authorities for Peace and Human Rights

The National Coordination of local authorities for peace and human rights is an association founded in 1986, including Municipalities, Provinces and Regions committed, in Italy, to promoting peace, human rights, solidarity and international cooperation. More than 700 members among Municipalities, Provinces and Regions have adhered to the Coordination. The Chair of the National Coordination is Marco Vinicio Guasticchi, President of the Province of Perugia; the Director is Flavio Lotti.

The Coordination's main aims are to promote constant commitment by local authorities and the Regions in favour of peace, solidarity and international cooperation, by supporting and facilitating their initiatives; to promote national coordination and development of shared initiatives, through the exchange of information and experience regarding various peace issues; to further research and politico-juridical reflection on the tasks of local authorities fostering peace and human rights; to ensure liaison with the main European and international associations of local authorities and with associations of civil society operating toward such goals; to promote the development of peace- and solidarity-oriented culture and behaviour among the population, especially the young.

The Coordination promotes and supports the Peace Roundtable (*Tavola della Pace*), a permanent forum for confrontation and collaboration among civil society organisations and local authorities. It has organised the *Perugia-Assisi Peace March* in cooperation with the Roundtable and, since 1995, the Assembly of the Peoples' UN which anticipates the March.

The Coordination is a member of the World Council of United Cities and Local Government (UCLG), and of the executive committee of the Municipal Alliance for Peace in the Middle East. Moreover it manages the administrative office of the European Network of Local Authorities for Peace in the Middle East (COEPPO).

In 2010 the Coordination has participated together with the Peace Roundtable in organising the Perugia-Assisi Peace March which took place on 16 May 2010. Among collateral events, the Coordination organised the Forum of Peace (*Forum della pace*), held in Perugia on 14-15 May 2010, offering a meeting-point for schools, volunteer associations and local authorities.

The Coordination has also held a series of seminars addressed to local administrators, concerning peace and human rights issues. Together, again, with the Peace Roundtable, it has promoted the national school programme for peace and human rights education entitled *My school for peace* (*La mia scuola per la pace*). Beginning in June 2010, and following on events linked to the humanitarian mission of assistance for Gaza named "Freedom Flotilla", the Coordination has distributed to local authorities and Regions the outline of a deliberation entitled *Let's make peace in the Middle East.* The text proposes participation in two international initiatives fostered by the Coordination itself: the programme *100 cities for peace in the Middle East* and the European Network of Local Authorities for Peace in the Middle East.

Region of Veneto

The Region of Veneto has been operating organically for the promotion of human rights, the culture of peace and international cooperation, ever since 1988, the year when the first specific law on such issues was adopted: regional law 30 March 1988, No. 18 (Regional measures for the promotion of a culture of peace). During the same year, the Regional Council instituted the Ombudsman (r.l. 28/1988) and the Commissioner for children and adolescents (r.l. 42/1988).

The "peace human rights norm" (see Part I, Italian law, III), formulated for the first time in art. 1 of this law and spread out into the statutes of thousands of Italian territorial authorities from 1991 on, is present today in Veneto in the statutes of 233 Municipalities – among the 264 existing with a population over 5,000 inhabitants – and in all seven Provinces.

In 1999, regional law 18/1988 was replaced by the current r.l. 16 December 1999, No. 55, on "Regional measures for the promotion of human rights, a culture of peace, development cooperation and solidarity".

Art. 1 of r.l. 55/1999 reasserts the Region's commitment on such issues, further reiterated in the more recent Regional Council resolution 40/2007, adopted on the 60th anniversary of the Universal Declaration of Human Rights and of the Italian Constitution. On that occasion, which has also marked the 25th anniversary of the Human Rights Centre of the University of Padua, the Council met for the first time outside its usual institutional site: in the Aula Magna of the University of Padua.

In virtue of r.l. 55/1999, the Committee on Human Rights and the Culture of Peace (art. 12-13) and the Committee on Development Cooperation (art. 14-15) operate to fulfil their mandate of formulating *three-year programmes* and *annual plans* of implementation according to their respective areas of competence and intervention. In addition, the law reconfirms the Regional Archive "Pace Diritti Umani – Peace Human Rights" (art. 2) and the Venice for Peace Research Foundation (art. 17).

Finally, every two years, the Regional Government convenes a regional Conference serving as a meeting-point enabling the exchange of experiences among regional actors working in the area of cooperation and international solidarity (art. 20). The fourth such meeting, entitled *Veneto today for the world of tomorrow (Il Veneto di oggi per il mondo di domani)*, took place in Treviso on 10 and 11 December 2009 in the framework of the celebrations for the tenth anniversary of r.l. 55/1999. On this occasion a report of the same title was presented, illustrating the projects promoted by the Region since the law was adopted, in the area of human rights and development cooperation (*Veneto today for the world of tomorrow. 10 years of the regional law for the promotion of human rights, peace culture, development cooperation and solidarity. Project report*, 3rd edition, 2010, available in English).

Besides the above-mentioned regional Commissioner for Children and Adolescents and the Ombudsman, the integrated regional infrastructure also presents the Commission for the Realisation of Equal Opportunities between Men and Women, instituted by r.l. 30 December 1987, No. 62, and a series of regional Observatories of particular usefulness in establishing human rights policies. Among them, it is worth taking into consideration, in particular, the Integrated Network of Regional Observatories on Social Policies and the Regional Observatory on Immigration, instituted in 2007 pursuant to r.l. 30 January 1990, No. 9.

To complete the picture, it must be added the promotion and support for the European Master's Degree in Human Rights and Democratisation (E.MA) by way of r.l. 28 December 1998, No. 33.

With the adoption of r.l. 22 January 2010, No. 6 (Measures in support of fair trade organisations and modifications of r.l. 55/1999), the Region has recognised the social and cultural value of fair trade, proclaiming its support for autochthonous products of economically disadvantaged areas in developing Countries, guaranteeing greater diffusion of fair trade products, and offering more information to consumers in order to encourage responsible consumption.

As years have passed, through its action the Region of Veneto has gradually assumed the aspect of organic policy-maker in matters of peace and human rights. It has furthered this tendency through the active collaboration of organisations and operators of civil society, with full respect for their autonomy.

In the sphere of the Regional Government human rights-related competencies pertain to the Councillor on human rights and gender policies, Marialuisa Coppola. Measures and activities connected to international relations and development cooperation respond directly to the Regional Governor, Luca Zaia. Luciano Falcier, appointed in 1988, was the first Councillor on human rights in Veneto.

I. Department for International Relations, International Cooperation, Human Rights and Equal Programmes

The Regional Department is the central administrative structure dealing with implementation of r.l. 55/1999. The Director managing this structure is Diego Vecchiato. The Department has a staff of 30.

The Regional Department is dedicated to overseeing a good portion of the international activities taken up by the Region, including: the management of international relations, the signature of memoranda of understanding with national and foreign institutions, the participation in international bodies and initiatives, the promotion of international solidarity, and of all sorts of activities concerning human rights, the culture of peace, the promotion of equal opportunities and the protection of linguistic minorities. The Department head office also hosts the Veneto regional Committee for UNICEF.

Besides promoting activities and projects favouring development cooperation and human rights, in collaboration with institutions, associations and public and private bodies active in applying r.l. 55/1999 throughout regional territory, the Department offers, in the specific area of human rights, technical support to the Committee for human rights and the culture of peace; it oversees the organisation of several important events, including the *Biennial Conference for human rights and development cooperation* and the Prize, *Veneto for peace and solidarity among peoples*; it participates in activities performed by the Venice Commission of the Council of Europe; and it fulfils obligations linked to the Region's participation in the European Master Programme in Human Rights and Democratisation (E.MA).

The role of the Department in the regional activities realised during the year 2010 has therefore been transversal to the bodies discussed in the following paragraphs.

II. Committee for Human Rights and the Culture of Peace

Established pursuant to art. 12 of r.l. 55/1999, the Committee concurs in setting up pertinent triennial programmes and annual plans regarding of the initiatives promoted by the Region of Veneto on these issues (art. 13). The Committee comprises representatives from local administrations, civil society, the university, entrepreneurs and social sectors.

Pursuant to art. 3 of the above-mentioned r.l. 55/1999, the Regional Council, on proposal by the Regional Government and based on indications given by the Committee, approves a *three-year programme* defining objectives and priorities, as well as criteria for selecting human rights initiatives and the modes used for regional funding, in accordance with the indications emerging at the international level. Based on the three-year programmes, after hearing the Committee, the Regional Government approves the *annual plan of action*, which identifies the cultural and informational initiatives in matters concerning human rights and the culture of peace. Such initiatives are carried out both via direct commitment by the Region of Veneto and by assigning funds to external bodies.

On 12 January 2010, with deliberation 5, the Regional Council adopted the new three-year programme covering the period 2010-2012. The general goals defined by this programme concern the promotion and development of coordinating networks on human rights culture, with a view to spreading information on normative sources. More specifically, its goals are to foster reciprocal knowledge among human rights actors and activities; to promote a human rights culture based on non-discrimination and respect for women, children, adolescents, minorities and vulnerable groups, consistent with international human rights conventions; to promote a culture favouring peace and integration, based on intercultural and interreligious dialogue; to promote the peaceful transformation of conflicts, and the reciprocal knowledge of ethnic, religious and linguistic diversities.

With deliberation No. 607 of 9 March 2010, the Regional Government adopted the *plan of action for 2010*. This not only confirmed the Region's commitment pursuant to r.l. 55/1999 concerning the Archive "Pace Diritti Umani – Peace Human Rights", the Venice Peace Research Foundation, and the Regional Prize *Veneto for peace and solidarity among peoples*, but also approved 16 direct initiatives for the year 2010, and financed a number of initiatives demanding funding, allotting a total of 600,000 euros.

Direct initiatives financed by the Region for 2010:

– in the area of schools: *Project Peace 2009-2010, 6th year* by the Fabio Besta Professional Institute in Treviso; the *European campus for students in Veneto 2010* by the regional school office of Veneto; the project The *school and the town: telling, doing, knowing*, by the Municipality of Rovigo; the project *In and Out*, by the Municipality of Jesolo;

– in the area of training: the *Summer School in applied anthropology 2010* by the Municipality of Portogruaro; the *Regional network for human rights and the culture of peace* by the regional school office of Veneto; the programme *Citizenship and Constitution: problems and perspectives for new teaching*, by the Concetto Marchesi High School in Padua; the programme *First steps by COMPASITO: teachers actively promoting human rights education among school children in the Province of Padua*, by the Comprehensive High School of Vigodarzere; the project *Human rights painted green. Man, environment and sustainability*, by the Province of Venice;

– in the area of citizenship awareness: *ImmaginAfrica 2010* by the Department of history of the University of Padua; the project *The rights of children and adolescents today for the world of tomorrow, between reality and utopia: local policy and international strategies*, by the Italian Committee for UNICEF; the scholastic itinerary The *sixth Millennium Development Goal: access to health – Combating HIV/AIDS, malaria and other diseases*, by the provincial school office of Padua; the project *The ABCs of human development. 100 words for exploring the topic of human development, starting with the family*, by the Municipality of Ponzano Veneto; the activities relating to *Information initiatives and participation in fairs and exhibitions*, by the Department for International Relations, International Cooperation, Human Rights and Equal Opportunities of the Region of Veneto; the project *Belluno, a city for children*, by the Municipality of Belluno;

– in the area of research: the project *Italian Yearbook of Human Rights* (*Annuario italiano dei diritti umani*), by the Human Rights Centre of the University of Padua.

III. Archive "Pace Diritti Umani – Peace Human Rights"

The Regional Archive was created pursuant to r.l. 18/1988 and reconfirmed by the successive r.l. 55/1999. The Archive is managed by the Human Rights Centre of the University of Padua according to special agreement with the Region, in application of art. 2 of the forementioned law. The Archive is one of the principle instruments by which the Region of Veneto promotes the culture of human rights, peace, development cooperation and solidarity in Italy and in other Countries.

The Archive works to collect, elaborate and make publicly available documents, thematic databases, and informational resources on topics regarding regional law, particularly through the regular updating of the portal "Archivio Pace Diritti Umani" (http://unipd-centrodirittiumani.it/en) and by spreading human rights awareness through multi-media tools and social networks. In addition, it oversees publication of books, teaching aids, in-depth study packets and multi-media, and ensures techno-scientific support for persons most closely interested to the promotion and to the realisation of the culture of peace.

The Archive offers seven databases which respectively collect: legal instruments of international human rights, humanitarian, criminal and refugees law, translated into Italian; the publications edited from 1982 to today by the Human Rights Centre of the University of Padua; data on institutional norms concerning the establishment of the Ombudsman in Italian Municipalities (with populations over 5,000 inhabitants), Provinces and Regions; norms on peace, human rights and equal opportunities in Italian Municipalities (with populations over 5,000 inhabitants) Provinces and Regions; the associations and NGOs active in Veneto in matters of human rights and development cooperation; documentation and publications relating to the rights of the persons with disabilities; and the volumes collected at the Piergiorgio Cancellieri library of the Human Rights Centre. Noteworthy contents offered by the portal include "thematic dossiers" presenting in-depth studies and updated information on important issues related to peace and human rights; and the webpages dedicated to the activities of the Jean Monnet European Centre of Excellence, "Human rights, intercultural dialogue and multi-level governance" and of the UNESCO Chair "Human rights, democracy and peace" of the University of Padua.

During 2010, the Archive has presented the new version of its web portal, further strengthening its information and communications activities; the new site includes a specific independent version in English. Moreover, the Archive has undertaken the publication of three issues of the four-monthly review "Pace diritti umani/Peace human rights", and organised a series of initiatives in collaboration with regional and international institutions and organisations. Among the most noteworthy:

- participation in carrying out the activities promoted in the sphere of the joint peer to peer programme between the European Union and the Council of Europe, entitled *European National Preventive Machinery against Torture (NPM) Project* (January-March 2010);
- organisation of the intensive CiMiC (*Civil-Military Cooperation*) training module for a group of students of the Master's Degree in Institutions and Policies of Human Rights and Peace of the University of Padua; the training took place from 19 to 21 October 2010 at the Mario Fiore military barracks in Motta di Livenza (Treviso), headquarters of the NATO's Multinational CiMiC Group;
- organisation of an encounter between representatives from civil society and members of the Council of Europe's European Commission against Racism and Intolerance (ECRI); the encounter took place on 24 November 2010 at the Human Rights Centre of the University of Padua, in connection with the preparation of the fourth Report on Italy;
- organisation of the conference *Extreme poverty and human rights: the rights of the poor*, which took place at the University of Padua on 10 December 2010 during the International Human Rights Day, and in conclusion of the European Year for the fight against poverty and social exclusion. The United Nations independent expert on human rights and extreme poverty, María Sepúlveda Carmona, participated in the event.

Finally, during 2010 the Archive provided the necessary documentary and technical data-processing support for special high education courses for teachers and school principals, on the topic *Civic education, human rights, citizenship and constitution*, organised by the Human Rights Centre and the UNESCO Chair "Human rights, democracy and peace" of the University of Padua.

IV. Venice for Peace Research Foundation

Like the Regional Archive, the Venice for Peace Research Foundation was instituted by r.l. 18/1988 and reconfirmed successively by r.l. 55/1999. The Foundation's main goal is to carry out research, partly in collaboration with national and international institutions, on matters of security, development and peace.

In recent years its activities have focused on two themes in particular: the role of memory in peace-building and in the process of European integration, and guaranteeing access to natural resources, starting with the problem of access to water and proceeding to deal with the issue of climate change and sustainable development. From 2001 to 2008, the Foundation promoted *Progetto Iride* (Iris Project), encompassing publication of the *Annuario geopolitico della pace* (*Geopolitical yearbook of peace*) and the Salon of peace publications.

V. Commissioner for Children and Adolescents

The regional Office of the Commissioner for children and adolescents (*Ufficio di protezione e tutela pubblica dei minori*) was created by r.l. 9 August 1988, No. 42. The Commissioner is elected by the Regional Council, to which he or she presents a detailed yearly report on the activities performed. The Commissioner works toward the non-conflictual, non-jurisdictional protection of children and adolescents' rights, freely and independently with respect to other public institutions. It is a monocratic authority which collaborates with a staff of experts and collaborators from various professions and disciplines; the Commissioner operates free of charge. From 2001 to 2010 the Commissioner for children and adolescents of the Region of Veneto was Lucio Strumendo. During that period, in carrying out its institutional activities, the Office received assistance from the Human Rights Centre of the University of Padua, pursuant to specific agreements. On 7 December 2010 the President of the Regional Council appointed Aurea Dissegna as the new regional Commissioner.

Regional law 42/1988, the United Nations International Convention on the Rights of the Child and the Council of Europe Convention on the Exercise of Children's Rights constitute the paradigm which founds and orients the action by the Commissioner for children and adolescents. His or her functions are disciplined by art. 2 of the above-mentioned regional law. They include: awareness-raising, training and support for volunteer legal guardians for children; promoting a culture fostering children's and adolescents' rights in collaboration with local authorities and in connection with public opinion and the information media; listening to children involved in situations of distress, risk or prejudice, in cases brought to the Office's attention, and undertaking orientation, mediation and consultation measures; vigilance over guardianship given to minors living outside their family of origin; notification to the competent administrative and legal authorities as well as to social services regarding situations of risk or prejudice to minors; collaboration with public administrations in order to foster goal-sharing; support for the assumption of responsibility by individuals, professionals and institutions operating in favour of children and adolescents; network-building among figures dedicated to the protection of minors.

As years have passed, the regional Commissioner for children and adolescents has provided training and on-the-job support to over 900 volunteer legal guardians throughout the territory of Veneto. In 2010 the Office continued its training activities, organising five new basic training courses in the same number of ULSS (public health care services), in Veneto. The documents now available (updated to June 2010) report 139 requests for volunteer guardians made by the judiciary authority; approximately 60 requests for telephone consultancy were handled, and 17 individual files were opened. During the two-year period from 2009-2010, moreover, the Commissioner managed the legal guardianship of 45 unaccompanied foreign minors transferred from Lampedusa to Jesolo in January 2009.

The Commissioner's office coordinated the publication of "guidelines" for social and health care services in Veneto concerning the management and notification of children-related problems. In 2010 it has assisted in implementing and revising them pursuant to Regional Government (*Giunta*) deliberation 8 August 2008, No. 2416 (Regional guidelines in developing services for the protection and guardianship of children and adolescents). In addition, the Office presented "orientation guidelines" regarding communications between schools and social health services; between April and October 2010 it hosted a training course on this topic in collaboration with the MIUR, the Regional Department for social services and the Human Rights Centre of the University of Padua. Approximately 80 participants from the entire region attended, including school principals, teachers, employees and professionals working in social and health care services region-wide.

As regards activities of listening, mediation and consultancy, data relative to the period from January to November 2010 document the opening of 406 files (approximately 436 for the entire year; around 50 more than in the preceding year) relative to requests coming predominantly from Municipalities (50%). The problems emerging involved, in particular: neglect (23%), mistreatment (15%), parental conflict (14%) and foster care (14%). The types of intervention generally made by the Office in responding to such requests involved consultancy with the social worker (69%), mediation (13%), information (11%) and notification to judicial and/or administrative bodies (5%).

Of particular importance, among activities of cultural promotion and research: the regional conference *A look toward the future for the children's Commissioner. Results and perspectives regarding the experience of Commissioner for children and Adolescents of Ve*neto, held on 21 June at the University of Padua; and initiatives aiming to promote participation of children and adolescents in community care structures. In addition, pursuant to Regional Government deliberation 5 June 2010, No. 1595, and in collaboration with the Regional Communications Committee (Co.re.com) of Veneto, the Commissioner joined the working group for the European project *Friends on line*, which aims to prevent and fight cyber-bullying.

On 30 April 2010, the Commissioner for children and adolescents of Veneto, together with the regional Commissioners for children and adolescents of Lazio, Marche, Campania, Friuli-Venezia Giulia and Molise, participated in the establishment of the Network of Children's Commissioners (see Part II, Structure at a Sub-national level, IV).

VI. Ombudsman

The Ombudsman of the Region of Veneto was established with r.l. 6 June 1988, No. 28. Supported by a specific office, this monocratic authority carries out his or her activity freely and independently, in defence of citizens' rights and interests, in cases of dysfunction or abuse by the public administration. He or she operates free of charge. The Ombudsman of the Region of Veneto is elected by the Regional Council, to which he or she presents a detailed annual report on the activity performed. From 2001 to 2010 the office was held by Vittorio Bottoli. On 7 December 2010 the President of the Regional Council appointed Roberto Pellegrini as the new regional Ombudsman.

> The Ombudsman has the following tasks: to intervene in cases of dysfunction or abuse by the public administration; to protect common interests; to request exhibition of any necessary act or document, even if secret; to promote the creation of roundtables for confrontation and agreements (service conferences); to direct the citizen toward the most pertinent structures and advise him on initiatives or remedies to adopt; to promote the conciliatory resolution (mediation) of controversies; to solicit those responsible for proceedings; to request activation of disciplinary proceedings against negligent functionaries; to stimulate and advice public administrations when adopting measures.

VII. Commission for Equal Opportunities between Men and Women

The Commission was instituted by regional law 30 December 1987, No. 62. It is a regional consultative body on gender policies aimed at the actual implementation of the principle of parity and equal opportunities, stated by the Constitution and by the regional statute. Pursuant to Regional Government deliberation No. 1231 of 30 April 2004, the Commission receives administrative assistance from the Regional Department for international relations, international cooperation, human rights and equal opportunities. The Chair of the Commission is Simonetta Tregnago.

> The Commission's main function is to carry out inquiries and research on the condition of women in Veneto, with particular reference to matters involving employment, labour and professional training, and to spread information about this sphere. It may formulate opinions on the current status of compliance with laws, and on law proposals, and prepare its own proposals. The Commission of Veneto carries out its activities partly in coordination with other Commissions on the local, regional and national level, and with other bodies committed to realizing parity.

Among the activities performed during 2010, the Commission has begun a mapping of community shelters and centres of reference active in the regional territory, in which women who are victims of domestic violence may find support and assistance and it has published a manual for social workers entitled *Guardiamo avanti con sicurezza. Come individuare la violenza domestica* (*Let's look ahead with confidence. How to detect domestic violence*). The Commission has also published a study on *Women's associations and politico-cultural debate in Veneto from 1944 to today*. In May 2010 it organised a training session on stalking, and has published the related documentation on the Commission website.

VIII. Integrated Network of Regional Observatories on Social Policies

From 1999 on, the Region of Veneto has disciplined the activation of a network of seven regional Observatories, created with the aim to monitor and define new modalities of response to the growing complexity of social policies. Pursuant to art. 21 of the law 8 November 2000, No. 328 (Framework law for the creation of an integrated system of social measures and services), and to Regional Government deliberation 19 December 2006, No. 4139, the integrated Network of Observatories was reorganised with the aim to overcome the fragmentary nature of its single components. The Network, which depends on the Regional

Department for social services, encompassed three Observatories in 2010.

– *Observatory on new generations and the family.* This is a point of reference for all those who act professionally or on the basis of personal commitment, to promote the rights of children, adolescents and the family in the region. Among its various tasks, the Observatory strives to construct a complete, updated awareness framework regarding the condition of children, adolescents, young adults and the family, in close collaboration with other socially-oriented agencies present throughout the territory; to become a point of documentation, research and analysis capable of providing the regional infrastructure with information allowing it to plan and programme measures and policies favouring children. The Observatory is dedicated to guaranteeing widespread diffusion of information to all operators, favouring the circulation, appreciation and efficacy of territorial experiences.

– *Observatory on the condition of the elderly and of persons with disabilities.* This is a knowledge, understanding and operative instrument that systematically documents problems hinging on social relations, social assistance, cultures and health in the world of the elderly and of persons with disabilities, and ways of confronting such issues. The Observatory aims to publicise information, experiences and the results of research and initiatives carried out at the local level; to promote human rights by informing elderly persons and persons with disabilities of programmes designed to strengthen their capabilities, and to favour processes and behaviour tending to maintain their welfare, autonomy and health for as long as possible, in hopes of improving their life quality. The Observatory also aims to study the evolution of the request for services in favour of the elderly and persons with disabilities, and the availability of such services; and to promote the cultural growth of care providers.

– *Observatory on dependency and social marginalisation.* This is an instrument of inquiry with a transversal, multi-dimensional approach to the issues of dependency, marginalisation and social exclusion. In particular, the Observatory aims gradually to construct a shared patrimony of knowledge concerning Venetian prisons a, situations of social deviancy, sexual abuse and exploitation, and the dynamics linked to them. It aims to create modes and strengthen forms of collaboration among local health care offices, local authorities, the third sector and all social actors operating in the sphere of dependency and social marginalisation; to promote and sustain development of a cultural, methodological and operative approach toward the protection and promotion of the person, the family and the local community.

With deliberation 2077 of 3 August 2010, the Regional Government has given further structuring to the Network, by constituting a new, single Regional Observatory on Social Policies, meant to substitute, beginning in 2011, the three Observatories described above.

IX. Regional Observatory on Immigration

The Observatory is overseen by the Department of public security and migratory flows (Councillor's office on migratory flows policies). Its establishment was foreseen by the *three-year programme 2007-2009* comprising immigration measures, and by the *annual plan of action for 2007*, adopted in application of that programme, pursuant to art. 3 of r.l. 9/1990 (Measures for the immigration sector).

The Observatory is defined as a techno-scientific instrument aiming to monitor, analyse and diffuse data and information on migratory movements and integration. To this end, it ensures collaboration with other regional observatories interested in various aspects of the migration phenomenon; it ensures the constant operation and data input for databases, the monitoring of immigration dynamics, and in-depth inquiry into specific phenomena. It examines the living conditions and socio-scholastic integration of children as well as their education and training. It ensures updated acknowledgment of special norms, proposing training sessions in order to facilitate awareness of them and correctness in their application.

In November 2010 the Observatory published its annual report, which updates the analysis of migratory flows and the presence of foreigners in the Region, with particular attention to the impact of the economic crisis on the immigrant population. The report is divided into parts specifically dedicated to the presence of foreigners in the school system and in the world of labour.

According to data contained in the report, at the end of 2009 there were 490,000 foreigners resident in Veneto (for 2010, the estimate is over 500,000), amounting to 10% of the total regional population. In 2009 the number of resident foreigners in Veneto increased by about 35,000. As regards the Country of origin, 25% of foreigners residing in Veneto are from European Union Countries (especially Romania), 31% from other Countries in Eastern Europe, 24% from Africa, and 16% from Asia.

Part III

Italy in Dialogue with International Human Rights Institutions

The United Nations System

I. General Assembly

The United Nations General Assembly is articulated in six main Committees, each made up of all UN Member States. Human rights issues are discussed mainly within the Third Committee (Social, Humanitarian and Cultural Committee). This Committee has competence in dealing with issues such as torture and other degrading, inhuman or cruel punishment or treatment; advancement of women; rights of refugees and displaced persons; promotion and safeguarding of children's rights; rights of indigenous people; elimination of racism, racial discrimination, xenophobia and related intolerance; rights to self-determination; social development.

In the framework of the activities of the General Assembly and the Third Committee, Italy's effort in relation to human rights have primarily focused in the following issues:

– *Promotion of the rule of law and strengthening of democracy.* Italy is a member of the Community of Democracies which organises a yearly conference at the ministerial level focusing on a selected topic. In 2010, the conference was on *The role of women as a crucial factor in democratic governance.* In addition, Italy is one of the chief donors to the United Nations Democracy Fund (UNDEF).

– *Fight against torture, xenophobia, racism and other forms of discrimination, with particular attention towards religious discrimination and intolerance.* Italy is one of the main supporter of the resolution sponsored by the European Union, presented and approved by consensus during the 65th session of the General Assembly, on the *Elimination of all forms of discrimination.* Italy is also a member of the Group of Friends of the Alliance of Civilisations, an initiative launched by Spain and Turkey under the auspices of the United Nations aimed at the promotion of intercultural and interreligious dialogue.

– *Protection of children's rights.* Italy is among the main sponsors of the annual resolution on children's rights sponsored by the European Union. In recent years, moreover, Italy has also assumed a key role in raising the international community's awareness concerning the issue of children involved in armed conflict.

– *Abolition of death penalty.* Thanks to Italy's contribution, in 2007 the General Assembly passed resolution A/RES/62/149 establishing a moratorium on capital punishment (104 votes in favour). In 2008, again thanks to Italy's fundamental role, a second resolution on the issue, A/RES/63/168, was adopted recording 106 votes in favour. Italy has pursued its commitment and, together with its European Union partners and other supporters, it was particularly active in promoting a third resolution, A/RES/65/206, at the 65th session of the General Assembly in 2010. This time, 109 Member States voted in favour, confirming the international trend toward abolition.

– *Fight violence against women and female genital mutilation.* During the 65th session of the General Assembly, Italy worked alongside various African partners, including Egypt, in building consensus on a resolution against female genital mutilation. In this regard, Italy organised several informal meetings, as well as a "side-event" on the ministerial level, together with Egypt, Burkina Faso and Senegal, chaired by the Minister for Equal Opportunities, Carfagna. The meeting took place in March 2010, in concomitance with activities of the United Nations Commission on the Status of Women. Italy also supports the joint UNICEF/UNFPA programme on female genital mutilation; in 2010 the programme was financed by a contribution of one million Euros.

In 2010, Italy's Permanent Representative at United Nations headquarters in New York is Cesare Maria Ragaglini; Luca Zelioli is responsible for monitoring the Third Committee's human rights activities. The following chart shows the most important interventions by the Italian delegation and by Italian Government representatives in General Assembly meetings during 2010.

Date	Event	Statements
19 January 2010	Informal Plenary of the GA	Statement by Amb. Ragaglini concerning inter-governmental negotiations on Security Council reform
17 February 2010	Informal Meeting of the GA	Statement by Amb. Ragaglini on the 2010 review of the Peacebuilding Commission
22 March 2010	High-Level Interactive Dialogue on Water, (International Decade "Water for Life: 2005-2015")	Statement by Min. Plen. Serpi, Special Envoy of the Italian Ministry of Foreign Affairs
12 May 2010	Commission on Sustainable Development of the GA	Statement by the Minister of the Environment Prestigiacomo
14 May 2010	Informal Plenary of the GA	Statement by the Minister of the Environment Prestigiacomo on piracy

17 June 2010	High-Level Segment on the Palermo Convention	Statement by the Minister of Justice Alfano
17 June 2010	High-Level Segment on transnational organised crime	Statement by the Minister of Interior Maroni
19 August 2010	Plenary Meeting of the GA on strengthening coordination of humanitarian and disaster relief assistance of the United Nations	Statement by Amb. Iannucci, Special Envoy of the Italian Minister of Foreign Affairs
21 September 2010	High-Level plenary meeting of the GA on the Millennium Development Goals	Statement by the Minister of Foreign Affairs Frattini
24 September 2010	High-Level plenary meeting of the GA on development strategies of Small Island Developing States (SIDS)	Statement by the Minister of the Environment Prestigiacomo
25 September 2010	65th Plenary session of the GA	Statement by the Minister of Foreign Affairs Frattini
21 October 2010	Informal Plenary of the GA	Statement by Amb. Ragaglini concerning inter-governmental negotiations on Security Council reform
4 November 2010	65th Plenary session of the GA on the situation in Afghanistan	Statement by Amb. Ragaglini
11 November 2010	65th Plenary session of the GA	Statement by Amb. Ragaglini concerning the position of Italy on the Security Council reform
14 December 2010	Informal Plenary of the GA	Statement by Amb. Ragaglini concerning inter-governmental negotiations on Security Council reform

Source: Permanent Italian Representative's Office at the United Nations, New York

A. Human Rights Resolutions Sponsored by Italy

On 21 December 2010, during its 65th session, the General Assembly adopted 52 resolutions on human rights which had been previously discussed and approved by the Third Committee during the months of October and November. In this occasion, Italy presented a proposal for the resolution "*Strengthening the United Nations Crime Prevention and Criminal Justice Programme in particular its technical cooperation capacity*", which was later approved by the General Assembly by consensus (A/RES/65/232); it also sponsored 29 resolutions, and was called upon to express a vote on 16 of them.

Subject	Resolution	Resolution's main sponsor	Information regarding Italy	Results of the voting process in plenary session
Social development	A/RES/65/182 Follow-up to the Second World Assembly on Ageing	Yemen	Co-sponsor of the resolution	Adopted without a vote
	A/RES/65/183 United Nations Literacy Decade: education for all	Mongolia	Co-sponsor of the resolution	Adopted without a vote
	A/RES/65/184 Cooperatives in social development	Mongolia	Co-sponsor of the resolution	Adopted without a vote
	A/RES/65/186 Realizing the Millennium Development Goals for persons with disabilities towards 2015 and beyond	Philippines	Co-sponsor of the resolution	Adopted without a vote
Advancement of women	A/RES/65/187 Intensification of efforts to eliminate all forms of violence against women	France and the Netherlands	Co-sponsor of the resolution	Adopted without a vote
	A/RES/65/188 Supporting efforts to end obstetric fistula	Malawi	Co-sponsor of the resolution	Adopted without a vote
	A/RES/65/190 Trafficking in women and girls	Philippines	Co-sponsor of the resolution	Adopted without a vote
Refugees, displaced persons and humanitarian issues	A/RES/65/193 Assistance to refugees, returnees and displaced persons in Africa	Sierra Leone	Co-sponsor of the resolution	Adopted without a vote
	A/RES/65/194 Office of the United Nations High Commissioner for Refugees	Sweden	Co-sponsor of the resolution	Adopted without a vote
Report of the Human Rights Council	A/RES/65/195 Report of the Human Rights Council	Mali	Abstention	123 in favour, 1 against, 55 abstentions
	A/RES/65/196 Proclamation of 24 March as the International Day for the Right to the Truth concerning Gross	El Salvador	Co-sponsor of the resolution	Adopted without a vote

	Human Rights Violations and for the Dignity of Victims			
Promotion and protection of the rights of children	A/RES/65/197 Rights of the child	Uruguay and Belgium	Co-sponsor of the resolution	Adopted without a vote
Indigenous issues	A/RES/65/198 Indigenous issues	Bolivia	Co-sponsor of the resolution	Adopted without a vote
Elimination of racism, racial discrimination, xenophobia and related intolerance	A/RES/65/199 Inadmissibility of certain practices that contribute to fuelling contemporary forms of racism, racial discrimination, xenophobia and related intolerance	Russian Federation	Abstention	129 in favour, 3 against, 52 abstentions
	A/RES/65/240 (adopted on 24 December 2010) Global efforts for the total elimination of racism, racial discrimination, xenophobia and related intolerance and the comprehensive implementation of and follow-up to the Durban Declaration and Programme of Action	Yemen and China	Against	104 in favour, 22 against, 33 abstentions
Rights of peoples to self-determination	A/RES/65/202 The right of the Palestinian people to self-determination	Egypt	In favour	177 in favour, 6 against, 4 abstentions
	A/RES/65/203 Use of mercenaries as a means of violating human rights and impeding the exercise of the right of peoples to self-determination	Cuba	Against	127 in favour, 52 against, 5 abstentions
Torture and other cruel, inhuman or degrading treatment or punishment	A/RES/65/204 Committee against Torture	Denmark	Co-sponsor of the resolution	Adopted without a vote
	A/RES/65/205 Torture and other cruel, inhuman or degrading treatment or punishment	Denmark	Co-sponsor of the resolution	Adopted without a vote

Human rights-related issues, including alternative approaches aimed at improving the effective enjoyment of human rights and fundamental freedoms	A/RES/65/206 Moratorium on the use of the death penalty	Croatia	Co-sponsor of the resolution; In favour	109 in favour, 41 against, 35 abstentions
	A/RES/65/207 The role of the Ombudsman, mediator and other national human rights institutions in the promotion and protection of human rights	Morocco	Co-sponsor of the resolution	Adopted without a vote
	A/RES/65/208 Extrajudicial, summary or arbitrary executions	Finland	Co-sponsor of the resolution In favour	122 in favour, 1 against, 62 abstentions
	A/RES/65/209 International Convention for the Protection of All Persons from Enforced Disappearance	France	Co-sponsor of the resolution	Adopted without a vote
	A/RES/65/210 Missing persons	Azerbaijan	Co-sponsor of the resolution	Adopted without a vote
	A/RES/65/211 Elimination of all forms of intolerance and of discrimination based on religion or belief	Belgium	Co-sponsor of the resolution	Adopted without a vote
	A/RES/65/213 Human rights in the administration of justice	Austria	Co-sponsor of the resolution	Adopted without a vote
	A/RES/65/214 Human rights and extreme poverty	Peru	Co-sponsor of the resolution	Adopted without a vote
	A/RES/65/215 Elimination of discrimination against persons affected by leprosy and their family members	Japan	Co-sponsor of the resolution	Adopted without a vote
	A/RES/65/216 Globalization and its impact on the full enjoyment of all human rights	Egypt	Against	132 in favour, 54 against, 0 abstentions
	A/RES/65/217 Human rights and unilateral coercive measures	Cuba	Against	131 in favour, 53 against, 0 abstentions

	A/RES/65/219 The right to development	Cuba	Abstention	133 in favour, 24 against, 28 abstentions
	A/RES/65/220 The right to food	Cuba	Co-sponsor of the resolution	Adopted without a vote
	A/RES/65/221 Protection of human rights and fundamental freedoms while countering terrorism	Mexico	Co-sponsor of the resolution	Adopted without a vote
	A/RES/65/222 Promotion of peace as a vital requirement for the full enjoyment of all human rights by all	Cuba	Against	127 in favour, 54 against, 4 abstentions
	A/RES/65/223 Promotion of a democratic and equitable international order	Cuba	Against	126 in favour, 54 against, 5 abstentions
	A/RES/65/224 Combating defamation of religions	Morocco	Against	79 in favour, 67 against, 40 abstentions
Situation of human rights and reports by Special rapporteurs and Special representatives	A/RES/65/225 Situation of human rights in the Democratic People's Republic of Korea	Belgium	Co-sponsor of the resolution; In favour	106 in favour, 20 against, 57 abstentions
	A/RES/65/241 (adopted on 24 December 2010) Situation of human rights in Myanmar	Belgium	Co-sponsor of the resolution; In favour	85 in favour, 26 against, 46 abstentions
	A/RES/65/226 Situation of human rights in the Islamic Republic of Iran	Canada	Co-sponsor of the resolution; In favour	78 in favour, 45 against, 59 abstentions
International drugs control	A/RES/65/233 International cooperation against the world drug problem	Mexico	Co-sponsor of the resolution	Adopted without a vote

Source: United Nations, General Assembly

II. Human Rights Council

With resolution 60/251 of 15 March 2006, the United Nations General Assembly created the Human Rights Council (HRC) as its subsidiary organ, in substitution of the previous Human Rights Commission. The HRC is made up of 47 UN Member States appointed by rotation by the General Assembly, for an initial period of three years, renewable for no more than two consecutive mandates. Normally, it meets in Geneva three times per year, for an overall time period of ten working weeks. Though it is an inter-governmental body, the Council is open to contribution from non-governmental organisations endowed with consultative status which may participate in meetings and present written documents.

In order to carry out the mandate assigned it, the Council has instituted several internal "mechanisms" and procedures (resolution A/HRC/RES/5/1, June 2007) among which the most significant are: the Universal Periodic Review, the Special Procedures, the Advisory Committee and the Complaint Procedure.

Italy was first elected to the Human Rights Council in May 2007. Its candidacy was supported by a memorandum prepared by the Government (doc. A/61/863) containing *voluntary pledges and commitments* assumed by Italy in respect of human rights on both the domestic and international level. On the international level, its commitments concerned the promotion of the rule of law and democracy; the fight against any form of discrimination (sex-based in particular); the fight against torture; protection of children's rights; the abolition of the death penalty. On the national level, Italy committed itself to completing the normative process for the implementation of the Statute of the International Criminal Court; to ratifying and implementing the Optional Protocol to the Convention against Torture and Other Cruel, Inhuman or Degrading Treatment or Punishment; to establish a National Independent Commission for the Promotion and Protection of Human Rights and Fundamental Freedoms. It is interesting to note, however, that as of 31 December 2010, the last two commitments had not yet been fulfilled.

During its mandate at the Human Rights Council, Italy gave an important contribution in preparing the *United Nations Declaration on Human Rights Education and Training*; together with Morocco, Costa Rica, the Philippines, Senegal, Slovenia and Switzerland it set up a *Platform for Human Rights Education and Training*, an informal group of Countries whose role has been to promote the discussion over the text of the Declaration and to facilitate its adoption. With this goal in mind, the Platform organised three informal consultancies open to States, United Nations Agencies, and members of civil society, respectively on 24 June, 3 September and 14 December 2010. In July 2010, Italy, represented by Counsellor Roberto Vellano, participated in the *International Seminar of Experts on the Project for the United Nations Declaration on Human Rights Education and Training* in Marrakech; participants included Professor Marco Mascia (on the topic *The right to human rights education and training: the responsibility of public and private sectors*); and Professor Antonio Papisca (on the topic *Reflections on important aspects of the integrated approach to human rights education and training*).

In 2010, Italy was represented at the Human Rights Council by Ambassador Laura Mirachian, Permanent Representative to the International Organisations in Geneva, by Counsellors Roberto Vellano and Paolo Cuculi and by Chief Secretary Roberto Nocella. The following chart shows the main instances of intervention by the Italian delegation to the Human Rights Council during 2010.

Date	Event	Statements
27 January 2010	Special session of the Human Rights Council on Haiti	Request of the Special Session co-sponsored by Italy and statement by Amb. Mirachian during the session
8-19 February 2010	7th session of the UPR	Statements with reference to the review of the human rights situation in the following States: El Salvador, Gambia, Fiji, San Marino, Angola, Madagascar, Slovenia, Iraq, Bosnia-Herzegovina
2 March 2010	13th session of the Human Rights Council	Statement by Amb. Mirachian on the opportunity of a United Nations declaration on human rights education and training
3 March 2010	13th session of the Human Rights Council	Statement by Amb. Mirachian on the occasion of the General Segment
11 March 2010	13th session of the Human Rights Council	Statement by Counsellor Vellano during the debate with the Special rapporteur on religious freedom and belief
15 March 2010	13th session of the Human Rights Council	Statement by Amb. Mirachian during the debate on the situation of human rights in Myanmar
23 March 2010	13th session of the Human Rights Council	Statement by Amb. Mirachian during the Council debate on religious freedom
3-14 May 2010	8th session of the UPR	Statements with reference to the review of the human rights situation in the following States: Kyrgyzstan, Laos, Lesotho, Spain, Armenia, Turkey, Kuwait, Belarus
31 May 2010	14th session of the Human Rights Council	Statement by Counsellor Vellano on the occasion of opening statements
1 June 2010	14th session of the Human Rights Council	Statement on the situation on the Middle East
7 June 2010	14th session of the Human Rights Council	Statement by First Secretary Nocella during the debate on human rights of women
10 June 2010	14th session of the Human Rights Council	Statement by First Secretary Nocella on the occasion of the adoption of the UPR report on San Marino
14 June 2010	14th session of the Human Rights Council	Statement by Amb. Mirachian during the general debate on the situation on the Middle East

15 June 2010	14th session of the Human Rights Council	Statement by Counsellor Vellano on the follow-up of the Vienna Declaration and Programme of Action
16 June 2010	14th session of the Human Rights Council	Statement by Amb. Mirachian during a panel on medical care for children affected by AIDS/HIC, organised by Comunità Papa Giovanni XXIII and Caritas Internationalis and co-sponsored by Italy.
18 June 2010	14th session of the Human Rights Council	Statement by Amb. Mirachian on the occasion of the end of the mandate of in the Human Rights Council
14 September 2010	15th session of the Human Rights Council	Statement by Counsellor Cuculi on children and armed conflicts
22 September 2010	15th session of the Human Rights Council	Statement by First Secretary Nocella on the occasion of the adoption of the UPR report on Armenia
29 September 2010	15th session of the Human Rights Council	Statement by Amb. Mirachian during the debate on the situation in Somalia
29 September 2010	15th session of the Human Rights Council	Side event mother-child health, organised by Italy and co-sponsored by Burkina Faso, Colombia and New Zealand, as well as by the World Trade Organisation and by the Partnership for Newborn, Child and Maternal Health
14 October 2010	8th session of the Inter-governmental Working Group on the effective implementation of the Durban Declaration and Programme of Action	Statement by First Secretary Nocella to present the pilot project launched in Rome to ameliorate the situation of Roma people
15 October 2010	Informal dialogue	Informal dialogue on the problem of female genital mutilations, organised by the United Nations Fund for Population (UNFPA) and UNICEF, in cooperation with the permanent representatives of Burkina Faso, Italy and Norway
1-12 November 2010	9th session of the UPR	Statements with reference to the review of the human rights situation in the following States: Liberia, Malawi, Mongolia, Panama, Bulgaria, Honduras, United States, Jamaica, Croatia, Mauritania, Lebanon
25 November 2010	Seminar	Statement by First Secretary Nocella on the occasion of the experts workshop entitled "Elimination of all forms of violence against women – challenges, good practices and opportunities", organised by the OHCHR

Source: Permanent Italian Representative's Office at the United Nations, Geneva

A. Resolutions Sponsored by Italy

During the year 2010, Italy participated to the 13th Special Session of the Human Rights Council on the continued support to the recovery process in Haiti and the importance of integrating a human rights approach, and in three regular Council sessions, including two – the 13th and 14th – as a Member State, and one (the 15th) as observer.

During the Special Session on Haiti, Italy sponsored the final resolution, A/HRC/S-13/L.1, later adopted by the Council by consensus.

During the 13th regular session of the Council (1-26 March 2010), 27 resolutions were adopted: Italy sponsored one and co-sponsored nine, including eight adopted by open vote; they appear as follows:

Resolution	State presenting the resolution	Information regarding Italy	Outcome of the voting process
A/HRC/RES/13/1 Composition of staff of the Office of the United Nations High Commissioner for Human Rights	Cuba	Against	31 in favour, 12 against, 3 abstentions
A/HRC/RES/13/3 Open-ended Working Group on an optional protocol to the Convention on the Rights of the Child to provide a communications procedure	Thailand	Co-sponsor of the resolution	Adopted without a vote
A/HRC/RES/13/5 Human rights in the occupied Syrian Golan	Pakistan	Abstention	31 in favour, 1 against, 15 abstentions
A/HRC/RES/13/6 Right of the Palestinian people to self-determination	Pakistan	In favour	45 in favour, 1 against
A/HRC/RES/13/7 Israeli settlements in the Occupied Palestinian Territory, including East Jerusalem, and in the occupied Syrian Golan	Pakistan	In favour	46 in favour, 1 against
A/HRC/RES/13/8 The grave human rights violations by Israel in the Occupied Palestinian Territory, including East Jerusalem	Pakistan	Against	31 in favour, 9 against, 7 abstentions
A/HRC/RES/13/9 Follow-up to the report of the United Nations Independent International Fact-Finding Mission on the Gaza Conflict	Pakistan	Against	29 in favour, 6 against, 11 abstentions
A/HRC/RES/13/10 Adequate housing as a component of the right to an adequate standard of living, in the context of mega-events	Germany and Finland	Co-sponsor of the resolution	Adopted without a vote

A/HRC/RES/13/11 Human rights of persons with disabilities	Mexico	Co-sponsor of the resolution	Adopted without a vote
A/HRC/RES/13/12 Rights of persons belonging to national or ethnic, religious and linguistic minorities	Austria	Co-sponsor of the resolution	Adopted without a vote
A/HRC/RES/13/13 Protection of human rights defenders	Norway	Co-sponsor of the resolution	Adopted without a vote
A/HRC/RES/13/14 Situation of human rights in the Democratic People's Republic of Korea	Japan and Spain	Co-sponsor of the resolution; In favour	28 in favour, 5 against, 13 abstentions
A/HRC/RES/13/15 United Nations declaration on human rights education and training	Morocco	Main sponsor of the resolution	Adopted without a vote
A/HRC/RES/13/16 Combating defamation of religions	Pakistan	Against	20 in favour, 17 against, 8 abstentions
A/HRC/RES/13/19 Torture and other cruel, inhuman or degrading treatment or punishment: the role and responsibility of judges, prosecutors and lawyers	Denmark	Co-sponsor of the resolution	Adopted without a vote
A/HRC/RES/13/21 Strengthening of technical cooperation and consultative services in the Republic of Guinea	Nigeria	Co-sponsor of the resolution	Adopted without a vote
A/HRC/RES/13/24 Protection of journalists in situations of armed conflict	Egypt	Co-sponsor of the resolution	Adopted without a vote

Source: United Nations, Human Rights Council

During the 14th regular session of the Council (31 March-18 June 2010), 16 resolutions were adopted: Italy sponsored three, co-sponsored six, and had to participate to three voting procedures. They appear as follows:

Resolution	**State presenting the resolution**	**Information regarding Italy**	**Outcome of the voting process**
A/HRC/RES/14/1 The grave attacks by Israeli forces against the humanitarian boat convoy	Pakistan	Against	32 in favour, 3 against, 9 abstentions
A/HRC/RES/14/2 Trafficking in persons, especially women	Germany and Philippines	Co-sponsor of the resolution	Adopted without a vote

and children: regional and subregional cooperation in promoting a human rights-based approach to combating trafficking in persons			
A/HRC/RES/14/3 Promotion of the right of peoples to peace	Cuba	Against	31 in favour, 14 against, 3 abstentions
A/HRC/RES/14/4 The effects of foreign debt and other related international financial obligations of States on the full enjoyment of all human rights, particularly economic, social and cultural rights	Cuba	Against	31 in favour, 13 against, 3 abstentions
A/HRC/RES/14/5 The role of prevention in the promotion and protection of human rights	Ukraine	Sponsor of the resolution	Adopted without a vote
A/HRC/RES/14/6 Mandate of the Special Rapporteur on the human rights of internally displaced persons	Austria and Uganda	Co-sponsor of the resolution	Adopted without a vote
A/HRC/RES/14/10 Enforced or involuntary disappearances	France and Morocco	Co-sponsor of the resolution	Adopted without a vote
A/HRC/RES/14/11 Freedom of religion or belief: mandate of the Special Rapporteur on freedom of religion or belief	Spain	Co-sponsor of the resolution	Adopted without a vote
A/HRC/RES/14/12 Accelerating efforts to eliminate all forms of violence against women: ensuring due diligence in prevention	Canada	Co-sponsor of the resolution	Adopted without a vote
A/HRC/RES/14/13 Question of the realization in all Countries of economic, social and cultural rights: follow-up to Human Rights Council resolution 4/1	Portugal	Co-sponsor of the resolution	Adopted without a vote
A/HRC/RES/14/14 Technical assistance and cooperation on human rights for Kyrgyzstan	Kyrgyzstan and United States	Sponsor of the resolution	Adopted without a vote
A/HRC/RES/14/15 Addressing attacks on school children in Afghanistan	Afghanistan and United States	Sponsor of the resolution	Adopted without a vote

On 18 June 2010, Italy concluded its first mandate as member of the Human Rights Council. In leaving, it issued a verbal note addressed to

the Secretariat of the Council (doc. A/HRC/14/G/3), reserving the possibility of presenting its candidacy for a successive mandate, starting in 2011.

At any rate, Italy participated as an observer (devoid, therefore, of the right to vote) at the 15th regular Council session (13 September-1 October 2010), sponsoring one resolution and co-sponsoring 14:

Resolution	State presenting the resolution	Information regarding Italy	Outcome of the voting process
A/HRC/RES/15/2 Special Rapporteur on contemporary forms of slavery	United Kingdom	Co-sponsor of the resolution	Adopted without a vote
A/HRC/RES/15/3 Independence and impartiality of the judiciary, jurors and assessors and the independence of lawyers	Hungary	Co-sponsor of the resolution	Adopted without a vote
A/HRC/RES/15/4 The right to education: follow-up to Human Rights Council resolution 8/4	Portugal	Co-sponsor of the resolution	Adopted without a vote
A/HRC/RES/15/5 Forensic genetics and human rights	Argentina	Co-sponsor of the resolution	Adopted without a vote
A/HRC/RES/15/8 Adequate housing as a component of the right to an adequate standard of living	Finland and Germany	Co-sponsor of the resolution	Adopted without a vote
A/HRC/RES/15/9 Human rights and access to safe drinking water and sanitation	Germany and Spain	Co-sponsor of the resolution	Adopted without a vote
A/HRC/RES/15/10 Elimination of discrimination against persons affected by leprosy and their family members	Japan	Co-sponsor of the resolution	Adopted without a vote
A/HRC/RES/15/11 World Programme for Human Rights Education: adoption of the plan of action for the second phase	Costa Rica	Co-sponsor of the resolution	Adopted without a vote
A/HRC/RES/15/17 Preventable maternal mortality and morbidity and human rights: follow-up to Council resolution 11/8	New Zealand	Co-sponsor of the resolution	Adopted without a vote
A/HRC/RES/15/18 Arbitrary detention	France	Co-sponsor of the resolution	Adopted without a vote
A/HRC/RES/15/19 Draft guiding principles on extreme poverty and human rights	France	Co-sponsor of the resolution	Adopted without a vote
A/HRC/RES/15/20 Advisory services and technical assistance for Cambodia	Japan	Co-sponsor of the resolution	Adopted without a vote

A/HRC/RES/15/21 The rights to freedom of peaceful assembly and of association	Maldives and United States	Co-sponsor of the resolution	Adopted without a vote
A/HRC/RES/15/23 Elimination of discrimination against women	Colombia e Mexico	Co-sponsor of the resolution	Adopted without a vote
A/HRC/RES/15/28 Assistance to Somalia in the field of human rights	Nigeria	Sponsor of the resolution	Adopted without a vote

Source: United Nations, Human Rights Council

B. Universal Periodic Review

The 7th session of the Universal Periodic Review (UPR) of the Human Rights Council took place in Geneva from 8 to 19 February. During the session, reports from 16 Countries were review: Angola, Egypt, Madagascar, Gambia, Qatar, Fiji, Iran, Iraq, Kazakhstan, Bolivia, Nicaragua, El Salvador, Italy, San Marino, Slovenia, Bosnia-Herzegovina.

Italy's review session was scheduled on 9 February 2010. The interactive dialogue was conducted before the UPR Working Group of the Human Rights Council and was facilitated by a *troika* formed by Slovakia, Argentina and Ghana.

In that occasion, Italy was represented by a high-level delegation composed of 25 officials from various Ministries and headed by the Vice Minister of Foreign Affairs, Vincenzo Scotti and by the Chairman of the Inter-Ministerial Committee on Human Rights, Valentino Simonetti.

Italy national report	A/HRC/WG.6/7/ITA/1
Compilation of United Nations information	A/HRC/WG.6/7/ITA/2
Summary of stakeholders' information (NGOs and Council of Europe)	A/HRC/WG.6/7/ITA/3
Report of the Working Group on the Universal Periodic Review – Italy	A/HRC/14/4
Views on conclusions and/or recommendations, voluntary commitments and replies presented by Italy	A/HRC/14/4/Add.1
Date of the Universal Periodic Review	9 and 11 February 2010
Date of adoption of the final report by the Human Rights Council	9 June 2010, during the 14th regular session of the Council (31 May-18 June 2010)

During the presentation of the national report, Vice Minister Scotti stressed that Italy is meeting a number of challenges mainly due to its transformation from a Country of emigration to one of immigration. Topics discussed in the report were:

– *normative and institutional framework*: respect for human rights within the constitutional framework, in ordinary law and in the judiciary system as well as in connection with activities carried out by the judiciary, executive and legislative powers;

– *specific human rights*: civil and political rights; asylum and immigration; human trafficking; integration policies; dialogue with religious communities; protection from torture; fight against xenophobia; minorities; Roma and Sinti communities; gender equality and violence against women; human rights and the fight against terrorism; economic, social and cultural rights;

– *achievements and best practices*: dialogue and cooperation with civil society; human rights education and training; accountability of public officials; international development cooperation;

– *national priorities*: policy against discrimination, policy for migrants' integration; promotion of the rights of persons with disabilities.

During the *interactive dialogue* which followed, and which lasted for approximately three hours, the Italian delegation had to respond to questions, concerns and suggestions expressed by representatives of the Human Rights Council Member States as well as by observer States. As many as 64 Countries asked to intervene but, due to time limits, only 51 were actually able to take the floor. The documents on which the review is based and which form the basis for the discussion are the national report prepared by the State under review and the two reports prepared by the Office of the High Commissioner for Human Rights. The first of these two documents presents a summary of all recommendations addressed to Italy by Treaty Bodies and Special Procedures concerning the human rights situation in the Country over the four previous years; the second one, a synthesis of additional information sent by other "stakeholders" such as, in the Italian case, non-governmental organisations and the Council of Europe. The NGOs submitting information for the Italian UPR were: Amnesty International; the Comitato per la promozione e protezione dei diritti umani; European Roma Rights Centre; Franciscans International; Global Initiative to End All Corporal Punishment of Children; Human Rights Watch; International Commission of Jurists; Index on Censorship; ArciGay, Ilga Europe, Crisalide and others (in a joint report) and the Unione forense per la tutela dei diritti dell'uomo. Italy also had to take into account the written requests for clarification sent in advance by Austria, Denmark, Norway, Sweden, the United Kingdom, the Czech Republic, Germany and the Netherlands.

The intervening Countries, in particular, expressed concerns and formulated specific recommendations on the following issues:

- the increase in xenophobic attitudes, racial discrimination and hate speech attributed to politicians against migrants, Roma and Sinti communities;
- gender discrimination on the labour market, especially in terms of equal pay for equal work; and the inadequate representation of women in politics;
- increase in the number of human trafficking cases and modern forms of slavery;
- need to reconsider the criminalisation of irregular migrants and to take adequate legislative measures in order to de-criminalise the status of irregular migrants;
- lack of independence in the media, and objective, transparent criteria for regulating the system of broadcasting licences;
- lack of a definition, in domestic law, of the crime of torture, as required by the Convention against Torture;
- absence of initiatives ensuring the independence of the judiciary system;
- absence of condemnation and of an effective determination to pursue those responsible for discrimination and violence based on sexual orientation;
- need to set up an independent National Human Rights Commission in accordance with the "Paris Principles";
- need to ratify as soon as possible the United Nations Convention on the Protection of Rights of All Migrant Workers and Members of their Family, the International Convention for the Protection of All Persons from Enforced Disappearance, the Optional Protocol to the Convention against Torture and the Council of Europe Convention on Action against Trafficking in Human Beings.

At the conclusion of the interactive dialogue, on 11 February 2010 the UPR Working Group provisionally adopted the report A/HRC/14/4, submitting it to the Human Rights Council for final approval. The report contains 92 recommendations to the Italian Government for possible measures – legal, political and institutional – to adopt in order to strengthen the national system for promoting and protecting human rights.

The Human Rights Council gave final approval to the report on 9 June 2010, during its 14th regular session. During the session in particular, Italy was called upon to give exhaustive response for each of the 92 recommendations and to specify the reasons why it accepted or declined to accept the specific recommendation.

Italy *fully accepted* 78 recommendations. 44 of these are considered already implemented or under implementation; they are No. 3, 5, 6, 7, 9, 10, 11, 12, 13, 15, 23, 24, 25, 26, 28, 29, 30, 32, 33, 34, 35, 37, 41, 42, 43, 53, 55, 57, 60, 67, 68, 76, 77, 78, 79, 80, 82, 83, 84, 85, 86, 87, 88 and 92. More specifically, Italy committed to ratifying Optional Protocol to the Convention against Torture and to setting up the specific national prevention machinery (recommendation 4).

Two recommendations were *partially accepted*: No. 21 and 75. As regards No. 21, Italy reiterated its commitment to eradicate any form of racism but, at the same time, it declared it was not in the position to adopt or endorse the Outcome Document of the 2009 Durban Review Conference since it had chosen not to participate in that event.

Finally, Italy *rejected* 12 recommendations: No. 1, 2, 8, 14, 17, 38, 49, 56, 58, 72, 73 and 81. Among these, the following are of particular relevance:

– *Recommendation 2 on the ratification of the Convention on the Protection of the Rights of All Migrant Workers and Their Families*. Italy rejected this recommendation with the following reasoning: "The Italian legislation already guarantees most of the rights contained in the UN Convention on the Protection of the Rights of All Migrant Workers and Their Families. However, Italy is not in a position to ratify this instrument because it does not draw any distinction between regular and irregular migrant workers and the signature and ratification could only be planned jointly with the other European partners as many provisions of the Convention fall within the European Union domain".

– *Recommendation 8 on the incorporation of the crime of torture into national legislation*, pursuant to art. 2 and 4 of the 1984 Convention against Torture and Other Cruel, Inhuman or Degrading Treatment or Punishment (ratified by Italy in 1988). Italy rejected this recommendation on the following ground: "In Italy, torture is punishable under various offenses and aggravating circumstances [...]. Even though it is not typified as one specific offence under the Italian criminal code, both the constitutional and legal framework already punish acts of physical and moral violence against persons subject to restrictions of their personal liberty. Both provide sanction for all criminal conducts covered by the definition of torture, as set forth in art. 1 of the relevant Convention".

– *Recommendation 14 on the creation of National Human Rights Institutions* by the end of 2010, in compliance with General Assembly resolution 48/134 of 20 December 1993. Italy rejected this recommendation with the following motivation: "A Bill on the establishment of a National Human Rights Institution will be submitted to the Parliament as soon as the required budgetary resources are made available. However, in accordance with the principle of the separation of powers, the

Government is not in a position to commit the Parliament to act within a specific deadline".

– *Recommendations 72, 73, 81 on the elimination of legislative provisions which criminalise irregular immigration* (with particular reference to law 94/2009). Italy rejected these recommendations with the following motivation: "The management of large migratory flows remains a very serious challenge for any State. In this context, it is crucial to put in place the necessary tools to fight against human trafficking and regular migration. The 2009 legislation has the two-fold aim: of ensuring that migrants – those who are not entitled to any form of protection – are effectively returned to their Country of origin, and of preventing their involvement in organised crime networks. These measures are meant to curb criminal behaviour of individuals and no provision at all is envisaged against any community, group or class nor is linked to any forms of discrimination and xenophobia. Along these lines, the aggravating circumstances under reference are solely meant to prevent the involvement of illegal migrants in organised crime".

The interactive discussion which followed saw the intervention not only of several States, but also of ten non-governmental organisations commenting on stances taken by the Italian Government. The NGOs included Volontariato internazionale per lo sviluppo (VIS), Human Rights Watch, Charitable Institute for Protecting Social Victims, International Federation for Human Rights Leagues, Amnesty International, Save the Children, Rencontre africaine pour la défense des droits de l'homme, Reporters without Borders, European Federation of Gays and Lesbians and Franciscans International.

Finally, it can be mentioned that, during the 8th UPR session (3-14 May 2010), Italy was a member of the *troika* in the Universal Periodic Review of Grenada together with Gabon and Qatar.

C. Special Procedures

All Special Procedures, in the framework of the activities carried within their specific mandate, shall submit an annual report to the Human Rights Council. The report includes a summary of communications sent by the Special Rapporteur, replies received from the Governments and observations of the Special Rapporteurs concerning alleged human rights violations. During the year 2010, Italy was involved in seven of such reports.

Council Session	Date	Symbol	Title
13	22/02/2010	A/HRC/13/20/Add.1	Report of the Special Rapporteur on adequate housing as a component of the right to an adequate standard of living, and on the right to non-discrimination in this context, Raquel Rolnik – Addendum – Summary of communications sent and replies received from Governments and other actors
13	24/02/2010	A/HRC/13/22/Add.1	Report of the Special Rapporteur on the situation of human rights defenders, Margaret Sekaggya – Addendum – Summary of cases transmitted to Governments and replies received
14	16/04/2010	A/HRC/14/30/Add.1	Report submitted by the Special Rapporteur on the human rights of migrants, Jorge A. Bustamante – Addendum – Communications sent to Governments and replies received
14	17/05/2010	A/HRC/14/25/Add.1	Report of the Special Rapporteur on the right to education, Vernor Muñoz – Addendum – Communications sent to and replies received from Governments
14	21/05/2010	A/HRC/14/43/Add.1	Report of the Special Rapporteur on contemporary forms of racism, racial discrimination, xenophobia and related intolerance, Githu Muigai – Addendum – Summary of cases transmitted to Governments and replies received
14	01/06/2010	A/HRC/14/23/Add.1	Report of the Special Rapporteur on the promotion and protection of the right to freedom of opinion and expression, Frank La Rue – Addendum – Summary of cases transmitted to Governments and replies received
14	18/06/2010	A/HRC/14/24/Add.1	Report of the Special Rapporteur on extrajudicial, summary or arbitrary executions, Philip Alston – Addendum – Communications to and from Governments

Source: United Nations, Human Rights Council

– 22 February 2010: *Report by the Special Rapporteur on adequate housing as a component of the right to an adequate standard of living and the right to non-discrimination in this context*, Raquel Rolnik. The report contains an urgent appeal sent to the Italian Government on 23 April 2009 by the Rapporteur on adequate housing together with the Independent Expert on minorities issues, requesting information on the forced eviction of a community of about 140 Roma peoples which took place in the municipality of Milan on 1 July 2009. The report also contains the Italian Government's response, according to which the eviction was carried out in full compliance with the Italian criminal code and was necessary due to the poor security conditions of the Roma camp.

– 24 February 2010: *Report by the Special Rapporteur on the situation of human rights defenders*, Margaret Sekaggya. The report contains an urgent appeal sent to the Italian Government on 9 January 2010 by the Special Rapporteur on the situation of human rights defenders together with the Special Rapporteur on the promotion and protection of the right to freedom of opinion and expression, concerning the status of the police investigations into the death threats issued against the journalist and writer, Roberto Saviano. The report also contains the Italian Government's response, dated 3 March 2009, giving updated information on the investigative and judicial proceedings under way.

– 16 April 2010: *Report by the Special Rapporteur on the human rights of migrants*, Jorge Bustamante. The report contains an urgent appeal sent to the Italian Government on 11 January 2010, by the Special Rapporteur on the human rights of migrants and the Special Rapporteur on contemporary forms of racism, racial discrimination, xenophobia and related intolerance, Githu Muigai, concerning xenophobic violence targeting African migrant workers in the town of Rosarno, Calabria, at the beginning of January, 2010. The Government answered on 9 March 2010, drawing attention to the prompt intervention by the Police, as well as Public Prosecutor's Office, who immediately started investigations. The report also contains the letter of allegation sent to the Italian Government on 31 December 2009 by the Special Rapporteur on the human rights of migrants together with the Special Rapporteur on the right to education, Vernor Muñoz, in connection of some legislative developments in Italy, including law 15 July 2009, No. 94, on public security; law-decree 23 February 2009, No. 11; law 24 July 2008, No. 125 and law 31 July 2005, No. 155. The two Special Rapporteurs maintained that, based on the information received, these laws may have a negative impact on the rights of migrants, including: irregular migration status as an aggravating factor in sentencing; the offence of illegal entry and stay; expulsion of aliens; extension of administrative detention for migrants; restrictions on money transfers; modification of the Civil Code affecting irregular migrant's right to marry; restrictions in the right to birth registration. On 31 March 2010 the Government responded to such allegations affirming that these measures are meant to curb criminal behaviour of individuals and no provision at all is envisaged against any community, group or class nor is it inspired by forms of discrimination and xenophobia.

– 1 June 2010: *Report by the Special Rapporteur on the promotion and protection of the right to freedom of opinion and expression*, Frank La Rue. The report contains a letter of allegations sent to the Italian Government on 1 March 2010 together with the Special Rapporteur on the situation of human rights defenders, seeking information on the sentencing of Roberto Malini and Dario Picciau, Co-Chairmen of EveryOne Group, a non-governmental organisation working to promote the rights of persons belonging to minorities, including Roma, on the basis that "in complicity with each other, they cause the interruption, or at least disturbed a police operation aimed at identifying three foreign citizens". At the end of 2010, the Special Rapporteur regretted that no response had been received to this communication.

– 18 June 2010: *Report by the Special Rapporteur on extrajudicial, summary or arbitrary executions*, Philip Alston. The report contains the letter sent to the Italian Government on 12 February 2010 by the Rapporteur on arbitrary executions and the Rapporteur on torture, inquiring into the current state of progress of investigations relating to the death of seven persons while they were imprisoned (Stefano Cucchi, Aldo Bianzino, Federico Aldrovandi, Marcello Lonzi and three others who were not identified, detained respectively in the penitentiaries of Velletri, Imperia and Lecce), between 2003 and 2009. In the Rapporteurs' view, these deaths might be imputable to torture, negligence, the excessive use of force, or conditions of detention considered a threat to the life of the prisoners. By the end of 2010 the Italian Government had not yet provided any answer on the issue.

In addition to such reports, during 2010 Italy was mentioned in two communiqués issued by some of the Special Rapporteurs:

– *12 January 2010.* Special Rapporteurs Bustamante and Muigai issued a public communiqué condemning the violence broke out in the Calabrian town of Rosarno. In their opinion, violence, be it perpetrated by Italians or migrant workers, must be addressed in the most vigorous manner through the rule of law and human rights should always be protection, regardless of immigration status. According to the two Special Rapporteurs, the violence erupted in Rosarno is particularly worrying since it reveals serious and deep-rooted problems of racism against those migrant workers. The Rapporteurs therefore urged the Italian authorities to finding ways to improve the very poor living and working conditions of migrant workers, as well as to implement an immigration policy in full compliance with international human rights standards. While welcoming the initial steps taken by the authorities to inquire into the events, the Rapporteurs stressed the urgent need for the Italian authorities to strengthen anti-racist activities, to provide human rights education, to swiftly denounce hate speech and to prosecute the racist and violent actions perpetrated by some individuals.

– *13 July 2010.* Special Rapporteur on freedom of expression, Frank La Rue, urged the Italian Government to either abolish or revise bill No. 1415 on surveillance and eavesdropping for criminal investigations as, if adopted, it may undermine the enjoyment of the right to freedom of expression in Italy. According to the bill (Provisions on surveillance and eavesdropping), anyone who is not accredited as a professional journalist can be sentenced to imprisonment for up to four years for recording any communication or conversation without the consent of the person involved, and publicising such information. Such a severe penalty, according to La Rue, would seriously undermine the individuals' right to seek and impart information, in contravention of the International Covenant on Civil and Political Rights to which Italy is party. The specific reference here is to Covenant art. 19, stating that "everyone shall have the right to freedom of expression; this right shall include freedom to seek, receive and impart information and ideas of all kinds, regardless of frontiers, either orally, in writing or in print, in the form of art, or through any other media of his choice." La Rue also expressed concern regarding the introduction of a penalty for journalists and publishers who publish the contents of leaked wiretapped materials before the beginning of a trial. Such punishment included up to thirty days in jail and a penalty of up to 10,000 Euros for journalists and 450,000 for publishers. The Special Rapporteur therefore recommended the Government to refrain from adopting the draft law in its current form, and to engage in meaningful dialogue with all stakeholders, in particular journalists and media organisations. He also stood ready to provide technical assistance to ensure that the draft law aligns with international human rights standards on the right to freedom of expression.

During 2010, no Special Rapporteur visited Italy. The visits carried out in previous years, those agreed upon but not yet carried out, and those requested by Special Rapporteurs, appear in the following chart.

Visits carried out and reports	Agreed visits	Requested visits
Special Rapporteur on the independence of judges and lawyers (11-14/3/2002). Report: E/CN.4/2002/72/Add.3	Special Rapporteur on contemporary forms of slavery (agreed in December 2008, dates to be confirmed)	Special Rapporteur on the right to freedom of opinion and expression (requested in September 2009)
Special Rapporteur on the human rights of migrants (7-18 June 2004). Report: E/CN.4/2005/85/Add.3	Independent expert on extreme poverty and human rights (dates to agreed)	
Special Rapporteur on the right to freedom of opinion and expression (20-29 October 2004). Report: E/CN.4/2005/64/Add.1		
Special Rapporteur on contemporary forms of racism (9-13 October 2006). Report: A/HRC/4/19/Add.4		
Working Group on arbitrary detention (12-14 November 2008). Report: A/HRC/10/21/Add.5.		

III. High Commissioner for Human Rights (OHCHR)

The Office of the High Commissioner for Human Rights was created by the General Assembly in 1993 with resolution 48/141, following explicit recommendation formulated in the final Declaration of the World Conference on Human Rights held Vienna in June 1993. The Commissioner's task is to coordinate, strengthen and streamline the United Nations system in the field of human rights.

On 10 and 11 March 2010 the visit to Italy of the High Commissioner for Human Rights Navanethem Pillay represented the occasion to discuss a number of human rights issues representatives of the Government and other institutions. The focus was on immigration, forms of discrimination, the need to set up in a national human rights institution and the outcomes of the Universal Periodic Review. Discussions involved the strengthening of future cooperation and continued dialogue on issues of mutual concern. In particular, the High Commissioner met with the Minister of Justice, Alfano, the Minister of Interior, Maroni, the Undersecretary to the Presidency of the Council of Ministers, Letta, the Minister of Foreign Affairs, Frattini, the Chairman of the House of Representatives, Fini, and various representatives of non-governmental organisations. In addition, Ms Pillay gave a speech at the Lateran University, and was welcomed by the Senate Extraordinary Commission for the Protection and Promotion of Human Rights. Finally, she visited two Roma camps and an identification and expulsion centre (CIE) for migrants on the outskirts Rome.

Italy does not appear on the list voluntary contributors the Office of the High Commissioner for 2010; instead, it contributed approximately 270,000 dollars in 2009 and 2.4 million dollars in 2008 (source: Office of the High Commissioner for Human Rights).

IV. High Commissioner for Refugees (UNHCR)

The Office of the United Nations High Commissioner for Refugees was set up by the United Nations General Assembly on 14 December 1950 with resolution A/RES/428(V). The UNHCR is mandated to coordinate international action to protect refugees and to resolve refugee problems worldwide. Its main purpose is to safeguard the rights and well-being of refugees, ensuring that everyone can exercise the right to seek asylum and find refuge in another State, with the option to return home voluntarily, integrate locally or to resettle in a third Country. The UNHCR is also mandated to assist stateless people.

Since 1953 UNCHR has been present in Italy with its own office in Rome. The Italian Office in particular participates in the procedure for determining refugee status in the Country, carries out activity involving international protection, training and communication concerning refugees and asylum-seekers both Italy and in various crisis areas around the globe. It is also dedicated to raising awareness in public opinion and to soliciting funds from Governments, companies and private citizens. Since 2006 the Italian Office has worked as regional Office, responsible not only for Italy but also for Cyprus, Greece, Malta, Portugal, San Marino and the Holy See; and since 2009, for Albania as well.

According to data provided by UNCHR, as of January 2010, the persons under its mandate for protection in Italy numbered 60,123, including 54,965 refugees, 4,365 asylum-seekers and 793 stateless persons. During 2010, in addition to the ordinary activity of protection and assistance for these persons (registration of refugees, legal counselling, collection of personal data on asylum seekers, territorial distribution of protected persons for the enjoyment of protection and assistance, training for public and private operators), UNCHR activities included:

– *18 June 2010*: organisation of the Conference *HOME – A safe place to start over*, on World Refugee Day.

– *20 July 2010*: presentation of the outcome of the research paper *Il tempo delle rivolte*, carried out during the previous semester by the Observatory Carta (*Osservatorio Carta*) in Rome. The Observatory is a scientific structure created thanks to the Italian National Press Association (FNSI) and the Italian Journalist Association (*Ordine dei giornalisti*), in collaboration with UNCHR. It aims to monitor Italian information media dealing with immigration and asylum issues.

– *3 December 2010*: launching the campaign *UN'Impresa Speciale*, aiming to raise funds from small and medium-size enterprises in support of UNCHR activities.

– *29 December 2010*: visit to the former Embassy of Somalia in Rome which shelters from 120 to 140 Somali citizens, most of whom has been granted some form of international protection. At the end of the visit, the UNCHR staff expressed deep concern over the deteriorating conditions observed inside the building. The competent authorities – the Municipality of Rome (Social Policy Office) and Prefecture – were then asked to create a special advisory board seeking an urgent, sustainable solution capable of restoring dignity of the Somali refugees, and access to acceptable living conditions.

In 2010, Italy contributed to the UNCHR budget with approximately 11.5 million dollars, around 4 million dollars less than the year before. In 2008 Italy's contribution to UNHCR amounted to 44 million dollars.

V. Treaty Bodies

The core international human rights instruments adopted by the United Nations are: the Convention for the Elimination of All Forms of Racial Discrimination (ICERD, 1965); the Covenant on Civil and Political Rights (ICCPR, 1966); the Covenant on Economic, Social and Cultural Rights (ICESCR, 1966); the Convention on the Elimination of All Forms of Discrimination against Women (CEDAW, 1969); the Convention against Torture and other Cruel, Inhuman or Degrading Treatment of Punishment (CAT, 1984); the Convention on the Rights of the Child (CRC, 1989); the Convention on the Protection of the Rights of all Migrant Workers and Members of Their Families (ICRMW, 1990); the Convention on the Rights of Persons with Disabilities (CRPD, 2006); the Convention for the Protection of All Persons from Enforced Disappearance (CPED, 2006). Italy has ratified seven Conventions and their related Optional Protocols (see chart below) while it has signed the CPED (2007), the Optional Protocol to CAT (2003) and the Optional Protocol to ICESCR (2009). It has not yet signed the ICRMW.

Convention	Deposit date of ratification instrument	Declarations/Reservations	Recognition of specific Committee competencies
ICERD	05/01/1976	Yes (art. 4)	Individual communications (art. 14): Yes
ICESCR	15/09/1978	No	-
ICCPR	15/09/1978	Yes (art. 15.1 and 19.3)	Inter-State communications (art. 41): Yes
OP – 1	15/09/1978	Yes (art. 5.2)	-
OP – 2	14/02/1995	No	-
CEDAW	10/06/1985	Yes (general)	-
OP	22/09/2000	No	Inquiry procedure (art. 8 and 9): Yes
CAT	12/01/1989	No	Individual communications (art. 22): Yes Inter-State communications (art. 21): Yes Inquiry procedure (art. 20): Yes
CRC	05/09/1991	No	-
OP – AC	09/05/2002	Binding declaration in accordance with art. 3: 17 years old	-
OP – SC	09/05/2002	No	-
CRPD	15/05/2009	No	-
OP	15/05/2009	No	Inquiry procedure (art. 6 and 7): No

Legend: OP = Optional Protocol; OP – AC = Optional protocol to the Convention on the Rights of the Child on the involvement of children in armed conflict; OP – SC = Optional protocol to the Convention on the Rights of the Child on the sale of children, child prostitution and child pornography.

Each of these conventions has established a committee of experts to monitor the implementation of the treaty provisions by its States Parties, the so-called Treaty Bodies. Each committee is composed from 10 to 23 independent experts, selected according to their recognised experience in human rights issues. In 2010, two Italian experts were members, respectively, of two Committees: Luigi Citarella, Committee on Rights of the Child, and Alessio Bruni, Committee against Torture.

First of all, the Committees examine periodical reports submitted by contracting States (usually once every 4 or 5 years).on the status of implementation of the internationally agreed rights. The Committees also publish their interpretation of the content of human rights provisions (the so-called "General Comments").

Italy is subject to monitoring by the Committees, as indicated in the chart below.

Italy's cooperation with United Nations Treaty Bodies

Committee	**Total number of reports**	**Latest report**	**Latest concluding observations**	**Reporting status**
Committee on the Elimination of Racial Discrimination	15	March 2006	May 2008	XVI, XVII and XVIII combined report: to be submitted in February 2011
Committee on Economic, Social and Cultural Rights	4	April 2003	November 2004	V report: overdue, since June 2009
Human Rights Committee	5	March 2004	April 2006	VI report: overdue, since October 2009
Committee on the Elimination of Discrimination against Women	6	December 2009	-	VI report: submitted and awaiting for discussion (scheduled for July 2011)
Committee against Torture	4	May 2004	July 2007	VI report: to be submitted in June 2011
Committee on the Rights of the Child	4	January 2009	-	III and IV combined report: submitted and awaiting for discussion
OP – AC	2	January 2009	-	The information about the implementation of the Protocol are included in the III and IV combined report submitted in 2009
OP – SC	2	January 2009	-	The information about the implementation of the Protocol are included in the III and IV combined report submitted in 2009
Committee on the Rights of Persons with Disabilities	-	-	-	I report: to be submitted in June 2011

In the following sections, the most recent recommendations addressed to Italy by each Committee, according to time sequence, are presented. As regard the Committee for the Elimination of All Forms of Discrimination against Women and the Committee for the Rights of the Child, reference is made to the latest reports elaborated by the Italian Government, presented but not yet discussed.

A. Committee on Economic, Social and Cultural Rights

Latest report presented by Italy

Reporting round	Fourth periodic report
Scheduled date for the submission of the report	30/06/2001
Actual date of submission of the report	23/04/2003
Report	E/C.12/4/Add.13
List of issues	E/C.12/Q/ITA/2
Reply of the Government to list of issues	HR/CESCR/NONE/2004/3
Summary of the discussion	E/C.12/2004/SR.38; .39; .40
Concluding observations	E/C.12/1/Add.103
Date of discussion of the report	15 November 2004, during the 33rd session of the Committee (8-26 November 2004)

The Committee on Economic, Social and Cultural Rights examined the fourth Italian Periodic Report during its 33rd session (8-26 November 2004). It adopted the following conclusive observations and recommendations.

Among the *positive aspects*, the Committee underlined:

- the adoption of the law 30 May 2003, No. 1 modifying art. 51 of the Italian Constitution, which introduces the principle of equal opportunity for men and women in respect of access to political office;
- the adoption of law 228/8, of August 2003 on human trafficking;
- the establishment under the Ministry for Equal Opportunities of the National Office against Racial Discrimination (UNAR) in November 2004;
- extension to irregular migrants of the coverage by the National Sanitary Plan (2003-2005).

The Committee expressed *reasons for concern* and formulated *recommendations* in the following areas:

– *Judicial enforceability of economic, social and cultural rights.* The Committee is concerned that Italy still considers that some economic, social and cultural rights, including the right to adequate housing, are not justiciable: a fact reflected in the scarcity of court decisions in which the Covenant has been expressly invoked. Instead, the Committee maintains that Party States are under an obligation to give full effect to the Covenant provisions, in line its "General Comment 9" on the domestic application of the Covenant. Therefore, the Committee urges Italy to recognise the binding nature of the Covenant provisions and to provide appropriate training to the judiciary, prosecutors and other officials responsible for the implementation of the rights enshrined in the Covenant.

– *Human rights education.* The Committee encourages Italy to prepare school programmes for human rights education at all teaching levels and to foster public awareness campaigns regarding the international rights norms.

– *National independent institution.* The Committee urges Italy to create a national independent institution and to prepare an integrated human rights plan of action, pursuant to Part II, para. 71 of the 1993 Vienna Declaration and its Plan of Action.

– *Racism and discrimination.* Pursuant to legislative decree No. 286, 25 July 1998, the Committee urges Italy to establish, besides UNAR, monitoring bodies throughout the national territory and to provide them with adequate human and financial resources. Moreover, concerned over the increasing difficulty for disadvantaged or marginalised persons, immigrants and Roma in particular, in renting or acceding to public housing, the Committee urges the Government to make greater efforts in combating discriminatory or racist phenomena affecting access to adequate housing.

– *Migrants' rights.* In the Committee' view, law 189/2002, by introducing a strong link between the labour contract and the length of the residence permit, may hamper the enjoyment of rights enshrined in the Covenant by migrant workers and members of their families. The same goes for the excessive time taken by the authorities to renew the residence permit (particularly as regards freedom of movement and access to social services). Therefore, the Committee urges Italy to ratify as soon as possible, the International Convention on the Protection of the Rights of All Migrant Workers and Members of their Families and to undertake measures to expedite the process of renewing the residence permit. Moreover, in reaffirming its concluding observations of May 2000, the Committee asks Italy to build more permanent housing for Roma immigrants and to promote their integration.

– *Asylum.* Noting the persistent lack of organic legislation on asylum, the Committee urges Italy to start up a process for adopting a comprehensive legislation as soon as possible.

– *Right to work.* The Committee urges Italy to expedite the procedure for ratifying the International Labour Organisation Convention No. 174 of 1993 on the Prevention of Major Industrial Accidents and immediately implement Covenant art. 7, para. 2, on the principle of equal pay for work of equal value.

– *Struggle against poverty.* The Committee urges Italy to integrate economic, social and political rights into the national plan of action on poverty and social exclusion and to establish, nationally, the "minimum income" (*reddito minimo d'inserimento*) necessary to tackle social exclusion.

– *Women's rights.* The Committee urges Italy to intensify its efforts to combat domestic violence, in particular through information and education campaigns and to extend the network of childcare services.

B. Human Rights Committee (civil and political rights)

Latest report presented by Italy

Reporting round	Fifth periodic report
Scheduled date for the submission of the report	01/06/2002
Actual date of submission of the report	19/03/2004
Report	CCPR/C/ITA/2004/5
List of issues	CCPR/C/84/L/ITA
Reply of the Government to list of issues	List of Issues, by the Inter-ministerial Committee on Human Rights of the Ministry for Foreign Affairs (CIDU), CCPR/C/84/L/ITA
Summary of the discussion	CCPR/C/SR.2317; 2318
Concluding observations	CCPR/C/ITA/CO/5
Date of discussion of the report	20 and 21 October 2005, during the 85th session of the Committee (17 October-3 November 2005)

The Human Rights Committee examined the fifth Italian Periodic Report during its 85th session (17 October-3 November 2005). It adopted the following conclusive observations and recommendations:

Among the *positive aspects*, the Committee welcomed:

- Italy's position that the guarantees in the Covenant on Civil and Political Rights also apply to the act of Italian troops and police officers stationed abroad, whether in a context of peace or armed conflict;
- the amendments to art. 51 of the Constitution (constitutional law 1/2003) on equal opportunity between man and women in respect of access to political offices;

The Committee expressed *reasons for concern* and formulated *recommendations* in the following areas:

– *National Human Rights Institution* (art. 2). The Committee urges Italy to create an independent National Human Rights Institution in line with the "Paris Principles"; with that goal in mind, it should organise consultations with civil society.

– *Excessive use of force* (art. 7). While approving the start of criminal proceedings against police officials in relation to the demonstrations in Naples and Genoa of 2001, the Committee urges Italy to carry out prompt and impartial investigations wherever there is reasonable ground to believe that an act of ill-treatment has been committed by one of its agents. Particular consideration should be given to cases involving vulnerable groups such as Roma, foreigners and Italians of foreign origin.

– *Racial discrimination and intolerance* (art. 20). The Committee expresses concern over information it has received regarding hate speeches, including statements attributed to several politicians referring to foreign citizens – Arabs and Muslims – and persons of Roma ethnicity. The Committee warns that hate speeches must be outlawed and urges Italy to take urgent measures in order to bring those responsible to justice.

– *Preventive detention* (art. 9 and 14). Italy ought to reduce the length of detention awaiting trial: excessive duration may constitute violation of the right to be presumed innocent and the right to a fair trial. Preventive detention should be limited to cases of absolute necessity.

– *Treatment of asylum-seekers and non-citizens* (art. 7, 10, 13). The Committee calls attention to the absolute nature of the right of each person not to be expelled to a State where she or he may face serious threat of torture or mistreatment and to the harbouring State's consequent obligation to process each migrant's situation individually. Moreover, the Committee asks Italy to provide detailed information on readmission agreements concluded with third Countries, Libya in particular, and on guarantees contained in agreements, relative to the rights of deported persons.

– *Prison conditions* (art. 10). Italy should give priority to any intervention necessary for reducing overcrowding in prisons, including alternative measures to detention.

– *Independence of judges* (art. 14). Italy should guarantee the independence of the judiciary with respect to the executive power and ensure that the ongoing reform of the judiciary system do not jeopardise such independence.

-*Freedom of expression* (art. 19). In the Committee's view, Italy should ensure that defamation is no longer punishable by imprisonment.

Moreover, the Committee asks Italy to provide detailed information on the concrete results achieved through the implementation of law 3 May 2004, No. 112 (on television broadcasting and RAI), and law 20 July 2004, No. 215 (on conflict of interests).

– *Rights of persons of Roma origin* (art. 12, 26 and 27). The Committee urges Italy, in consultation with representatives of Roma communities, to put an end to the camp-based residential segregation policy against Roma and to adopt specific programmes fostering Roma full participation in mainstream society at all level. The Committee is also worried over the fact that the Roma are not protected as a minority, on the basis that they do not have a connection with a specific territory. In this regard, the Committee recalls its General Comment 23 (1994) on Covenant art. 27, stating that the absence of connection with a specific territory does not bar a community from qualifying as a minority.

Finally, the Committee appreciates Italy's announcement of its intention to withdraw some of the reservations to the Covenants[1]; however, the Committee deplores that the withdrawal of reservation to art. 14, para. 3[2]; 15, para. 1[3]; and 19, para. 3[4], is not part of the process.

---

1 In December 2005 Italy notified the United Nations Secretary General of its decision to withdraw the reservations concerning art. 9, para. 4 and art. 14, para. 5.

2 Art. 14, para. 3 declares that "In the determination of any criminal charge against him, everyone shall be entitled to the following minimum guarantees: […] d) to be tried in his presence, and to defend himself in position or through legal assistance his own choosing; to be informed, if he does not have legal assistance, of this right; and to have legal assistance assigned to him, in any case where the interests of justice so require, and without payment by him in any such case if he does not have sufficient means to pay for it; […]" At the moment of ratification, the Italian Government stated that "The provisions of letter d) of paragraph 3, art. 14 are interpreted as being compatible with the existing Italian legislation regarding the presence of the accused at the trial; the legislation defines the cases in which self-defence is permitted and those demanding the assistance of defending counsel."

3 "With reference to art. 15, paragraph 1, last sentence 'if, subsequent to the commission of the offense, provisions is made by law for the imposition of a lighter penalty, the offender shall benefit thereby', the Italian Republic deems this provision to apply exclusively to cases in progress. Consequently, a person who has already been convicted by a final decision shall not benefit from any provision made by law, subsequent to that decision, for the imposition of a lighter penalty."

4 Art. 19, para. 3 declares that "The exercise of the rights provided for in paragraph 2 of this article carries with it special duties and responsibilities. It may therefore be subject to certain restrictions, but these shall only be such as provided by law and are necessary: a) for respect of the rights or reputations of others; b) for the protection of national security or of public order, or of public health or morals". At the moment of ratification, the Italian Government declared that "The provisions of art. 19, paragraph 3, are interpreted as being compatible with the existing licensing system for national radio and television and with the restrictions laid down by the law for local radio and television companies and for stations relaying foreign programmes."

C. Committee against Torture

Latest report presented by Italy

Reporting round	Fourth periodic report
Scheduled date for the submission of the report	10/02/2002
Actual date of submission of the report	04/05/2004
Report	CAT/C/67/Add.3
List of issues	CAT/C/ITA/Q/4/Rev.1
Reply of the Government to list of issues	CAT/C/ITA/Q/4/Rev.1/Add.1
Summary of the discussion	CAT/C/SR.762; .765; .777; .778
Concluding observations	CAT/C/ITA/CO/4
Date of discussion of the report	4 and 7 May 2007, during the 38th session of the Committee (30 April-18 May 2007)

The Committee examined the fourth Italian Periodic Report during its 38th session (30 April-18 May 2007). It adopted the following conclusive observations and recommendations:

– *Definition and introduction of the crime of torture.* Throughout the years, the Committee has repeatedly urged Italy to introduce the crime of torture into its domestic law, adopting a definition of "torture" that covers all the elements identified by art. 1 of the Convention;

– *Preventive detention.* Italy should adopt urgent measures to reduce the length of preventive detention and limit its use where strictly necessary;

– *National Human Rights Institution.* Like the other treaty bodies, the Committee against Torture urges Italy to establish an independent National Human Rights Institutions;

– *Treatment of asylum-seekers and non-citizens.* The Committee urges Italy to ensure that detention of asylum-seekers and non-citizens is used only in exceptional circumstances or as a measure of last resort, and only for the shortest possible time. The Committee also urges Italy to adopt a comprehensive legislation on political asylum, and to guarantee that all asylum-seekers have access to a fair and prompt asylum procedure. Finally, in expressing particular concerns over forcible and collective expulsion to Libya (*refoulement*) of persons not of Libyan origin, the Committee asks Italy to fully comply with art. 3 of the Convention against Torture, setting forth the absolute nature of the right of any person not to be subject to torture, inhuman or degrading treatment or punishment in the Country where he/she would be returned to;

– *Universal jurisdiction.* Pursuant to art. 5 of the Convention, Italy should carry out prompt, impartial and effective investigation into all allegations of torture and ill-treatment committed by law enforcement officials and Italian troops, in Italy or abroad; try perpetrators and impose appropriate sentences on those convicted;

– *Conditions of detention.* Italy should alleviate the overcrowding of penitentiary institutions, possibly by applying alternative measures to detention, establishing additional prison facilities, and appointing additional prison staff, especially in the educational and health sectors. Moreover, Italy should take effective measure to further improve living conditions in the immigration centres. An independent body for the monitoring of these centres should be set up;

– *Excessive use of force.* In expressing deep concern over the number of allegations of mistreatment by law enforcement officials, the limited number of investigations carried out by Italy into such cases and the very limited number of convictions at the conclusion of such investigations, the Committee urges Italy to send to all levels of the police force hierarchy and to prison staff a clear and unambiguous message that torture, violence and mistreatment are unacceptable. Italy is then asked to consider the possibility of introducing a code of conduct for such operators and to ensure that prompt, impartial and effective investigation into all allegations of torture and ill-treatment are carried out by an independent body. In the event of *prima facie* case of torture, the suspect should as a rule be suspended or reassigned for the duration of the inquiry, especially if there is a risk that he or she might impede the investigation. Victims of torture and ill-treatment should be able to accede to compensation, redress and rehabilitation programmes;

– *Vulnerable groups.* Italy should intensify its efforts to combat any form of racial discrimination, xenophobia and related intolerance, as well as any form of ill-treatment of vulnerable groups, including Roma, foreigners and Italians of foreign origin.

D. Committee for the Elimination of Racial Discrimination

Latest report presented by Italy

Reporting round	XIV and XV periodic report (combined)
Scheduled date for the submission of the report	04/02/2001
Actual date of submission of the report	15/03/2006
Report	CERD/C/ITA/15
List of issues	Unclassified document
Reply of the Government to list of issues	List of Issues, by the Inter-ministerial Committee on Human Rights of the Ministry for Foreign Affairs
Summary of the discussion	CERD/C/SR 1851; .1852; .1867 e.1868
Concluding observations	CERD/C/ITA/CO/15

Date of discussion of the report	20 and 21 February 2008, during the 72nd session of the Committee (18 February-7 March 2008)

The Committee on the Elimination of Racial Discrimination examined the joint Periodic Report of Italy – XIV and XV – during its 72nd session, 18 February-7 March 2008.

Among the *positive aspects*, the Committee welcomed:

- the adoption of legislative decree 9 July 2003, No. 215, which converted into law the European Council directive 2000/43/CE on the principle of equal treatment of all people regardless of their race and ethnic origin;
- the creation of the National Office against Racial Discrimination (UNAR) under the Ministry of Equal Opportunities;
- institution of the figure of language mediator in support, in particular, of foreign prisoners;
- the adoption of law-decree 17 August 2005, No. 162, providing for new measures aimed at combating act of racially motivated violence during sports events, including the setting up of a national observatory on sports events.

Reasons for concern and *recommendations* were formulated in the following areas:

– *Rights of persons of Roma and Sinti origin* (Convention art. 2, 3, 5 and 7). In recalling its General Comment 27 on discrimination against Roma, the Committee recommends Italy to adopt and implement a comprehensive national policy and legislation regarding Roma and Sinti; to put an end to the residential segregation of these communities in isolated nomad camps, and to involve the Roma communities and associations in housing project construction, rehabilitation and maintenance; to act firmly against local discriminatory measures; to prevent the use of illegal force by law enforcement officials against persons of Roma origin and to punish any racially motivated offence against Roma, Sinti, or foreigners in general; to promote the inclusion of Roma children in schools, while addressing the causes of dropout rates, including early marriage, which affect girls in particular. In confronting such issues the active collaboration from Roma parents, teachers and associations in the local communities is needed. Italy should encourage the media to oppose negative stereotypes and prejudices affecting Roma communities, and promptly adopt the code of conduct of journalists (the so-called "Charter of Rome"), drafted by the Italian Journalist Association (*Ordine dei giornalisti*) and the Italian National Press Association (FNSI) in collaboration with UNAR and the United Nations High Commissioner for Refugees.

– *National Human Rights Institution* (art. 2). This Committee, as well, recommends its establishment.

– *Hate speech* (art. 4). Expressing concern over information received regarding hate speech, including statements attributed to politicians targeting foreign nationals and Roma, the Committee urges Italy to prevent and effectively punish such phenomena as well as any recourse to racist propaganda for political purposes.

– *Rights of non-citizens* (art. 5). Recalling its General Comment 30 on non-citizens, the Committee urges Italy to take measures to eliminate discrimination in working conditions, and to prevent and redress the some serious problems commonly faced by non-citizens workers, including debt bondage, passport retention, illegal confinement and physical assault. Italy must improve living conditions in receptions and identification centres for migrants and asylum-seekers; it must monitor such centres and, in any case, ensure that non-citizens are not returned or removed to a Country where they may be subject to serious human rights violations. Italy is then strongly invited to ratify the international Convention on Migrant Workers.

Finally, the Committee urges Italy to take into consideration the relevant parts of the Durban Declaration and Programme of Action, adopted in September 2001 by the World Conference against Racism, Racial Discrimination, Xenophobia and Related Intolerance (A/CONF.189/12).

E. Committee for the Elimination of Discrimination against Women

Latest report presented by Italy

Reporting round	Sixth periodic report
Scheduled date for the submission of the report	10/07/2006
Actual date of submission of the report	16/12/2009
Report	CEDAW/C/ITA/6
List of issues	CEDAW/C/ITA/Q/6
Scheduled date for the discussion of the report	July 2011, during the 49th session of the Committee

In its latest report, Italy states that prohibition of discrimination on the ground of sex is one of the pillars of its legal system, as authoritatively stated more than once the Constitutional Court. The *principle of non-discrimination* is recognised in art. 3 of the Italian Constitution and in other relevant constitutional provisions, including art. 35 (protection of labour), art. 37 and art. 51 (equal opportunity between men and women in acceding to public office). The Italian Government's actions in this sphere are promoted and coordinated by the Minister and Department for Equal Opportunities.

On the legislative level, legislative decree No. 198 of 11 April 2006 introduces into the Italian legal system the so-called *Code of equal opportunities between men and women*, concerning measures against any gender-based discrimination which have the effect of impairing or preventing the recognition, enjoyment or exercise of human rights and fundamental freedoms in the political, economic, social, cultural or civil or any other field (art. 1). The following legal measures were reported as well:

- Law 4 April 2001, No. 154 (Measures against violence within the household), introducing the possibility of forced expulsion of the violent spouse from the family home;
- Law 9 January 2006, No. 7 (Provisions on the prevention and prohibition of the practice of female genital mutilation). The law introduces into the criminal code the specific offense of female genital mutilation, punishable even if committed outside Italy, and regardless of the victim's consent; moreover, the legislation promotes and finances rehabilitation programmes for victims and activities aimed to prevent, inform and train;
- art. 19, para. 3 of Legislative decree No. 223, 4 July 2006, amended by law 4 August 2006 No. 248. It institutes, under the Presidency of the Council of Ministers, the Fund for policies on rights and equal opportunities;
- Legislative decree No. 196, 6 November 2007 (which converted European Council directive 2004/113/CE on the principle of equal treatment for men and women as regards access to goods and services and their supply).

In order to combat any form of *violence against women*, the Ministry for Equal Opportunities prepared two bills (No. 1440 and 1424, approved by the Council of Ministers on 18 June 2008). They first merged into decree-law No. 11, 23 February 2009 and then converted into law 23 April 2009, No. 38, entitled "Urgent measures concerning public security and the struggle against sexual violence, as well as acts of persecution". Some provisions concern stalking (repeated acts of molestation and persistent harassment arousing, in the person offended, fear for their safety, and for the safety of persons tied to them by bonds of kinship or affection, causing them to modify their life style to an important degree). These provisions foresee introducing into the penal code, the crime of "persecutory acts" (art. 612-*bis*), as well as a specific cautionary measure; they foresee instruments facilitating investigation (in particular, telephone interception). The same law, moreover, strengthens the criminal protection against sexual violence, introducing aggravating circumstances, imposing increased punishment in the event of recidivism, and introducing mechanisms to speed up the proceedings.

Moreover, in 2006, the Department for Equal Opportunities launched the "Arianna Project" in support of women who are victims of family or non-family violence, and stalking; the Project aims to create a National Anti-Violence Network, supported by a number of public utility (No. 1522). Finally, a ministerial decree of 23 January 2008 instituted a National Observatory against Sexual and Gender – based Violence aiming to: monitor the phenomenon and the public administration's measures in combating it; raise public awareness of the issue; provide assistance to local authorities, anti-violence centres and other actors operating in this field.

As regards the phenomenon of *prostitution*, at the end of 2008, the Council of Ministers approved bill 1079 (Measures against the prostitution), on proposal by the Ministers for Equal Opportunities, Interior and Justice. The law aims to introduce the crime of "prostitution in public places or in places open to the public". In addition, the following monitoring instruments are now operating to oppose human trafficking and other grave forms of exploitation: Inter-Ministerial Commission for the Support of Victims of Trafficking, Violence and Exploitation (under the Department for Equal Opportunities); Coordinating Committee of the Government Actions against Human Trafficking (instituted by ministerial decree on 21 March 2007); Observatory on Human Trafficking (instituted by the Ministry for Equal Opportunities on 21 March 2007).

Finally, as regards *women's participation in public life*, the report acknowledges that Italy still presents evident marginalisation of women in political and decision-making processes; in order to invert this tendency, the Government has promoted various educational and awareness campaigns, including the projects *Women, politics and institutions – Educational Patterns for Gender Equality* (2005-2007); and *L'Europe pour les femmes*.

Beside the Italian national report, the Committee also received a parallel report prepared by *Lavori in corsa – 30 anni CEDAW* ("Work on the Run: 30 years of CEDAW"), an Italian network of associations and individual women committed to research and training in women's rights and gender analyses. This "shadow-report" outlined several matters of concern not brought out in the national report, with particular reference to the following issues: absence of public consultation and Parliamentary discussion concerning the preparation of the report; lack of a gender perspective in the overall governmental action, in gender mainstreaming and budgeting; persistence of gender prejudices and stereotypes; marginalisation of women on the political and decision-making level;

absence of adequate policies for poor and unemployed women; lack of adequate guarantees for free access to health services, including those connected to sexual and reproductive health; lack of adequate instruments of prevention, protection or compensation for the victims of violence.

F. Committee on the Rights of the Child

Latest report presented by Italy

Reporting round	Third and fourth periodic report (combined)
Scheduled date for the submission of the report	04/10/2008
Actual date of the submission of the report	30/01/2009
Report	CRC/C/ITA/4

In its latest report, Italy presented the legislative and administrative measures enacted in the Country during the last years for the implementation of the Convention and its two Optional Protocols.

– *Resources for children.* Expenditure for children and adolescents can be subdivided into three main areas: social assistance, health care, and education and training. The latest available data for these three sectors date back to 2005, when the overall expenditure amounted to around 15 billion euros, or 4.4% of overall social expenditure and 1.1% of Gross domestic product (GDP) (source: EUROSTAT, *Social protection in the European Union*, No. 46/2008, Statistics in Focus, Brussels 2008).

Monitoring and coordinating bodies. The most important institutions having generated actions for the knowledge, coordination, promotion and protection of children's rights are: the Italian National Observatory on Children and Adolescents; the National Observatory on the Family; the Inter-Ministerial Coordinating Committee for Government Action against Trafficking in Human Beings, (coordinated by the Department for Equal Opportunities); the Inter-Ministerial Committee for the Coordination of the Fight against Paedophilia (CICLOPE); Observatory on Prostitution and the Crimes connected to it (Ministry of Interior); Observatory on Youth Problems Connected to Addictions (established at the Ministry of Social Solidarity); National Observatory for the Integration of Foreign Pupils; Observatory for the Fight against Paedophilia and Child Pornography; Coordination Table between Government and social partners for the fight against the exploitation of child labour; regional and provincial Observatories on bullying (upon initiative of the local education authorities). On 1 August 2008, moreover, on proposal by the Minister for Equal Opportunities, the Council of Ministers approved a bill introducing the National Commissioner for Children and Adolescents.

National Plan of Action. In 2000, Italy approved two national plans of action guaranteeing the rights and development of minor-age individuals, respectively for 2000-2002 and 2002-2004.

Best interest of the child (Convention art. 3). Explicit reference to the best interest of the child appears not only in the national plans of action, but also in national legislation, in particular in the provisions regarding separated parents and shared custody (law 8 February 2006, No. 54, establishing that the child has the right to maintain a balanced and continuous relationship with each of the separated parents, and to receive care, education and training from both), and with respect to the hospitality of people seeking asylum (legislative decree 30 May 2005, No. 140, implementing directive 2003/9/CE).

As to the case law, the principle of the best interest of the child has been assigned particular attention by the Constitutional Court, especially in cases of adoption (provision 14 June 2001, No. 192), with respect to criminal matters (judgment 149/2003), and in relation to national regulatory measures to support motherhood (judgment 385/2005: with this decision the Court reiterates that "the institutions established to protect motherhood, in particular maternity leaves and days offs, no longer have, as it was in the past, the main and exclusive objective to protect the woman", but are designed to the protection of the child's best interest).

Rights of the child to preserve their identity. This right touches on aspects of individual identity, such as nationality, name, and family relationships. It finds full recognition in art. 30 of the Italian Constitution, and was reiterated on the occasion of the reform while occurred with law 149/2001 on adoption.

Privacy protection and representation of children in the media. To tackle these issues, Italy has followed a guidance for co-regulation aimed at introducing specific mechanisms to give a sense of responsibility and self-regulation to communication professionals and as well as specific committees of vigilance and protection. At the beginning of 2000 there existed 13 self-regulatory codes. With the aim to rationalise the matter, in 2007 the Ministry of Communications prepared a draft of a single *code on minors and the media*, while the presidential decree No. 72 of 14 May 2007 transformed the TV and Children Committee into the Committee for the application for the Media and Children Code of self-regulation.

Roma, Sinti and Travellers children and adolescents. The Italian national report discusses a civil protection order signed on 30 May 2008. The order, envisaging an imminent and progressive census of Italian

Roma, Rumanians Roma, non-EU Roma and non-EU citizens belonging to other nations, had the objective, among other, to protect children in order to remove them from their illegal alien status and from degrading conditions. Italy asserts that the census was carried out according to guidelines issued by the Ministry of Interior on 22 July 2008, in full compliance with the fundamental rights and laws which safeguard personal dignity and privacy, and in compliance with the EU directives and the Italian law in force (public safety laws Consolidation Act). In particular, for people over 14 years of age, by taking fingerprints in cases where identity documents are missing and when there are no other means of identification. For children aged 6 to 14, finger prints may be obtained only for the purpose of issuing a residence permit when requested by those who have parental authority over them (art. 4-*ter* of EU regulation No. 380 of 18 April 2008 establishes that it is compulsory to obtain fingerprints from the age of 6 years), or, in case of necessity, contacting the competent Public Prosecutor at the Juvenile Court through the Investigative Police. Below this age group, fingerprints can be obtained, upon agreement between the Public Prosecutor and the Juvenile Court, only in exceptional cases of children who are in a state of neglect or who may have been the victims of a crime. The European Commission has considered such measures to be non-discriminatory and in line with the European legal system.

Policies for the reconciliation of work and family life. Law 8 March 2000, No. 53 as implemented by legislative decree 26 March 2001, No. 151 (Consolidated act on legal provisions on the protection and support of motherhood and fatherhood), envisaged financial contributions in favour of companies that plan actions of positive flexibility, and independent workers or entrepreneurs who wish to develop projects to reconcile family life and the work.

Separated parents. As regard the preservation of the relations between parents and children, the above-mentioned law 54/2006 intervened on the issue of shared custody, reaffirming the principle according to which children have the right to maintain a continuing and balanced relation with both parents evening case of disintegration of the family unity.

Separation of the child from his family due to parents detention. Italian legislation establishes a series of actions in support of parental relationships, especially when detention involves the mother. In this perspective, Italian legislation has introduced home detention for pregnant women and mothers (but also fathers) of children less than 10 years old (art. 4, law 165/1998). Law 40/2001 extends the application of the law to individuals with sentences of over four years, in addition with the opportunity of a daily release from the prison in order to care for their children. When such rules are not applicable, the children of women prisoners may remain with their mother until the age of three.

Violence, abuse and neglect. Italy has ratified the following international acts: ILO Convention No. 182 on the Prohibitions and Immediate Actions for the Elimination of the Worst Forms of Child Labour; the European Convention on the Exercise of Children's Rights; the United Nations Convention against Transnational Organised Crime and relative Protocols; the Council of Europe Convention on Cybercrime.

Sex crimes. Law 6 February, 2006 No. 38 (Provisions concerning the fight against the sexual exploitation of children and child pornography, also via Internet) introduces several new crimes concerning pornography on the Internet, incorporating into the Italian legal system several EU provisions. The Italian report also mentions law 9 January 2006, No. 7 (Provisions concerning the prevention and prohibition of the practice of female genital mutilation). Finally, thanks to the periodic report to Parliament prepared by the Presidency of the Council of Ministers on the implementation of law 3 August 1998, No. 269 (Provisions against the exploitation of prostitution, pornography, and sexual tourism to the detriment of minors: the new forms of slavery), a comprehensive monitoring on activities against sexual exploitation of children is yearly undertaken.

Educational and informational health campaigns. From 2000 to 2007, the Ministry of Health carried out various educational and informational campaigns regarding AIDS, vaccinations, nourishment, smoking and life styles. Of particular note, the *9th Informational preventive campaign against AIDS*; the *Special campaign on vaccination against measles-mumps-rubella*; the *Campaign on children's health and prevention of domestic accidents among the young*; the *Campaign for correct nourishment and promotion of physical activity*.

Measures against poverty. In Italy, strategies for combating poverty and social exclusion affecting children are included in the national plan of action in favour of children and adolescents, and the national plan of action against poverty and social exclusion.

Foreign children at school. Between 1997 and 2007, the presence of foreigners in Italian schools went from 0.8% to 5.6% of all students. Specific training programmes have been set up for teachers and administrators in schools having a high percentage of foreign students, focusing on the teaching of Italian as a second language and placing greater value on students' mother tongues. Among instruments aiming to promote the integration of foreign students, the Office for the integration of foreign students, instituted in June 2004 at the Central Office of student services at the Ministry of Public Education. In addition, the National Observatory on the integration of foreign students was set up in December 2006.

Children with disabilities. 2007 marked the 30th anniversary of law 517 of 4 August 1977 which still at the forefront in the scholastic integration of students with disabilities. Governmental actions in favour of students with disabilities extend over two different fronts: increase the opportunities for autonomous learning, and spread a culture of inclusion in school. These goals are pursued through several projects of national scope, including the project *Disabilities and the new technologies*, begun in 2005; the project *I care*, begun in 2007; and the project *E-inclusion.* Since 1996, moreover, a National Observatory for the integration of the disabled has been in operation at the Ministry of Education, Universities and Research.

Unaccompanied foreign minors seeking asylum. In this domain, a number of provisions implementing European Union directives were approved between 2000 and 2007. Of particular note, the presidential decree 303/2004, containing the regulations governing the procedure for the recognition of refugee status; legislative decree 140/2005 on the implementation of directive 2003/9/CE (on minimum regulations concerning the reception of asylum-seekers in Member States); legislative decree 251/2007, on the implementation directive 2004/83/CE (establishing that children who have refugee of complementary protection must have the same access to any type or level of schooling as an Italian citizen); legislative decree 25/2008 on the implementation of directive 2005/85/CE (providing for a series of guarantees for unaccompanied minors, including the fact that a person who has expressed the intention of applying for international protection be provided with the necessary assistance to present the application, such as the assistance of a legal guardian at every stage of the procedure).

Children victims of economic exploitation. The Government report states that law 296/2006 raises the minimum age for employment from 15 to 16 years (as it does for compulsory education). In addition, 2006 saw the reintroduction of negotiations between the Government, trade unions and employers to combat exploitation of child labour; the negotiations had first started in 1998. In 2006 the participants achieved a preliminary re-formulation of the "Charter of Commitments" aiming to promote the rights of children and adolescents, and to eliminate the exploitation of child labour.

Other forms of exploitation. New instruments combating the exploitation of minors in begging activities were offered by law 11 August 2003, No. 228 (Measures against human trafficking), which amended the crime prescribed by art. 600 of the criminal code, now defined as "the placing or holding of persons in slavery or servitude".

The Italian report also contains sections regarding the two Optional Protocols to the Convention on the Rights of the Child.

Optional Protocol on the sale of children, child prostitution and child pornography.

– *Monitoring and coordinating bodies.* The aforementioned law 6 February 2006, No. 38, introduced two institutions: the Observatory for the Fight against Paedophilia and Child Pornography, under the Presidency of the Council of Ministers, and the Italian National Centre for Combating Child Pornography on the Internet, under the Ministry of Foreign Affairs, Postal and Communications Police Service. In addition, the year 2007 saw the institution of an Observatory on Prostitution and Related Crimes (ministerial decree 18 January 2007), set up within the Ministry of Interior, an instrument of support for central administrations' actions preventing and opposing such phenomena, which involve both adults and children. Finally, between 2007 and 2008, the Department for Equal Opportunities hosted the institution of the Coordinating Committee for Government Actions against Trafficking in Human Beings, the Inter-Ministerial Commission for the Support of Victims Trafficking, Violence and serious Exploitation, and the Observatory on Trafficking in Human Beings.

– *Prohibition against the sale of children, child prostitution and pornography representing children.* On the legislative level, the central point of reference in the fight against sexual exploitation of children and child pornography is law 38/2006. Moreover, with law 18 March 2008, No. 48, Italy adopted the Council of Europe Convention on Cybercrime, an important international instrument against such criminal activity. Finally, the Italian legislation punishes the crime of "Tourism initiatives aimed at exploiting child prostitution" (art. 600-*quinquies* of the criminal code), committed by "anyone organising or promoting trips aimed at enjoying prostitution activities involving children or which in any case, encompass such activity".

International activity. At the European and international level, the central operative services of the Central Anti-Crime Department of the State Police carries out activities of prevention, victims support and repression of crimes connected with sexual exploitation of children and child pornography, in collaboration with other States and international investigative bodies.

Optional Protocol on the involvement of children in armed conflict.

Law 2/2000 set a minimum limit of 18 years for voluntary enlistment in the military conscription service (later interrupted in Italy since 1 January 2005). Current legislation – *de facto* – does not allow direct employment of minors in armed conflict.

The recruitment of children under the age of 15 years into the armed forces constitutes a war crime pursuant to art. 8 of the Statute of International Criminal Court, ratified by Italy with law 232/1999. Italian legislation excludes this hypothesis: the minimal age to enlist volunteers in the Armed Forces is 18 (art. 4 law 226/2004) and to enlist in initial careers in the *Carabinieri* is above 18 because only Armed Force volunteers can join (art. 16 law 226/2004).

The minimum age to take part in competitions to become warrant officers in the Armed Forces and *Carabinieri* is, respectively, 17 and 18 (art. 11 legislative decree. 196/1995, art. 14 legislative decree 198/1995, and art. 1 ministerial decree 188/1999); while the minimum age to take part in competitions to become officers of the Armed Forces is 17, the appointment cannot be made before the age of 18 (art. 3 and 4, legislative decree 490/1997).

If the recruitment of a minor has been performed by armed groups pursuing terrorist aims, art. 270-*bis*, 270-*quater* and 270-*quinquies* of the criminal code apply. These provisions provide for penalties up to 15 years' imprisonment for anyone creating, promoting, organising, heading or financing associations which pursue terrorist aims.

VI. Specialised United Nations Agencies

A. International Labour Organisation (ILO)

The International Labour Organisation is the international organisation responsible for drawing up and overseeing international labour standards. Instituted in 1919 with the Treaty of Versailles, the ILO was the first specialised agency of the United Nations in 1946 (see the Agreement between the United Nations and the International Labour Organisation, New York, 30 May 1946).

Since its institution, the ILO has adopted 188 conventions covering a vast array of issues: freedom to associate and right to collective bargaining; equal opportunities and treatment; abolition of forced labour and child labour; promotion of employment; professional training; social security; working conditions; labour administration and inspection; prevention of work accidents; protection of maternity care; protection of migrants and specific categories of workers such as maritime labourers, medical assistants, plantation labourers. Among the conventions, ILO considers 8 to be "fundamental": No. 29, on forced labour (1930); No. 87, on freedom of association and the right to organise (1948); No. 98, on the right to organise and collective bargaining (1949); No. 100, on equal remuneration for men and women workers for work of equal value (1951); No. 105, on the abolition of forced labour (1957); No. 111, on discrimination in respect of employment and occupation (1958); No. 138, on the minimum age for admission to employment

(1973); No. 182, on the prohibition and immediate action for the elimination of the worst forms of child labour (1999).

Italy has been a member of ILO since 1919 and, indeed, is among the founding members; in 1937 it withdrew from the Organisation, and then once again became a member, a permanent one, in 1945. ILO has an office in Italy in Rome since 1920 and an international training centre, set up in Turin in 1965. Italy has ratified 111 conventions adopted by the ILO, including all the fundamental ones. Among these, the following conventions are particularly significant for human rights:

Convention	**Date of deposit of instrument of ratification**
1 – Hours of Work (Industry), 1919	06/10/1924
2 – Unemployment, 1919	10/04/1923
3 – Maternity Protection, 1919	22/10/1952
4 – Night Work (Women), 1919	10/04/1923
6 – Night Work of Young Persons (Industry), 1919	10/04/1923
11 – Right of Association (Agriculture), 1921	08/09/1924
12 – Workmen's Compensation (Agriculture), 1921	01/09/1930
14 – Weekly Rest (Industry), 1921	08/09/1924
18 – Workmen's Compensation (Occupational Diseases), 1925	22/01/1934
19 – Equality of Treatment (Accident Compensation), 1925	15/03/1928
29 – Forced Labour, 1930	18/06/1934
42 – Workmen's Compensation (Occupational Diseases) (Revised), 1934	22/10/1952
44 – Unemployment Provision, 1934	22/10/1952
45 – Underground Work (Women), 1935	22/10/1952
48 – Maintenance of Migrants' Pension Rights, 1935	22/10/1952
52 – Holidays with Pay, 1936	22/10/1952
79 – Night Work of Young Persons (Non-Industrial Occupations), 1946	22/10/1952
81 – Labour Inspection Convention, 1947	22/10/1952
87 – Freedom of Association and Protection of the Right to Organise, 1948	13/05/1958
89 – Night Work (Women) (Revised), 1948	22/10/1952
90 – Night Work of Young Persons (Industry) (Revised), 1948	22/10/1952
95 – Protection of Wages, 1949	22/10/1952

Convention	Date of deposit of instrument of ratification
97 – Migration for Employment (Revised), 1949	22/10/1952
98 – Right to Organise and Collective Bargaining, 1949	13/05/1958
100 – Equal Remuneration Convention, 1951	08/06/1956
102 – Social Security (Minimum Standards), 1952	08/06/1956
103 – Maternity Protection (Revised), 1952	05/05/1971
105 – Abolition of Forced Labour, 1957	15/03/1968
106 – Weekly Rest (Commerce and Offices), 1957	12/08/1963
111 – Discrimination (Employment and Occupation), 1958	12/08/1963
115 – Radiation Protection, 1960	05/05/1971
117 – Social Policy (Basic Aims and Standards), 1962	27/12/1966
118 – Equality of Treatment (Social Security), 1962	05/05/1967
122 – Employment Policy, 1964	05/05/1971
135 – Workers' Representatives, 1971	23/06/1981
138 – Minimum Age, 1973	28/07/1981
143 – Migrant Workers (Supplementary Provisions), 1975	23/06/1981
148 – Working Environment (Air Pollution, Noise and Vibration), 1977	28/02/1985
159 – Vocational Rehabilitation and Employment (Disabled Persons), 1983	07/06/2000
182 – Worst Forms of Child Labour, 1999	07/06/2000
183 – Maternity Protection, 2000	07/02/2001

In order to monitor the application of conventions ratified by States, in 1926 the ILO created the Committee of Experts on the Application of Conventions and Recommendations, a body made up of 20 eminent specialists in social and legal areas, independent of Governments and appointed individually. The monitoring mechanism requires every Member State to present a periodical report on measures adopted, in law and in practice, in the application of each ratified convention. At the same time, it must send a copy of the report to employers' and workers' organisations, who have the right to provide further information. The Government reports are first examined by the Committee of Experts, which may adopt two different types of measures: *observations* and *direct requests*. The observations contain comments on fundamental issues emerging with the application of a particular convention by a State, and are published in the Committee's annual report. The direct requests, instead, refer to issues of an essentially technical nature, or else aim to request information; they are not published in the annual report, but are directly transmitted to the Governments involved.

After the examination, the Committee submits to the International Labour Conference – the most highly representative body of the ILO, with representation from all ILO Member States – an annual report containing its observations and recommendations. The report is closely examined by the Conference Committee of the Conference on the Application of Standards, a tripartite body composed of representatives from the Government, employers and workers. The Committee selects a certain number of observations from the report for in-depth discussion. The Governments called upon in such observations are urged to present their own comments before the Conference Committee. In many cases, the Conference Committee adopts conclusions urging States to take specific measures in order to remedy a problem, to ask the ILO to carry out missions in their territory, or to request technical assistance.

In 2010, the Committee of Experts on the Application of Conventions and Recommendations addressed 16 direct requests and four observations to Italy.

Through the *direct requests*, the Committee wished to obtain more complete information on legal, administrative and political instruments relative to the application of the following conventions: No. 9 – Establishing facilities for finding employment for seamen, 1920; No. 23 – Repatriation of seamen, 1926; No. 29 – Forced labour, 1930; No. 69 – Certification of ships' cook, 1946; No. 105 – Abolition of forced labour, 1957; No. 106 – Weekly rest (commerce and offices), 1957; No. 108 – Seafarers' national identity documents, 1958; No. 117 – Social policy (aims and basic standards), 1962; No. 122 – Employment policy, 1964; No. 134 – Prevention of occupational accidents to seafarers, 1970; No. 143 – Migrant workers (supplementary provisions), 1975; No. 149 – Nursing personnel, 1977; No. 152 – Safety and health (dock work), 1979; No. 164 – Health protection and medical care (seafarers), 1987; No. 175 – Part-time work, 1994; No. 183 – Maternity protection, 2000.

The *observations* concerned the following conventions: No. 81 – Labour inspection, 1947; No. 129 – Labour inspection (agriculture), 1969; No. 143 – Migrant workers (supplementary provisions), 1975; No. 147 – Merchant shipping (minimum standards), 1976. Among these, two attain closely to the human rights sphere.

Convention 81 on labour inspections

– As regards Convention art. 3, para. 2 ("Any further duties that may be entrusted to labour inspectors shall not be such as to interfere with the effective discharge of their primary duties or to prejudice in any way the authority or impartiality which are necessary to inspectors in their relations with employers and workers"), the Committee recalls that the role of labour inspectors, pursuant to the provisions of the Convention, is to monitor not the legality of the employment relationship but the conditions in which the work is performed and that the system of labour inspection must apply to all employees or apprentices, however they may be remunerated and whatever the type, form or duration of their contract. Any form of cooperation with the immigration authorities should be carried out cautiously, keeping in mind that the primary purpose of labour inspectors is to protect the rights and interests of all workers and to improve their working conditions. In this connection, the Committee believes that the role assigned to labour inspectors as *Carabinieri* of the criminal police may severely jeopardise the performance of their original duties. The Committee urges Italy to distinguish with sufficient clarity the powers and working methods of labour inspectors from those of the officials of other bodies responsible for combating illegal employment and migration, though such separation in no way excludes the possibility of establish a form of cooperation among the various competent authorities.

– As regards art. 20 and 21 of Convention 81, concerning the State's obligation to prepare and publish a detailed annual inspection report, the Committee – noting the Italian Government's decision not to publish the report in the immediate future on account of institutional reform concerning the methods for the collection of statistics – nonetheless reiterates that compilation of the report is an international obligation, and urges the Italian State to comply with it as soon as possible.

Convention 143 on migrant workers (supplementary provisions)

The Committee expresses concern over information it has received concerning the widespread conditions of exploitation affecting irregular migrant workers, and asks Italy to undertake a detailed analysis of recent legislative initiatives targeting irregular immigration and to the measures to ensure that migrant workers who are in an irregular situation were able to enjoy basic human rights. The Committee calls the Government's attention to the fact that the measures advocated in Part I of the Convention (art. 2-6) primarily targeted at the demand for clandestine labour rather than the supply. In particular, the goal of art. 6, para. 1, is to define and apply sanctions against organisers of clandestine movements of migrants and against employers in cases of illegal employment, and not against irregular migrant workers. Art. 1-9 of the Convention aim to guarantee that migrant workers enjoy a minimum level of protection with respect to their fundamental human rights, regardless of their condition as irregulars. In this connection, the Committee urges the Government to conduct a detailed analysis on the impact of recent legislative measures aimed at combating irregular migration. In addition, the Italian Government is asked to indicate how it is ensured that migrant workers, who are in an irregular situation, especially those who are the subject of an expulsion order, can judicially recur against such order. The Committee asks the Government to provide information on the concrete results obtained by programmes aiming to promote equality of opportunity and treatment in respect of employment and occupation (art. 10), with particular reference to discrimination between migrants lawfully in the Country and nationals, and discrimination against workers of Roma origin.

However, during 2010 none of these observations was selected for in-depth discussion by the Conference Committee on the Application of Standards.

In 2010, Italy contributed approximately 5% to the ordinary ILO budget, amounting to around 19.7 million Swiss francs. In addition, during that year Italy signed an agreement with ILO to give further, voluntary contribution amounting to around 300,000 dollars during the two-year period 2010-2011.

B. United Nations Educational, Scientific and Cultural Organisation (UNESCO)

Italy has been a Member State of UNESCO since 1948. The chart below shows the conventions most closely tied to human rights issues adopted by the Organisation, which Italy has ratified.

Convention	Date of deposit of instrument of ratification
Universal Copyright Convention, with Appendix Declaration relating to art. XVII and resolution concerning art. XI, 1952	24/10/1956
Protocol 2 annexed to the Universal Copyright Convention concerning the application of that Convention to the works of certain international organizations, 1952	24/10/1956
Protocol 3 annexed to the Universal Copyright Convention concerning the effective date of instruments of ratification or acceptance of or accession to that Convention, 1952	24/10/1956
Convention for the Protection of Cultural Property in the Event of Armed Conflict with Regulations for the Execution of the Convention, 1954	09/05/1958
Protocol to the Convention for the Protection of Cultural Property in the Event of Armed conflict, 1954	09/05/1958
Convention concerning the International Exchange of Publications, 1958	02/08/1961
Convention concerning the Exchange of Official Publications and Government Documents between States, 1958	02/08/1961

Agreement on the Importation of Educational, Scientific and Cultural Materials, with Annexes A to E and Protocol annexed, 1950	26/11/1962
Convention against Discrimination in Education, 1960	06/10/1966
Protocol Instituting a Conciliation and Good offices Commission to be Responsible for Seeking the settlement of any Disputes which may Arise between States Parties to the Convention against Discrimination in Education, 1962	06/10/1966
Protocol 1 annexed to the Universal Copyright Convention concerning the application of that Convention to the works of stateless persons and refugees, 1952	19/12/1966
International Convention for the Protection of Performers, Producers of Phonograms and Broadcasting Organizations, 1961	08/01/1975
Convention on Wetlands of International Importance especially as Waterfowl Habitat, 1971	14/12/1976
Convention for the Protection of Producers of Phonograms against Unauthorized Duplication of their Phonograms, 1971	20/12/1976
Convention concerning the Protection of the World Cultural and Natural Heritage, 1972	23/06/1978
Convention on the Means of Prohibiting and Preventing the Illicit Import, Export and Transfer of Ownership of Cultural Property, 1970	02/10/1978
Universal Copyright Convention as revised at Paris on 24 July 1971, with Appendix Declaration relating to art. XVII and resolution concerning art. XI, 1971	25/10/1979
Protocol 1 annexed for Universal Copyright Convention as revised at Paris on 24 July 1971 concerning the application of that Convention to works of Stateless persons and refugees, 1971	25/10/1979
Protocol 2 annexed for the Universal Copyright Convention as revised at Paris on 24 July 1971 concerning the application of that Convention to the works of certain international organizations, 1971	25/10/1979
Convention relating to the Distribution of Programme-Carrying Signals Transmitted by Satellite, 1974	07/04/1981
Convention on the Recognition of Studies, Diplomas and Degrees in Higher Education in the Arab and European States Bordering on the Mediterranean, 1976	14/04/1981
Protocol to the Agreement on the Importation of Educational, Scientific or Cultural Materials, with Annexes A to H, 1976	02/07/1981
Convention on the Recognition of Studies, Diplomas and Degrees concerning Higher Education in the States belonging to the Europe Region, 1979	20/01/1983
Protocol to amend the Convention on Wetlands of International Importance especially as Waterfowl Habitat, 1982	27/07/1987
Convention on the Protection and Promotion of the Diversity of Cultural Expressions, 2005	19/02/2007
Convention for the Safeguarding of the Intangible Cultural Heritage, 2003	30/10/2007

International Convention against Doping in Sport, 2005	27/02/2008
Second Protocol to the Hague Convention of 1954 for the Protection of Cultural Property in the Event of Armed Conflict, 1999	10/07/2009
Convention on the Protection of the Underwater Cultural Heritage, 2001	08/01/2010
Convention on the Recognition of Qualifications concerning Higher Education in the European Region, 1997	01/10/2010

As a member of UNESCO, Italy is obliged to respect the principles guaranteed in the declarations and recommendations adopted by its bodies.

In 2010, Italy was a member of the Executive Board; it was also represented in the Inter-governmental Oceanographic Commission, in the International Coordinating Committee for the Safeguarding of the Intangible Cultural Heritage and in the following consultative bodies of the General Conference: International Coordinating Council of the Man & Biosphere Programme; Inter-governmental Council for the International Hydrological Programme; Inter-Governmental Committee for Promoting the Return of Cultural Property to its Country of Origin or its Restitution in cases of illicit appropriation; Inter-Governmental Council of the International Programme for the Development of Communication; Legal Committee; Commission for UN Model Rules for the Conciliation of Disputes between States, which might arise among States Parties to the Convention against Discrimination in Education (Francesco Margiotta-Broglio is a member).

In addition, Ambassador Maurizio Enrico Serra, Italian Permanent Representative at UNESCO, acted as Chair of the Committee on Conventions and Recommendations, a consultative organ of the Executive Board in charge of monitoring national-level application of the Convention against Discrimination in Education, the Convention on the Means for Prohibiting and Preventing the Illicit Import, Export and Transfer of Ownership of Cultural Property, and the Convention on Technical and Professional Education, as well as 11 over recommendations. On 1 July 2010 Francesco Bandarin was appointed Assistant Director-General for Culture.

In 2010, Italy contributed approximately 5% to UNESCO's ordinary budget, amounting to around 16 million dollars, gaining the sixth place among contributors. In addition, again in 2010, Italy is in second place (surpassed only by Japan) for voluntary contributions; amounting to around 9.5 million dollars, the sum is distributed among programmes benefiting the following regions: Africa (around 3.4 million dollars; Italy is the prime contributor here); Arab Countries (205,000 dollars);

Asia and the Pacific (573,000); Europe and North America (726,000); Latin America and the Caribbean (341,000); inter-regional and global programmes (around 4.3 million dollars).

In December 2010 UNESCO sent a mission of experts to the World Heritage Site of Pompei, Ercolano and Torre Annunziata, after the *Schola Armaturarum* started to cave in on 6 November 2010, prior to the partial ruin of three other structures belonging to the World Heritage Site. The mission included experts on Roman mural paintings, ancient architecture, and mural painting techniques from the International Council on Monuments and Sites, one of the consultancy bodies for the UNESCO World Heritage Centre. A report on the results of the three-day mission (2-4 December) will be presented during the next session of the UNESCO Commission on World Heritage, in Bahrein, June 2011.

In addition, during 2010, the General Director of UNESCO, Irina Bokova, made two visits to Italy, respectively on 7 October, when she was conferred a *Laurea honoris causa* in European and International Politics at the Catholic University of Milan, and 22-23 November, in order to discuss UNESCO reform policies, Italy's role in the Organisation, and the situation of the site at Pompei, Ercolano and Torre Annunziata, with the Italian authorities.

Finally, as regards the topic of education, in 1991 the 26th General Conference at UNESCO set up the programme International University Cooperation (IUC), with has at its core the realisation of UNESCO as a laboratory of ideas and as catalyst for international cooperation between universities and educational and scientific institutions coming from all over the world. With this goal in mind, the Programme attempts to foster the creation of a network of centres of excellence (UNESCO Chairs) undertaking training and research activities, with particular attention to UNECSO major programmes areas: peace, human rights, democracy and intercultural dialogue.

Mora than 650 UNESCO Chairs exist throughout the world; Italy hosts 13 Chairs, three of which are specifically dedicated to human rights, a term figuring in their denomination: the Chair "Human Rights, Democracy and Peace", instituted in 1999 at the University of Padua (Chair Antonio Papisca); the Chair "Human Rights and Ethics of International Cooperation", instituted in 2003 at the University of Bergamo (Chair Felice Rizzi); the Chair "Bioethics and Human Rights", instituted in 2009 at the Pontifical Atheneum "Regina Apostolorum", European University of Rome (Chair Alberto García).

Council of Europe

With the entry into force of the 1950 European Convention for the Protection of Human Rights and Fundamental Freedoms (ECHR) and of its successive Additional Protocols (the most recent being Protocol XIV, which came into force on 1 June 2010), the Council of Europe (CoE, 47 Member States) has developed the first and most advanced regional system for the promotion and protection of human rights, characterised, in particular, by the establishment of the European Court of Human Rights (ECtHR). Further legal instruments include the European Social Charter (1961, a revised version was adopted in 1996), which has created a monitoring system centred on the role of the European Committee of Social Rights (ECSR); the European Convention against Torture and Inhuman or Degrading Treatment or Punishment (1987), which instituted the European Committee for the Prevention of Torture and Inhuman or Degrading Treatment or Punishment (CPT); the Framework Convention for the Protection of National Minorities (1995), which created the Advisory Committee on the fore-mentioned Convention, and the European Convention on the Exercise of Children's Rights (1996), with its relative Standing Committee.

The institutional architecture of the Council of Europe, whose principal bodies are the Court, the Committee of Ministers and the Parliamentary Assembly, is completed by the following: the Commissioner for Human Rights, the European Commission against Racism and Intolerance (ECRI), and the European Commission for Democracy through Law (Venice Commission).

The Directorate-General of Human Rights and Legal Affairs monitors the functioning of the various regional human rights treaties and their relative follow-up machinery, and provides assistance and support in such matters to the bodies of the Council of Europe and to Member States. Italy's Permanent Representative is Ambassador Sergio Busetto.

I. Parliamentary Assembly

18 members of the Senate and House of Representatives, plus 18 substitutes, represent Italy in the Parliamentary Assembly of the Council of Europe (PACE). The Chair of the Italian delegation is Luigi Vitali, who is also one of the 20 Assembly Vice-Presidents. In 2010 the first Vice Chairperson of the Committee on Migration, Refugees and Population has been Giacomo Santini.

In 2010, PACE activities involving Italy focused mainly on the issue of Roma and Sinti communities, and on the governance of migratory movements.

On 26 February 2010 a report was presented to the PACE Committee on Legal Affairs and Human Rights, concerning the situation of Roma in Europe and important measures taken by the Council of Europe in this connection (doc. 12174, rapporteur: Berény). Its explicative memorandum reports several examples of violent attacks against Roma in Italy occurring between 2007 and 2009. The discussion on this report led to the adoption of resolution 1740, on 22 June 2010, in which the Parliamentary Assembly exhorts Member States to acknowledge their responsibilities and to deal with the Roma issue in a serious, sustainable manner, through a series of measures aimed at protecting and respecting their human rights.

The explicative part of a following report, on the topic of Roma asylum-seekers in Europe (doc. 12393, rapporteur: Pupovac), presented on 6 October 2010 to the Committee on Migration, Refugees and Population, acknowledges that numerous positive projects relating to Roma have been developed in Italy, thanks, in particular, to non-governmental organisations and religious communities. However, according to the report, such progress does not exempt the CoE from pointing out the institutional shortcomings existing in Italy. The report makes explicit reference to declarations from high-level Italian Government representatives who, in the summer of 2010, described migrants of Roma ethnicity as "criminals". The operative part of the report was adopted by PACE with resolution 1768, on 12 November 2010. The document focuses mainly on the situation of Roma asylum-seekers in Member States of the Council of Europe, who fled from Kosovo after the wars of the 1990s and who now, after several years, are constrained to face forced returns to that Country. The Parliamentary Assembly proposes a holistic approach to the issue, in respect for the rights and responsibilities of the Roma, involving all States of the region, the European Union, the Council of Europe and the civil society. In resolution 1768, PACE urges all politicians of the 47 Member States to condemn, publicly and vigorously, all forms of racism and discrimination against Roma.

Aside from the documents mentioned above, the Assembly referred directly to Italy in resolution 1702 of 26 January 2010, on the action of the Council of Europe against trafficking in human beings, in which it urges Italy and other Member States of the Organisation to ratify as soon as possible the 2005 Convention against Trafficking in Human Beings. On 29 November 2010, Italy ratified this Convention, whose provisions will become binding for the Country, starting from 1 March 2011.

As regards the activities carried out in 2010 by Italian representatives involved in the Parliamentary Assembly Committees, it is worth noticing: two reports by Piero Fassino to the Committee on Political Affairs, discussing, respectively, the situation in the Middle East (11 January 2010, doc. 12117) and the flare-up of tension in the Middle East (22 June 2010, doc. 12308); the report by Pietro Marcenaro to the Committee on Legal Affairs and Human Rights on achievements, deficiencies and failures in the fight against extremism (8 July 2010, doc. 12337); the two reports by Luca Volonté to the Committee on Social Affairs, Health and Family, discussing, respectively, investment in family cohesion as a development factor in times of crisis (19 January 2010, doc. 12103) and the promotion of volunteering in Europe (27 October 2010, doc. 12430).

During its first plenary session of 2010 (25-29 January), PACE elected Guido Raimondi judge of the European Court of Human Rights, in substitution of Vladimiro Zagrebelsky, who had concluded his mandate.

II. Committee of Ministers

In the area of human rights, the Committee of Ministers (CM) consults the Steering Committee for Human Rights, an inter-governmental body composed of representatives from the 47 Member States plus a number of observers, whose functions include standard-setting and follow-up measures.

As regards the activities involving Italy, on 3 June 2010, in the framework of its responsibilities in supervising the execution of judgments, the CM adopted interim resolution CM/ResDH(2010)83 concerning the case *Ben Khemais v. Italy* (application 246/07, judgment of 24 February 2009; see also Part IV, Case-law of ECtHR, V). In this resolution the Committee deplores Italy's conduct relative to the deportation to Tunisia of the applicant (and other applicants in similar cases), in violation of the provisional measures indicated by the Court, based on art. 39 of its rules. The Committee reiterates Italy's obligation to respect the interim measures indicated by the Court, and exhorts the Italian authorities to adopt effective measures sufficient to prevent violations of this kind in the future.

Concerning the same issue, on 21 April 2010 the Committee adopted the response to written question 571, presented by a member of the Parliamentary Assembly, Herta Däubler-Gmelin (Germany), on Italy's persistent non-compliance with the interim measures ordered by the European Court of Human Rights. In the question, presented to the Committee of Ministers on 20 August 2009, following the fourth case of Italy's deportation of an applicant in violation of the Court's interim measures to suspend deportation, the then Chairman of the PACE Committee on Legal Affairs and Human Rights, Däubler-Gmelin, asked the CM for information on measures taken up to that moment, and those that it intended to take, in order to censure Italy's conduct in the matter. In its reply (CM/AS(2010)Quest571final), the CM highlights that in several similar cases, the Italian State has complied with the ECtHR's orders by taking a measure alternative to deportation; it reasserts Italy's need to clarify whether such measures will be applied in all similar cases, and to prevent, in any event, similar violations of ECtHR provisions.

On 21 October 2010 the Committee of Ministers adopted resolution CM/ResChS(2010)8 relating to application 58/2009 presented against Italy, pursuant to the Additional Protocol to the European Social Charter Providing for a System of Collective Complaints, by the international non-governmental organisation Centre on Housing Rights and Evictions (COHRE) (see Part III, Council of Europe, V). In its resolution the CM takes note of the complaint filed by COHRE, the decision by the European Committee of Social Rights, and the relative declaration and information given by the Italian Government and welcomes the commitment shown by the authorities to comply to the standards set by the revised European Social Charter, also with regards to members of the Roma community. The CM looks forward to Italy reporting that, at the time of the submission of the next report concerning the relevant provisions of the revised European Social Charter, the situation is in full conformity with the revised European Social Charter

Interim resolution CM/ResDH(2010)224, on the execution of ECtHR judgments regarding the excessive length of judiciary proceedings in Italy, was adopted by the Committee of Ministers on 2 December 2010. The document is the latest in a long series of previous resolutions of analogous content adopted since 1997. In particular, it refers to 2,183 applications presented on this subject, and to 24 cases regarding bankruptcy proceedings. Recalling the analogous resolution of 2009 (CM/ResHR(2009)42), the CM calls upon Italy urgently to adopt *ad hoc* measures to reduce the civil and penal backlog, to finance reforms adequately and to take into consideration any measure capable of improving the efficiency of justice. The Committee reiterates that excessive delays in the administration of justice constitute a serious threat to respect for the rule of law, and an infringement of the ECHR. After expressing concern over the fact that, since the latest resolution adopted in 2009, no information has arrived allowing the Committee to make an effective assessment of the Country's progress, the CM exhorts the Italian authorities to deal with the problem at the highest political level, and to take all suitable technical and budgetary measures. As soon as possible, the CM must be provided with elements of an effective strategy, together with updated data and statistics.

During 2010 the Committee of Ministers has elected Francesco Palermo as member of the Advisory Committee on the Framework Convention for the Protection of National Minorities (resolution CM/ResCMN(2010)8, June 2010) and Giuseppe Palmisano as member of the European Committee of Social Rights (resolution CM/ResChS (2010)9, 10 November 2010). The latter will take office in January 2011.

III. European Court of Human Rights

The European Court of Human Rights (ECtHR) is the first example of an international Court created specifically for the protection of human rights in a given region of the world. Since 1998, with the entry into force of Additional Protocol XI and later, Additional Protocol XIV to the ECHR, the structure and functioning of the Court have been reformed in order to satisfy the increasing number of individual applications lodged.

The Italian judge currently sitting in the Court is Guido Raimondi (see Part III, Council of Europe, I). The other Italian judges that previously held this position at the Strasbourg Court are, in chronological order, Giorgio Balladore Pallieri (1959-1980), who was also its President, Carlo Russo (1981-1998), Benedetto Conforti (1998-2001) and Vladimiro Zagrebelsky (2001-2010).

The most recent information bulletin on Italy published by the Court (1959-2010) states that ECtHR activity involving Italy – from the first judgment (*Artico v. Italy*) of 13 May 1980 until 1 January 2010 – amounts to a total of 2,023 judgments. In 1,556 of them, the Court found violation of the rights guaranteed by the ECHR; in 48 of them, the Court found no violation. In addition, the ECtHR delivered 8,988 decisions of inadmissibility (pursuant to ECHR art. 35) for individual applications filed against Italy, while the number of applications pending is 7,158.

Part IV presents an in-depth analysis of the Court's activities and judgments which involved Italy in 2010.

IV. European Committee for the Prevention of Torture

The European Committee for the Prevention of Torture and Inhuman or Degrading Treatment or Punishment (CPT) was instituted in 1987 by the respective Convention, conceived as complementary to the provision on the prohibition of torture set forth in art. 3 ECHR.

The CPT is a body made up of independent experts; there is one member for each State Party to the Convention for the Prevention of

Torture (ratified, as of today, by all Member States of the Council of Europe). The independent expert from Italy, and current CPT President, is Mauro Palma. His mandate will end on 19 December 2011. The first Chairman of CPT, in 1989, was Antonio Cassese.

Till today the CPT has made nine visits to Italy: from 15 to 17 March 1992, from 22 October to 6 November 1996, from 13 to 25 February 2000, from 21 November to 3 December 2004, from 16 to 23 June 2006, from 14 to 26 September 2008, from 27 to 31 July 2009 and from 14 to 18 June 2010.

In virtue of the principle of confidentiality, the most recent report that can be publicly consulted is the one based on the visit made in 2009 (CPT/Inf(2010)14), published on 28 April 2010, together with relative observations by the Italian Government.

The main motivation for this visit was to examine recent immigration measures adopted by the Italian authorities, consisting in intercepting at sea migrants who are approaching the southern maritime border of Italy and pushing them back toward Libya or other non-European Countries. The report examines seven such push-back operations, occurring between 6 May and 31 July 2009.

The CPT delegation examined the protection system currently in force in Italy to ensure – in respect for the so-called "principle of *non-refoulement*" – that no migrant be turned back toward a Country where there is good reason to believe his/her life or freedom are threatened, or that he/she might be subjected to torture, or cruel, inhuman or degrading treatment or punishment. In addition, the delegation examined the treatment reserved for migrants during their detention in centres of identification and expulsion (CIE).

The delegation notes the high degree of cooperation obtained at the local level, while as regards the central authorities, it deplores the lack of access to several documents requested (for example, logbooks from the ships involved in the operations): this lack violates art. 3 (principle of cooperation) and art. 8.2 (States' facilities to help the Committee to carry out its task) of the European Convention for the Prevention of Torture. The delegation also complains that the Italian authorities did not inform it of a push-back operation occurring during the visit. The report, then, states that on the whole, the Italian authorities did not behave in the cooperative spirit required and expresses hope for greater cooperation in the future.

The report's authors have detected cases of suspected mistreatment and the wounding of several migrants by personnel involved in the operations, and have asked the Italian Government to make in-depth inquiries, informing them of the results.

In listing the protection measures benefiting migrants intercepted at sea, the CPT stresses that the prohibition against torture is a peremptory, inalienable norm of international law incorporating the principle of *non-refoulement* extended – according to the case-law of the Strasbourg Court – to all persons who might be exposed to a real risk of torture or inhuman treatment in the non-European Country where they might be deported. As regards the operations considered, the Committee identifies such a risk threatening persons sent back toward Libya, where they are destined to be detained or again deported to their Country of origin, or to another State. The CPT's analysis of data provided by governmental sources and by civil society organisations met with during the visit, leads the Committee to conclude that the current Italian policy of pushing back migrants at sea (in particular toward Libya) violates the principle of *non-refoulement*, and therefore, art. 3 ECHR. According to the Committee, Italy has a duty to respect this principle anywhere it exercises its jurisdiction, and therefore, even when State agents operate outside of its territorial waters.

The CPT notes that the persons pushed back toward Libya during the operations considered were generally denied the right to obtain individual assessment of their case and real access to the international protection system (asylum procedures). The Italian authorities deliberately pushed back groups of persons who were particularly vulnerable (pregnant women and children) and persons who would presumably have been able to obtain refugee status.

In conclusion, then, the Committee exhorts the Italian authorities to reconsider, in an immediate, substantial manner, the current practice of interception at sea and successive pushing back of migrants, so as to ensure that all persons submitted to Italian jurisdiction, including those intercepted outside territorial waters by ships under the control of Italian personnel, receive the humanitarian and medical assistance required by their condition, and have real access to protection procedures capable of guaranteeing respect for the principle of *non-refoulement*. Even in light of the legal instruments on which Italy bases the international legitimacy of such operations (the United Nations Convention against Transnationally Organised Crime of 2000, and a series of bilateral agreements signed by Italy and Libya from 2000 to 2009), the Committee stresses that their implementation in no way limits Italy's obligations pursuant to art. 3 ECHR.

The press release issued by the CPT regarding its report based on the 2010 visit gave preliminary notice that the delegation had dealt with three main issues: the provisions relative to health care in prisons after the transfer of responsibility from the Prison Administration to the National Health Service; the policies adopted and measures taken to reduce the incidence of suicides and acts of self-harm in prison; the current system in place to investigate cases of alleged ill-treatment of arrested and/or detained persons.

V. European Committee of Social Rights

The European Committee of Social Rights of the Council of Europe (ECSR) was established pursuant to art. 25 of the 1961 European Social Charter, with the purpose of determining whether the Member States comply, in law and practice, with the provisions of the European Social Charter, its Protocols, and the revised European Social Charter (ESC-R).

Currently, the Committee is composed of 15 independent experts elected by the Committee of Ministers for a six-year mandate, renewable only once. Since 10 November 2010, Giuseppe Palmisano has been a member of the ECSR; he will hold office until 31 December 2016.

Italy ratified the European Social Charter in 1965, and the revised European Social Charter in 1999, accepting 97 of its 98 numbered paragraphs. The only provision not accepted concerns art. 25 ESC-R, which guarantees the right of workers to the protection of their claims in the event of the insolvency of their employer.

Between 1967 and 2010 the Italian Government presented 20 reports concerning the application of the 1961 Charter and 10 on the application of the revised Charter. The latest conclusions, adopted and published by the Committee of Social Rights in December 2010, refer to the ninth report, presented on 26 January 2010, which regards the Charter provisions accepted by Italy concerning a set of workers' rights (art. 2, 4, 5, 6, 21, 22, 26, 28 and 29 ESC-R) during the period 2005-2008.

In the chapter concerning Italy in its *Conclusions 2010*, the ECSR stresses, first of all, the three-month delay beyond the deadline in the Government's presentation of the ninth report. The Committee analyses Italy's position relative to 22 provisions, recognising 12 situations of compliance (while expressing, in some cases, the need for more detailed information) and 10 of non-compliance.

Concerning art. 2 ESC-R (the right to just conditions of work), the Committee concludes that Italy's situation is in compliance with para. 3 (annual holiday with pay), 5 (weekly rest period), 6 (information on the work contract) and 7 (night work). On the contrary, Italy's situation is not in compliance with para. 1 (reasonable working hours), on the ground that regulations permit weekly working time of up to 72 hours in the fishing industry; with para. 2 (public holidays with pay), since work done on public holidays is not adequately compensated; and para. 4 (elimination of risks in dangerous or unhealthy occupations), since there is no prevention policy for the risks in inherently dangerous or unhealthy occupations and it has not been established that the right to just conditions of work in case of risks in inherently dangerous or unhealthy occupations is guaranteed.

As regards art. 4 ESC-R (right to a fair remuneration), the Committee recognises Italy's non-conformity with all its paragraphs except para. 3 (non-discrimination between men and women with respect to remuneration), since it is dealt with by the Committee in conjunction with art. 20. The non-conformities regard para. 1 (decent remuneration), since it has not been established that the minimum wage can guarantee a decent standard of living; para. 2 (increased remuneration for overtime work), because time off granted to compensate overtime is not sufficiently long under the collective agreement in the food industry sector; para. 4 (reasonable notice of termination of employment), because – in textile, private metal-working and mechanical industries as well as food-processing sector – the notice period is not adequate; para. 5 (limits to deduction from wages), since it has not been established that deductions from wages will not deprive workers and their dependence of their very means of subsistence.

As regards art. 5 ESC-R (right to organise), the Committee concludes that the situation in Italy aligns with Charter provisions.

As regards art. 6 ESC-R (right to bargain collectively), the ECSR observes that the Italian situation is in conformity with the first three paragraphs (joint consultation, negotiation procedures, conciliation and arbitration), but not with para. 4 (collective action), since it has not been demonstrated that the Government's right to issue ordinances restricting strikes in essential public services falls within the limits of art. G of the revised Charter, and since the requirement to notify the duration of strikes concerning essential public services to the employer prior to strike action is excessive. Nor is the situation in Italy in compliance with art. 21 ESC-R (right of workers to be informed and consulted), since it has not been established that the rules relating to information and consultation cover the majority of employees concerned. Also, as regards art. 22 ESC-R (right of workers to take part in the determination and improvement of working conditions and working environment), the situation found by the Committee is one of non-conformity, since it has not been proven that the majority of employed workers actually enjoy this right.

As regards art. 26 ESC-R (right to dignity in the workplace), the ECSR finds compliance of the Italian situation both with para. 1 (sexual harassment) and para. 2 (moral harassment). The same assessment is given relative to art. 28 ESC-R (right of workers' representatives to protection in the undertaking and facilities to be accorded to them) and art. 29 ESC-R (right to information and consultation in procedures of collective redundancy).

The tenth report on the application of the revised Social Charter was presented in two parts, on 29 October and 3 December 2010; it refers to the provisions accepted by Italy concerning the social rights of children, families and migrants, during the period 2005-2009. In particular, it concerns art. 7 ESC-R (right of children and young persons to protection), 8 ESC-R (right of employed women to protection of maternity), 16 ESC-R (right of the family to social, legal and economic protection), and 27 ESC-R (right of workers with family responsibilities to equal opportunities and equal treatment), for a total of 19 provisions. The observations by the ECSR regarding this report will be published in the *Conclusions 2011*.

As regards the Additional Protocol to the European Social Charter of 1995, Italy has not yet presented a declaration allowing national non-governmental organisations to present collective complaints to the ECSR. However, from the coming into force of the Protocol for Italy (1997) until 2010, four collective complaints were presented by international non-governmental organisations. In two cases – *European Federation of Employees in Public Services (EUROFEDOP) v. Italy* (No. 4/1999) and *World Organisation against Torture (OMCT) v. Italy* (No. 19/2003) – the Committee found no violation. On the contrary, in the other two – *European Roma Rights Centre (ERRC) v. Italy* (No. 27/2004) and *Centre on Housing Rights and Evictions (COHRE) v. Italy* (No. 58/2009) – the ECSR found violations of the provisions indicated in the complaints. The *decision* regarding the last collective complaint was issued on 25 June 2010.

In lodging its complaint, the COHRE had stated that the condition of the Roma and Sinti in Italy violates art. 16 ESC-R right of the family to social, legal and economic protection), 19 ESC-R (right of migrant workers and their families to protection and assistance), 30 ESC-R (right to protection against poverty and social exclusion) and 31 ESC-R (right to housing); as well as art. E ESC-R (non-discrimination) taken in conjunction with each of the preceding provisions. In particular, the COHRE had asked the Committee to acknowledge that the adoption of the "Pacts for Security" (November 2006), of the so-called Nomad "state of emergency" decrees (21 May 2008) and their respective implementation orders and guidelines, constitutes a deliberate retrogressive steps with respect to guarantees previously declared, and does not take into account the violations found by the Committee on the occasion of the complaint presented by the ERRC in 2004. According to the COHRE, the *de facto* and *de jure* residential segregation of which Roma and Sinti are victims, like the obstacles preventing them from gaining or retaining legal status, have worsened their living conditions, whereas the revised European Social Charter requires a coordinated approach in order to combat poverty and social exclusion. The COHRE had asked the Committee to recognise that the policy and practice of segregating Roma and Sinti families in "ghettos" by using discriminatory identification procedures, has denied them access to adequate housing and to the protection of family life. In addition, the view tending to present "nomads" as a threat to national security has fanned the flames of racist, xenophobic propaganda against members of these communities.

On its part, the Italian Government delegation had countered that the condition of Roma and Sinti in Italy shows no violation by the State of the revised Social Charter.

In its decision – which is based on its own case-law, on the Strasbourg Court's case-law, and on the latest reports by various regional and international bodies for the promotion and protection of human rights (in particular, reports by the Commissioner for Human Rights, the ECRI, the OSCE High Commissioner on National Minorities and the United Nations Committee on the Elimination of Racial Discrimination) – the Committee establishes the violation of all the provisions indicated by the COHRE. In particular, as regards art. E ESC-R taken in conjunction with art. 31 ESC-R, the Committee finds that the living conditions of Roma and Sinti in nomad camps have worsened after the adoption of the measures contested. The situation that has arisen tends to stigmatise the Roma and Sinti communities, and therefore constitutes discriminatory treatment. The ECSR believes that evictions of Roma and Sinti continue to be carried out in Italy without respecting the dignity of the persons concerned, and without providing alternative accommodation. In addition, the Italian Government has not provided credible evidence to refute the claims that the Roma have suffered unjustified violence during such evictions. Raids into the settlements have not been systematically denounced, and some of those responsible for such acts have not been identified, nor investigated or condemned. In particular, the Committee believes that the lack of protection measures and of inquiries in cases of generalised violence against Roma and Sinti camps, even when those presumed responsible are public officials, implies responsibility by the State. Though it acknowledges that the Italian authorities have allocated considerable financial resources for initiatives and projects, the Committee says it has not been proven that such resources are aimed at favouring non-discriminatory access to social housing for the Roma and Sinti.

As regards art. E ESC-R taken in conjunction with art. 30 ESC-R, the Committee maintains that the Italian Government has not proved that it has invested real efforts to prevent or eradicate the condition of poverty afflicting Roma and Sinti population, in particular the persons evicted, who did not receive any form of social assistance and found themselves living in a severely deprived context. In addition, the Committee observes that Italy has not been capable of adopting an overall and coordinated approach to promoting effective access to housing; and that the condition of segregation and poverty afflicting most of the Roma and Sinti population in Italy is linked to social and civil marginalisation. This condition is tied to the failure of the authorities to address Roma and Sinti's lack of identification documents, and is further aggravated by the condition of segregation in which they live. All these elements combined prevent them from access to residence and citizenship documents and to exercise civil and political participation, causing their marginalisation and social exclusion. As regards art. E ESC-R taken in conjunction with art. 16 ESC-R, the Committee assesses that art. 16 ESC-R and 31 ESC-R partly overlap. The Committee notes that the Italian authorities' procedures of identification and census of Roma and Sinti were not accompanied by the due safeguards for privacy, and are open to abuse by the authorities themselves. Such procedures end up causing undue interference into private and family life, in violation of art. 16 ESC-R. The Committee believes that the Italian authorities have not demonstrated that the contested security measures respect the principle of proportionality, are necessary in a democratic society, and have been used to benefit the communities. The Committee concludes that, in light of the specific discriminatory context in which information has been recorded and retained, the measures adopted by the Italian authorities were exclusively based on theoretic security reasons (the "*emergenza nomadi*") and were of no use to enlighten any social problem. In addition, the emergency conditions in which such operations have been performed constituted an obstacle to real protection against arbitrariness.

As regards art. 19 ESC-R, taken in conjunction with art. E ESC-R, the Committee believes that declarations by several public officials have created a discriminatory atmosphere. The ESCR holds that deceptive racist propaganda against migrants, Roma and Sinti, whether indirectly allowed or directly expressed by the Italian authorities, constitutes serious violation of the revised Social Charter. As regards the expulsions of migrants, the ESCR believes that the contested security measures, favoured by the so-called "nomad emergency", have been an excuse for recourse to collective forms of repression and expulsion which have specifically affected Roma and Sinti, including those with Italian citizenship or citizenship of other European Union Countries.

VI. Commissioner for Human Rights

The Commissioner for Human Rights of the Council of Europe is an independent non-judicial institution created with the Committee of Ministers' resolution (99)50 of 7 May 1999. Since 1 April 2006 this office has been held by Thomas Hammarberg (Sweden).

Until today, the Commissioner for Human Rights has made two visits to Italy, in 2005 (from 10 to 17 June; report published on 14 December 2005 – CommDH (2005)9); and in 2008 (from 19 to 20 June; report published on 28 July 2008 – CommDH (2008)18). A follow-up visit was made in 2009 (from 13 to 15 January 2009; the relative report was published on 16 April 2009 – CommDH (2009)16).

It is also worth mentioning three letters recently sent to the Minster of Interior, Maroni, and to the Minister of Foreign Affairs, Frattini. Two of them are dated 2 July 2010; in both of these, the Commissioner stresses his concern relative to the possibility, raised by a series of independent reports reaching his Office, that several individuals, including migrants who had attempted to reach Italy to ask for international protection and had been pushed back toward Libya, could have been further deported to Eritrea, where they risked being exposed to serious human rights violations, or to Sudan. The Commissioner asks the two Ministers to cooperate in order urgently to clarify with Libya, the situation of such persons.

The most recent visit made to Italy was dedicated to monitoring and assessing progress made by the Italian authorities relative to the four topics on which the previous visit, in 2008, had focused: the struggle against racism and xenophobia; the protection of human rights for Roma and Sinti; the protection of human rights for migrants and asylum seekers; and foreign nationals' forced returns. Particular attention was given to Italy's compliance with requests by the Strasbourg Court, pursuant to art. 39 of its rules (interim measures).

As regards the first topic, the Commissioner approves several positive measures adopted by Italy in the effort to combat racism and xenophobia, such as law 6 June 2008, No. 101, which provides for an explicit shift of the burden of proof from the complainant to the respondent in cases of discrimination; and the new programmes of the Ministry of Education, characterised by an intercultural approach.

However, the Commissioner expresses particular concern aroused by reports that continue to reflect an increase in racist and xenophobic manifestations in Italy, occasionally supported by members of local authorities, which have given rise to violent acts against migrants, Roma, Sinti or Italian citizens who are of migrants descent. The Commissioner urges immediate response by the authorities, and strong condemnation of all such manifestations of intolerance, as well as stronger legislation against discrimination. Hammerberg also urges the authorities systematically to promote education and awareness measures on human rights issues, targeting, in particular, the police and judicial authorities; to create a National Human Rights Institution without delay; and to oppose racism in sport and on the Internet.

As regards the second topic (Roma and Sinti), the Commissioner welcomes the Italian Government's commitment in following recommendations contained in the previous report, and in taking specific measures, such as support for *DOSTA!*, the Council of Europe campaign against anti-Roma prejudice. A significant effort has also been made to foster the access of Roma and Sinti to housing and education. However, visits made to several settlements in Rome, and encounters with representatives of such communities, have confirmed the existence of a climate of intolerance towards Roma and Sinti, the lack of institutionalized dialogue between the authorities and communities' representatives, and the persistence of unacceptable living standards in some of the settlements visited, especially those inhabited by migrants and their families. The Commissioner expresses deep concern, as well, over census-taking methods in Roma and Sinti camps, managed by police authorities in an atmosphere of emergency and widespread public alarm. While appreciating the commitment shown by the Mayor of Rome in consulting with representatives of Roma communities, and by the representative of the Ministry of Interior in dealing with the issue of stateless Roma children, the Commissioner asks the authorities to create consultation mechanisms at every level with members of the Roma and Sinti communities, to avoid evictions, and to adopt and implement an organic national plan to be adequately financed and congruent with Council of Europe's recommendations.

Concerning problems created by irregular immigration, the Commissioner expresses worry over the new legislative measures, such as the law that criminalises the letting of accommodation to irregular migrants ("security packet" 2008), and the rumoured proposal to oblige Italian health care personnel to report to the authorities irregular migrants who have access to the Italian health care system. There is criticism, as well, against the decision by the Ministry of Interior to examine asylum requests directly on the island of Lampedusa, which causes overcrowding in the reception centre located on the island. Finally, the Italian authorities are urged to reconsider immigration laws, adopted or in a preparatory state, which raise serious questions of compatibility with international human rights standards; to devote special attention to the needs of migrant children; and to ratify the CoE Convention against trafficking in human beings (this was done during the year 2010).

Finally, as regards the topic of expulsions towards Countries which offer no guarantee for the respect of human rights, the Commissioner's report expresses deep concern over several cases of expulsion toward Tunisia. The Commissioner refers, in particular, to two cases dealt with by the European Court of Human Rights (*Ben Khemais v. Italy* and *Trabelsi v. Italy*: see Part IV, Case-law of the ECtHR, V), in which deportation occurred even though the ECtHR had ordered Italy to suspend execution of the measure until settlement of the application pending before the Court itself. The Commissioner reiterates his strong aversion to the practice of forced returns, even when occurring under the umbrella of diplomatic assurances, toward Countries which – in light of reliable, consolidated information – diffusely use practices definable as torture, and might use them against the repatriated person. He therefore asks the Italian authorities urgently to reconsider their immigration policies, and to comply with binding interim measures ordered by the ECtHR.

VII. European Commission against Racism and Intolerance

The European Commission against Racism and Intolerance (ECRI), established in 1993, is a monitoring body of the Council of Europe specialised in combating any form of racism, xenophobia, anti-Semitism and intolerance, in a human rights perspective.

The members of the ECRI remain in office for five years. They are selected for their moral authority and their recognised experience in the field of combating racism, xenophobia, anti-semitism and intolerance; they act on an individual basis and independently. The Commission is composed by a member and, if a Government so wishes, a deputy member for each Member State of the Council of Europe.

The experts in respect of Italy are Vitaliano Esposito (actual member) and Antonio Mura (deputy member). Both will remain in office until January 2013.

From its creation to the end of 2010, the ECRI has made four visits to Italy. The latest was effected during the month of November 2010, and observations concerning it will be published during the year 2011. The main topics focused on during the fourth visit have been: the reception and legal status of regular migrants; access to public services (schooling, housing, health care); discrimination in the employment market; incidents based on racism and xenophobia; irregular immigrants and the "crime" of clandestine status; asylum-seekers; the condition of Roma and Sinti populations and Muslim communities; protection for the victims of trafficking in human beings; conduct of the media; provisions disciplining the issue of residence permits; education and awareness initiatives. In accordance with its usual procedure, the delegation met with public authorities, representatives of NGOs, and members of the academic community. Official encounters were organised by the Inter-Ministerial Committee for Human Rights in Rome, Venice and Naples. By request of the ECRI, the consultative meeting with civil society organisations operating in Veneto was held at the Human Rights Centre of the University of Padua. Participants in the encounter included the following associations and academic institutions: Giuristi Democratici (Padua section), Migrantes, Caritas, CISL Veneto, Consulta regionale immigrazione, CGIL Treviso, Associazione per l'autogestione dei servizi e la solidarietà (AUSER), Centro studi immigrazione (CESTIM), ACLI Veneto, Associazione diritti umani-sviluppo umano (ADUSU), Associazione Opera Nomadi, Associazione per gli studi giuridici sull'immigrazione (ASGI-Veneto), University of Padua, Ca' Foscari University of Venice, University of Trieste.

Until now, therefore the Commission has prepared three reports concerning Italy. The first was published on 15 June 1998 (CRI(98)48), the second on 23 April 2002 (CRI(2002)4), and the third on 16 May 2006 (CRI(2006)19). Besides these documents, on 20 June 2008 the ECRI adopted a declaration expressing its concern over violent and discriminatory incidents emerging in Italy against Roma and immigrants. The latest report published covers the Italian situation until 16 December 2005.

The first part of the report offers observations concerning the implementation of recommendations contained in the previous report. In this section, the Commission acknowledges that Italy has made progress in the fight against racism and intolerance, in particular through the institution of the National Office for Racial Discrimination (UNAR – see Part II, National Human Rights-related bodies, II, E). Advancements have also been recorded in the field of education and in the protection of the victims of trafficking in human beings. However, the report finds that some recommendations have not been put into effects, or have been only partially. Among the aspects mentioned in negative feedback, in particular, is the increase in recourse to racist or xenophobic statements by the politicians, referring specifically to non-EU citizens, Roma, Sinti and Muslims, and the lack of a general political orientation aiming to improve their status. In addition, stress is laid on the lack of an organic legislation on asylum, and on the absence of any national programme for the integration of refugees.

In the second part of the report, the Commission provides a series of recommendations.

Concerning the acceptance of pertinent international legal instruments, the Commission recommends ratifying Protocol XII to the ECHR, the European Charter for Regional or Minority Languages, the European Convention on Nationality, the Additional Protocol to the Convention on Cybercrime and the International Convention on the Protection of the Rights of All Migrant Workers and their Families.

As regards the *overall legislative framework*, the ECRI recommends introducing the necessary reforms to facilitate the attribution of Italian citizenship both to children of foreign origin born on national territory, and to long-term residents, and to ascertain whether naturalisation measures are applied in a transparent, non-discriminatory manner.

As regards provisions of criminal, civil and administrative law, the Commission exhorts the Italian Government to improve the application of current guarantees against racism and racial discrimination, and to foster knowledge about them among persons operating in all the pertinent sectors.

As regards the *administration of justice*, the recommendations concern the need to study the reasons for the excessively high quota of non-citizens among the prison population in Italy, ensuring that this situation does not depend on any form of direct or indirect discrimination; and in any event, guaranteeing all prisoners without Italian citizenship access to translation and interpreting services and, if necessary, proper legal aid at State expense.

As regards *specialised bodies and institutions*, the Commission stresses the need to ascertain that the UNAR is able to offer victims of racially discriminatory acts, the most effective protection possible. It exhorts the Government to institute regional monitoring centres on racial discrimination in all regions, as required by law, and to ensure their coordination by way of the UNAR's activity.

As regards *awareness-raising*, the ECRI urges Italy to pursue and intensify its efforts to combat racism both among the general public and specific groups. In addition, it exhorts the Government to continue in its commitment to intercultural and human rights education for both students and educators.

As regards *reception and the legal status of non-citizens*, the recommendations focus on the modalities for issuing resident permits. That must not result in direct or indirect discrimination against individuals on grounds covered by the ECRI's mandate. In addition, it is necessary to strengthen and rationalise political and institutional commitment on a central level, in support of local initiatives fostering integration between citizens and non-citizens.

As regards *access to public services*, the Commission's concern is to ensure that there is equal educational opportunities for non-Italian students, comprising good-quality teaching of Italian and the adoption of provisions which avoid any stigmatisation against students who do not attend lessons on the Catholic religion; alternative teaching should be proposed for them.

Concerning the *right to housing*, the ECRI asks Italy to apply at the national level, local-level best practices in immigrants' access to housing. It recommends favouring access to health care services by minority groups. In particular, the Commission reiterates the need to deal with this issue in relation to the Roma and Sinti communities, in collaboration with representatives from these communities. On the issue of *work and employment*, as well, Italy is asked to adopt further provisions for reducing disparities between citizens and non-citizens.

On the topic of *racial, xenophobic and anti-semitic-based incidents*, the Commission strongly encourages Italian authorities to make greater efforts, especially in the area of sports events and in contrasting the spreading of racist propaganda via the Internet. It also recommends raising awareness in the media – without, however, interfering with their independence – on their duty to abstain from contributing to an atmosphere of hostility against the members of any minority.

Measures against *manifestations of prejudice, discrimination and violence* are requested to protect the members of Islamic communities, victims of trafficking, and Jewish communities. The report encourages the authorities to institute an independent Commission to investigate into accusations of discriminatory acts directed against police officers, and to improve technical instruments for monitoring and collecting information on the status of minority groups in respect for privacy and informed consent with special attention to combating gender discrimination.

As regards *immigrants and asylum-seekers*, the ECRI urges Italy to adopt an organic legislation on the right to asylum and to guarantee adequate treatment for asylum-seekers during examination of their requests. The Commission also exhorts the authorities to take urgent measures in order to guarantee respect for the principle of *non-refoulement*, especially regarding immigrants intercepted at sea or arrested at the moment of their illegal entry into Italy.

Finally, concerning the situation in the *Centres for Temporary Stay and Assistance* (CPTA), the ECRI recommends guarantees for adequate living conditions, the furthering of inquiries into episodes of presumed mistreatment, and an increase in the transparency of such structures, facilitating access to them by organisations for the protection of human rights of refugees and asylum-seekers.

VIII. Advisory Committee on the Framework Convention for the Protection of National Minorities

The Committee is a monitoring body instituted pursuant to art. 26 of the Council of Europe Framework Convention for the Protection of National Minorities. It is composed of 18 independent experts with recognised expertise in the field of the protection of national minorities. They shall serve on the Committee in their individual capacity, for a period of four years.

Having ratified the Convention in 1998, Italy participated in the first monitoring cycle and presented its report (ACFC/SR(1999)007) on 3 May 1999; the opinion of the Committee (ACFC/IF/OP/I(2002)007) was adopted on 14 September 2001 and the resolution by the Committee of Ministers (ResCMN(2002)10) on 3 July 2002. The second cycle opened with the presentation of the Italian report (ACFC/INF/OPII (2004)006) on 14 May 2004; the relative opinion (ACFC/INF/OP/II (2005)003) dates back to 24 February 2005, and the consequent resolution by the CM (ResCMN(2006)5) to 14 June 2006.

The Committee's latest activity concerning Italy falls into the third monitoring cycle, still in progress, opened on 21 December 2009 with presentation of the Italian Government report (ACFC/SR/III(2009)011). The Committee's opinion was adopted on 15 October 2010, but has not yet been made public, while the resolution by the Committee of Ministers is expected during 2011.

The latest Government report reiterates the great importance attributed by Italy to protecting linguistic minorities; this fact is reflected in art. 2 Const., 3 Const., and 6 Const., and in legal instruments protecting the right of persons belonging to a minority to use their own language, in particular: law 15 December 1999, No. 482 (Provisions safeguarding historical linguistic minorities) and law 23 February 2001, No. 38 (Provisions in favour of the Slovene minority in Friuli-Venezia Giulia). The report also underlines the safeguarding provisions emanated by nearly all the Regions inhabited by minority-language communities, within the sphere of competence assigned them by the Italian Constitution.

In a more generally context, in response to the Committee's observations, the report focuses on the most recent measures taken by Italy in the area of language teaching in schools, in the widening of university curricula, in the use of minority languages in the public administration, in the adaptation of place names in national signs, in the creation of radio and television programmes using the minority language, in the financing of activities aiming to safeguard the language, and in the creation of specialised institutes. In addition, the report stresses that there exists no definition of "national minority" either in the Framework

Convention or in the Italian legal system, and that Italian laws grant special protection only to *linguistic minorities which have been settled in a delimited territory since ancient times*. For this reason, the Roma and Sinti minorities, over whose condition the Committee had expressed particular concern, do not belong to groups protected by law 482/1999, since they are not concentrated within specific areas, but are spread out over the entire Italian territory. However, the report stresses that, in order to favour their integration, the Department for Civil Liberties and Immigration has begun a national monitoring process in order to discover critical points, and any suitable measures to adopt in the areas of education, housing and employment; and it mentioned a great number of positive initiatives put into effect by local authorities: in particular, in favouring recourse to cultural mediators and promoting internships and work grants. In the same field, on State level, the report sheds light on several projects aiming to improve Roma and Sinti living standards, social and scholastic inclusion, and the right to housing; the projects are financed by the Ministry of Interior and the Ministry of Labour and Welfare. In addition, the report notes the organisation of the 2008 European Conference on the Roma Population, held with the aim to find an effective strategy for social inclusion of Roma; participants included representatives of the Roma community.

Among the project initiatives financed pursuant to law 482/1999, the report sheds light on the institution and implementation of linguistic "windows" in Municipalities with linguistic minorities, and numerous other initiatives of a cultural nature (creation of linguistic archives, collection of bibliographic itineraries, and textbooks for compulsory education).

The report notices a decidedly positive overall result ten years after the law came into force; its effects can be measured, in particular, in the considerable increase in requests to use minority languages, greater awareness of the value of diverse languages and cultures, and the promotion of dynamic bilingualism.

Finally, the report notes the frequent collaborative relations and cultural exchanges with minority groups' Country of origin, resulting in official visits by foreign politicians, and in the respective Governments' approval of activities promoted by Italy internationally, regarding the protection of national minorities.

IX. Standing Committee of the European Convention on the Exercise of Children's Rights

The Committee is provided for in art. 16 of the European Convention on the Exercise of Children's Rights (1996). It is composed of one or more representatives for each Member State. The observers attending its sessions may include experts from other States, from the United Nations Committee on the Rights of the Child, from the European Union, and other international organisations having competence in children' rights issues.

The first meeting of the Committee was held on 8 and 9 June 2006, following the launch of the programme *Building a Europe for and with children*, during the third summit of Government leaders from Member States of the Council of Europe, held in Warsaw in May 2005.

Simonetta Matone, Deputy Public Prosecutor at the Youth Court in Rome, was elected Committee Chair until the next meeting.

On this occasion, participants shared their own experiences concerning developments in the exercising of children's rights on the national level; they discussed reports and reflected on the possibility of contradiction between the European Convention and the United Nations Convention on Children's Rights. In addition, the Committee's rules of procedure were adopted, and the decision was made to invite Member States' National Commissioners for Children, as well as representatives of UNICEF, to the next meeting (initially planned for 2009).

X. European Commission for Democracy through Law

Known as the "Venice Commission", this is the Council of Europe's consultative body for constitutional issues. It was established in 1990 and has played a leading role in the widespread adoption, in Europe – particularly in eastern and Balkan areas – of constitutions aligned with European standards

Since 2009 the Chair of the Venice Commission has been Gianni Buquicchio. Two other Italians participate in the Commission activities as substitute members: Sergio Bartole and Guido Neppi Modona.

The Venice Commission's latest activity concerning Italy dates back to 2005. During its 63rd plenary session (10-11 June 2005), on request by PACE (resolution 1387(2004)), the Commission adopted an *opinion* (CDL-AD(2005)017) concerning the compatibility of the so-called "Gasparri law" (law 3 May 2004, No. 112 and the so-called "Frattini law" (law 20 July 2004, No. 215) with Council of Europe standards as regards freedom of expression and pluralism in the media. In the following paragraphs the conclusions presented by the Commission are grouped, according to the topic discussed.

Generally speaking, the Commission maintains that as regards the "Gasparri law" provisions whose purpose is to protect pluralism in the media, the mere increase in the number of channels that will be brought with the introduction of digital television is not, in itself, sufficient in guaranteeing pluralism. Instead, that goal is served well by provisions prohibiting discrimination between independent suppliers of content and those linked or linkable to controlled companies and by AGCOM decisions ensuring access to networks of independent content providers. As regards provisions concerning the switchover from analogical channels to digital ones, the Commission holds that the law has taken the approach of attempting to hold back on finding a real solution to the problem of media concentration in the television market until some future point in time and it relies heavily on the point when digitalisation will come into full effect. The Commission considers this approach insufficient, since if the status quo is maintained, Mediaset and RAI would most probably remain the dominant actors in the Italian television market, whereas dominant positions in the media are forbidden, as such.

As regards the public broadcasting service, the Commission notes that access to airtime seems to be regulated democratically, although the entitlement of the Presidency of the Council of Ministers to obtain free airtime on request, seems formulated in excessively vague terms. As regards the privatisation of RAI, which should lead to a lower degree of politicisation in the public service, the Commission notes that the change, instead, will allow the Government control over the public service for an unforeseeable length of time. Therefore, Prime Minister Berlusconi will have a certain amount of control, as well, over the three channels of public television, besides the three private channels. The Commission expresses its concern over the risk that this atypical situation might aggravate the threat of monopolisation and therefore, according to the Strasbourg Court's case-law, constitute unjustified interference in freedom of expression.

Finally, as regards the printed press, the Commission recommends that it be provided with greater State support, given the growing concentration of the advertising market in television broadcasting.

In the part of the *opinion* focusing on the "Frattini law" which deals with conflict of interest, the Commission notes that this law does not seem to offer general regulation for situations where public officials have personal or financial interests that would make it difficult for them to fulfil their duties with just the public interest in mind; furthermore, the law fails to consider conflicts of interest that might arise in connection with legislative measures targeting a specific category of individuals to which a member of the Government might belong, or targeting a category of business in which a member of the Government may have proprietary interests. In the Commission's opinion, the law does not contain sufficient measures for preventively resolving a potential conflict of interest; therefore it puts excessive onus on the Antitrust Authority, which must decide *ex post* and case by case. In addition, the

Commission criticises the fact that the law fails to require potential members of the Government to remove a conflict of interest, but instead, merely establishes the obligation to inform the competent authorities of the critical situation. While, on one hand, the "Frattini law" assumes that there exists a general incompatibility between management of a company and the holding of public office, on the other, it does not assert the incompatibility between the ownership as such and public office; this fails to alter conflict of interest, as it currently emerges in Italy. Not even the foreseen penalties seem entirely adequate. In particular, the impact of political penalties, which in principle might seem effective, risks being annulled if the political party supporting the Government member suspected of conflict of interest, predominates in Parliament. In conclusion, therefore, the Commission states that the "Frattini law" has few chances of significantly affecting the current situation in Italy, and encourages the authorities to continue studying such problems in hopes of finding an appropriate solution.

European Union

I. European Parliament

The European Parliament (EP), together with the Commission and the Council of the European Union, exercises a fundamental role in the promotion and implementation of the Union's human rights policies.

Among the permanent EP Committees closely concerned with human rights issues, figures the Sub-Committee on Human Rights (Italian member: Vittorio Prodi) within the Committee on Foreign Affairs (Chair: Gabriele Albertini). The Sub-Committee takes human rights initiatives and provides a permanent discussion forum on the human rights situation and the development of democracy in third Countries. One of its main goals is to contribute toward integrating human rights issues into all facets of the EU's foreign relations and, therefore, into the Union's enlargement, foreign trade, development, as well as neighbourhood policies. The Parliament carefully monitors compliance with the human rights clauses which are systematically included by the European Union in every commercial agreement with third Countries.

The Committee on Civil Liberties, Justice and Legal Affairs (Vice Chairman: Salvatore Iacolino; other Italian members: Sonia Alfano, Roberta Angelilli, Rita Borsellino, Maro Borghezio, Rosario Crocetta) is dedicated mainly to human rights issues within the European Union. Other Committees closely related to human rights issues are the Juridical Committee (Vice Chairmen: Luigi Berlinguer, Raffaele Baldassarre; other Italian members: Alfredo Antoniazzi, Francesco Enrico Speroni); the Committee on Employment and Social Affairs (Italian members: Maria Bizzotto, Sergio Cofferati, Licia Ronzulli); the Committee on the Environment, Public Health and Food Safety (Italian members: Paolo Bartolozzi, Sergio Berlato, Elisabetta Gardini, Vittorio Prodi, Oreste Rossi, Salvatore Tartarella); the Committee on Development (Vice Chair: Iva Zanicchi); the Committee on Women's Rights and Gender Equality (Vice Chair: Barbara Matera; other Italian member: Silvia Costa); and the Committee on Petitions, which is presented below.

Between 15 and 17 February 2010, a delegation from the EP (Committee on Civil Liberties, Justice and Legal Affairs) conducted a fact-finding mission in Rosarno, after the riots involving migrant workers in the Calabrian town in early January 2010. The data collected by the delegation were presented to the Parliamentary Committee on 4 March 2010 (report EP439.312v01-00).

Committee on Petitions

Among the citizenship rights recognised in the EU Charter of Fundamental Rights, figures the right to present a petition to the European Parliament (art. 44 CFREU, as well as art. 24 and art. 227 TFEU), which is guaranteed by an apposite Parliamentary Committee. […] The Chair of the Committee on Petitions is Erminia Mazzoni.

The European Parliament received 1,506 petitions in 2007, 1,849 in 2008, 1,924 in 2009 and 1,655 in 2010 (a 14% decrease compared to the preceding year). As regards the year 2010, 864 petitions were considered admissible and 586 inadmissible, while 205 were not registered. According to the working document on the Committee deliberations in 2010, 182 petitions came from Italy in that year, amounting to 9.9% of the total.

Moreover, a delegation from the Committee carried out a fact-finding mission in *Campania*, between 28 and 30 April 2010, in order to verify declarations contained in 15 petitions, received between the end of 2009 and January 2010, on the situation of waste disposal in the region. In the resulting document, after meeting with representatives of the local authorities and the petition's authors, and hearing the opinion of independent researchers, the delegation gave a series of recommendations aiming at enabling the passage from crisis management to *actual waste management.* Among them: to transform the *Guidelines for the management of solid waste (2010-2010)* adopted by Campania's Regional Government in February 2010, into a concrete and detailed plan of action with short- and long-term objectives; to rebuild dialogue between citizens and authorities and among the different levels of governance; to allocate appropriate resources on both the national and regional level; to implement the plan for waste management while giving priority to the hierarchy of the waste cycle (in particular, to prevention, reduction, reuse and recycling); to create only incinerating systems compatible with EU waste management guidelines, with particular attention to the management of industrial, toxic and special waste, and to inform the citizens about the environmental impact of such systems.

II. European Commission

The European Commission has a central role in the development and implementation of European Union policies, including human rights policies, both within the Union and in relation to third Countries.

The European Instrument for Democracy and Human Rights (EIDHR), established with regulation EC 1889/2006, is a fundamental tool for the promotion of human rights in the EU. The EIDHR replaces the previous European Initiative for Democracy and Human Rights, launched in 1994.

The Instrument provides Communitarian assistance through bilateral development cooperation and contributes to the development and the strengthening of democracy, the rule of law and to the respect of human rights and fundamental freedoms in non-EU Countries. Among the various financed initiatives, the EIDHR supports operating costs of the European Inter-University Centre for Human Rights and Democratisation (EIUC), in particular for the European Master's Degree Programme in Human Rights and Democratisation and the EU-UN Fellowship Programme, fully accessible to nationals of third Countries.

On 19 October 2010, the Commission adopted the *Communication on a Strategy for the effective implementation of the Charter of Fundamental Rights by the European Union* (COM(2010)573def). The Communication sets the goal of developing a policy to make the Charter's fundamental rights as effective as possible within the EU. Among the activities foreseen in this framework, the Commission will publish an annual progress report on the Charter's application. Further details on the Commission's action are available in the section discussing EU legislation and case-law during 2010 (see Part I, International Human Rights Instruments, IV, B).

III. Council of the European Union

Starting in 1998, the Council has adopted and updated a series of "human rights guidelines" which constitute a framework of reference for the promotion and protection of human rights in third Countries, in the context of EU's common foreign and security policy.

Until today eight guidelines have been adopted, focused on the following topics: *death penalty* (1998, updated in 2008); *torture and other cruel, inhuman or degrading treatment or punishment* (2001, updated in 2008); *human rights dialogues with third Countries* (2001, updated in 2008); *children and armed conflict* (2003, updated in 2008); *human rights defenders* (2004, updated in 2008); *promotion and protection of the rights of the child* (2007); *violence against women and girls, and combating all forms of discrimination against them* (2008); *international humanitarian law* (2005, updated in 2009).

Within the Council there is the Human Rights Working Group (COHOM) created in 1987 as an instrument dealing with human rights in foreign relations of the European Union. The group is composed of the representatives from the units concerned with fundamental rights within the Ministry of Foreign Affairs of the 27 member Countries and from the Commission. Its agenda includes the various aspects of EU human rights policy: in particular, its action in international forums, the "dialogues" with third Countries, various thematic issues, as well as emergency situations of human rights violations.

Since 1999 the Council of the European Union has adopted an annual report on human rights and democracy in the world. The report presented in 2010, referring to the period 2008-2009, was prepared by the European External Action Service.

IV. Court of Justice of the European Union

Over time, the Court of Justice has played an essential role in maintaining that human rights are an integral part of the Communitarian juridical system.

In 2010, the members of the EU Court of Justice with respect to Italy have been Antonio Tizzano, as judge, Paolo Mengozzi, as general attorney and Enzo Moavero Milanesi as judge in the General Court.

On ECJ case-law in 2010, see Part I, International Human Rights Instruments, IV, B.

V. European External Action Service

In the exercise of his functions, the High Representative of the European Union for Foreign Affairs and Security Policy/Vice President of the European Commission (HR/VP) finds support in the European External Action Service (EEAS), a sort of European Ministry of Foreign Affairs composed of officials in the competent services of the General Secretariat of the Council and of the Commission, and by detached personnel from the national diplomatic services (art. 27 TEU).

On 10 May 2010 the EEAS presented the report *Human rights and democracy in the World*, concerning the activities promoted by the EU externally during the period July 2008-December 2009. It is worth noticing that the report also mentions the European Master in Human Rights and Democratisation (E.MA), located in Venice, which has now reached its 14th academic cycle; the programme is indicated as a successful example among EU-sponsored activities promoting post-graduate education in human rights, and as an inspiration for other Master's programmes focusing on the same issues, in other regions of the world.

VI. Fundamental Rights Agency

The European Union's Fundamental Rights Agency (FRA) is an advisory body instituted by Council regulation (EC) 168/2007 on 15 February 2007, and has been operative since 1 March 2007. The FRA was created in order to expand the mandate of the preceding European Monitoring Centre on Racism and Xenophobia (EUMC), which it legally succeeds. The Agency Director is Morten Kjaerum (Denmark). Since December 2009 the Italian participants in the FRA Management Board have been Daniela Bas (member) and Lorenza Violini (alternate member), who have replaced, respectively, Elena Paciotti (who was also a member of the Agency's Executive Board) and Marina Callon; both had held office during the two-year period 2007-2009.

Among its functions, the Agency collects data relating to issues of racism, xenophobia and relative intolerance, by way of the "focal-point" network, RAXEN, created in 2000. The focal points have the task of instituting, maintaining and regularly revising a national information network that includes the main actors in the field. In addition, they coordinate and structure the database in relation to their own Country, and transmit the information to the FRA following specific guidelines. The focal point for Italy is COSPE (Cooperazione per lo sviluppo dei Paesi emergenti).

In addition, since 2007, the FRA has managed FRALEX, a network of legal experts highly qualified in the area of human rights. The experts prepare reports and studies on the national level, which are published and utilised for further comparative analyses. The legal expert in respect of Italy is Marta Cartabia.

The Agency collaborates with the Council of Europe, the human dimension machinery of OSCE, the UN High Commissioner for Refugees, and UNESCO, and acts in network with civil society organisations, in particular through the Fundamental Rights Platform (FRP), a network for cooperation and information exchange launched by the FRA in 2008, open to all qualified, concerned actors which have their office in one of the EU Member States. The organisation and functioning of the FRP are supported by an advisory panel composed of nine Platform members, who remain in office for a two-year period. Since April 2010 Barbara Terenzi has been a panel member, as representative of the Italian NGOs Network named *Comitato per la Promozione e Protezione dei Diritti Umani*.

The scientific quality of the Agency's work and publications is ensured by a scientific committee whose members include Stefano Rodotà.

The FRA has presented general and specific reports comparing data relating to Italy's human rights situation with respective data from the other 26 EU Member States. In addition, at the end of 2008, FRA presented an incident report entitled *Violent attacks against Roma in the Ponticelli District of Naples.* The information used in this report was collected by the COSPE.

The report gives a summary account of aggressions against Roma and their camps between May and June 2008, and against other persons belonging to foreign communities, not only in the capital city of Campania, but throughout the Italian territory. In addition, it provides brief general data on the events, and describes the Italian authorities' response in the form of normative measures. The report also sheds light on the climate of intolerance generated throughout the Country by the events in Ponticelli, and gives several examples of critical reactions by the national and European civil society and international bodies, to the events and to the Italian authorities' response.

In its conclusions, the Agency highlights that the incidents in Italy reflect the more generalised problems faced by Roma communities throughout Europe. It therefore stresses the fact that despite the commitment of European institutions and of other regional organisations, such as the Council of Europe, Roma, Sinti and Travellers remain the most vulnerable groups in Europe. Their problems include poor and segregated housing conditions, discrimination and forced evictions in over one half of the European Union Member States.

Drawing from the events which occurred in Italy, the report also sheds light on the fact that a significant number of Roma camps in the areas where the incidents broke out was unauthorised; it therefore emphasises the urgent need to replace illegal settlements with authorised sites in all Member States. Through commitment by the local authorities, the sites must be provided with adequate sanitary structures guaranteeing water supply, sanitation, electricity and access to public transport.

According to the Agency, the violent, discriminatory events reported in Italy against Roma are evidence that in order to safeguard the fundamental rights in the European Union, Governments must fulfil their duty to respect, protect and promote such rights not only by providing the necessary legal safeguards, but also by ensuring its effective application by the local, regional and national public authorities. The report refers, in particular, to directive 2000/43/EC of 29 June 2000 and claims that achieving equal treatment for Roma and Traveller groups throughout the European Union requires strong political commitment and urgent action on the ground, in the context of a holistic approach developing long-term strategies, policies and measures for all areas of social life.

VII. European Ombudsman

The right to make a complaint to the European Ombudsman is recognised as one of European Citizenship rights, by art. 43 of the CFREU, as well as art. 24 and 228 TEU.

The Ombudsman works together with the European Network of Ombudsmen, which includes all the national and regional Ombudspersons of the Member States and of the candidate Countries, along with the Ombudspersons of Norway and Iceland, and the national Committees on Petitions.

The complaints lodged before the Ombudsman and falling into the sphere of his mandate numbered 870 in 2007, 802 in 2008, 727 in 2009 and 744 in 2010. In 2010, the European Ombudsman began 335 investigations (compared to 339 in 2009), and completed 326 of them within the year (compared to 318 in 2009). In all, during 2010 the Ombudsman handled over 3,700 complaints and requests for information. In 2010, 132 complaints came from Italy, amounting to 4.9% of the total, with a ratio between claims and population of 0.4.

Since April 2003 the European Ombudsman has been Nikiforos P. Diamandouros, former National Ombudsman of Greece.

Organisation for Security and Cooperation in Europe

The Director of the Italian mission at Organisation for Security and Cooperation in Europe (OSCE) is Ambassador Gianfranco Varvesi. Thirteen members of the House of Representatives and of the Senate sit at the Parliamentary Assembly of the Organisation. The Director of the Italian Parliamentary delegation, Riccardo Migliori, was elected Vice Chair of the Assembly on 10 July 2010.

Among the positions of Personal Representative of the OSCE Chairperson in office it is worth mentioning that on *fighting racism, xenophobia and discrimination against Christians and members of other religions*, which, during the two-year period 2009-2010, was held by Mario Mauro who was recently succeeded by Massimo Introvigne.

I. Office for Democratic Institutions and Human Rights (ODIHR)

Established in 1990 as the Office for Free Elections and later reorganised in name and mandate, today the Office for Democratic Institutions and Human Rights (ODIHR, with headquarters in Warsaw) is the main OCSE institution dealing with the "human dimension" of security. Its goal is to assist Member States in implementing their commitments in the fields of elections, human rights and democratisation.

The first Director of the Office was Luchino Cortese, who held the mandate from 1991 to 1994.

The ODIHR's most recent mission for electoral observation in Italy was carried out for the political elections of 13 and 14 April 2008, on request from the Italian delegation at OSCE. During the preceding elections of 2006, a similar mission had been requested.

The general considerations contained in the final report, published on 5 September 2008, indicate that the elections were conducted in a correct, efficient manner, although it was pointed out that several polls directors and several scrutinisers had failed to show up on election day. Although acknowledging that a good number of voters had come to the polls, the mission reports a certain amount of discontent over the current electoral law, especially over the fact that, in the current system, voters can no longer express preference for an individual. This shortcoming aggravates distrust toward the electoral system itself.

The ODIHR mission notes that while the two election processes were held according to the same electoral legislation, the recommendations made in the report on the 2006 elections were largely ignored, specifically as regards several key aspects of the normative framework, such as the fact that the newly elected Parliament is the body of final appeal for complaints concerning election results. The political campaign was pluralistic, competitive, and conducted in a fairly calm atmosphere. Freedom of expression and assembly were respected, and voters were offered a genuine choice among various political options. The candidates held rallies and presented their programmes in a free environment respectful toward civil and political rights.

As regards *media behaviour*, the report notes that they generally focused their attention on the two main contending parties; for that reason, smaller parties complained of receiving scarce attention from the media. The national broadcast and the print media gave in-depth coverage to the elections and, on the public television channels, all parties enjoyed equitable access to programmes specifically dedicated to election day. However, the mission found clear bias in favour of the coalition of the *Popolo delle libertà* (PdL) on two television channels owned by Mediaset.

As regards the *presence of women in the incoming Parliament*, the mission notes that they represent only 21% of House seats and 17% in the Senate. In addition, women are poorly represented in the leadership positions within political parties.

Aside from the general assessment of the electoral process, the mission gave recommendations for improving electoral operations.

As regards the legal framework, the ODIHR recommends adopting a single, integrated and consolidated text of electoral legislation and considering the possibility of lowering the voting age to 18, for the Senate as well. In addition, it suggests excluding the possibility of anonymous donations to political parties and single candidates, in order to improve transparency in their financing systems; eliminating the possibility for candidates to present themselves in all electoral constituencies; eliminating the system of closed lists, in order to allow a closer tie between candidates and voters; and cancelling the majority bonus, given the unforeseeable nature of its effects.

Concerning the *impact of the media in covering the electoral process*, the mission urges Italy to implement the recommendations contained in the 2005 report by the OSCE Representative on Freedom of the Media entitled *Visit to Italy: the Gasparri law* (see Part III, OSCE, III). It also suggests that the Italian authorities grant more powers to the Communications Regulatory Authority (AGCOM), in order to implement its decisions.

Concerning the *absence of a competent body to decide on pre election day complaints*, the ODIHR report urges the new Parliament to consider measures capable of providing timely and impartial resolution of electoral disputes before election day.

Finally, as regards the *participation of vulnerable groups in the democratic process*, the mission stresses that parties should include a greater number of women in the most important positions in candidate lists, and that Italian citizens of Roma origin should be informed of their rights and responsibilities, should not be discriminated against, and should be encouraged to vote.

The Office's most recent activity regarding Italy concerns a visit made in July 2008, in collaboration with the High Commissioner on National Minorities.

II. High Commissioner on National Minorities

The Office of the High Commissioner on National Minorities was set up in 1992 with the purpose of responding to the increasing number of violent episodes on the continent, imputable to ethnic conflict. Today Knut Vollebaek of Norway holds this post, and has done so since 2007. His mandate, renewed in 2010, will expire in 2013.

Between 20 and 26 July 2008, a delegation composed of representatives from the Office of the High Commissioner on National Minorities, the ODIHR, and the Council of Europe's Office of the Commissioner for Human Rights made a visit to the cities of Milan, Rome and Naples. The purpose of their mission was to assess both the violent incidents that had broken out in preceding months against members of Roma and Sinti communities residing in Italy, and the measures taken by the Italian authorities in confronting these episodes. The resulting report was published on 6 March 2009. During the mission the delegation met with representatives of the Italian authorities, civil society, and Roma and Sinti communities. The recommendations addressed to the Italian authorities include: to increase efforts to apply the provisions of the 2003 OSCE Plan of Action for improving the condition of Roma and Sinti and reconsider current policies dealing with these populations; to intensify efforts to develop and enact a strategy aiming to integrate Roma and Sinti in Italy; to strengthen anti-discriminatory legislation and provide effective remedies; to strengthen protection of Roma and Sinti in Italy by recognising them as a minority group; to abstain from using the term "nomads", preferring, instead, the denomination "Roma and Sinti"; to ask local and regional authorities to take initiatives in integrating Roma and Sinti populations, making use of local, regional, national and European funds; to establish a governmental body coordinating integration policies for Roma and Sinti, with adequate participation by representatives of the respective communities; to engage in direct dialogue with Roma and Sinti representatives, partly through support and training by civil society groups within their communities; to reconsider emergency measures which have a disproportionate effect on such populations, in consideration of international standards in the area of human rights and non-discrimination; to ensure that any piece of information collected by way of the 2008 census of the Roma and Sinti populations be used only in order to favour integration and be protected according to European and international standards; to provide information to the OSCE on how the results of the 2008 census are to be used in planning integration policies; to adapt to national and international standards for what regards expulsions, and ensure that expulsion orders are based on careful, objective examination of the situation of individuals involved and that they are subject to judiciary control; to find a lasting solution to the problem of "*de facto* statelessness" among Roma from the western Balkans.

In this connection, the delegation encourages the Italian authorities to consider guaranteeing citizenship for humanitarian reasons for Roma children born in Italy, and for their families. It urges authorities to improve cooperation with the Romanian Government in order to improve the integration of Roma and Sinti in both Countries. It recommends avoiding the practice of evictions, while respecting juridical and administrative protective measures and providing alternative housing. The report encourages the State to cope with the problem of housing for Roma and Sinti while taking into account that, on the long-term, the habitual resort to camps and temporary shelters should be abandoned; to commit itself to ensuring that all Roma and Sinti children have access to quality education favouring their full integration into Italian society; and to oppose manifestations of hate against Roma, as well as other xenophobic behaviour, even if expressed in the private sphere.

III. OSCE Representative on Freedom of the Media

The OSCE Representative on Freedom of the Media was established in December 1997 with the purpose of ensuring a high level of conformity with the norms and standards accepted by the Member States of the Organisation concerning freedom of expression and freedom in the media. Since March 2010 this office has been held by Dunja Mijatovic, of Bosnia-Herzegovina.

The OSCE Representative visited Italy in 2004. The report that followed, entitled *Visit to Italy: the Gasparri law*, was published on 7 June 2005. The mission's motivation was to assess the situation in Italy in the telecommunications sector after the adoption of the "Gasparri law" (law

3 May 2004, No. 112), the first overall regulation for radio and television media, and the "Frattini law" (law 20 July 2004, No. 215), on conflict of interest. These two laws have also been examined in an *opinion* adopted by the Council of Europe's Venice Commission, in 2005 (see Part III, Council of Europe, X).

According to the report of the Representative (at the time of the visit, the Hungarian, Miklós Haraszti), freedom of expression and freedom of the press in Italy are, generally speaking, in good health although the television market continues to be anomalous. The persistent duopoly held by RAI and Mediaset, and especially the quasi-monopoly of Mediaset within the commercial television market, have deprived Italian audiences of effective variety of information, thus weakening guarantees for pluralism in the Country. In his observations, the Representative on Freedom of the Media stresses that, in Italy, the influence of Governments and political parties is especially strong in the public television service. The fact that the Prime Minister is also the principal national entrepreneur in the media sector, television in particular, further aggravates such concern.

As regards the "Gasparri law", the Representative concludes that despite the innovations it introduces, it will not be capable of correcting the television anomaly and will not result in a de-monopolised television environment. He therefore recommends that the new law be carefully revised in order to resolve the current anomalies. In particular, the Representative encourages the legislator to fully de-politicise RAI's management structures. Concerning the second law discussed, while acknowledging that the conflict between the public office of Prime Minister Berlusconi and the media in his holdings is settled from a legal point of view by the "Frattini law", the Representative observes that this conflict of interest continues to raise concern, since the legal formula chosen does not completely separate the Prime Minister from his media holdings. The Representative maintains that the conflict of interest in the media must be dealt with by stricter measures in order to strengthen the public's trust in the correctness and transparency of political competition. The system recommended is that of a "blind trust" with a custodian.

In more recent times, on 15 June 2010, the current Representative on Freedom in the Media commented on the status of freedom of expression in Italy after the Senate approved bill No. 1611, also known as the "wiretap law", on 10 June 2010.

In a public declaration, Dunja Mijatovic expresses concern over a measure that might seriously hinder investigative journalism in Italy, and which does not take into account previous warnings made by her Office. In its current form, the bill contradicts OSCE commitments. Specifically, several measures seem particularly questionable: severe restrictions in the possibility to publish documents related to Court proceedings or police investigations prior to the beginning of a trial; the introduction of a penalty up to 450,000 euros for publishers, and up to 30 days' imprisonment and a penalty up to 10,000 euros for journalists who publish leaked wiretappings before the beginning of the trial; the possibility of a prison sentence for anyone who is not a professional journalist and records or films a person without that person's prior consent.

IV. Special Representative and Co-ordinator for Combating Trafficking in Human Beings

The OSCE Office of the Special Representative and Co-ordinator for Combating Trafficking in Human Beings was set up with the purpose of assisting States in in the implementation of the commitments and in the full usage of the recommendations proposed by the OSCE Action Plan to Combat Trafficking in Human Beings, adopted in 2003 through decision No. 2 of the Council of Ministers.

Maria Grazia Giammarino was appointed Special Representative and Co-ordinator for Combating Trafficking in Human Beings in December 2009, and has begun to operate in January 2010.

In 2010, the Representative published her yearly report on the topic *Combating trafficking in human beings as a modern form of slavery: a question of rights, freedoms and security*.

International Humanitarian and Criminal Law

I. Adapting to International Humanitarian and Criminal Law

Italy has signed all the major international conventions on the law of armed conflict and international criminal law. In 2010 it ratified the Protocol on Explosive Remnants of War (Protocol V), annexed in Geneva on 28 November 2003 to the Geneva Convention on Conventional Weapons, adopted on 10 October 1980. Authorisation for ratification had been given by law 12 November 2009, No. 173, while the relative instrument was registered on 11 February 2010. In addition, during the year 2010, the ratification process for the Oslo Convention prohibiting cluster bombs, signed in 2008, continued its Parliamentary procedure. The ratification of this important treaty is foreseen for 2011.

As for the domestic implementation of international humanitarian law, especially in regards to the formulation of specific war crimes, an organic intervention of the wartime military criminal code (WMCC) is still awaited. The legislator and the Constitutional Court, despite having modified or amended the WMCC in a number of occasions, did not coherently reformed it. Indeed, art. 165 of the WMCC, which introduces the section on crimes against the laws and uses of war, states that its provisions apply "pending the issuing of rules organically regulating the matter".

The obligation to provide training for Italian military personnel in the field of international humanitarian law and international criminal law, including the Statute of the International Criminal Court, was reiterated by legislative decree 66/2010 (Code of the Military System).

Italy was also among the first Countries to ratify the Rome Statute establishing the International Criminal Court. It did so with law 232/1999. In addition, with law 130/2006, Italy ratified the Agreement on the Privileges and Immunities of the International Criminal Court. Despite this, Italy has not yet fully implemented into its domestic legal order the measures necessary for the practical enforcement of provisions set forth in the Rome Statute. Several bills were presented during the last two legislatures, based on the work of four Ministerial Commissions operating between 1998 and 2004. At the end of 2010, the bills pending before the Justice Commission of the House of Representatives were: C. 1439 (Melchiorre), C. 1782 (Di Pietro), C. 2445 (Bernardini) and C. 1695 (Gozi). The trend emerging in the Justice Commission during that year has been to limit the process of adaptation only to provisions of procedural nature, leaving aside the substantial changes needed to fully align the Italian criminal system with the obligations set forth in the Rome Statute.

Two Italian nationals occupy institutionally eminent positions in the International Criminal Court structure: Registrar Silvana Arbia, appointed in 2008 for a five-year mandate and Cuno Tarfusser, appointed as judge in 2009, with a mandate lasting nine years. Between 2003 and 2009, Mauro Politi was Court judge.

Italian nationals have also played highly significant role in the activities of the two ad hoc International Tribunals set up to provide accountability for international crimes committed respectively in the Former Yugoslavia and Rwanda.

As regards the International Criminal Tribunal for the Former Yugoslavia (ICTY), established by the United Nations Security Council with resolution 827/1993, Antonio Cassese was its first President, from 1993 to 1997, and sat as judge until 2000. Since 2000 Fausto Pocar has been an ICTY judge; he also presided over the Tribunal from 2005 to 2008. Since 2007, Flavia Lattanzi has acted as judge *ad litem* at this tribunal and has been involved in very important cases, such as the Seselj trial. She was also judge at the International Criminal Tribunal for Rwanda (2003-2006). Italy was among the first Countries to implement a law on the cooperation with the Yugoslavian tribunal (law 120/1994), and in 1999 it ratified the agreement signed with the United Nations for the enforcement in Italy of sentences of imprisonment decided by the ICTY. Five convicted individuals are currently serving sentences in Italy: Goran Jelisic, Milorad Krnojelac, Dragan Nikolic, Vinko Marinović, and Mladen Naletilić.

As for the cooperation with the International Criminal Tribunal for Rwanda, created by the United Nations Security Council with resolution 954/1994 to judge international crimes – war crimes, crimes against humanity and genocide – committed in 1994 in the territory of Rwanda and neighbouring States, laws 181/2002 and 64/2006 provided the necessary legislative framework.

Worth to mention is also the appointment, since 2009, of judge Antonio Cassese as President of the Special Tribunal for Lebanon, the mixed criminal tribunal instituted by the Security Council on 30 May 2007 with resolution 1757 (2007) to hold trials for those guilty of the dynamite attack which in 2005 killed the former Prime Minister of Lebanon, Rafik Hariri, along with several other persons.

Lastly, it seems relevant to recall that, since 2008, Italy has been involved in a controversy with Germany in regard to several Italian courts decisions ordering Germany to pay compensation to victims of war crimes committed by the Third Reich during World War II (the basis for these decisions is the well-known 2004 judgement of the Court of Cassation in the *Ferrini* case). Germany reacted instituting a procedure against Italy before the International Court of Justice (ICJ) for failing to respect its jurisdictional immunity as a sovereign State. The basis for the jurisdiction of the ICJ is the European Convention for the Peaceful Settlement of Disputes, adopted by the Council of Europe in 1957 and ratified by Italy and Germany respectively in 1960 and 1961. In 2010 the International Court of Justice rejected Italy's counter-claim requesting the Court to adjudicate and declare that Germany had violated the international obligation of reparation owed to the Italian victims of war crimes perpetrated during World War II. By majority (the Brazilian judge, Antônio Conçado Trindade, voting against) the Court held that the counter-claim submitted by Italy, relating to facts and situations existing prior to the entry into force of the 1957 European Convention (deportations took place between 1943 and 1945) fell outside the Court's jurisdiction.

II. The Italian Contribution to Peace-keeping Missions and Other International Missions

In 2010, with two law-decrees then converted into law (law-decree 1/2010, converted with law 30/2010; law-decree 102/2010, converted with law 126/2010), Italy refinanced the participation of Italian military and civilian personnel to several international missions taking place in regions torn by conflict or political tensions where, at least potentially, international humanitarian law applies. In all such missions, including those carried out in situations of armed conflict, the law establishes the non-applicability of the WMCC. It is the peacetime military criminal code (PMCC), integrated by Italian, international law and local norms (regulating the status of foreign troops in the ground), which represents the applicable legal framework. All international missions in particular, are subject to art. 4, paragraph 1-*sexies* of law-decree 152/2009, converted with law 29 December 2009, No. 197. Integrating the justifications laid out by the Italian criminal code and the PMCC, which are deemed to align with international criminal and humanitarian law (in particular, self-defence), this provision seems to provide a new ground to exclude criminal responsibility. The new justification is described as follows: "The military who […] in conformity with directives, rules of engagement or legitimate orders, makes use of or orders the use of weapons, force or other means of physical coercion which is necessary for military operations, is not punishable". The overall effect of this norm has yet to be clarified.

In the following chart, the military and police missions to which Italy committed by deploying its personnel in 2010 are listed. Italy's participation ranges from a presence of over 3,500 soldiers in Afghanistan – increased by around 1,000 during the course of that year – to missions involving few individuals, in other contexts. The most numerically significant mission, that in Afghanistan, was financed with more than 700 million euros. Worth to mention is that the intelligence activities protecting the security of the missions are carried out by the External Intelligence and Security Agency (AISE). In 2010, 11 Italian soldiers lost their lives in Afghanistan.

Country/Geographic Area of Intervention	**Italy's Mission and Activities**
Afghanistan	International Security Assistance Force (ISAF) (military and police component)
	EUPOL AFGHANISTAN (military and police component)
Lebanon	United Nations Interim Force in Lebanon (UNIFIL), which includes the use of naval units in the UNIFIL Maritime Task Force
Kosovo/Balkans	Multinational Specialized Unit (MSU) of KFOR (NATO), in support of the European Union Rule of Law Mission in Kosovo (EULEX Kosovo)
	Operation Joint Enterprise (NATO) Security Force Training Plan in Kosovo
	Cooperation programmes of Italian police forces in Albania and in the Countries of the Balkan area
	Participation of State Police officers, judges, prison police and administration officers to the mission EULEX Kosovo
	Participation of State Police officers to the United Nations Mission in Kosovo (UNMIK)
Bosnia-Herzegovina	Integrated Police Unit (IPU) in the framework of the European Union ALTHEA operation
	Participation of officers from the *Arma dei Carabinieri*, the State Police and the Judiciary in the European Union Police Mission (EUPM)
Eastern Mediterranean	Mission Active Endeavour in the Mediterranean (NATO)
Occupied Palestinian territories	Temporary International Presence in Hebron (TIPH2);
	Participation of State Police officers and of a judge to the European Union Police Mission for the Palestinian Territories (EUPOL COPPS)

Occupied Palestinian territories/Egypt	European Union Border Assistance Mission in Rafah (EUBAM Rafah)
Sudan	United Nations/African Union Mission in Darfur (UNAMID)
Democratic Republic of the Congo	Mission EUPOL RD CONGO
Cyprus	United Nations Peacekeeping Force in Cyprus (UNFICYP)
Albania	Italian Delegation of Experts – activity in support of the Albanian armed forces.
Georgia	European Union Monitoring Mission in Georgia – EUMM Georgia
Somalia/Indian Ocean	European Union ATALANTA military mission
	NATO operation to combat piracy
Iraq	Consulting, education and training activities for Iraqi armed and police forces
United Arab Emirates	Task Force Air in support of the operations in Afghanistan and Iraq (Abu Dhabi, Bahrain and Tampa – USA)
Haiti	Participation of officers from the *Arma dei Carabinieri* to the United Nations Stabilization Mission in Haiti (MINUSTAH)
Somalia-Uganda	Participation to the European Union Training Mission to contribute to the training of Somali security forces (EUTM SOMALIA) (activities in Uganda and Kenya)
Libya	Participation of officers from the Financial Police to the mission in Libya, in order to guarantee the ordinary maintenance and the efficiency of the naval units given by the Italian Government to the Libyan Government, implementing the cooperation agreements signed by the Italian Republic and the Great Socialist People's Libyan Arab Jamahiriya, in order to face the phenomena of illegal immigration and of trafficking in human beings
Afghanistan and other States	Participation of officers from the *Guardia di Finanza* (Financial Police) to the Joint Multimodal Operational Units (JMOUs) established in Afghanistan, United Arab Emirates and Kosovo

Part IV

National and International Case-law

Human Rights in Italian Case-law

Part IV presents a selection of the case-law produced by the Italian Constitutional Court, the Court of Cassation and the Council of State (the highest administrative court) during the year 2010 which closely involves issues linked to internationally recognised human rights. The Italian case-law discussed in the first section is complemented in the second section by a systematic review of the European Court of Human Rights decisions adopted in 2010 involving Italy as the responding State.

As already mentioned in relation to Italian law (Part I, International Human Rights Instruments, IV), the selection of topics and case-law relating to human rights dealt with by Italian courts and published during 2010, is in no way exhaustive. Indeed, the issues that may have direct or indirect impact on the enjoyment of human rights are numerous. The judicial cases reviewed here have been selected according to the presence, in the final judgement settling the dispute, of explicit references to international human rights norms such as the European Convention on Human Rights (ECHR). This methodological choice renders the two parts of present section, the one on the Italian case-law and other on Italy's standing before the Strasbourg Court, strictly interconnected.

In the case-law of the Italian courts, including the Constitutional Court, the number of references to the sources of International human rights law has steadily increased. This reflects a growing willingness, on the part of the Italian judiciary system, to acknowledge the capacity of such international norms to affect domestic law, whether directly or by imposing a given interpretation of current national legislation. In any case, the year 2010 could well mark a turning point in this field, thanks to the coming into force, on 1 December 2009, of the new EU treaties: respectively, on the European Union (TEU) and on the functioning of the European Union (TFEU), as reformed by the Treaty of Lisbon. The so-called "Communitarisation" of human rights is the first topic dealt with in the present section of the *Yearbook*.

Other subjects regarding which the Italian courts have most extensively referred to international human rights standards are: dignity of the person (non-pecuniary loss, bio-law issues, torture); discrimination (racial, gender, minority-based, religious, linked to disability); immigration; children's rights (especially those of foreign minors); asylum seekers; criminal law ("harsh imprisonment" measures, trial by default, European arrest warrant, etc.); right to peaceful enjoyment of property and expropriation for public use; reasonable length of trials.

I. The "Communitarisation" of International Human Rights Norms

Only a few days after the new treaties on the EU came into force, the Constitutional Court's judgement 317, 4 December 2009, in extensively recalling its own previous, well-known judgements 348/2007 and 349/2007, reiterated the fact that, based on art. 117(1) of the Constitution (as deeply amended in 2001), the norms of international conventions duly ratified by Italy supplement the parameters of constitutionality already present in the Constitution. In particular, as regards human rights agreements – specifically, the 1950 ECHR – this means that "the ordinary judge is called upon to interpret domestic laws in harmony with international norms [...]. Should that prove impossible, or should the judge be in doubt about compatibility of the domestic provision with the 'interposing' international norm, he must refer to the Constitutional Court the question of the constitutional legitimacy with regard to the parameter of art. 117, paragraph 1, Const." (par. 6.2 of the "as to the law" part).

The judgement however, though delivered after 1 December 2009, does not say anything over the potential impact of the entry into force of the Treaty of Lisbon on the matter. In particular, it does not take into account the possibility for ordinary courts to "disapply" domestic norms conflicting with ECHR as it already happens in case of domestic norms in contrast with EU law (as it is well-known, if a national court is in doubt about the interpretation or validity of an EU law, it is the European Court of Justice, thought the preliminary ruling procedure *ex* art. 267 TFEU, and not the Constitutional Court the competent body to set the issue). Similarly, Constitutional Court's judgement 311, 26 November 2009, delivered just a few days before the entry into force of the Lisbon Treaty, do not pronounce on the point, except to declare that ECHR provisions cannot prevail over domestic conflicting norms as, currently, this is only possible for EU norm having direct effect.

> This point had been clarified in the Constitutional Court's judgement 348/2007: "the European Convention on human rights does not create a supra-national legal order [as in the case, instead, of EU founding treaties], and does not therefore produce norms directly enforceable in contracting States legal system. The Convention can be seen as a multi-lateral international treaty [...] setting forth "obligations" for the contracting States but not incorporating of the Italian legal system into a wider system whose de-

liberative organs may issue, *omisso medio*, norms binding for all the domestic authorities of the Member States".

After 1 December 2009, however, the juridical framework forming the basis for the Constitutional Court position may well be modified. In fact, the new art. 6 of the EU Treaty not only gives the EU Charter of fundamental rights binding legal force, but establishes that "the Union shall accede to the European Convention for the Protection of Human Rights and Fundamental Freedoms", and that "Fundamental rights, as guaranteed by the European Convention for the Protection of Human Rights and Fundamental Freedoms and as they result from the constitutional traditions common to the Member States, shall constitute general principles *of the Union's law*" (in the previous version, art. 6(2) stated "the Union *shall respect* fundamental rights, as guaranteed by the European Convention for the Protection of Human Rights and Fundamental Freedoms;" [emphasis added]).

The Italian Government itself had already acknowledged that "the position of the Constitutional Court does not appear to be fully compatible with the new structure of the EU as delineated by the recent Treaty of Lisbon, which completes the so-called "Communitarisation" of ECHR principles. This process would actually mean that "all ECHR provisions would become directly enforceable in the national legal systems of Member States, to the degree and with the force of EU norms; i.e., pursuant to art. 11 of the Constitution [...], and no longer as sub-constitutional norms pursuant to art. 117, para. 1 of the Constitution; with the further, foreseeable consequence that conformity of national legislation to the ECHR could become subject to control by the European Court of Justice, and not by the Constitutional Court" (see the *2007 Report on the Strasbourg Court decisions*, the Department of juridical and legislative affairs, Presidency of the Council of Ministers, p. 21).

In some cases, Italian judges have adopted this interpretation, acknowledging that the Treaty of Lisbon, along with the new art. 6 TEU and in full recognition of the European Charter of fundamental rights (CFREU), has furthered the process of conformity between EU law and international human rights law, particularly as regards standards established by the ECHR. It follows that the national judge must take into account international human rights norms, both because they are considered in national case-law (through the incorporation of customary law and treaty law operated respectively by art. 10, para. 1, Const. and art. 117, para. 1 Const.), and because they are general principles of EU law accepted in Italy by way of art. 11, Const.

Perhaps the most explicit affirmation of this position can be found in the judgement of 18 May 2010, No. 11984, TAR of Lazio Region (the Lazio TAR – Regional Administrative Tribunal – has nation-wide jurisdiction).

The administrative judge states that "the recognition of fundamental rights enshrined in the European Convention on human rights as principles inherent in EU law [...] has extremely important, immediate consequences, since the norms of the Convention, according to EU law, instantaneously become operative in the national judicial systems of EU Member States and therefore in the Italian one (through art. 11 Const.). This process sheds light on the wide-ranging, decades-long jurisprudential evolution which has eventually led to the obligation, on the part of the national judge, to interpret national norms in conformity with EU law, that is to immediately and directly disapply contrasting national norms, possibly following adjudication by the EU judge, but without the need to domestically review the constitutionality of the norm." The TAR of Lazio also observes that given the pre-eminent role of the European Court of Human Rights (ECtHR) in interpreting the ECHR, case-law produced by the ECtHR is destined to gain extraordinary importance in the Italian legal system. This should occur regarding "all the fundamental rights declared by the European Convention on Human Rights, and no longer, as in the past, merely cases in which a fundamental right in the Convention has acquired special relevance in EU law through acceptance of a given EU law provision, or through its use as a general principle of law in a ruling of the Luxembourg Court".

The Lazio TAR's point of view is based on a preceding judgement by the Council of State (section IV, 2 March 2010, No. 1220), declaring, with no in-depth discussion, that the supreme administrative judge is obliged to "apply principles of effective judicial protection, as indicated in art. 24 Const. and in art. 6 and 13 ECHR (*which became directly applicable in the national system after modification of EU Treaty art. 6*, as arranged by the Treaty of Lisbon, which came into force on 1 December 2009)" [emphasis added]. This passage reappears, for example, in Lombardy TAR (Brescia), section II, 20 May 2010, No. 2070. A similar formulation, along with further reference to the Constitutional Court's interpretation of art. 117(1) Const. in the fore-mentioned rulings of 2007, appears in Council of State judgements 3760 and 7200, which shall be consider later in discussing the deportation of foreign citizens and refusal to renew their residence permit.

The stance of the administrative judge has been criticised by legal scholars as it seems to take for granted something the EU has not yet finalised, that is the formal accession to the ECHR, today made possible as the Treaty of Lisbon and ECHR Protocol XIV have come into force (the latter on 1 June 2010).

The Tribunal of Novara delivered a judgement concerning the validity of a matrimonial bond between an Italian (husband) and a Russian citizen (wife) after the man was imprisoned due to a complaint filed by the woman herself. At stake was the woman's request to renew her residence permit. The court made extensive reference to an important decision by the European Court of

Justice (19 January 2010, C-555/07, *Kükükdeveci*) concluding that "today, the national judge dealing with national norms which are in potential conflict with any of the human rights declared by the European Convention on human rights, and finding it impossible to adopt an 'interpretation in conformity' with EU law (which should always be the first solution to consider), finds himself facing two possibilities: one, to raise the question of constitutional legitimacy pursuant to art. 117 Const., with arguments grounded on ECtHR case-law; the other, [...] to refer to the same principle as approved by the Charter of Nice (that wholly overlaps the ECHR), and then to refer the case to the European Court of Justice for a preliminary ruling, it being understood that, pursuant to EU Charter on Fundamental Rights art. 51, the censured national norm must concern one of the norms originating in EU law. In applying for a preliminary ruling, the national judge may also argue on the basis of ECtHR case-law".

In judgement No. 2352, 2 February 2010, the Court of Cassation, civil division, in remitting to the trial judge the definition of a lawsuit demanding payment of damages for behaviour defined as "mobbing" within a hospital structure, points out that "with the coming into force of the Treaty of Lisbon [...], which gives the Charter of Nice provisions the status of primary law as the EU Treaties [...], trial judges must consider the principles mentioned in art. 1 of the Charter of Nice, ruling on the value of human dignity (which includes professional dignity), and in art. 15, on the right to engage in work as an inviolable right, belonging to the value category of freedoms". The Court of Cassation, in short, even in matters extraneous to EU legislation, declares that it includes in its interpretative scope the process of "conforming national and constitutional rights to the non-conflicting, promotional principles in the Treaty of Lisbon and the Charter of Nice, which it considers as the basis for common European law". The Court suggests that the conformity process certainly did not begin on 1 December 2009, but has been evolving for a number of years, even though it has found only partial response in EU law: at least until recent years.

In other rulings, on the contrary, the Court of Cassation explicitly denies that the ECHR can be considered an integral part of the EU legal framework. In particular, it is inadmissible that doubts concerning conformity between domestic norms and the ECHR can be resolved by way of preliminary ruling of the European Court of Justice, as foreseen by the Treaty on the functioning of the EU (TFEU), art. 267: the national judge can neither disapply domestic norms incompatible with the ECHR, nor resort to the Court of Luxembourg in order to obtain interpretation of that Convention; at most, it may raise the question of constitutionality (see judgements 11124/2010 and 6500/2010, Court of Cassation, civil division).

In light of the case-law as it evolved during 2010, Italian judges appear to believe that the process of "Communitarisation" affecting international human rights law (the ECHR in particular) has not yet been fully accomplished. The same message comes from the case-law of the

Constitutional Court where, albeit only in passing and as *obiter dicta*, it observes that when the trial judge is unable to proceed toward an interpretation of the domestic norm which harmonizes it with the ECHR norm, it is his/her duty to raise the question of constitutionality, "since he[/she] cannot disapply the domestic contrasting norm" (judg. 93/2010, para. 4 of the pertinent part).

In particular, it is not clear when the ECHR provisions should be considered as norms of international law to which domestic law must conform (art. 117(1) Const.), in compliance with the interpretation given it by the ECtHR, for possible use as an "interposing norm" in judging the constitutionality of a domestic norm; and when, instead, it should be considered as a norm complementing EU law, and as such autonomously valid in the legal systems of Member States, introduced into Italy by way of art. 11 Const., and whose interpretation is the prerogative of the EU Court of Justice (and of the Strasbourg Court as well). One might suppose that the decisive factor would hinge on the subject matter of the internal norm at stake or of the judicial dispute: whether the matter falls within the EU competence (e.g., discrimination among EU citizens, or anti-trust), or instead, is strictly within the single State's competence (a good portion of criminal law issues, for example).

With the EU's accession to the European Convention on human rights, a move requiring full involvement and the consent by all Member States as well, an important step will be taken toward the "merging" of ECHR parameters and those of EU law. At that point it will appear reasonable to eliminate any discrepancy between human rights-related issues over which the EU has competence, and issues not directly dealt with in EU law or in the case-law of the European Court of Justice, since the same standards would apply to both spheres. If there is uncertainty over the compatibility of domestic norms with EU law, the national judge will be entitled to make a reference for a preliminary ruling by the European Court of Justice, whose judgement on the matter will, in turn, be subject to examination by the ECtHR. The domestic norm incompatible with the European one will be disapplied, if one can recur to a valid EU law provision of equal scope. Moreover, if there is incompatibility between a domestic law and the ECHR, the national judge himself may raise the question of constitutional legitimacy; the ECHR, again as interpreted by the Strasbourg Court, shall function in this case as a source of international law capable of supplementing, by way of an interposing norm, the judgement of constitutionality centralised at the Constitutional Court and aimed at abolishing the incompatible legal norm with retroactive effect (*ex tunc*).

In any case, the ECHR and the norms of the other human rights treaties, as well as the Charter of Nice, understood as an expression of universal values shared also by the EU, nowadays provide criteria for interpreting domestic norms, and are already binding for judges and public administration agencies, that must strive to prevent any possible conflict between the domestic legal system, on one hand, and international and EU human rights principles and standards, on the other.

II. Dignity of the Person

A. Compensation for Non-pecuniary Loss

The principle of dignity, enshrined in art. 1 of the Charter of Nice (CFREU), has been referred to by recent Italian case-law in order to establish the right to indemnity for non-pecuniary damages (moral, "biological", "existential", or at any rate, a loss concerning non-economic interests of the person) in tort cases. The principle set out by art. 1 of the CFREU and art. 2 Const. taken together, in fact, impose the extensive interpretation of art. 2059, Italian Civil Code. This article, according to an interpretation of the Court of Cassation, especially in judgements 26972 and 26975, 11 November 2008, limits the operational scope of art. 2043, Civil Code ("Any intentional wrong-doing or negligence causing unlawful damage to someone else, obliges the person who has committed the act to compensate the damage") merely to pecuniary damages, in the sense that only in the presence of given torts expressly indicated by the law, or of criminal offences as established by art. 185, criminal code, can there be a claim for compensation of non-pecuniary loss. The constitutionally-oriented interpretation adopted by the Unified Sections of Cassation in the fore-mentioned judgements, however, makes it possible to claim compensation for non-pecuniary damages when constitutionally relevant interests of the person are affected, unless the damages are of very light entity.

During last year, many judgements touching on such issues have applied this principle, mentioning art. 1 of the Charter of Nice. Among them: Tribunal of Nola, sec. II, judg. 18 August 2010; Tribunal of Sulmona, judg. 21 July 2010; Tribunal of Varese, sec. I, judg. 12 April 2010, No. 488 and judg. 10 February 2010; justice of the peace of Ceglie Messapico, judg. 18 February 2010, No. 15; Tribunal of Tivoli, judg. 17 February 2010, No. 263; Tribunal of Bari, sec. III, judg. 1 February 2010, No. 263; Tribunal of Mondovì, judg. 27 January 2010.

The Tribunal of Palermo recognises that pursuant to ECHR Protocol I, the right to property is a fundamental right whose violation justifies the victim's claim to reparation for non-pecuniary damages consequential to infringement of the right (judgement of 18 June 2010). The same judgement assumes that with the Lisbon Treaty's coming into force, there must also be an innovative interpretation of art. 42 Const. which strengthens the characterisation of the right to property as a human right.

The value of dignity was also taken into account in a claim to the Court of Cassation in which persons convicted for rape who, after the crime, had paid the victim the sum of 10,000 euros, complained that this payment had not been considered at all as a mitigating element in the sentencing. In judgement 28658/2010, section II of the Court of Cassation (penal division) applies the meta-principle of personal dignity, as recognised by the Charter of Nice (though the case did not concerned EU law); it therefore rejects the appeal, stating that to accept any free, private-level monetisation of personal dignity would lead to an unacceptable restriction of the principle itself.

The principle also emerges in judgement 24401/2010, Court of Cassation, sec. III, which confirms the sentencing of a health care administration to pay non-pecuniary damages linked to the grave cerebral dysfunctions inflicted on a new-born baby girl by the poor hygienic conditions of a clinic in the province of Verona (the event dates back to the 1990s): in this case, as well, damages must be paid regardless of whether any crime has been ascertained.

Finally, the principle of personal dignity is evoked in the above-mentioned judgement 2352, civil division of the Court of Cassation, which recognises, among other elements, the right to compensation for non-pecuniary damages suffered by a surgeon who was victim of an abuse of power ("mobbing"). In this case, along with Charter of Nice art. 1, art. 15 of the same instrument is cited as well (freedom to choose an occupation and right to engage in work).

B. Personal Autonomy and Bio-law Issues

The issue of the "living will" and recognition of individuals' right to decide on health measures they are to receive if/when they are unable to express their consensus, has emerged repeatedly before Italian judges in recent years, sometimes in relation to highly dramatic, controversial cases. One particular aspect of the problem concerns the possibility for an individual to entrust a third figure, the *amministratore di sostegno*, a judicially appointed guardian/trustee (art. 404 ff., Civil Code, introduced with l. 6/2004) with responsibility for medical choices that might concern him or her, during any period of time in which the concerned individual is deprived of the capacity to give or deny his or her consent for treatment.

With a decree of 25 August 2010, the Tribunal of Varese (citing the well-known Court of Cassation ruling 21748/2007 in the *Englaro* case) held that in the Italian legal system, there is no element preventing a mentally capable individual from appointing, for the time period in which he or she may remain deprived of his/her mental faculties, a person who functions as guardian/trustee, empowered to make the necessary choices regarding health treatment in faithfulness to what would have been the will of the concerned person. According to the Varese judge, the ECHR norms and those of the

Charter of Nice, not to mention those of the Oviedo Convention on biomedicine (though the judgement does not specifically name the latter instrument), recognise the free, informed consensus of the patient as the parameter which medical practitioners must observe, overcoming any authoritarian or paternalistic conception of the physician's role. On another front, the right to choose medical treatment (art. 32 Const.) ensures compatibility between the Italian law (which admittedly contains prohibition against acts dealing with one's own body in such a way as to cause permanent damage: art. 5, Civil Code) and manifestations of the individual's will prior to the possible or foreseeable loss of his capability to understand and decide (the so-called "living will"). In this perspective, it is therefore admissible for an elderly person to designate by solemn act, a guardian/trustee with the task of providing consensus for medical treatments which health care personnel may advise for the person in their care, in respect for the convictions expressed by the patient before losing his/her ability to understand (in the case at hand, the patient manifested a conviction contrary to any form of euthanasia). The judge also states that the appointment of the guardian/trustee cannot occur "now for then", i.e., under condition that the foreseen circumstances will actually occur: however, the act designating the prospective guardian/trustee, like the specification of indications the latter must consider when carrying out his/her duties, provides elements which the guardianship judge must take into account in appointing the actual guardian/trustee when appropriate.

Similarly rules a decree of 22 December 2010 issued by the guardianship judge of the Tribunal of Florence. In this case the magistrate proceeds to appoint the guardian/trustee for the applicant, in the person of the latter's spouse, accepting the specifications agreed on by the two individuals according to which, upon loss of the capacity for self-determination and insurgence of merely vegetative conditions of survival, the guardian/trustee is authorised to deny consensus for therapeutic treatment or forms of resuscitation, ventilation or forced artificial nourishment, and to request any pertinent palliative treatment, even though it might hasten the death of the beneficiary.

C. The Crime of Reduction to Slavery

As regards the crime of enslavement and holding persons in a state of slavery or servitude, as considered by art. 600, criminal code (amended by art. 1 of l. 228/2003), in judg. 18072/2010 the Court of Cassation observed that this crime was to be considered a continuing offence even before its reformulation in 2003, since its interpretation proceeded in coordination with the definition of slavery deriving from the 1926 Geneva Convention against slavery and the 1956 supplementary Convention for the abolition of slavery, both ratified by Italy. Moreover, the offence may be committed – as in the case under consideration – even by the parent of the minors victims of the facts; accomplices in the crime may also include third parties to whom children reduced to slavery are handed over; moreover, motives grounded on traditional culture or custom cannot exclude the "psychological aspect (*mens rea*) of the crime". The Court does not even give any relevance to the defence that the thefts which the little slaves were forced to commit served to give their "masters" the resources to provide sustenance to the group to which the victims themselves belonged.

D. Medically Assisted Procreation

Law 40/2004 prohibits recourse to medically assisted procreation techniques of heterologous type. Among the reasons for this prohibition (whose violation calls for a pecuniary administrative penalty solely against the health professional who practises such intervention), is the need to prevent the creation of atypical family bonds, or to prevent the birth of children having "two mothers" (a natural one and a genetic one), the risk of exploiting women (in the case of "rented uterus") and the need to protect the child's identity. Such arguments, however, were recently discussed and discarded by the ECtHR, when dealing with a case regarding Austrian citizens. The Court's reasoning is easily adaptable to the Italian situation as well. In the judgement *S.H. and others v. Austria*, 1 April 2010, the Strasbourg judges stated that legislation which, in regulating assisted procreation techniques, introduces limits on heterologous forms of assisted procreation with respect to homologous ones, fails to respect art. 8 of the ECHR, and also violates art. 14 of this Convention (Austria requested the case be referred to the Grand Chamber). This led the Tribunal of Catania, dealing with a case concerning, again, the application of l. 40/2004, to raise the question of constitutionality for violation of art. 117, para. 1 Const. (order of 21 October 2010). Law 40/2004 had already been censured by the Constitutional Court which, in judgement 151/2009, had found unconstitutional the mechanism defined in its art. 14: without including protection of the woman's health among the criteria to follow, it strictly limited to three the number of fecundated embryos which could be transferred to the uterus after a treatment cycle of ovarian stimulation.

The Tribunal of Salerno (judg. 191, 9 January 2010) held that, according to a constitutionally oriented reading of art. 4 and 13 of law 40/2004, access to techniques of medically assisted procreation and, in particular, to a diagnosis of embryos prior to implantation, obtained from couples through *in-vitro* fecundation, must apply not only to sterile couples (as art. 4 specifically indicates), but also to couples who are at risk of generating children with grave, incurable, genetically transmittable diseases, such as type 1 spinal muscular atrophy.

III. Discrimination

A. Gender Discrimination, Homosexual Marriage

In 2008, the registrar of the Municipality of Venice rejected a homosexual couple's request to publish marriage banns. A similar event had occurred to another homosexual couple in Trent. The Tribunal of Venice and the Trent's Court of Appeals, to which the couples respectively resorted, maintained that the question raised by the would-be spouses' complaints concerning the unconstitutionality of a series of Civil Code articles which would appear to exclude same-sex marriages (art. 93, 96, 98, 107, 108, 143, 143-*bis*, 156-*bis*), was not manifestly ill-founded. The norms violated would appear to be art. 2, 3, 29 and 117(1) Const. (this last article, in that it refers to the ECHR, art. 8, 12 and 14; and to the Charter of Nice, art. 7, 9, 21). In ruling No. 138, 15 April 2010, the Constitutional Court rejected the case of unconstitutionality. The Court regarded as inadmissible the question raised in connection with art. 2 and 117(1) Const. (the cited provisions of the Charter of Nice and of the ECHR being considered as interposing norms). According to the judges, in fact, the Constitutional Court is not competent to satisfy the aspiration to extend "civil matrimonial discipline to homosexual unions in such a way as to close the gap resulting from the fact that the legislator did not consider the issue of homosexual marriage [...]". Instead, "it is up to Parliament, in exercising its discretion, to find forms guaranteeing and recognising [homosexual] unions, while the Constitutional Court can only intervene on a case-by-case basis" (par. 8 of the "as to the law" consideration). Moreover, as regards ways of exercising the right to marry and form a family, the cited norms of the Charter of Nice and the ECHR refer to national law, without imposing (nor excluding) the equal application of norms concerning marriage between a man and a woman, to homosexual unions (see para. 10, "as to the law" consideration). With respect to art. 29 Const., the judges deny that its paragraph 1 can be interpreted in such a way as to encompass homosexual unions in the constitutional concept of marriage: "it is true that the concepts of marriage and family cannot be considered 'crystallised' in conformity to the epoch in which the Constitution came into effect [; however,] one must conclude that [the drafters of the Constitution] had in mind the concept of matrimony as defined by the [1942] Civil Code [...] which [...] stipulates (and still does) that spouses must be persons of different sex [...]. This meaning of the constitutional rule cannot be overcome hermeneutically, because such a process would not entail a mere reinterpretation of the system, or the abandoning of a mere interpretative method, but instead, the undertaking of creative interpretation". Since "homosexual unions cannot be considered homogeneous to marriage", it follows that in current legislation, there occurs no violation of art. 3 Const. (gender discrimination). Nor does there exist any disparity of treatment between homosexuals and transsexuals, who are allowed to marry persons of the same biological sex, after the modification of their sexual traits as authorised by the Tribunal: l. 14 April 1982, No. 164 (Norms concerning the modification of sexual attributes). In fact, "recognition of the right to marry for those who have undergone sex change […] constitutes, if anything, an argument confirming the hetero-sexual nature of matrimony, as defined in current legislation" – see para. 9 of the "as to the law" section.

B. Racial Discrimination

The Court of Cassation, judgement 28282, 9 July 2010, applied and reiterated the meaning of doctrine expressed by the penal division of the same Court of Cassation in 2009 (judg. 49694), according to which the aggravating circumstance constituted by the aim to discriminate and express ethnic, national, racial or religious hate, occurs when the expression used is "objectively" discriminatory: i.e., "when, according to common usage, it is linkable to a manifest prejudice proclaiming the inferiority of a single race". The *subjective* interpretation given by the actor is not relevant, nor is it necessary that the discriminatory conduct appear as such externally, arousing the danger of further discriminatory conduct or emulative acts; for if that were true, the aggravating factor could not be contested in any case where the discriminatory act takes place in the absence of third parties.

With an order of 29 June 2010 settling a suit for discrimination as defined by art. 43 and 44, legislative decree 286/1998 (Consolidated act on immigration), the monocratic judge of Udine ordered the Municipality of Latisana to disapply the provisions of the regional law 7 July 2006, No. 11, of Friuli-Venezia Giulia, regarding the childbirth grant (the so-called "baby bonus", *bonus bébé*), since the law did not include among the recipients of the bonus, the claimant, a Romanian citizen father of a baby born in 2007; according to the regional law, the only foreigners who can receive the bonus were those who have resided for at least ten years in Italy, and at least five in Friuli-Venezia Giulia.

The judge held that the regional law resulted in indirect discrimination against non-Italian EU citizens, in contrast with art. 18 TFEU and art. 21 CFREU, as well as directive 2004/38/EC on EU citizens' right to move and reside freely in EU States. In fact, the limits set by the regional law were such as to exclude nearly all foreign families from enjoyment of what that same law presented as a real social right that Municipalities are obliged to acknowledge. The criterion of long-term residence actually discriminated against any foreigner, including Romanians, who were EU citizens (on this point there is abundant case-law by the European Court of Justice: regarding

Italy, can be cited judgement C-388/01). Moreover, nation-based discrimination accompanied the ethnic and racial discrimination considered in directive 2000/43/EC (transposed in Italy with legislative decree 215/2003). Not only does the discriminatory result actually – or at least potentially – stem from application of the cited regional law; indeed, the purpose of excluding non-Italian parents from the measure supporting the family, children and parenthood was explicitly pursued by the regional legislator. This was confirmed by the following regional law of Friuli-Venezia Giulia, 18/2009, which extended the benefit to Friulians resident abroad, to their descendants who have established residence in the Region (with no duration limit), and to all those serving in the armed forces or the police on regional territory. The order of the Udine judge obliged the Municipality of Latisana to assign the "baby bonus" to the claimant as well, disapplying the regional norm which prevented its assignation.

Deciding on a claim in the interest of the law submitted by the chief prosecutor (*procuratore generale*) at the Court of Cassation, the Unified Sections of the same court declared that a decree of suitability for international adoption issued by the Juvenile Court (*Tribunale per i minori*) cannot contain reference to the race or ethnic origin of children being adopted (judgement 13332, 1 June 2010).

The decision is based on a complain submitted by an association involved in international adoptions, which had pointed out that in a decree attesting the suitability of a couple to adopt children through the international adoption procedure, a passage appeared in which the would-be adoptive parents expressed their unwillingness to adopt children with dark skin or a "non-European" appearance. The Court of Cassation recognises that similar specifications must not be expressed in a decree issued pursuant to the law on adoption (l. 184/1983, modified several times, in particular following ratification of the 1993 Hague Convention on Intercountry Adoptions). Such specifications, in fact, would be in conflict with human rights principles (art. 2 Const.) and principles of non-discrimination (art. 3 Const.), as well as with international norms in force in the Italian legal system (art. 10 Const. and art. 117 Const., paragraph 1), contained, in particular, in treaties such as the ECHR (art. 14), the 1965 International Convention against racial discrimination, the Convention on the rights of the child, the Charter of Nice and the EU Treaty. They would also conflict with the anti-racism norms of legislative decree 286/1998 (Consolidated act on immigration) and with the above-mentioned legislative decree 215, which applies directive 2000/43/CE, not to mention law 184/1983 on adoption. According to the Court of Cassation, the adopting couple's expression of attitudes reflecting racial or ethnic discrimination, must be considered in assessing whether they are suitable to adopt children.

In judg. 134/2010, the Constitutional Court established the constitutional illegitimacy of the regional law which, in connection with the Liguria Region's commitment against any form of racism or discrimination, declared the Region's unwillingness to host an Identification and Expulsion Centre (CIE) on its territory. In this case, the Region was actually intervening in a matter – immigration – which art. 117 Const., paragraph 2) attributes to exclusive State competence.

The Constitutional Court (judg. 247/2010), in examining the constitutionality of a law provision of the Region of Veneto forbidding street peddling in public areas of historical centres in municipalities having more than 50,000 inhabitants (a norm that had justified the adoption, among others, of a municipal measure in Venice ordering the removal of numerous immigrants away from zones of major tourist areas), concluded that the norm does not breach the Constitution and, in particular, cannot be understood as a discriminatory act, even though most of the persons in the category defined by the norm are indeed non-EU peddlers.

C. Linguistic Minorities

As regards minority languages, in 2010 the Constitutional Court adopted judgement 170/2010, which extensively reiterates its previous ruling 150/2009 and confirmed its findings. In 2009 the topic had been dealt with by legislation in Friuli-Venezia Giulia, which tended to extend protection of the minority languages used in the Region, outside the geographic area of settlement of the linguistic minority groups. The 2010 judgement closely examines a law of the Piedmont Region (r.l. 11/2009) which, alongside measures aimed at the historico-cultural valorisation of Piedmont's linguistic heritage, proposed parity between the Piedmontese language and "other" minority languages spoken in regional territory: Occitan, French, Franco-Provençal and Walser. In so doing, the Regional Council was exercising a power, that of recognising minority languages, strictly attributed to the State by art. 6 Const. By way of law 482/1999, the State Parliament had already compiled the list of the Italian linguistic minorities, that does not feature a Piedmontese minority group. Therefore, the regional legislation foreseeing the introduction of Piedmontese language in the media, alongside the minority languages recognised in national legislation must be considered as unconstitutional as it breaks the boundaries of regional competence. Moreover, the Constitutional Court once again stated that the possibility of proposing the use of a given minority language in public offices pertains to administrations located in the geographic area inhabited by members of the minority, and cannot be extended generically to the entire regional territory (especially if the State does not officially recognise the language as a minority language). Instead, regional law provisions foreseeing the use of local idioms historically spoken in the area to complement Italian toponyms, are lawful, even when the idioms are not included among the languages of historic minorities recognised by national legislation).

In judg. 2352/2010, the Council of State deliberated that, contrary to what occurs in Trentino-Alto Adige, for the Friuli-Venezia Giulia Region, the employees of local administrations are not obliged to speak a minority language (in this case, Slovene) in addition to the Italian language; therefore, public officers fluent in both languages are not entitled for that reason to supplementary pay.

D. Minorities and Regional Elections

In judgement 6778, 15 September 2010, the Council of State, Section V, dealt with the appeal presented by the political party "*Venetie per l'autogoverno*" against the decision by which the Veneto Regional Administrative Tribunal (TAR) had denied the party admission to the regional elections of 2010. The decision was motivated by the lack of a requisite established by current norms on electoral matters (l. 108/1968) as necessary in order to participate in the elections with a separate list, i.e., the obligation to collect and submit a certain number of signatures of citizens enrolled on the regional electoral lists. Essentially, "*Venetie per l'autogoverno*" was requesting the supreme administrative court to declare the incompatibility of the requisite with international instruments relating to the principle of non-discrimination and protection of national minorities' rights, since such conditions hamper the formation of direct political representation for groups such as the "Venetian people". The claim seems particularly pertinent in the Veneto Region, since art. 2 of the regional statute (l. 340/1971) reads: "Self-government by the *Venetian people* proceeds in accordance with its historical characteristics and traditions" (emphasis added). The Council of State confirms rejection of the appeal. In particular, it rules that the obligation to deposit a certain number of residents' signatures (and not signatures only by autochthonous "Venetians") before presenting electoral lists, is justified by the need to prove the list's representativeness; the requisite also affects electoral lists claiming for minority rights (in the Council of States' view, this does not imply recognition of the existence of a Venetian national minority in accordance with, for instance, the 1995 Framework Convention of Council of Europe for the protection of national minorities).

Recalling the case-law of the Constitutional Court, the judges reaffirm the principle according to which "the protection of (linguistic) minorities proceeds by way of the principle of territoriality, i.e., by application of the protecting measures in the territories where there is a sufficient number of citizens belonging to the minority, and not by way of the personality principle; therefore a protecting legislation cannot be claimed by a member of the minority when he/she finds him/herself outside the territory of settlement of the minority". As regards the formula used in art. 2 of the current Statute of the Region of Veneto, the Council of State denies that the term "people" (*popolo*) it uses has a different meaning from that of "population", which is devoid of any political connotation alluding to a right to self-determination; the concept of "self-government", moreover, must not be confused with that of "sovereignty" (reference is made to the Constitutional Court judgement 7 November 2007, No. 365).

E. Persons with Disabilities

In judgement 80/2010, the Constitutional Court declared the constitutional illegitimacy of the norm in the 2008 financial law (art. 2, paragraphs 413 and 414) where it sets a maximum limit on the number of assistant teachers for students with disabilities, and excludes the possibility of appointing untenured assistant teachers in order to meet the needs of students with particularly serious disabilities. The norm aimed to reduce the number of assistant teachers for students with disabilities to 70%, by school year 2010-2011, of those employed in 2006-2007. In the case at hand, by effect of the disputed norms, a girl with serious disabilities was assigned an assistant teacher for only 12 hours a week. The Court recognised that the provisions of the financial law might overturn the right to education and attending school, from nursery to university, guaranteed in Italy by l. 104/1992 and qualified by the Court as a fundamental right (ruling 215/1987). In particular, art. 12 of l. 104/1992 implements art. 38, para. 3 Const. ("The disabled and the handicapped [*minorati*, *sic*] have the right to education and to professional training"), and regulate the right to education of persons with disabilities, also guaranteed by the 2006 United Nations Convention on the Rights of Persons with Disabilities, ratified with l. 18 of 2009. Budgetary cuts in the assistance services for children with disabilities, moreover, cannot be made without allowing adaptation of the service to the specific needs of each student.

The principle set by the Constitutional Court was applied by TAR of Lazio in judgement 1804, 15 April 2010, which orders the administrations concerned to supplement scholastic assistance for a student with disabilities, bringing it to 24 hours per week, instead of the 12 hours originally established. The TAR of Campania ruled similarly, in decisions 2054/2010 and 8328/2010, in a case where a single teacher had been assigned for a limited number of hours to assist two children with serious disabilities attending a primary school class, and in a case where an assistant teacher had been assigned a schedule incompatible with the real needs of the child, without planning an individualised education project (PEI). Among other things, the judges observed that "the provision assigning hours of special teaching assistance for the current school year [...] does not appear to have been adopted in light of the clinical situation resulting from the health care documentation attached by the claimant, which reveals the need for special, continuing assistance; instead it appears to be justified only by the insufficiency of resources allotted to schools and by limits imposed on the number of personnel; such motivation appears as wholly legally untenable in light of recent Constitutional Court judgement 80/2010". Consistent with the just cited TAR Campania judgement, see also TAR Calabria, case No. 2547/2010. Concerning the obligation to plan the PEI and to re-fine it from year to year according to the real assistance needs of children with disabilities, see TAR Campania, decision 17222/2010.

In judgement 581/2010, the TAR of Lombardy (Brescia) applies art. 13 of the mentioned l. 104/1992, a norm recognising the right of the disabled child not only to an assistant teacher, but also to a personal assistant who helps him or her on the social and communicative level – not on a strictly didactic level – to develop autonomy and integrate into the scholastic context; the task of arranging such service is attributed to the Municipalities. The Municipality obliged to provide such *ad personam* assistance service, pursuant to l. 328/2000 on social services, is the one where the minor legally resides. Citing the Convention on the rights of persons with disabilities, the TAR emphasises the minor's right to qualified social assistance, aiming at favouring the child's integration, in coordination with teaching activities carried out by the assistant teacher.

The right to health (art. 32 Const., art. 35 CFREU) of persons with disabilities (art. 26 CFREU) is an inviolable right (art. 2 Const.) which must be guaranteed according to the principle of social solidarity. This implies – the Court of Cassation (judg. 18378/2010) affirms – that the local institution must reimburse expenses incurred by the family for placing a minor with a psychiatric illness into a protected facility, including any sums advanced during the period prior to conclusion of the procedure for ascertaining the minor's disability. The right to health, in fact, "cannot be hampered and fragmented in awaiting conclusion of the relative ascertainment and other assessment procedure carried out by the competent agency, especially when the minor needs immediate assistance or therapy". It is understood that the right to medical treatment or to the economic benefit does not arise automatically at the moment when the health care need emerges, but instead, demands the ascertainment of the state of need, whose effects nevertheless must tend to extend retroactively – according to the solidarity principle – to the moment when the pathology or the cause of disability arose.

In judgement 51/2010, the Constitutional Court points out that competence for proceeding to the appointment of a guardian/trustee (*amministratore di sostegno*) rests in part with the Italian Consul abroad, even though this mandate is not expressly stated in provisions relating to the consular powers (p.d.r. 200/1967).

F. Religious Discrimination

The Council of State took position on an issue regarding the role of teachers of Catholic religion in high schools, recognising the possibility for them to participate in decisions by the Class Council when it assigns the scholastic credits qualifying the student applying to take the final State examination, even though Catholic religion teachers do not issue marks or grades. This possibility would allegedly favour students enrolled in the Religion course over those who are not. Only in theory, in many cases, does the latter group actually access alternative study courses, since in the majority of schools, such alternative courses have not been activated. According to the TAR of Lazio, this situation induces students to opt for the course on Catholic religion not out of personal conviction, but on opportunistic grounds; it ends up by weakening religious freedom, and constitutes discrimination. The appeal to the Council of State was proposed by the Presidency of the Council of Ministers and, by incidental remittal, by the Italian Council of Bishops. Council of State judgement 2749/2010 rules in favour of the appellants. In fact, judges observe that students (and families) who decide not to avail themselves of religious teaching and who do not follow any alternative course, cannot consider as discriminatory the fact that the other students are evaluated in part by teachers of the subjects which the first group has declined to follow (after all, the religion teacher's assessment is not necessarily positive). The norms regulating the attribution of scholastic credits (that only integrate the final assessment, which is based on the average of marks) do not favour students who attend optional courses, with respect to those who do not.

After having pronounced in favour of the appeal and therefore quashing the TAR ruling, the Council of State adds several significant paragraphs in which it complains that the schools' widespread failure to activate courses alternative to Catholic religion education can be detrimental to religious freedom of students and families; the judges therefore urge the Government to fill this gap, for though such courses are optional, their institution must be considered compulsory.

IV. Immigrants' Rights

A. Deportation and Right to a Family

One of the most important provisions of the Italian legislation regarding foreigners is art. 19, legislative decree 286/1998, defining cases in which it is forbidden to deport an immigrant (unless in exceptional circumstances involving national security and only by intervention of the Minister of domestic affairs). Minor age and the existence, in the

State, of genuine family relations with Italian citizens ("it is forbidden […] to deport c) foreigners cohabiting with relatives to the second degree of kinship or with a spouse having Italian citizenship", art. 19, paragraph 2) are among the criteria most widely applied. The right to family unity is also taken into account, especially in cases involving the migrant's right to reunite with the family, as well as the protection of the reunited family member.

In judg. 18527, 3 February 2010, the Court of Cassation, in quashing the judge's order of deportation of a foreigner, applied the parameter of respect for family life. The expulsion order, issued as an accessory penalty for crimes related to drug trafficking after the applicant served his prison sentence, was decided without taking into account his family bonds in Italy (he was married to an Italian citizen, and had children), or the effective threat he posed to the society as factors that should temper-ate the issue of national security.

This judgement amply reviews the case-law by the Constitutional Court and the ECtHR and opposes a previous interpretation of the Cassation itself (e.g. judg. 26938, 2004), which systematically gave prevalence to the judicial measures of expulsion over the right to family unity. In the 2010 ruling the Supreme Court mentions art. 8, ECHR and relative case-law by the Strasbourg Court, see in conjunction with art. 2 Const. where it links protection of the individual's human rights to safeguarding the social entities where his/her personality develops: first of all, in the family, also protected, among others, by art. 29, 30 and 31 Const. In discussing protection of the family, the judgement also refers to art. 10, International Covenant on Economic, Social and Cultural Rights; to art. 23 and 24, International Covenant on Civil and Political rights; to art. 3, 9 and 10, Convention on the Rights of the Child; art. 7, 9, and 24 of the CFREU. Of course, the condition necessary for applying the *favor familiae* criterion is the actual (*effettiva*) existence of a family relationship: i.e., cohabitation of spouses and progeny.

But how should the parameter of *actual* family life be interpreted? In the fore-mentioned judgement of 1 March 2010 by the Novara Tribunal, the judge invalidate the decree by the State police provincial chief (*Questore*) of that city that rejected a demand for a permanent residence permit submitted by a Russian women married with an Italian. The refusal was motivated by the lack of cohabitation between the spouses, due to the husband's imprisonment after the wife herself had accused him of ill-treatment. The judge ascertained that the lack of cohabitation was not due to the absence of *affectio coniugalis.* The Tribunal interprets the norm in art. 19 of legislative decree 286/1998 in accordance with art 8, ECHR, and pertinent case-law of the Strasbourg Court: "the differing interpretation used by the *Questura* created clear discrimination against the non EU citizen with respect to Italian women, putting her, unlike the Italian woman, in the inadmissible condition of choosing either to undergo abuse by her spouse without reacting, or to run the risk – after filing a legal suit for harassment – to be deported from the State where, as in this case, she had built up a network of affective, economic and work relationships".

Pursuant to current immigration legislation, when it is impossible either to deport an irregular foreigner or to hold him/her in an Identification and Expulsion Centre (CIE) (e.g., due to the expiry of the maximum period of confinement in the CIE, extended in 2009 to up to 180 days: see legislative decree 286/1998, art. 14, paragraph 5), the chief of the State police provincial department (Questore) issues and order mandating the foreigner to leave national territory within five days; if the person fails to comply with the order without a justified reason, he commits an offence punishable by detention (legislative decree 286/1998, art. 14, paragraphs 5-*bis* and 5-*ter*). Cassation case-law has clarified that the order at hand must be motivated (it is not sufficient to cite generically its legal basis; for 2010, see judg. 10240, 25 February). The Tribunal of Monza (judg. 4 May 2010, No. 839), referring to paragraph 3 of art. 6, ECHR, also points out that the order for deportation must be written in a language known by the foreigner; otherwise, non-compliance with the order cannot be considered an offence. The foreigner present in the Italian territory who has been reached by a deportation order not translated into a language he knows, must be absolved of the offence of non-compliance with the order.

In Cassation case-law, however, if the offence subsists, deportation must be enforced automatically. In judgement 13197/2010, e.g., the legality of the expulsion order issued against a foreign woman who, in failing to comply with a previous order of leaving the Italian territory, is confirmed. The woman in fact was committed the offence of illegal residence in the State, despite the fact that the she was the mother of a two-year-old girl regularly resident in Italy. In this case – unlike cases ruled by art. 13, paragraph 2-*bis* and art. 29, paragraph 3 of the Consolidated act on immigration, which protect from deportation foreigners benefiting from provisions relative to family reunification – the irregular foreigner, together with the minor-age child, must leave the Country and the cautionary measures meant to protect family life cannot prevent deportation. Case-law does not seem to have taken into account the possible effects on this legislation of EU directive 2008/115 ("the return directive"), whose very *ratio* appears to conflict with the logic underlying the Italian criminal sanction.

In the sphere of administrative justice as well, art. 8 ECHR and the principle of respect for family unity were extensively applied, but this time to exclude denial or revocation of a residence permit in the presence of a foreigner's family bonds, even outside the sphere expressly indicated by art. 5, paragraph 5, legislative decree 296/1998 (reunification with the family). See, on this point, Council of State judgements 29 September 2010, No. 7200;

15 June 2010, No. 3760; 30 March 2010, No. 1480; 31 March 2010, No. 1469; 31 March 2010, No. 1468; 10 February 2010, No. 691; 3 February 2010, No. 537. In particular, judgement 3760 states that the administration cannot deny renewal of the residence permit based on the fact that a previous renewal had been granted in the absence of the necessary requisite, when in the meantime, situations have emerged (particularly in the family sphere) which would portray the denied renewal as a disproportionate interference in the personal and family life of the foreigner. Judgement 7200 applies the same principle to the case of a Chinese worker whose application for renewal of the residence permit had been rejected, because several years earlier, he had declared income inferior to the minimum required by art. 29, paragraph 3 (b) of legislative decree 286/1998, and therefore, during that period, had not been entitled to renewal of the residence permit. If the residence permit had been previously issued in the absence of conditions prescribed by the law – based, e.g., on the foreigner's declaration asserting the existence of a work contract in Italy which in reality was lacking – the police authority can still legitimately deny the renewal and order deportation of the person, if he does not appear to have created particular social or family relations in Italy: all the more so if the foreigner has committed offences in Italy (see, for example, TAR Milan Lombardy, judg. 310, 9 February 2010, also cited below).

As regards whether or not deportation of a foreign offender is automatic, case-law has witnessed some oscillation.

The Consolidated act on immigration connects the issuance or renewal of a residence permit to ascertainment that the foreigner is not "a threat to public order or State security" (art. 4, paragraph 3, legislative decree 286/1998): i.e., he/she has not incurred criminal convictions, although still under appeal or decided through plea bargaining, for the crimes in art. 380, criminal procedure code; i.e., for crimes linked to drug trafficking, human trafficking, aiding clandestine immigration, etc. Council of State decision 543/2010 rules that the steady character of this barring clause can be overcome pursuant to art. 5, paragraph 5 of legislative decree 286/1998 (as amended by a law of 2007), according to which the automatic denial of issuance or renewal of the residence permit may be bypassed when "new elements have emerged" whereby the existence of a social threat inferred from the previous conviction (for theft, in the considered case) is untenable (the Council of State found that no such new elements emerged). However a similar plea by a foreign immigrant woman in a case judged by the Council of State, had a positive outcome (judgement 4774/2010). A woman, now well integrated into Italian society and mother of a baby girl, was seeking validation of her residence permit; years earlier, however, she had plea bargained a conviction for theft. Her application should have been rejected. The judges, nonetheless, citing case-law by the ECtHR and the European Court of Justice, as well as provisions in the Constitution and the Convention on the Rights of the Child on the fundamental rights of minors and the family, observed that the "reasons supporting deportation do not emerge, or must recede, when it clearly and unequivocally appears that the foreigner has established and consolidated in Italy a dignified, normal relational life, or that he or she is, at any rate, a bearer of non-renounceable, inviolable rights, and that the provision might harm the life of an innocent child". In accordance with this ruling, see also Council of State judgement 4904/2010, that reminds the importance of a factor which must not be overlooked when deciding deportation of a convicted foreigner, namely he or she might have previously been permitted to exercise the right to reunification with his family. The last cited ruling also mentions Constitutional Court judgement 148/2008, which interprets the "automatic expulsion" clause as a rights-protecting measure, that is an "indispensable safeguard of the [...] rights [of foreigners] as it prevents any possible arbitrariness on the part of the administration". the TAR Lombardy judgement 310/2010 does not contrast with such case-law; it confirms the revocation of the residence permit of an immigrant who, besides having lied about the existence of a job in Italy, had not been able to prove that he was socially integrated into the Country, nor that he could invoke the right to protect his family life.

The position taken by the Council of State is thus contrary to the "automatic expulsion" clause; a contrasting solution was followed by the TAR, Valle d'Aosta, in judgement 14 July 2010. The claimant, who had been living in Italy for years, married and father of three minor-age children, had been denied renewal of his residence permit for work motives, because of a previous conviction for theft. The judges upheld. Moreover, they declared that the question of constitutionality here was manifestly unfounded: the issue was raised by the immigrant's defending counsel based on a presumed disparity of treatment between the foreigner who has entered Italy for the sake of family reunification, who cannot be deported without due consideration of his right to live in a family, and the foreigner present in Italy for other reasons (holding e.g., a work permit), who is subjected to the "automatic expulsion" clause. TAR Lazio seems to follow similar reasoning in judgement 9914/2010, confirming the rejection of a application for renewal of a residence permit based on a mere promise of employment filed by an immigrant after his previous permit, awarded for expected employment, had expired. The foreigner had also claimed his right not to be separated from his family members legally residing in Italy, including his minor-age son. The judges observed that the need to keep the family united was satisfied, since the individual can ask to re-enter Italy through a ordinary procedure for family reunification, or through the procedure of art. 31, legislative decree 286/1998 (see below).

Another ground justifying the invalidation of an expulsion order is the circumstance that the deported person might be exposed, in the Country of return, to inhuman treatment or torture, or even to capital punishment. This danger, however, must personally concern the individual subject to deportation, at least potentially, in a more intense degree with respect to any inhabitant of the State where he is returned.

The Court of Cassation therefore upheld the deportation order of a Chinese female citizen to China, although, as is widely known, in that Country capital punishment is applicable and prison conditions are harsh, since the person had no particular reason to fear being affected by such treatments (judg. 25466, 3 December 2009).

Another aspect connected to the right to family unity is the issue of temporary permit to enter or reside in Italy pursuant to art. 31, legislative decree 286/1998, favouring the family member of a foreign minor with special psycho-physical needs. This topic will be discussed in the following paragraph on children's issues.

B. Unconstitutionality of the Aggravating Circumstance Linked to the Status of the Irregular Immigrant

Constitutional Court judgement No. 249, 8 July 2010, declared the unconstitutionality of art. 61, No. 11-*bis*, criminal code, a norm introduced by law 24 July 2008, No. 125, in conversion of law-decree 92/2008 ("security packet 2008"). Among circumstances aggravating the commission of any offence, the abrogated norm included the fact "of the convicted person's having committed the offence while illegally present on national territory". With l. 94/2009 ("security packet 2009"), the circumstance was limited to foreigners who are not EU citizens, and to stateless persons. According to the Constitutional Court, the norm introduces discrimination based on "personal and social conditions" (art. 3 Const.) of the convicted person, which have nothing to do with the contested fact constituting the offence; in this way, the law assumes as a conclusive presumption the greater threat posed by irregular immigrants. The aim of combating illegal migratory flows is not considered capable of justifying such an aggravating circumstance, since it is dishomogeneous with respect to the aims pursued by the criminal law and likely to be applied to a wide variety of criminal offences. This is all the more true following the introduction, by cited l. 94/2009, of the crime of irregular entry and residence that aims at punishing the same situation (see following paragraph).

"The foreigner who is not an EU citizen," observes the Court, "is punished first on ground of his illegal entry or residence on national territory, but due to the persistent duration of his status of irregular alien he undergoes one or more further sanctions associated with any other offences he may commit, whatever their number; such offences may harm interests and values which have nothing to do with the problem of controlling migratory movements" (see "as to the law" part of motivations, para. 6). This implies unreasonable, discriminatory treatment contrary to art. 3 Const., paragraph 1. In examining the norm from the perspective of art. 25 Const., the Court observes, moreover, that the "definition of 'irregular' immigrant – associated to the illegal entry into Italian territory or with permanence after expiry of the residence permit, even in consequence of the negligent failure timely to renew the permit – becomes a 'stigma' tending to create the premise for differentiated penal treatment regarding the subject, whose behaviour now appears, generically and with no reservation or distinction, as marked by stronger antagonism against law". Finally, the position of the irregular immigrant is not comparable to that of the fugitive from justice (who voluntarily absconds from a warrant of arrest), nor to that of the habitual offender (who has already undergone convictions for criminal offences of the same type), conditions which, at least theoretically, may well count as aggravating circumstances.

C. Non-unconstitutionality of the Offence of Irregular Immigration

Constitutional Court, in judgement 250/2010, also of 8 July, ruled on the offence of illegal entry and residence on the part of the immigrant, introduced by the so-called "security packet" of 2009, through amended art. 10-*bis* of legislative decree 286/1998. The penalty foreseen is a fine from 5,000 to 10,000 euros, which can be substituted by deportation and a five or more year ban to re-entry the Country. The tribunals involved (Justices of the Peace in Lecco and Turin) had raised doubts of unconstitutionality of this provision for infringing numerous articles of the Constitutional Charter. In particular, they had maintained that the norm punished a merely personal and social status of the individual, and at any rate, a non-offensive behaviour, thus violating art. 25 Const., paragraph 2. The Constitutional Court rejects this interpretation; it holds that it is not unreasonable for the legislator to consider the conduct of one who enters and resides in Italy in violation of the immigration laws, as deserving criminal sanction; the legal good protected, in fact, is the State's interest in managing migratory flows, with an aim to safeguarding various other public values and goods (security, health, public order, etc.) which the State has a duty to guarantee in the exercise of its sovereignty. The constitutional provision allegedly infringed was art. 25 Const., partly in relation to art. 3 Const., since the criminalisation of illegal entry or residence was thought to introduce a presumption of the immigrant's social dangerousness. This doubt, too, is rejected by the Constitutional Court, which retains identifiable in the conduct of the illegal immigrant, specific behaviour susceptible to criminal punishment. The call for solidarity mentioned in art. 2 Const. is not nullified by the norm, since other legal provisions are designed to satisfy it (i.e., legislation on the right to asylum, on family reunification, etc.): therefore, not even art. 2 is violated by the provision. Further objections raised by the remitting judges were also dismissed, in particular those pointing out that the criminal offence mentioned in art. 10-*bis* virtually equated the administrative offence of art. 13, paragraph 2, also in legislative decree 286/1998, sanctioned with deportation order issued by the Prefect (the official representing the State Government at the provincial level). The Constitutional Court stated that the issue addressed the political advisability, rather than the legitimacy, of the choice made by the legislator. Finally, the Constitutional Court denies that there is any conflict between art. 10-*bis* and art. 117(1) Const. as to incompatibility with provisions in EU directive 2008/115/CE ("return directive"), which requires States to arrange repatriation of illegal non-EU immigrants mainly on a voluntary basis. According to the Constitutional Court, first of all the directive had not yet been incorporated into the Italian legal system; and secondly, it does not interfere with the State's right to intervene using criminal law measures. Other grounds of unconstitutionality envisaged by the remitting judges (including the failure to foresee "reasonable motives" capable of excluding the offence, or to expressly exempt school authorities from the obligation to report irregular immigrants) are rejected by the Court, either because they are ill-founded or because they are not pertinent to the impugned article.

D. Unconstitutionality of the Irrelevance of Reasonable Motives in the Irregular Immigrant's Failure to Comply with the Order to Leave the State Territory

Constitutional Court judgement 359/2010 declared the unconstitutionality of art. 14, paragraph 5-*quater* in the Consolidated act on immigration punishing the foreigner who, after being served with a police order of deportation from national territory, has not complied with it, and so has received a further order to leave the Country within five days time (the rule derives from paragraphs 5-*bis*, 5-*ter* and 5-*quater* of art. 14, as amended by the recent l. 94/2009). While the law explicitly acknowledges (art. 14, paragraph 5-*ter*) that "reasonable motives" may have prevented compliance with the expulsion order, and accordingly the foreigner has not committed the offence of irregular permanence in Italy, the "safety clause" is omitted in paragraph 5-*quater* in the case of an immigrant who has received two or more deportation orders. The immigrant who reiterates non-compliance with a deportation order, moreover, is punished more severely (imprisonment from one to five years, instead of one to four). The stricter disposition depended on the greater offensiveness of the conduct and the graver social alarm associated with the repeated failure to meet the obligation to leave the national territory. The case sparking off the judgement of unconstitutionality concerned an immigrant woman who did not comply with four deportation orders given her absolute indigence (she slept under stairways in the dead of winter). The extreme indigence, the unavailability of a carrier, the difficulty in acquiring travel documents, are some of the circumstances judicially recognised as "reasonable motives" that free the perpetrator from committing the offence of unlawful permanence in the State. In upholding the arguments of the remitting judge, the Constitutional Court considers as unreasonable the legislator's choice to exclude such motives in cases of repeated non-compliance with the order to leave Italy. In fact, the state of extreme indigence might be of long duration, or emerge after receiving the second deportation order: that would not necessarily make the foreigner's conduct more blameful as unreasonable. Art. 3 Const. has thus been violated. Concerning other grounds of unconstitutionality mentioned by the remitting judge (violation of art. 2 Const., as well as art. 25 Const. and 27 Cont.), the Court gives no specific reasoning, holding them to be included in the area considered.

E. Extradition and Risk of Ill-treatment

On several occasions, Italian judges have refused the extradition or deportation of foreign citizens toward Countries where there exists a real risk that the person may undergo torture or cruel, inhuman or degrading treatment prohibited by international human rights law (in particular art. 3 ECHR). The Court of Cassation (judg. 20514, 28 April 2010), in quashing on various grounds a judgement for crimes of terrorism, also pointed out that the measure of deportation, once an individual has served his sentence, toward a Country such as Tunisia, already considered by the European Court of Human Rights as incapable of effectively guaranteeing respect for the fundamental rights of persons charged with crimes of terrorism (in particular, see the case *Saadi v. Italy*, 2008), cannot be ordered unless a change in the current situation of alarm is demonstrated; in the absence of such proof, deportation must be substituted by a different security measure. In the case concerning one of the accused foreigners, who on 13 April 2010 filed an application to the ECtHR, the Italian Government was then issued with a note of the Court urging it not to enforce the deportation order before the case had been heard; should it not comply with the request, the Italian State would be responsible for violating art. 34 ECHR. The Cassation Court points out that "any institutional structure of the Republic must ensure rigorous respect for art. 3 of the ECHR", including the judiciary. This principle must also apply to accused persons who have not taken a case to the Strasbourg Court.

F. Social Rights of Immigrants and Regional Policies

Constitutional Court judgement 187/2010 has declared the illegitimacy – given its conflict with the principle of non-discrimination affirmed by the ECHR, and its consequent violation of art. 117 Const., paragraph 1 – of a provision contained in the 2001 financial law (l. 388/2000). The norm concerned established that the monthly indemnity paid by the national social security agency (INPS) to those who have an invalidity of 75% and therefore cannot work, must not be paid to foreign immigrants unless they are long-term residents (having been living in the Country for at least five years). The Court pointed out that the right to this benefit must be understood as essential to the survival of persons who, because of serious disability, are unable to work, even though they might be foreigners holding a mere temporary residence permit. The enjoyment of the right cannot be subordinate to the terms of the residence permit (namely, for of a long-term residence permit, five years' presence and availability of a certain income). The judgement makes ample reference to the ECHR, both in affirming that entitlement to invalidity benefit is a right (pursuant to art. 1, Protocol I, ECHR), and in identifying the existence of an impermissible discrimination (art. 14 ECHR).

In 2009 the Region of Tuscany adopted a law (r.l. 29/2009) on the integration of foreign citizens that established some measures in the sphere of social and health care, culture, health care, etc., in favour of immigrant citizens – including the irregular ones and the so-called "neo-Communitarians". The regional act was impugned by the Presidency of the Council of Ministers for incompatibility with art. 117 Const., paragraph 2, letters a) and b), and paragraph 9, since it introduced several provisions conflicting with legislative decree 286/1998. In judgement 269/2010, the Constitutional Court declared the question raised by the Government in part inadmissible and in part unfounded. In fact, the judges maintain that on one hand, the regional norms limit themselves to regulate the access to rights, in the sphere of regional competence, which EU law attributes to all European citizens; on the other, it sets out measures facilitating access to the exercise of fundamental rights (children's health, vaccinations, protection for the mothers, etc., as well as support for information campaigns carried out by local authorities in favour of immigrants) belonging to everyone, including undocumented immigrants. The judges cite judgements No. 148/2008 of the same Court and, as regards the right to health, No. 252/2001, where it recognises that there exists "an irreducible nucleus of the right to health protected by the Constitution as an inviolable dimension of human dignity, which demands that we prevent the formation of situations devoid of protection, which may in fact hamper the implementation of that right"; the core aspects of that right must therefore be granted "to foreigners as well, whatever their position with respect to norms regulating entry and residence in the State, although the legislator may set out different modes for exercising the right". The registration with the regional health care service of foreigners whose application for refugee status, asylum or subsidiary humanitarian protection has been rejected, and who have appealed against the denial decision, is indeed foreseen by the Consolidated act on immigration; therefore, the detailed regulation of the procedure as contained in the Tuscan regional law, does not exceed the legislative competence as conferred to the Regions by the Constitution. As regards the Tuscany law provisions aimed at promoting initiatives in cooperation with national and international institutions on immigration issues, in particular those facilitating immigration in order to attend professional training courses or internships, the Constitutional Court recognises that these are "activities of international scope" within regional competence, provided they comply with the foreign policy guidelines established by the State.

Similar conclusions were reached in judgement No. 299/2010, the Constitutional Court issued concerning the Apulia r.l. 32/2009 (Norms for the reception, civil coexistence and integration of immigrants). The Court, while acknowledging that in most cases the Region had deliberated within its own sphere of competence, considers unconstitutional several provisions in art. 1 and 2 of r.l. 32/2009, aimed, respectively, at promoting regional policies "to guarantee legal help, in particular the effectiveness of the defendant's rights, for immigrants present for any reason on regional territory", and to further the application, in Apulia, of the norms of the International Convention on the rights of migrant workers and their family members, a treaty which Italy has not yet ratified.

V. Children

A. Court Hearings

Several Court of Cassation judgements have tackled the issue of children's hearing and participation in judicial adoption proceedings. A new legislation on adoptability procedures, defined in l. 149/2001, came into effect on 1 July 2007.

In judgement No. 7280, 26 March 2010, the father of children for whom the juvenile court of Turin had declared the state of adoptability – a provision upheld by the Court of Appeals – challenged the appeal's ruling on the ground that, among other factors, it had been adopted without having heard one of the two children, aged eight and a half years. The Court of Cassation observes that at any rate, the child was regarded as a legal party in the proceedings, legally represented by his guardian, pursuant to l. 184/1983, art. 8 (as amended by l. 149/2001). It also points out that direct hearing of the child in adoption procedures is mandatory only for children from the age of 12 years (and the adoption of a minor aged 14 years or more cannot be authorised without his or her consent); a child younger than 12 may also be heard directly by the judge, at the judge's discretion, taking into account his or her maturity, in order not to expose the child to further trauma. The judge considers this praxis in compliance both with the UN Convention on the Rights of the Child and with the 1996 Council of Europe Convention on the Exercise of Children's Rights; the latter expressly provides that the child may be heard by way of an appropriate body or representative; this, according to the Supreme Court, was done. The application was therefore rejected.

The hearing of a child in a procedure for adoptability is described by the Court of Cassation (see, in particular, judg. No. 7282/2010) not as an instrument of evidence, i.e., as testimony aiming to provide the judge with elements for reconstructing the facts on which to base the decision; but instead, as a "tool for directly gathering opinions as well as evaluations and needs expressed by the child in relation to the event in which he or she is involved [...], allowing the judge to perceive immediately [...] how to protect the child's crucial interests". The judge, then, may hear the child even without the presence of other parties. The hearing may take place either directly or by way of professionally qualified personnel, in compliance with the children's right to apply to be assisted by an appropriate person of their choice in order to help them express their opinions, as provided for by art. 5(a) of the Strasbourg Convention on the Exercise of Children's Rights.

Court of Cassation judgement 7281/2010 (and with the same orientation, also see judg. 12290/2010) presents ample discussion on the way in which the children's right to participate in adoptability procedures is currently configured, after the 2001 reform of l. 184/1983. The child is a necessary party in the proceeding: his failure to appear is cause of absolute, irremediable nullity of the proceeding which may be insisted upon by the parties or by the judge on its own motion at any moment. Since there exists a radical conflict of interest between the child and his or her "natural" legal representatives, i.e., the parents, the judge is obliged (in juvenile courts) to appoint an *ad litem* guardian (*curatore speciale*) who will represent the child's interests; the same obligation exists if the child has no parents and does not have a legal guardian. If, instead, a legal guardian has been assigned to the child, it is a guardian's duty to care for the child's interests; in exceptional cases only, if a conflict of interest should arise during the proceedings between the child and the guardian, the judicial authority may proceed to appoint a *curatore speciale*. In this case, the proceeding will not be radically null; only the acts performed after emergence of the conflict of interest will be repeated. In particular, it is the guardian's duty (or the *ad litem* guardian's, in the circumstances considered above) promptly to appoint a counsel for the technical defence of the rights of the child; in any event, the child's legal guardian and his lawyer are both required in order to grant the substantial and procedural protection of the child; both of them, e.g., can separately oppose or decline to oppose the judgement on adoptability (on this point, see also Court of Cassation judgements 16870/2010 and 14063/2010). Italian regulations are deemed to comply with the 1996 Strasbourg Convention principles.

As regards the child's full participation in the adoption procedure, the Court of Cassation also adopted judgements 3804 and 3805, 17 February 2010. In the cases considered, the Milan Court of Appeals had annulled and remitted to the juvenile tribunal a declaration of adoptability because it found that in the first phase of the proceedings it had been the Mayor of the Municipality where the children waiting for adoption resided who, as their legal guardian, appointed their counsel. The Court of Cassation rules that the child needs not to take part in legal proceedings by way of a counsel (appointed by the judge *motu proprio*): if a legal guardian has been appointed and there is no conflict of interest with the child, the guardian can represent the child in the procedure of adoptability. While for a natural parent or a guardian belonging to the child's family of origin, a conflict of interest is presumed, a legal guardian who has no family bonds with the child – including when the guardian is public institution, for example a Municipality represented by its Mayor – is not necessarily in a conflict of interest.

The children's right to be heard in judicial procedures appeared, as well, in a Court of Cassation judgement issued in application of the 1980 Hague Convention on Civil Aspects of International Child Abduction. The case regarded two children for whom a German tribunal determined shared custody by both their separated parents (the mother was Italian, the father German); they had been transferred to Italy on the mother's initiative, without permission by the German judge; the latter therefore granted temporary custody only to the father; as a response, the mother retained the children with her in Italy. The Milan juvenile court, to which the father had appealed seeking application of the 1980 Hague Convention, had arranged for the immediate return of the children to him in Germany. The Cassation Court (judg. 12293/2010) censures, on one hand, the Court of Appeals' failure to verify whether there was an effective impediment for the father to exercise his right to make regular visits to his children after their moving to Milan; and on the other hand, the judge's failure to arrange an hearing with the children. On this point, the Cassation Court, while acknowledging that the law does not impose the hearing of a child in such procedures, stressed that such a hearing was nevertheless opportune, and required by regulation CE 2201/2003. The juvenile court's unjustified failure to arrange for the hearing leads the Cassation Court to quash the decree.

B. Immigrant Children in Need and Temporary Residence Permit for Their Parents

Art. 31, paragraph 3 of the Consolidated act on immigration allows issuance of a temporary residence permit for the foreigner whose presence is considered indispensable in order to care for a under age family member – not subject to deportation – on Italian territory. In such an exceptional case, the legal status is attributed to the adult family member as a result of the provisions regulating the child, while the rule is the opposite: the child's status follows the parents'. Case-law applying art. 31, paragraph 3 has oscillated from an interpretation that gives wide scope to the notion of "grave motives connected to the psycho-physical development of the child" to one appearing, instead, quite restrictive.

The more restrictive interpretation (see, e.g., Court of Cassation, civil division, section I, judg. No. 747, 2007) grants a temporary permit to the adult family member only when the child is affected by particularly serious health or social conditions (severe pathologies, hospitalisation, situations of extreme social hardship, etc.), present at the moment when entry or residence permit is requested. According to a wider interpretation that stresses the child's "best interest" (see Court of Cassation judg. No. 22080, 2009), an entry of residence permit would be granted to the child's parent (or other care-giving adult) "exceptionally" (it is indeed a sort of inversion in the ordinary family reunification mechanism), not only in situations of health or social emergency, but also in relation to such situations as the child's very young age, or to his/her need for school integration, for example. In this regards, the circumstances to be taken into account are not just those present at the moment of the request, but also those reasonably foreseeable for the future. Ordinance 823/2010, also by Cassation, moves in this same direction.

On 10 March 2010, Court of Cassation judgement No. 5856 was deposited. It opposed the same Court's recent "extensive" interpretation which was disapproved as it referred exclusively to children's rights (as defined by the 1989 Convention) without counterbalancing such parameter with requirements of public security and the governance of immigration. The criticised wide interpretation, indeed, is considered in this pronouncement capable of favouring the manipulation of children, whose mere presence on national territory would end up being exploited by the adult family members irregularly residing in the State, in order to obtain a surreptitious form of regularisation of their own position.

On this point, the Plenary of the Court of Cassation intervened with judgement No. 21799, 25 October 2010, and with the analogous judgement No. 21803, on the same date. In these cases the Court rejects both the restrictive and the wide interpretation of art. 31. According to the Plenary, therefore, which cites in support both EU law (directive 2008/115/EC) and ECtHR case-law, the issuing of a temporary residence permit pursuant to art. 31, paragraph 3 of the Consolidated act on immigration is subordinate to the ascertained existence of grave harm, whether medical or otherwise, either present or reasonably foreseeable in the future, and which would befall the foreign child due to the absence of or separation from the family member, or to his or her uprooting from the ordinary living environment. The provision, however, is not designed to cope with long-term situations or, at any rate, to face a hardship linked to life events that could strike any individual. According to Cassation, a decision must be taken on a case by case basis, without necessarily opting for the choice which is most advantageous for the child, but rather for the one which reconciles the child's best interest with the demands of national security and immigration governance. That is, as for this last aspect, with the need to combat the increase in the number of immigrants needing to regularise their residence position. It is not clear whether countering the irregular immigration or residence of foreigners, on one hand, and protecting children's rights, on the other, are considered goals of equal value by the ruling, or whether, instead, children's rights are given some priority (as would seem the case).

C. Family Reunification and **Kafalah**

In recent years, the possibility for immigrants to bring to Italy children placed under *kafalah* (an institution of Islamic law broadly analogous to foster placement) by way of the family reunification procedures as defined by legislative decree 286/1998, art. 29, paragraph 2, has become an issue of particular interest.

> *Kafalah* is a measure for the protection of children by which a couple or a single person (the *kafil*) is awarded custody of child in need (*makful*) – often a child born outside marriage; the *kafil* supports the child, sometimes permanently, even though the relationship does not imply adoption (inadmissible under Islamic law). After some oscillation, the Court of Cassation recognised the capability of *kafalah* (when ordered by a judiciary authority of the Country of origin, and not merely constituted on a private contract) to perform as a ground for family reunification as defined by the Consolidated act on immigration (see, e.g., judg. No. 18174/2008). In 2010, this jurisprudence was upheld, always concerning children from Islamic Countries (Morocco) involved in family reunification programmes with nationals residing in Italy (see Court of Cassation judg. No. 1073/2010). The Court acknowledged the analogy between (judicial) *kafalah* and foster placement: an analogy also grounded on art. 20 of the Convention on the Rights of the Child expressly mentioning *kafalah.*

The Court of Cassation also raised the question of extending this interpretation to include cases of entry into Italy of children under *kafalah*, in order to reunite with EU nationals, including Italian citizens. In judgement No. 4868 of 2010, the Supreme Court gave a negative answer. The case of an EU citizen claiming the right to bring to Italy a child placed in *kafalah* is, in fact, regulated not by the 1998 Consolidated act on immigration, but by legislative decree 30/2007, which transposes directive 2004/38/EC on the right of citizens and their family members to move and reside freely within the EU. This legislation contains no trace of any possibility to recognise, as entitlement for entry into Italy or Europe, any form of international foster care arrangement or *kafalah*, since for Italy and other EU Member States, only (internationally) adopted children can be reunited to a family that is not his or her natural one. An EU citizen who claims the right to "family reunification" of a child in *kafalah* according to the law of a Country admitting this institution, ought therefore to convert *kafalah* into adoption.

The Court of Cassation precedent was not followed by the Court of Tivoli's ruling on 22 June 2010. The case involved a baby girl abandoned by her parents shortly after her birth and placed in *kafalah* in her early days to an Italian couple temporarily residing in Morocco for reasons of work. The *kafalah* was arranged thanks to action taken by a local humanitarian association to which the couple had previously expressed their desire to help children in need. After approximately a year of cohabitation, the two Italians had to entrust the little girl to the association's care, since they were obliged to return to Italy. Since then, attempts to have the baby girl enter Italy for the sake of family reunification have been frustrated by the Italian consular authorities of Morocco that refused to issue the baby a visa, because her position was not comparable to that of a non EU citizen's *makful*, and therefore the provision in art. 29, paragraph 2, legislative decree 286/1998 did not apply. The Tivoli judge to whom the two Italians applied in order to obtain an entry visa for the purpose of family reunification, despite the absence of a permission from the Italian consulate in Morocco, pointed out the differences between the case at hand and that ruled on by the Court of Cassation in judgement No. 4868/2010. The tribunal found that application of the Court of Cassation's *dictum* would inevitably have brought about a disproportionate restriction of the child's rights (the girls had never known any family environment outside the *kafalah*), thus conflicting with art. 2 Const. and with the principles of the Convention on the Rights of the Child. There was also a risk of discrimination (art. 3 Const.) between EU and non-EU citizens, to the detriment of the EU citizens. In the case at hand, judge underlines, *kafalah* presented characteristics highly similar to those of a pre-adoptive foster placement; moreover, there were no chance for the Italian couple to adopt the baby in Morocco, since adoption is not admitted by national law and the Italian law does not allow for intercountry "nominative" adoption (that is adoption of a child individually identified by the adopting adults before starting the adoption procedure). In conclusion, the Tivoli judge found that an interpretation of legislative decree 30/2007 in the light of the Constitution, required to consider, in the specific case, the person in *kafalah* as a "member of the family" to whom the more favourable provision of art. 29, paragraph 2 of the Consolidated act on immigration could be applied.

VI. International Protection, Asylum

Cases involving asylum, the recognition of refugee status and the granting of subsidiary protection have been dealt with by the Court of Cassation in a good number of rulings adopted – *in camera* or with particularly rapid procedures – on claims brought against the Court of Appeals' judgements concerning decisions of the territorial Commissions on asylum applications (see legislative decree 25/2008).

> The Court of Cassation order 17576/2010 annulled a ruling issued by the Milan Court of Appeals upholding the rejection by the territorial Commission of that city of a request for international protection submitted by a Turkish citizen, an activist in the Kurdish movement, reached by an arrest order issued *in absentia* by a Turkish court, for terrorism propaganda. The Court of Cassation criticized the total absence of preliminary inquiry as to the grounds of the asylum request. According to the Supreme Court, "political persecution subsists even when criminal sentences are legally inflicted as the result of a regular trial against a person who has expressed mere political opinions", which as such, are distinct from incitement to hatred or violence. Therefore, the judge must rule on this individual case, taking into account the situation actually existing in Turkey regarding freedom of expression, and not limit the assessment to the nature of crimes charged against the applicant.

The foreigner seeking protection in Italy claiming to be the victim of a persecution in his or her Country of origin, can apply for: refugee status, pursuant to the 1951 Geneva Convention; subsidiary protection, pursuant to EU directive 2004/83/CE; political asylum, as granted by art. 10, paragraph 3 Const.; or a residence permit on humanitarian grounds, pursuant to art. 5, paragraph 6, in the 1998 Consolidated act on immigration. In all such instances, besides the specific competence of territorial Commissions for recognition of international protection, still exists the jurisdiction by ordinary tribunals, as the matter involves fundamental human rights (see judgement No. 19394/2009 of the Plenary of Court of Cassation, civil division). In judgement No. 1220/2010, the Milan Tribunal also recalled Court of Cassation case-law which, in some cases, used the right to political asylum enshrined in art. 10, paragraph 3 Const. to the grant an individual the possibility of remaining in Italy while awaiting completion of procedures possibly leading to other forms of international protection. In any event, however, the attribution of such benefits must be grounded on the finding that the applicant has "unsuccessfully attempted to exercise concretely in his Country, the democratic liberties guaranteed by our Constitution": a claim for refugee status cannot be based on a mere statement that the exercise of such liberties, in a given Country, is generally hampered.

VII. Criminal Trial and Execution of the Penalty

A. 41-bis

In judg. No. 190/2010, the Constitutional Court ruled on a question of constitutionality regarding the new provisions introduced by the "2009 security packet", amending art. 41-*bis* of l. 354/1975 (the penitentiary act), which further harshen prison conditions for detainees convicted for Mafia crimes. In particular, the remitting judge held that the new provisions had excluded the possibility, for the judiciary (the Surveillance Tribunal, competent to supervise the execution of the sentence), to examine the legality of a Ministry decision suspending the ordinary treatment, and applying to a detainee the special regime regulated by art. 41-*bis*. A Constitutionally-oriented interpretation of the renewed article, says the Constitutional Court, should exclude this conclusion. Despite the amended provision does not envisage the possibility to challenge before the Surveillance Tribunal the decision to impose an art. 41-*bis* detention regime (while it is possible to challenge the extension of such measure before the Rome's Tribunal of Surveillance, nationwide competent) granting the detainee such a right stems from the general principles of the law. Therefore, l. 94/2009 (security package) has not violated art. 13 Const., as suggested by the remitting judge. The amended legislation also limits the Ministry discretion in shaping art. 41-*bis* measures applicable to the detained person.

B. Sentence Determination and the Obligation to Abide by the Judgements of the European Court of Human Rights

In ruling on a claim presented against Italy by a detainee sentenced to life imprisonment, the Strasbourg Court had recognised that the penalty of imprisonment for life inflicted on him was contrary to the *favor rei* principle and in conflict with art. 6 ECHR, as well as with art. 7 ECHR (non-retroactivity *in malam partem* of criminal law) (*Scoppola v. Italy* (2), judgement of 11 September 2009). In light of the Strasbourg Court's judgement, and facing the obligation to implement it with general measures, the Italian judiciary authority has tried to deal with the lack of a provision, in Italian law, which expressly permits the reopening of a closed case (*res iudicata*) if the ECtHR has found procedural irregularities amounting to a violation of the European Convention. The issue had arisen on several occasions in recent years (in particular, see the *Dorigo* case and related ruling by the Court of Cassation, penal division, section I, No. 2800, 1 December 2006), but a general solution is still missing. In the case at hand, at any rate, the Court of Cassation (judg. No. 16057, 11 February 2010) ruled that implementation in Italy of the Strasbourg Court's judgement in *Scoppola* (2) did not require any "reopening" of proceedings, but only a change in the sentencing. The Cassation Court just replaced the life sentence with a 30-year term.

C. Anti-Mafia Measures

Dispositions of two laws of 1956 and 1965, on preventive personal and property-related measures against members of Mafia organisations were found unconstitutional as far as they foresee that the adoption of such measures always occur *in camera* and not in a courtroom. With judgement No. 93/2010 the Constitutional Court, seized by the Tribunal of Santa Maria Capua Vetere, stated that, since they affect constitutionally protected rights (in particular, the right to personal freedom and to property), and since they have all the characteristics of a judiciary proceeding, such procedures must respect the fair trial parameters established in art. 111 Const. and spelled out in art. 6 ECHR, including namely the right to a public hearing. The absence of any specific reference to such a principle as applied to preventive measures in the Italian Constitution is remedied by the clear language found not only in the ECHR, but also in the International Covenant on Civil and Political Rights (art. 14) and the Charter of Nice (art. 47, para. 2 CFREU). The Constitutional Court found that the language of the impugned law was clear and did not leave room for a constitutionally-oriented interpretation, and that the remitting judge was not entitled to disapply the law by giving direct application to the provisions on the right to a public hearing enshrined in the ECHR. In alternative, the judge might have considered to apply the parallel provisions of the CFREU, but this point was not dealt with in the judgement. In conclusion, the impugned provisions are declared unconstitutional for violation of art. 117, paragraph 1 Const., through which art. 6 ECHR produces legal effects.

On the special regime for persons involved in Mafia-like criminal association, in judg. No. 139/2010 the Constitutional Court declared the illegitimacy of art. 76, paragraph 4-*bis* of d.p.r. 115/2002 (Consolidated act on judiciary service fees), introduced by the "security packet" of 2008, in the part where it construes as an irrebuttable presumption that those convicted for crimes of Mafia-like association (art. 416-*bis*, penal code), as well as those convicted for crimes involving tobacco smuggling and drug trafficking, exceed the asset ceiling determined for eligibility to legal aid. The fact that such persons are absolutely forbidden access to legal aid even in case of a successive criminal trial is an unreasonable measure curtailing the right to defence, of which access to technical defence, also guaranteed to "the poor" (art. 24, paragraph 3 Const.), is an integral part, pursuant also to art. 6 ECHR and art. 14 of the International Covenant on Civil and Political Rights.

D. Statutes of Limitations

The so-called "ex Cirielli" law (l. 251/2005), implementing a widely contested reform, modified the limitation period established by art. 157 criminal code for criminal offences, generally introducing shorter time limits for trials. A transitory norm, moreover, attempted to restrict the perverse effects of the reform by establishing that the shorter terms only applied to new prosecutions and to the pending proceedings in their pre-trial stage, but not to those already at the trial stage or pending at the Appeals Courts or in the Court of Cassation. This provision however ran contrary to the *favor rei* principle (it was apparently suggested by a merely political compromise devoid of any substantial systematic reasoning). The Constitutional Court (judg. 393/2006) had already found it was illegitimate and had virtually extended the benefit of the reform to all cases not yet at the appellate stage.

With order No. 22357/2010, issued in a trial concerning money laundering of Mafia profits, the penal division of the Court of Cassation stated that the question of constitutionality regarding the transitory norm described above, was not manifestly ill-founded. The Strasbourg Court, in fact, in its case-law on art. 7 ECHR, expanded the principle of non-retroactivity of incriminating criminal provisions to encompass the principle of retroactive application of the law most favourable to the accused (*favor rei*). The *favor rei* standard, though not explicitly included in art. 25 Const., is nevertheless granted not only by the ECHR, but also by art. 15 of the International Covenant on Civil and Political Rights, as well as by art. 49 CFREU ("If, subsequent to the commission of a criminal offence, the law provides for a lighter penalty, that penalty shall be applicable"). The Italian judge should therefore apply this parameter in order to avoid violating art. 117, paragraph 1 Const., and art. 3 Const. Failure to apply retroactively the less harsh provision can, however, be justified when in protection of another constitutional right (the efficient administration of justice, the protection of rights and interests of persons involved in the trial such as crime victims, etc.). This type of assessment, however, cannot be made by the trial court, but pertains to the Constitutional Court. Accordingly, the Court of Cassation decided to raise the question of constitutional legitimacy.

E. European Arrest Warrant

Constitutional Court judgement No. 227 of 24 June 2010 declared the unconstitutionality of art. 18, paragraph 1, letter r) of l. 69/2005, the law introducing in Italy the contents of the European Council framework decision 2002/584/JHA on the "European arrest warrant". The Italian provision sets forth the possibility for Italy of declining to arrest and surrender a convicted person on request by the judicial authority of another EU State where the person is supposed to purge the sentence, but only if the person is an Italian citizen. If the State request involves a non-Italian, the surrender would always be automatic, even if the non-Italian citizen has residence or *de facto* domicile in Italy. The framework decision allowed for States to treat foreigners resident or domiciled in their territory as Italian nationals, on the ground that the execution of the sentence in the State where the person actually lives and has established family bonds or other relationships, is generally preferable than serving the sentence in a different Country, including that of citizenship. The question of constitutionality had been raised in procedures regarding the surrender of Romanian and Polish citizens who have been living for long time in Italy where they have established family and social bonds.

> The Constitutional Court found that the judges could not disapply an Italian provision which is incompatible with the framework decision, since that EU instrument is not directly applicable in Italy absent a specific intervention by the national legislator: i.e., it is devoid of direct effect. The existing Italian legislation, however, appeared to conflict not only with the framework decision, but also with the principle of non-discrimination, established by art. 18 TFEU (formerly art. 12). In this regards, it would also violate art. 117, paragraph 1 Const., as read together with art. 11 Const. (the latter providing the legal basis of EU law supremacy over national law on issues within the competence of the EU). Doubts were also cast on the legitimacy of the Italian norm in light of Const. art. 117, para. 1, art. 3 and art. 27.

The contested norm was declared unconstitutional. The different treatment accorded to the Italian citizen compared to the non-Italian EU citizen, unmitigated by any consideration regarding the existence of a genuine and stable link with Italy of the non-Italian citizens, is an unreasonable form of discrimination. The parameter used by the Constitutional Court is consistent with that set out by the ECJ. In fact, the ECJ had ruled that an equal treatment between a national citizen and a foreigner who has resided in the Country for at least five years, as foreseen in the Dutch legislation, was not unreasonable (ECJ, 6 October 2009, case C-123/08, *Wolzenburg*; see also 17 July 2008, case C-66/08, *Kozlowski*).

F. Extradition

The 1957 European Convention on extradition is the legal basis for mutual surrendering of persons accused of crimes, or wanted for the execution of a detention sentence or other restrictive measure, between European Countries not bound by the EU provisions on the "European arrest warrant". This Convention, contrarily to l. 69/2005 implementing the EU framework decision on the European arrest warrant, does not take into account any particular needs of a "humanitarian" nature. The framework decision in particular, states that a mother living with her children aged less than three years cannot be extradited to the requesting Country. The Court of Cassation, penal division (sent. No. 20147/2010) has therefore quashed and remitted to another section of the Bologna Court of Appeals a decision to extradite to Ukraine a woman, mother of a child less than three years old on the ground that it was taken without having ascertained the existence, in Ukraine, of legislation on detained mothers implementing the standards set forth by the Convention on the Right of the Child and the CFREU.

An exposition of the person being extradited to the risk of torture or inhumane treatment contrary to art. 3 ECHR justifies dismissal of a request for extradition to Turkey in order to execute in that Country a sentence issued *in absentia* against a Turkish citizen for association to the PKK. The extradition of the same individual had already been denied by a Dutch tribunal, which had also ascertained that the person to be extradited had already been the victim of torture during a preceding prison term in Turkey, in 1989. The Rome's Court of Appeals decision, upheld by the penal division of the Cassation Court (judg. No. 32685/2010), was based on the ascertained persistence of inhuman prison conditions, as reported by Amnesty International and Human Rights Watch. The reliability of such information sources is also supported by the Strasbourg Court's frequent use of them, as in the case *Saadi v. Italy* in 2008.

G. Lawful Interceptions

With judgement No. 2374/2010, in a suit involving deception, the Court of Cassation ruled that in penal proceedings, evidence given in the form of a recorded conversation was not admissible. In the case at hand the recording had been made in agreement with the judicial police, but had not been authorised in any way by the judiciary branch (judge or prosecutor). After pointing out that the recording of a private talk by one of the participants in the conversation does not constitute interference in the private life of the interlocutors, as it merely documents the conversation (it is the disclosing of such documentation that constitutes violation of secrecy), the Cassation Court observed that some conditions have to be met in order to use a recording as evidence in a court. The recording stemming from investigative activity should be carried out in accordance with the right to secrecy in conversations (art. 15 Const. and art. 8 ECHR). When it does not involve wire-tapping or environmental interception, it demands no special procedure, but permission by the judge or public prosecutor remains necessary. The Court of Cassation then concludes that, lacking that permission, the document cannot be used in court.

H. Judgement in Default

Constitutional Court judgement No. 317/2009, cited above in connection to the "Communitarisation" of ECHR, has intervened (last in a series of rulings) concerning *in absentia* trials. Recent reforms of criminal trial procedure – induced by ECtHR decisions noting the existence, in the Italian legal system, of a "structural problem" in this area – have modified, in particular, art. 175 of the criminal procedure code, allowing the counsel of the defaulter to impugn the judgement regarding his or her client even without a defaulter's instruction. However – at least in the interpretation given by the Plenary of the Court of Cassation – the reform barred the accused from being given a new term to challenge once again the same judgement, in order to avoid an unreasonable delayed trial. The Constitutional Court therefore had to face a conflict, on one hand, between "living law" stemming from art. 175 of the criminal procedure code, which prevents the defendant who has eventually been notified that the proceeding against him or her started *in absentia* from appealing the judgement when the appeal was filed (unbeknownst to the accused) by the counsel assigned to him or her; and, on the other hand, the fair trial guarantees established by art. 6 ECHR which, instead (according to Strasbourg Court case-law) affirms this right.

The principle is upheld by the Constitutional Court, stating that its rulings "not only must not allow that, by way of art. 117, paragraph 1 Const., a lower protection [of individual rights] is introduced in domestic law compared with that provided by national legislation; it also must prevent a wider protection, potentially available by the same means, becoming inaccessible for persons entitled to a fundamental right". In fact, its mission is to aim "toward maximum expansion of the guarantees [of individuals]", while balancing them with the other constitutionally protected rights and interests, within the national margin of appreciation. In conclusion, the need to combat the excessive length of judicial proceedings cannot prevail over the right to a "fair" trial, i.e. capable of providing the defaulter with every opportunity to effectively exercise the right to defence.

VIII. Expropriations and the Right to Peaceful Enjoyment of Property

There has been a growing number of judicial decisions which, in applying a consolidated jurisprudence of the ECtHR, eventually upheld by the Constitutional Court as well, deal with disputes arising from the so-called "appropriative occupations" or "inverted accessions", also called "indirect expropriations", that is compulsory purchase of real properties by right of eminent domain through irregular procedures or *de facto* acquisition.

The cited TAR Lazio judgement No. 11984, 18 May 2010, found that the practice by which a public administration compulsorily purchases land from private owners, after public works have been implemented on the estate, even in the presence of irregularities in the expropriation process, is unlawful, for violation of the right to peaceful enjoyment of property (art. 1, Protocol I ECHR). The unlawfulness of the overall procedure is also acknowledged by art. 43, d.p.r. 327/2001 (Consolidated act on expropriations by right of eminent domain) which, even while admitting that a public administration may decide to purchase the private land on which it has unlawfully built structures, compels the public institution to pay for the unjust damage. According to TAR Lazio, moreover, the duty to guarantee the right to property demands application of this rule even in situations created before the coming into effect of d.p.r. 327/2001 (which began to produce its effects only in 2003), despite the literal content of the provision in art. 57 of the Consolidated act, in short, must simply be disapplied in situations covered by art. 43. Finally, again in an effort to interpret d.p.r. 327/2001 in a manner consistent with international and EU principles, the TAR of Lazio stated that "before proceeding to correspond the private owner damages for unlawful expropriation (which implies acquisition of property rights over the land by the public administration), the administration must verify the possibility of returning the property to its actual owner, at least in part", especially when the infrastructure of public interest built on the land was – as in the case at hand – an "isolated" road, "insufficient, by itself, to exclude restitution of the area pursuant to the Strasbourg Court jurisprudence" and in the light of "the principles, based on the European Community law, of reasonableness, adequacy, proportionality and subsidiarity"; in such a case, restitution instead of damage compensation was the better choice. TAR Liguria judgement No. 10405, 18 November 2010, points out that if the parties have agreed by contract on the transfer of property, the constitutional illegitimacy of the "indirect expropriation" may affect only the amount of reparations, which must be commensurate with the effective value of the good, even if the parties had previously agreed on a lower sum.

During the year 2010, art. 43, d.p.r. 327/2001, which had been interpreted by TAR Lazio in an effort to make it compatible with the ECHR and with EU legislation, was declared constitutionally illegitimate. Constitutional Court ruling No. 293/2010 radically annulled the norm allowing "amnesty" for a series of irregularities committed by various public administrations which, without bringing expropriation procedures to a close or even without beginning them, by the simple act of building on a private land infrastructures of a public character (roads, public buildings and facilities, etc.), obtained the result of acquiring ownership of the estate as well, paying the private owner an indemnity grossly disproportionate to market value. As observed above, art. 43 had linked acquisition of real estate to the obligation of compensating the owner; but it had made no distinction between situations of mere irregularity in the expropriation procedure, and other situations in which an administration had clearly abused its prerogatives (scholars have described the practice as "appropriative usurpation"); moreover, the disposition did not even contemplate the option of returning the good to its legitimate owner (restitution), but rather spoke of compensation. In acting thus, d.p.r. 327/2001, a decree based on the delegation of powers to the Government contained in art. 7, paragraph 5, l. 8 March 1999, No. 50, overstepped the limits of the delegation act, that requested a mere restructuring of current legislation. The provision is therefore unconstitutional since it violates art. 76 Const. ("The exercise of the legislative function can be delegated to the Government only if accompanied by the definition of principles and guiding criteria, and only for a limited time and with specified aims"). The Constitutional Court observed that the delegated legislator was not empowered to introduce an "innovative" norm such as art. 43, especially if by doing so, it aimed at legitimising a system of "living law", that of the so called "indirect expropriations", based on judge-made law and consistently censured by the Strasbourg Court. The remitting judges had actually asked the Constitutional Court to assess the constitutional legitimacy of art. 43, d.p.r. 327/2001 as infringing art. 117(1) Const., given its inconsistency with the ECHR. The Court however limited itself to considering the provision's incompatibility only with art. 76 Const., without discussing other grounds of constitutional legitimacy.

According to TAR Lombardy, which ruled in a dispute between private owners and ANAS, the State-owned company that manages most of the national road network (judgement No. 2070, 20 May 2010), the system of expropriation by right of eminent domain must take into account the increased importance of the right to peaceful enjoyment of property, emerging thanks to the ECHR and to the entering into force of the Lisbon Treaty. In light of these legal instruments, any interpretation of the Consolidated act on expropriations that considers the time-limits for implementing the work – once the declaration of public utility has been made – as merely directory, and not peremptory, should be rebutted. The same goes for any interpretations that subordinate works deadlines to the fulfilment of other tasks (in the case at hand, those required by the decree on environmental impact assessment), which have different deadlines.

Art. 1, Protocol I ECHR was also invoked before Italian courts by a private owner in the same position as many other victims or participants in the same fraud, who had purchased apartments and detached or semi-detached houses in a neighbourhood built up illegally by entrepreneurs linked to the *camorra* (a *mafia*-like criminal organisation) in the town of Giugliano, in Campania. The entire group of lots, built up in an area subject to archaeological protection (the area lies on part of the ancient Via Appia) and military limits, and reserved for hotels and other tourist facilities, had been put in the custody of the law as an *interim* measure. The plaintiff, who had bought the home prior to the sequestration, claims the right to enjoy property purchased in good faith. The Court of Cassation, penal division, judgement No. 45492, 23 November 2010, rejects this claim, noting that only an irreproachable third party can claim protection by the law, not the private person who has purchased a property while violating – deliberately or by negligence – obvious duties of obtaining information concerning the status of the real estate.

IX. Reasonable Length of Judicial Proceedings

The year 2010 has seen a great many rulings ascertaining the excessive length of judicial proceedings in the criminal, civil, and administrative matters. The Court of Cassation alone dealt with the problem in tens of petitions against decisions on excessive length adopted, pursuant to l. 89/2001 (the so-called "Pinto law"), by the Courts of Appeals. In particular, as regards calculation of damages for the violation of this right, Italian case-law generally aligns itself with that of the Strasbourg Court – as expressly required by l. 89/2001 – both on criteria for defining the reasonable duration of a trial, and on recognition of non-pecuniary damage as a normal consequence of violation of the right to a reasonably rapid trial (the duty to conform to the decisions of the ECtHR was expressly reiterated by the Court of Cassation in several of its early judgements of 2003-2004, namely in cases No. 1338/2004, 1339/2004, 1340/2004 and 1341/2004); on some points, however, the Italian judge detaches himself somewhat from the usual procedure followed by the Strasbourg Court. The most marked elements of non-convergence concern the criteria used in determining the period to be calculated, and the criteria used to define the sum payable to the victim.

As regards the first aspect, the ECtHR, in settling the amount of reparation for non-pecuniary damages caused by the violation of art. 6(1) ECHR, considers the entire period of the procedure's duration. The Italian judge, instead, in alignment with the "Pinto law" (art. 2), settles the just satisfaction taking into account only the time exceeding the limit of reasonable duration, which is determined on a case-by-case basis.

The Court of Cassation, in rejecting claims that impugned this lack of conformity as violation of supra-national norms, reaffirmed the nature of non-direct applicability informing the case-law of the ECtHR. In doing so it recalled pertinent Constitutional Court judgements, No. 348/2007 and 349/2007, excluding any directly binding effect of ECHR on national adjudication. In addition, the Court of Cassation clarifies that the "Pinto law", in implementing the Constitutional provision (art. 111 Const.) on fair trial, is mandatory for any national judge (Cassation, judg. No. 11030/2010), whose readiness to grant just compensation for damage caused by the infringement of the reasonable duration clause is by no means undermined by the different scheme adopted to calculate the amount (Cassation, judg. 6297/2010).

As regards the determination of non-pecuniary damages, the criteria applied in Italian case-law clearly differ from those followed by the ECtHR. Depending on the particularities of the single case, the ECtHR establishes just satisfaction sums ranging from 1,000 to 1,500 euros for each year of the proceeding, when the overall duration is ascertained as excessive; Italian courts, instead, set a minimum, mandatory limit of 750 euros payable for each of the first three years exceeding the standard length of the proceeding, and 1,000 euros for each successive year.

The reasoning followed by the Court of Cassation in justifying this difference is grounded on the case-law of the ECtHR itself. In judgement No. 16086/2009, the Court of Cassation stressed that the Strasbourg Court recognises the possibility for national tribunals to adjust the amount to be paid, according to the standard of living and the legal tradition in the concerned Country, and cites a series of cases regarding Italy in which the ECtHR had ruled that it was not unreasonable to liquidate a sum amounting to 45% of the indemnity that the ECtHR would have paid. In order to ensure that the liquidation adequately compensates for damage, but is not unduly lucrative, the Court of Cassation maintained that the national standard so far followed might be kept. In particular, it upheld the higher value (1,000 euros for each year) only for the years of delay successive to the first three; this further delay indeed is seen as a clear aggravation of the non-pecuniary damage and a cause of further psychological stress undergone by the claimant.

Moreover, while the Strasbourg Court held that for cases of particular importance to the claimant, including those concerning work and welfare issues, the amount of the non-pecuniary damages may rise as high as 2,000 euros per year (entailing a so-called "bonus"), the Court of Cassation, instead, rejected any automatism on this point, explaining that it is up to the judge concerned to ponder and assess any extraordinary aspects of the controversy (e.g., see judgements No. 1895/2010 and 20626/2010).

X. Right to Vote

In judgement No. 6984, 18 October 2010, the Lombardy TAR ruled on an application challenging the legitimacy of the decree proclaiming those elected in the regional elections of Lombardy in March 2010. The claimant, a member of the "Lista Marco Pannella" political group, alleged the illegitimate exclusion of this list's candidates from the electoral competition, along with other formal irregularities, in breach, among others, of art. 3, Protocol I ECHR. The Administrative Tribunal rejected the petition, noticing, among other things, that the provisions of law 120/1999 requiring political parties to collect a minimum number of signatures in order to field their candidates for the elections, was warranted to avoid presentation of any *lista civetta*, or "decoy list". The fact that even Municipal or Provincial Councillors might authenticate the signatures did not constitute an unlawful advantage to the same Councillors' own party since the function of authenticating signatures was not necessarily performed to the benefit of that party as Councillors could authenticate signatures of any electoral list. Therefore, current legislation provided for substantial parity for all lists of candidates in the collection of signatures.

Case-law of the European Court of Human Rights Concerning Italy

During the year 2010, the European Court of Human Rights (ECtHR) issued nearly 100 judgements concerning Italy. 687 applications were declared inadmissible or were struck from the list, and in 668 cases the application was declared admissible. Altogether, 3,852 individual claims regarding Italy were filed with the Strasbourg Court, in its various judicial formations.

During 2010, the Grand Chamber of the ECtHR held two hearings of particular interest for expert as well as for Italian and European public opinion. In both instances, the case had come before the Grand Chamber after the parties appealed the judgements pronounced by ordinary chambers, who had found Italy non-compliant with the ECHR. On 30 June 2010 a Grand Chamber hearing was held in connection with the case *Lautsi v. Italy*, also known as the "case of the classroom crucifix". A Court chamber had ruled on this case on 3 November 2009, affirming that by continuing to apply a regulatory norm of 1924 imposing the visual presence of a crucifix in all public school classrooms, Italy violated art. 2, Protocol I, ECHR in connection with art. 9 ECHR. On 28 January the Italian Government requested the Grand Chamber to re-examine that decision, on 1-2 March of the same year the panel of five judges instructed to filter appeals accepted the referral to the Grand Chamber. The final decision by the Grand Chamber is expected in 2011.

The second case, pleaded before the 17 judges of the Grand Chamber on September 29, 2010, was based on the application *Giuliani and Gaggio v. Italy*, a case concerning violence that broke out during the G8 summit in Genoa in 2001 and led to the killing of a young demonstrator, Carlo Giuliani. In this case, as well, the Italian Government, in a judgement pronounced on 25 August 2009, was found in violation of art. 2 ECHR, for not having adequately investigated into the circumstances of the killing. Appeals before the Grand Chamber were made both by the State and by the plaintiffs, relatives of Giuliani, and admitted by the panel of judges during the same meeting mentioned above. The final decision will be taken in 2011.

I. Excessive Length of Trials and "Pinto on Pinto" Cases

Several of the 98 judgements concerning Italy regarded the excessive length of judicial proceedings and, in particular, disputes over the application of the "Pinto law". In 44 cases, the Court found a violation of art. 6(1) ECHR.

Many of these judgements concerned individuals complaining that decisions taken by Italian judges in applying the "Pinto law" had awarded excessively low sums as just satisfaction.

In this area, among the various cases which altogether have involved hundreds of individuals and juridical persons, it is worth mentioning the judgement *Gaglione and others v. Italy* (21 December 2010). In this case, the ECtHR (Chamber II) found not only a violation of art. 6, paragraph 1, ECHR, but also a breach of the right to property (art. 1, Protocol I ECHR) as well as an infringement of the obligation to execute the judgements of the Court (art. 46 ECHR). The case concerned several hundred applications submitted in 2007 by 475 citizens who, between 2003 and 2006, had used the procedure established by the "Pinto law". On conclusion of the suit they were awarded indemnities for amounts ranging from 200 to nearly 14,000 euros. Since 2006-2007 the petitioners therefore have been claiming ascertained debts against the State for various sums. The State, however, liquidated its debts with delays ranging from 9 to 49 months, whereas the "physiological" delay permitted by the European Court is 6 months or less (on this point see the judgement *Cocchiarella v. Italy*, issued by the Grand Chamber in 2006). The individuals applied to the European Court claiming their right to be awarded without excessive delay the compensation for the loss resulting from the excessive length of civil proceedings to which they had been parties (such cases are named "Pinto on Pinto"). In ruling on *Gaglione and others*, the Strasbourg Court declared that this "shortcoming on the part of the State not only [was] an aggravating factor with regard to its responsibility under the Convention, but also a threat to the future of the system put in place by the Convention", creating a risk that a great mass of analogous cases may soon reach the Court. In fact, the judges observe, Italy is afflicted by a systematic lack of implementation of the "Pinto law". This fact is confirmed by the 3,900 pending applications involving Italy on that type of complaint, including more than 1,300 lodged between June and December 2010. Citing Italian sources, the Court points out that the cost of compensation payable by Italy in "Pinto law" proceedings passed from nearly 4 million euros in 2002 to 40 million in 2008; in six years, the State paid 81 million euros while 36 million remain payable. Worst then this, the situation is getting no better. By April 2009 there were nearly 9 million suits pending in Italian courts – civil and penal cases – most of which destined to last longer than the reasonable limit. Therefore, Italy must adopt general legislative measures (not just specific provisions merely linked to cases settle by the ECtHR) in order to comply with the obligation to conform to the Court's judgements, as recommended on various occasions by the Council of Europe's Committee of Ministers (most recently with resolution CM/ResDH(2009)42, 19 March 2009). Finally, the Court urged Italy to resume, once again, the reforming process of the judiciary system aiming, in particular, to reduce the duration of proceedings. The Court pointed out that is was not for it to make any suggestion concerning the bill's contents, but stressed the urgency of the reform, and lamented that since January 2010, the parliamentary treatment of the bill had ended up on a "blind track". As regards individual measures concerning the single appellants, the Court distances itself from the *Cocchiarella* jurisprudence, establishing for each of the 475 appellants a just satisfaction of 200 euros for moral damages, plus a total of 10,000 euros for the reimbursement of legal expenses. This decision, which undoubtedly favours the defendant State, was criticised by two of the seven judges of the Chamber: Justices Cabral Barreto and Popovic. The *Gaglione* judgement is noteworthy, too, for having rejected the inadmissibility plea made by the State in light of the new art. 35, ECHR, limiting the jurisdiction of the Strasbourg Court only to cases involving "significant disadvantage" to the individual applicant. The judges established that even claims for compensation amounting to a few hundred euros, in the case at hand, warranted the exercise of jurisdiction.

During the year 2010, the parties received notification of numerous petitions lodged in recent years, involving violation of art. 6 ECHR for excessive length of proceedings, including "Pinto on Pinto" cases (among others, *Quattrone v. Italy*).

II. Right to Property, "Indirect Expropriations" and Just Satisfaction

In many cases, the ECtHR deliberated only as to the awarding of just satisfaction, after ruling in favour of the petitioner. Most of these applications were linked to cases of "indirect expropriation" in breach of art. 1, Protocol I ECHR. In applying the criteria for equitable compensation defined by the ECtHR in *Guiso-Gallisay v. Italy* of 22 December 2009, the judgements at hand (see, e.g., *Maselli v. Italy*, 29 July 2010) establish that the indemnity must correspond to the value of the land at the moment when the private owner has lost its property, calculated in accordance with national procedures, adjusted taking into account the inflation and increased by the statutory interest due. Moreover, the claimant must be given equitably calculated indemnity for the loss of opportunity caused by the illegitimate taking of the land, along with non-pecuniary damages, also calculated on an equitable basis.

As regards the right to property, the ruling on *Plalam S.P.A. v. Italy*, pronounced on 18 May 2010, is particularly interesting. The case involved a firm which in the 1980s had obtained the right to receive public financing in support of entrepreneurship projects; later, however, the financing was partly blocked and retroactively annulled in light of law

No. 488, 19 December 1992. The Strasbourg Court ruled that the concept of a "good" protected by art. 1, Protocol I ECHR, encompassed claims against the State that enterprises or individuals had in connection with public subsidies, which therefore could not be annulled retroactively without the State's committing an unlawful act. A number of applications were communicated to parties in 2010, concerning an order addressed to a group of citizens in the town of Avola, in the early 1970s, preventing them from developing any construction on their land, because the Municipality had planned to taken it by right of eminent domain in order to establish a green zone. The local administration, however, has never accomplished an official expropriation, nor has it built the planned infrastructures. The plaintiffs complain that as years have passed, the situation has led to *de facto* expropriation without reparation, violating art. 1, Protocol I ECHR (see, e.g., *Scorpo and Costa v. Italy*).

The right to property (in particular, the right to salary or pension benefits) lies at the centre of several applications communicated to the parties in 2010. In particular, many petitions involve a dispute between the Italy and former INAIL employees (INAIL is a public agency assisting work accident victims and providing other services to workers), who complain that they have undergone pension cuts due to the budget law for 2000, which modified, with retroactive effect, the criteria for calculating pension fund contribution, allegedly in violation of art. 1, Protocol I (among various appeals pending, see *Tombesi and 65 others v. Italy*).

In *Mauriello v. Italy* (petition deposited in 2007, communicated to the parties in 2010), the Court is called to adjudicate as to the conformity with art. 1, Protocol I ECHR, of the situation created by national provisions dealing with pensions of public employees. The applicant points out that the current legislation not only withdrew her right to receive pension benefits, by introducing a requirement of at least 15 years in a job (she has been in service for less than it), but also barred her from continuing to work after the age of 60 in order to qualify for a pension.

In relation to art. 1, Protocol I, 24 cases are pending which were notified to parties in 2010. When the disputed facts occurred, the 24 were physicians specialising in various areas of medicine. They complain of the unfair salary conditions and the unfair employment and welfare schemes they were imposed, that seems to be discriminatory with respect to other medical doctors as well as to specialising physicians hired after 2006 (see *Celano and others v. Italy*, deposited in 2007).

Finally, the proceeding related to the case *Messeni Nemagna and others v. Italy* is likely to start shortly after the end of 2010. The case involved a dispute between the State and the heirs of Antonio Petruzzelli, who in the 19th century founded the theatre in Bari which bears his name. After the theatre was struck by fire in 1991, complex negotiations have been carried out between the heirs, the State, and the Municipality of Bari which, according to the applicants, have gravely impinged on their right to enjoy property.

III. Criminal Procedure, Prison System, Reduction to Slavery

In the cases *Bongiorno and others v. Italy*, concluded on 5 January 2010, and *Leone v. Italy*, decided on 2 February 2010, the Strasbourg Court, in accordance with, among others, *Bocellari and Rizza*, 2007, found that even procedures on execution of preventive measures (in the case at hand, the confiscation of assets available to persons charged with Mafia crimes: l. 575/1965 and later modifications) must respect the principle of publicity (art. 6, paragraph 1 ECHR). Therefore, they cannot be dealt with exclusively *in camera*. The Court rejected the point raised by the plaintiffs that the interim measure of confiscating their property, only based on suspected Mafia criminal activities, amounted to an excessive interference in the right to enjoy property and therefore was a violation of art. 1, Protocol I ECHR. The Court considered this measure proportionate, also in light of the particularly worrying dimension of the Mafia phenomenon in Italy.

In the case *Villa v. Italy*, 20 April 2010, the applicant complains that from 1999 to 2005, he was subjected to a series of security measures motivated by mental illness that in 1997 had led him to stab his father with a knife. The measures included confinement in a psychiatric hospital, periods of community sentence (*libertà controllata*) and of supervision order (*libertà vigilata*). According to the applicant, such measures constituted violation of art. 5 ECHR and of art. 2, Protocol IV ECHR (freedom of movement). The Court denied that the measures adopted constituted violation of art. 5 ECHR since only the confinement in a care and custody centre (*casa di cura e custodia*) can be characterised as a real deprivation of personal liberty; and in the case at hand, this measure was found lawful proportionate. Nor, in the case of other measures limiting freedom of movement, the EctHR found a violation of art. 2, Protocol IV ECHR, except in connection with the fact that the period of surveillance had been extended for approximately four months after the judge had ordered its cessation. Such a delay in the execution of the judicial authority's order motivated Italy's conviction; the applicant however was not awarded any compensation.

The application of the special prison regime set up for those convicted of crimes associated with Mafia activity (art. 41-*bis* of the Prison Administration Act) has continued to be a ground for applications to the ECtHR. In *Mole v. Italy* and *Barbaro v. Italy*, the claims were rejected as manifestly unfounded in reference to art. 3 ECHR (inhuman treatment), while they were admissible for violation of art. 6, paragraph 1 ECHR (fair trial). In this regard, the Court found that procedures before a surveillance judge through which the detainee challenged the legitimacy of orders establishing or renewing the special regime, were not, in some cases, effectively challenged, since the judicial control (by the Court of Cassation, acting as appeals judge) occurred when the implementation period for the special regime was already over. Lengthiness in the treatment of such claims deprived the prisoner of the right to effective judicial remedies.

In *Montani v. Italy*, another case involving a prisoner subject to the special prison regime provided for by art. 41-*bis*, the Strasbourg Court dismissed all alleged violations except the one related to art. 8 ECHR. The Court found that Italy failed to apply law 8 April 2004, No. 25, on the respect of the privacy in the correspondence between the prisoner and the ECtHR. In the case at hand, the letters sent by the individual to the Strasbourg Court arrived stamped with a mark of inspection by the penitentiary authorities. This was *ipso facto* violation of art. 8 ECHR.

Cases relating to prison conditions which in 2010 were communicated to the parties, and would therefore presumably soon undergo judicial examination, include: *Torreggiani v. Italy* (an application analogous to 33 others submitted by inmates of the prison at Busto Arsizio), where the fact of having available space measuring less than an average of three square metres is alleged to be inhuman treatment; *Carrella v. Italy* (lack of medical treatment in prison, in violation of art. 2 and 3 ECHR); *Rosmini v. Italy* (failure to terminate the high security regime despite the surveillance judge's order to do so: alleged violation of art. 6 and 13 ECHR).

Among the pending cases that the ECtHR will decide upon in the early months of 2011, is *Scoppola v. Italy* (this is the third application brought by the same individual to the Strasbourg judges: in 2009 the Court already ascertained violations of art. 6 and 7 ECHR, with the consequence, among others, that the Italian authorities ordered commutation of the life sentence to a term of 30 years; see Italian Case-law, VIII, B). The third *Scoppola v. Italy* case raised the issue of the compatibility with the ECHR (art. 3, Protocol I: right to free elections) of law provisions ordering automatic interdiction of the right to active vote of persons convicted in a final judgement, when the penalty goes beyond a certain limit in severity (in the Italian case, detention for more than five years or life sentence – *ergastolo*). With reference to similar cases concerning the United Kingdom, in particular, the ECtHR found that the automatic loss of the right to vote as a consequence of conviction, without considering the individual aspects of the case and therefore without specific motivation, constituted a disproportionate limitation of the fundamental right to political participation.

In 2010 the case *Milanova and others v. Italy* was communicated to the parties. In this case, a Roma family of Bulgarian citizens accuses the Italian authorities of failing to protect their right not to be subject of inhuman treatment (namely rape) and slavery, by preventing the criminal conduct of members of another Roma group of Serbian citizens. This second group had induced the defendants to travel to Italy where one of the claimants, a woman who was of minor age at the material time, was allegedly raped and reduced to slavery. The situation had been reported to the Italian police, but it was only after approximately two weeks that the police intervened, raiding the house where the crimes were committed. The Italian authorities, moreover, did not believe the version given by the Bulgarian family; the young woman who maintained she had been raped and reduced to slavery even after the facts had been reported to the police, was even accused for calumny. The police had apparently believed that the girls had been given away in marriage to one of the alleged kidnappers with her parents' consent. The ECtHR has to ascertain whether Italy bears responsibility for not having acted in time to protect victims of inhumane treatment (art. 3 ECHR) and reduction to slavery (art. 4 ECHR). The Italian conduct could also be potentially considered in light of the positive obligations stemming from the Council of Europe Convention against Human Trafficking even though at the time of facts Italy had not yet ratified it. In submitting that the reported facts amounted to trafficking in human beings, the *Milanova* case brings to mind the precedent of *Rantsev v. Cyprus and Russia* of January 2010.

IV. Fair Civil Trial

As regards civil proceedings, the ECtHR in *Calabrò v. Italy*, decision on 23 March 2010, declared there was no incompatibility between the ECHR and the Italian Court of Cassation's ordinary practice of dealing with disputes over jurisdiction *in camera* and not in the courtroom, without therefore taking into account memoranda submitted by the parties. This practice changed in 2002 following a ruling by the Plenary of the Court of Cassation which acknowledged the parties' right to be heard in an adversarial proceeding.

Many applications, lodged during 2008-2009 and communicated to the parties in 2010, concerned the consequences – for personnel serving as administrative technical assistant in public schools – deriving from their transfer, pursuant to a 1999 law provision, from the position of local administrations' employees to that of State ministry employees (see, e.g., *Colacione v. Italy*). The provision arranging for this transfer, as officially interpreted by Parliament with a law of 2005, established a salary scheme that did not fully consider the carrier of the public employee, with the result that individuals who had not brought a claim against the provision and obtained a final ruling before the enactment of the 2005 interpretative law, underwent cuts in their remuneration. According to the applicants, this implied violation of art. 6, paragraph 1 ECHR (right to a fair trial), art. 1, Protocol I ECHR (right to property) as well as other provisions (art. 8, art. 13, art. 14 ECHR).

Other cases submitted in recent years and communicated to the parties during 2010 concerning alleged violations of art. 6 ECHR, regard the competence of the Italian Authority Protecting Free Competition and the Market to impose penalties on corporate enterprises, a sanctionatory power subjected only to control on the merits by the judicial authority (*Menarini Diagnostics srl v. Italy*); the lack of publicity and the insufficiency of procedures for the reparation of a judicial error (*Lorenzetti v. Italy*); the less favourable pension scheme for administrative judges compared to ordinary judges, applied even to those who had judicially challenged the legitimacy of the provision, in violation of the "equitable" nature of the judicial procedure (*Guadagno and others v. Italy*).

V. Alien Deportations and the Risk of Torture or Inhuman Treatment

In *Trabelsi v. Italy* (application No. 50163/08), judgement issued on 13 April 2010, the ECtHR held the Italy had violated art. 3 ECHR (prohibition against torture and inhuman treatment). Italian authorities deported a Tunisian detainee to Tunisia, despite strong evidence of illegal practises afflicting inmates in the prison system of that Country. The Court also found that by not complying with the Court's request for suspension of the deportation order, Italy violated art. 34 ECHR. This judgement echoes the Court's rulings in the case *Ben Khemalis v. Italy* (application No. 246/07), decided on 24 February 2009, and in *Saadi v. Italy*, 2008.

On 28 November 2008 the Court applied art. 39 of its Rules (interim measures), indicating to the Italian authorities to refrain from deporting Trabelsi to Tunisia while waiting for his case to be dealt with in Strasbourg. In rejecting the application for political asylum made by Trabelsi, the Territorial Commission of Milan issued the advice of awarding him a residence permit for humanitarian protection, precisely in response to the request for interim measures emitted by the ECtHR. On 3 December, however, the Minister of Interior, exercising powers introduced by law 155/2005, art. 3, ordered the expulsion of Trabelsi for reasons of national security. The measure, later confirmed by the Pavia's Tribunal of Surveillance, was implemented on 13 December. Since then, Trabelsi has been in Tunisia, detained in the prison of Saouaf. The day before his deportation the Italian ambassador in Tunis asked the Tunisian Government for diplomatic assurances regarding Trabelsi's fair treatment and urged it to participate in the hearing over the case before the ECtHR, in support of the Italian State. The request received no answer. On 3 January 2009, however, the Tunisian Government sent a letter informing the Italian authorities of Trabelsi's position in the judicial procedures affecting him as well as providing assurances about his prison conditions.

The ECtHR, while noticing that such assurances came only after Italy had ordered (3 December 2008) and carried out (13 December) the deportation of the applicant, decided to ascertain their reliability all the same. The Court then, taking also into account reliable international sources on the prison condition in Tunisia (the CIA, Amnesty International, Human Rights Watch, etc.) concluded that they were not sufficient to eliminate the risk of the applicant being subject to torture or inhuman treatment. Italy, by deporting Trabelsi to Tunisia, had therefore violated art. 3 of the ECHR. Moreover, the Italian authorities failure to comply with the interim measure issued by the Court in accordance with art. 39 of its Rules of procedure was to be regarded as preventing the applicant from effectively carrying out his claim before the ECtHR and, accordingly, as violating art. 34 ECHR. In addition, the removal of the applicant from the Italian jurisdiction was deemed to constitute a serious impediment to the fulfilment of the State obligation under art. 1 ECHR as well as the Government duty to "abide by the final judgement of the Court". The expulsion of the applicant despite the Court's request for suspension nullified the effective exercise by the applicant of his right to individual petition, as guaranteed by art. 34.

Another case involving foreigners is *Hussun and others v. Italy.* The case arose from four applications presented by 84 foreigners who landed on the Island of Lampedusa from Libya between 13 and 25 March. Sheltered in the Centres of Lampedusa, Caltanissetta and Crotone, they had later fled or been deported. The case was not considered by the Court (it was struck from the list). After collecting the victims' signatures necessary for lodging an application before the Strasbourg Court, claiming that Italy had violated art. 2 and 3 ECHR (given the risks connected with deportation of the refugees to Libya); art. 13 ECHR (unavailability of effective remedies against non recognition of the refugee status); and art. 4, Protocol IV ECHR (collective deportation of foreigners), the counsel representing the 84 foreigners has not succeeded in establishing further contacts with their clients. Accordingly, the ECtHR was barred from dealing with the case, since no information was available concerning the fate of any single applicant; in particular, it proved to be impossible to know anything about what happened to those deported to Libya.

Concerning alien's condition, in *Udorovic v. Italy*, the ECtHR ruled that the application of art. 44, legislative decree 286/1998 (Consolidated act on immigration) is not contrary to the ECHR. The article states that orders by which the single judge imposes the cessation of discriminatory behaviour based on race, ethnicity, nationality or religion, must be adopted *in camera*, without a hearing in courtroom. On the other hand, in the case considered (referring to the removals of Roma families from several camps in Rome during the years 1995, 1996 and 1999), the Strasbourg Court found that Italy violated the right to fair trial, since in one of the judicial proceedings challenging the legality of the removals, the appeal judge had failed to examine some important facts invoked by the applicant.

Pending at the Strasbourg Court is also application No. 9961/10, submitted by Mohamed Ben Mohamed Mannai, a Tunisian citizen. The applicant, after completing a five-year prison term for conviction relating to criminal association, was expelled from Italy on the ground he was considered a threat to State security given his connections with Islamist groups. In February 2010 the ECtHR, applying its Rule 39, requested the Italian authorities to suspend the execution of the expulsive measure pending the conclusion of the proceeding in Strasbourg. The Italian judicial authorities, however, endorsed the deportation order, first to Austria (the Country where the applicant had been arrested in 2005), and then, eventually, to Tunisia. According to the plaintiff, Italy violated art. 3 ECHR, because of the risk of inhuman treatment he would have faced in that Country, and art. 34 ECHR, for not complying with the interim measure.

Another pending case is *Oribabor v. Italy*, concerning the deportation of a woman to Nigeria. The applicant, affected by HIV, claims a violation of art. 3 ECHR (inhuman treatment) given the virtual impossibility, in the Country of destination, to continue the anti-retroviral treatment she began in Italy.

Finally, Italy, like Greece, presents situations which harshly challenge the stability of the EU system protecting asylum seekers. The system is known as "Dublin II" and is broadly based on regulation 3343/2003 EC. Indeed, the Court is expected to examine two cases in which the applicants (Somali citizens) alleged violation of art. 3 ECHR both on the part of Italy – since it offered no concrete assistance after issuing them a residence permit for humanitarian protection – and on the part of the Netherlands, a Country which, in implementing the cited EU regulation, deported them to Italy, where they purportedly faced inhuman treatment (see. *Hasan Mahamed v. The Netherlands and Italy*; and also *Shukri Ibrahim v. The Netherlands and Italy*).

The Strasbourg Court might conclude that some EU Countries (namely Greece and Italy) actually contradict what declares Protocol 24 to the EU Treaty, i.e., that "[g]iven the level of protection of fundamental rights and freedoms by the Member States of the European Union, Member States shall be regarded as constituting safe Countries of origin in respect of each other for all legal ad practical purposes in relation to asylum matters".

VI. Parliamentary Immunity, Electoral Law

In 2010, the Strasbourg Court delivered the final judgment on the case *CGIL and Cofferati v. Italy*. The applicants, an Italian trade union federation (CGIL) and its then Secretary General, Sergio Cofferati, complained against the decision by the elections and parliamentary immunity board of the House of Representatives – decision later confirmed by the plenary on 30 June 2003 – denying authorisation for legal proceedings against the MP Carlo Taormina pursuant to art. 68 Const. The Tribunal of Rome disagreed and raised a conflict of State power before the Constitutional Court, which however, in 2007 declared the appeal inadmissible as having no factual basis. The judiciary wanted to prosecute Mr Taormina for the offence of defamation, in relation to several statements he gave to a press agency, in which he suggested there was a link between CGIL and its secretary general and the subversive groups which on 19 March 2002 had murdered Marco Biagi, an expert on labour law and consultant to the Ministry of labour. Relying on art. 6 ECHR, the applicants complained that the House's decision denying authorisation to the prosecution deprived them of their right to a trial.

The Court had already considered a similar case on the very same matter (statements evoking Marco Biagi's murder), again proposed by CGIL and its secretary. In that case, involving the parliamentary immunity granted by the Parliament to the MP Umberto Bossi, the Court declared that the Italy had violated art. 6 ECHR (*CGIL and Cofferati v. Italy*, judgement of 24 February 2009). In ruling on *CGIL and Cofferati v. Italy*, 6 April 2010, the ECtHR reiterates that the right of access to a court is not absolute. Limitations established by State may legitimately include the protection of Parliament members' right to express their opinions freely. However, according to the Court, in this case the principle of parliamentary immunity cannot be applied since the contested statement was released outside the legislative chamber and without any explicit reference to the debate held in the Houses (in which MP Taormina had participated neither orally nor in writing). The fact that the statement held to be defamatory had political implications did not bar from considering also its penal aspects. In conclusion (and in line with specific precedents, including the case *Cordova v. Italy*, 2003), the Court holds that Italy, in effectively preventing the applicants from ascertaining, before a tribunal, any civil or penal responsibility on the part of the member of the Parliament, violated their right, guaranteed by art. 6 ECHR, to have the alleged violation of their right determined in court.

Finally, 17 applications (see *Saccomanno and others v. Italy*), filed in 2008 and communicated to the parties in 2010, were brought in relation to the 2008 political elections and the application of law 270/2005. In the applicants' views, the law, which establishes blocked electoral lists and a majority bonus, violated art. 3, Protocol I, ECHR.

VII. Adoption and Foster Care

The issue of adoption has been dealt by the Court in two judgements concerning Italy. In *Moretti and Benedetti v. Italy* (judgement of 24 March 2010), it convicted the respondent State for shortcomings in the adoption proceedings which led to the removal from the applicants' home of a child they have had in custody for 18 months, and who they had wished to adopt, to a new foster family. Approximately a year after that traumatic separation, the juvenile court judge dismissed a request from the applicants as, in the best interest of the child, another change of custody would have constituted a further trauma. Relying in particular on art. 8 ECHR, the applicants filed a claim with the Strasbourg Court against the Italian State. The Court, besides recognising the violation, ordered the State to pay compensation for non-pecuniary damages. With this noteworthy decision, the Court recognised that between the foster couple and the child temporarily entrusted to their care, there may subsist a relationship qualifying as "family life" – protected as such by ECHR – if the duration of the cohabitation, in light of the child's age, exceeds a certain limit and if the quality of the relationship seems comparable to that existing between parents and children.

The Italian legislation on adoption lies at the centre, as well, of the case *Godelli v. Italy* (communicated to the parties in 2010, and not yet dealt with by the judges). Once she had become an adult, the appellant, adopted in 1949 with a form of affiliation – now abrogated – asked in vain to know the identity of her biological mother. Information of this kind, however, cannot be revealed (partly pursuant to current legislation: l. 184/1983) in cases where the biological parent declined to be named in the birth certificate or when he/she granted permission for immediate adoption on condition of anonymity. This legislation had been declared compatible with the Constitution, since it aims to allow mothers to give birth to their baby even in a situation of extreme precariousness. However, the applicant claims that such legislation conflicts with her right to privacy, which includes the right to know her biological parent and therefore, it is in contrast with art. 8. This case, which the Court will possibly adjudicate in 2011, addresses some issues already dealt with in *Odièvre v. France*, 2003. In its case-law, the Court has declared that in exceptional cases, a law establishing absolute secrecy concerning the parent's identity does not conflict with art. 8.

Another case concerning art. 8 ECHR is *Piazzi v. Italy*, ruled on 2 November 2010. After a divorce, the under-age son of a couple went to live with his mother and, despite the judicial authority had repeatedly declared the father's right to visit his son, for a period of more than four years all attempts to enforce the judge's orders were blocked by the ex-wife's refusal and by the lack of collaboration from the local health and social care services. According to the Strasbourg Court, the Italian authorities failed, on the whole, in their duty to take practical measures inducing the ex-spouses to cooperate in the best interest of the child.

VIII. Telephone and Environmental Interception

The case *Cariello and others v. Italy* was filed in 2007 and communicated to the parties during 2010. The case concerns wiretapping and environmental interception, ordered by the Tribunal of Rome, of communications between a judge and his family members. A *pentito*, i.e. a "repentant" criminal who collaborates with the judicial system, had accused the magistrate of corruption. Environmental interception devices had even been placed in chambers of the tribunal presided over by the claimant. Several extracts of the intercepted conversations were published by a widely circulating weekly magazine. Once the investigation was closed, the claimant presented a lawsuit against the surveillance measures taken against him. The interceptions were declared legitimate while the investigation on the information leak leading to the publication of inquiry documents ended without identifying any responsible person. The case before the Strasbourg Court will represent good opportunity to assess the implications stemming from a controversial legislation in light of the ECHR, particularly of its art. 8 (protection of private and family life), 6, paragraph 2 (presumption of innocence) and 13.

Table of Cases

Constitutional Court

Judg. 18 February 2010, No. 51
Judg. 26 February 2010, No. 80
Judg. 12 March 2010, No. 93
Judg. 15 April 2010, No. 134
Judg. 15 April 2010, No. 138
Judg. 28 May 2010, No. 190
Judg. 24 June 2010, No. 227
Judg. 8 July 2010, No. 249
Judg. 8 July 2010, No. 250
Judg. 17 July 2010, No. 252
Judg. 22 July 2010, No. 269
Judg. 8 October 2010, No. 293
Judg. 22 October 2010, No. 299
Judg. 17 December 2010, No. 359

Court of Cassation, Civil Division

Ord. Sec. I, 19 January 2010, No. 823
Ord. Sec. VI, 27 July 2010, No. 17576
Judg. Sec. I, 15 January 2007, No. 747
Judg. Sec. I, 16 October 2007, No. 21748
Judg. Sec. I, 2 July 2008, No. 18174
Judg. Sec. I, 8 July 2009, No. 16086
Judg. Sec. I, 16 October 2009, No. 22080
Judg. Sec. I, 3 December 2009, No. 25466
Judg. Sec. I, 21 January 2010, No. 1073
Judg. Sec. I, 28 January 2010, No. 1895
Judg. Sec. I, 17 February 2010, No. 3804
Judg. Sec. I, 17 February 2010, No. 3805
Judg. Sec. I, 1 March 2010, No. 4868

Judg. Sec. I, 10 March 2010, No. 5856
Judg. Sec. I, 15 March 2010, No. 6297
Judg. Sec. I, 17 March 2010, No. 6500
Judg. Sec. I, 26 March 2010, No. 7280
Judg. Sec. I, 26 March 2010, No. 7281
Judg. Sec. I, 6 May 2010, No. 11030
Judg. Sec. I, 7 May 2010, No. 11124
Judg. Sec. I, 19 May 2010, No. 12290
Judg. Sec. I, 28 May 2010, No. 13197
Judg. Sec. I, 11 June 2010, No. 14063
Judg. Sec. I, 19 July 2010, No. 16870
Judg. Sec. I, 4 October 2010, No. 20626
Judg. Sec. III, 2 February 2010, No. 235
Judg. Sec. III, 1 December 2010, No. 24401
Judg. Sec. VI, 8 July 2010, No. 32685
Judg. Plen., 26 January 2010, No. 1338
Judg. Plen., 26 January 2010, No. 1339
Judg. Plen., 26 January 2010, No. 1340
Judg. Plen., 26 January 2010, No. 1341
Judg. Plen., 11 November 2008, No. 26972
Judg. Plen., 11 November 2008, No. 26975
Judg. Plen., 9 September 2009, No. 19394
Judg. Plen., 1 June 2010, No. 13332
Judg. Plen., 25 October 2010, No. 21799
Judg. Plen., 25 October 2010, No. 21803

Court of Cassation, Penal Division

Ord. Sec. II, 27 May 2010, No. 22357
Judg. Sec. I, 25 February 2010, No. 10240
Judg. Sec. II, 21 May 2010, No. 28658
Judg. Sec. II, 9 July 2010, No. 28282
Judg. Sec. III, 3 February 2010, No. 18527
Judg. Sec. IV, 4 February 2010, No. 26938
Judg. Sec. V, 29 October 2010, No. 49694
Judg. Sec. V, 15 April 2010, No. 18072
Judg. Sec. VI, 28 April 2010, No. 20514
Judg. Sec. VI, 23 November 2010, No. 45492

Ordinary Tribunals

Justice of the Peace Ceglie Messapico, judg. 18 February 2010
Monocratic judge Udine Tribunal, ord. 29 June 2010
Tribunal of Catania, ord. 21 October 2010
Tribunal of Florence, decree 22 December 2010
Tribunal of Milan, judg. 1 February 2010, No. 1220
Tribunal of Monza, judg. 4 May 2010, No. 839
Tribunal of Nola, sec. II, judg. 18 August 2010
Tribunal of Novara, judg. 1 March 2010
Tribunal of Palermo, judg. 18 June 2010
Tribunal of Salerno, judg. 9 January 2010, No. 191
Tribunal of Sulmona, judg. 21 July 2010
Tribunal of Tivoli, judg. 22 June 20
Tribunal of Varese, decree 25 August 2010
Tribunal of Varese, judg. 10 February 2010
Tribunal of Varese, sec. I, judg. 12 April 2010

Supreme Administrative Council (*Consiglio di Stato*)

Sec. IV, judg. 2 March 2010, No. 1220
Sec. V, judg. 27 April 2010, No. 2352
Sec. V, judg. 15 September 2010, No. 6778
Sec. VI, judg. 5 February 2010, No. 543
Sec. VI, judg. 7 May 2010, No. 2749
Sec. VI, judg. 15 June 2010, No. 3760
Sec. VI, judg. 21 July 2010, No. 4774
Sec. VI, judg. 27 July 2010, No. 4904
Sec. VI, judg. 29 September 2010, No. 7200

Regional Administrative Tribunals (*TAR*)

TAR Brescia Lombardy, sec. II, judg. 4 February 2010, No. 581
TAR Brescia Lombardy, sec. II, judg. 20 May 2010, No. 2070
TAR Calabria, sec. II, judg. 8 September 2010, No. 2547
TAR Campania, sec. IV, judg. 20 April 2010, No. 2054
TAR Campania, sec. IV, judg. 24 May 2010, No. 8328
TAR Campania, sec. IV, judg. 3 August 2010, No. 17222
TAR Lazio, judg. 18 May 2010, No. 11984

TAR Liguria, sec. I, judg. 18 November 2010, No. 10405

TAR Milan Lombardy, sec. III, judg. 9 February 2010, No. 310

TAR Milan Lombardy, sec. IV, judg. 18 October 2010, No. 6984

European Court of Human Rights

Barbaro v. Italy, No. 16436/02, 16 February 2010

Ben Khemais v. Italy, No. 246/07, 24 February 2009

Bocellari and Rizza v. Italy, No. 399/02, 13 November 2007

Bongiorno and Others v. Italy, No. 4514/07, 5 January 2010

C.G.I.L. and Cofferati v. Italy, No. 46967/07, 24 February 2009

C.G.I.L. and Cofferati v. Italy (No. 2), No. 2/08, 6 April 2010

Calabrò v. Italy, No. 17426/02, 23 March 2010

Cariello and Others v. Italy, No. 14064/07

Carrella v. Italy, No. 33955/07

Celano and Others v. Italy, No. 14830/07

Cocchiarella v. Italy [CJ], No. 64886/01, ECHR 2006-V

Colacione v. Italy, No. 47348/08

Cordova v. Italy (No. 1), No. 40877/98, ECHR 2003-I 273

Gaglione and Others v. Italy, No. 45867/07, 21 December 2010

Giuliani and Gaggio v. Italy, No. 23458/02, 25 August 2009

Godelli v. Italy, No. 33783/09

Guadagno v. Italy, No. 61820/08

Guiso-Gallisay v. Italy, No. (just satisfaction) [CJ], No. 58858/00, 22 December 2009

Hasam Mahamed v. the Netherlands and Italy, No. 44517/09

Hussun and Others v. Italy, No. (striking out), No. 10171/05, 10601/05 and 17165/05, 19 January 2010

Lautsi v. Italy, No. 30814/06, 3 November 2009

Leone v. Italy, No. 30506/07, 2 February 2010

Lorenzetti v. Italy, No. 32075/09

Mannai v. Italy, No. 9961/10

Maselli v. Italy (just satisfaction), No. 63866/00, 29 July 2010

Mauriello v. Italy, No. 14862/07

Menarini Diagnostics srl v. Italy, No. 43508/08

Messeni Nemagna and Others v. Italy, No. 49199/06

Milanova and Others v. Italy, No. 40020/03

Mole v. Italy, No. 24421/03, 12 January 2010

Montani v. Italy, No. 24950/06, 19 January 2010

Moretti and Benedetti v. Italy, No. 16318/07, ECHR 2010

Odièvre v. France [CJ], No. 42326/98, ECHR 2003-III

Oribabor v. Italy, No. 34724/10

Piazzi v. Italy, No. 36168/09, 2 November 2010

Plalam S.P.A. v. Italy, No. 16021/02, 18 May 2010

Quattrone v. Italy, No. 13431/07

Rantsev v. Cyprus and Russia, No. 25965/04, 7 January 2010

Rosmini v. Italy, No. 5097/08

S.H. and Others v. Austria, No. 57813/00, 1 April 2010

Saadi v. Italy [CJ], No. 37201/06, 28 February 200

Saccomanno and Others v. Italy, No. 11583/08

Scorpo and Costa v. Italy, No. 36183/07

Shukri Ibrahim v. the Netherlands and Italy, No. 2301/10

Tombesi and 65 Others v. Italy, No. 31228/08264

Torreggiani v. Italy, No. 43517/09

Trabelsi v. Italy, No. 50163/08, 13 April 2010

Udorovic v. Italy, No. 38532/02, 18 May 2010

Villa v. Italy, No. 19675/06, 20 April 2010

European Court of Justice

Rec. 29 July 2010, *Commission v. Italy*

Judg. C-29/69, 12 November 1969, *Stauder*

Judg. C-4/73, 14 May 1974, *Nold*

Judg. C-11/70, 17 December 1979, *Handelsgesellschaft*

Judg. C-388/01, 16 January 2003, *Commission of European Communities v. Italian Republic*

Judg. C-66/08, 17 July 2008, *Kozlowski*

Judg. C-123/08, 6 October 2009, *Wolzenburg*

Judg.C-555/07, 19 January 2010, *Kücükdeveci*

Judg. C-92/09 and C-93/09, 9 November 2010, *Volker und Markus Schecke, Hartmut Eifert*

European Committee on Social Rights

COHRE v. Italy, No. 58/2009

ERRC v. Italy, No. 27/2004

EUROFEDOP v. Italy, No. 4/1999

OMCT v. Italy, No. 19/2003

Research and Editing Committee

Andrea Cofelice, MA, University of Padua, Institutions and Policies of Human Rights and Peace; PhD candidate, University of Siena, Political Science: Comparative and European Politics.

Paola Degani, University of Padua, Aggregate Professor, Human Rights and the Status of Women; Public Policy and Human Rights.

Pietro de Perini, MA, University of Padua, Institutions and Policies of Human Rights and Peace; Ph.D candidate, City University London, Department of International Politics.

Paolo De Stefani, University of Padua, Aggregate Professor, International Human Rights Protection; International Humanitarian and Criminal Law. National Director in Italy of the European Master's Degree in Human Rights and Democratisation.

Marco Mascia, University of Padua, Associate Professor of International Relations; Jean Monnet European Chair in the Political System of the European Union; Director of the Interdepartmental Centre on Human Rights and the Rights of Peoples of the University of Padua; Chair of the MA in Institutions and Policies of Human Rights and Peace; Coordinator of the Jean Monnet European Centre of Excellence at the University of Padua.

Antonio Papisca, University of Padua, Professor Emeritus, International Human Rights and Peace Organisation; UNESCO Chair Human Rights, Democracy and Peace. Editor in Chief of the review "Pace diritti umani/Peace human rights", published by Marsilio. Founder (1982) of the Interdepartmental Centre on Human Rights and the Rights of Peoples of the University of Padua. Member of the Inter-Ministerial Committee for Human Rights at the Ministry of Foreign Affairs, and of the Human Rights Commission at the Presidency of the Council of Ministers (1994-2002).

Human Rights Studies

Among the broad structural transformation processes at the global level, the international legal recognition of human rights occupies an exceptionally prominent position. The dimensions of this process include standard setting, the functioning of sophisticated machineries for the promotion and protection of human rights, the development of a specific international case-law as well as new priorities of the political agenda.

The human rights paradigm is at the heart of a new set of interrelated principles, which are equally valid at both the domestic and the international levels – such as the rule of law, democratic principles and the responsibility to protect – and of great strategic visions, as human development and human security. New functions, such as human rights monitoring, election observation, fact-finding and inquiry have already been admitted to international practice.

This series intends to foster the publication of volumes that investigate the multiple facets of a strongly evolving reality, and stimulate the production of new and innovative ideas. It offers to highlight how the human rights paradigm is at times used and at times disregarded or exploited in cases and situations that regard among others those belonging to vulnerable groups (immigrants, asylum seekers, persons with disabilities), NGOs and human rights defenders' advocacy, intercultural dialogue, governance of world economy, bio-technologies and peace operations. Those studies which adopt inter- and trans-disciplinary approaches, in accordance with the fundamental principle of interdependence and indivisibility of civil, political, economic, social and cultural rights, will be favored.